Verse by Verse Commentary on the Gospel of

JOHN

Enduring Word Commentary Series
By David Guzik

The grass withers, the flower fades,
but the word of our God stands forever.
Isaiah 40:8

Commentary on the Gospel of John
Copyright ©2019 by David Guzik
Printed in the United States of America
or in the United Kingdom
ISBN 987-1-939466-28-0

Enduring Word

5662 Calle Real #184
Goleta, CA 93117

Electronic Mail: ewm@enduringword.com
Internet Home Page: www.enduringword.com

Scripture references, unless noted, are from the New King James Version of the Bible, copyright ©1979, 1980, 1982, Thomas Nelson, Inc., Publisher.

Contents

John 1 - The Word and the Witness

A. John: The fourth Gospel.

1. The Gospel of John is the fourth section of what some call the four-fold gospel, with four voices giving different perspectives on the life of Jesus of Nazareth. Christian writers as early as Origen (A.D. 185-254) understood that there are not really four gospels, but there is one four-fold gospel.

a. The Gospel of John was probably the last of the four written, and written in view of what the previous three had already said. This is one reason why John's account of the life of Jesus is in many ways different from Matthew, Mark, and Luke.

b. There are significant events in the ministry of Jesus that Matthew, Mark, and Luke all include yet John leaves out, including:

- Jesus' birth.
- Jesus' baptism.
- Jesus' temptation in the wilderness.
- Confrontations with demons.
- Jesus teaching in parables.
- The Last Supper.
- The agony in Gethsemane.
- The Ascension.

c. The first three Gospels center on Jesus' ministry in *Galilee*. John centers his Gospel on what Jesus said and did in *Jerusalem*.

d. Each of the Gospels emphasizes a different origin of Jesus.

- Matthew shows Jesus came from Abraham through David, and demonstrates that He is the Messiah promised in the Old Testament (Matthew 1:1-17).

- Mark shows Jesus came from Nazareth, demonstrating that Jesus is a Servant (Mark 1:9).

- Luke shows Jesus came from Adam, demonstrating that Jesus is the Perfect Man (Luke 3:23-38).

- John shows Jesus came from heaven, demonstrating that Jesus is God.

e. However, it is wrong to think that the Gospel of John *completes* the story of Jesus. John wrote that the story of Jesus is so big that it can *never* be completed (John 21:25).

2. Matthew, Mark, and Luke are known as the three *synoptic* gospels. The word *synoptic* means "see-together" and the first three Gospels present the life of Jesus in pretty much the same format. The first three Gospels focus more on what *Jesus taught and did*; John focused more on *who Jesus is*.

- John shows us who Jesus is by highlighting seven signs (miracles) of Jesus. Six of these miracles are not mentioned in the first three gospels.

- John shows us who Jesus is by allowing Jesus to speak for Himself in seven dramatic *I Am* statements, which were not included in the first three gospels.

- John shows us who Jesus is by giving the testimony witnesses who testify about the identity of Jesus. Four of these witnesses speak in the first chapter alone.

3. John is a Gospel written for a specific purpose: that we might believe. A key verse for understanding the Gospel of John is found at the end of the book: *But these are written that you may believe that Jesus is the Christ, the Son of God, and that believing you may have life in His name* (John 20:31).

a. The Gospel of John has even helped scholarly skeptics to believe. The oldest surviving fragment of the New Testament is a portion of John 18, found in Egypt and dating well before A.D. 150 indicating wide circulation by that early date.

b. John doesn't tell us much about himself in the Gospel record he wrote, but we can put a few things together about him from the Gospel records.

- John's father was Zebedee

- John's mother was Salome, one of those to go to the tomb early on the morning the resurrection of Jesus was discovered

- John's brother was James

- John was a partner in the fishing business with Peter

- John and his brother James were given the nickname, "Sons of Thunder"

4. The Gospel of John is a beloved gospel. Because of its paradoxical combination of both simplicity and depth, John has been called "a pool in which a child may wade and an elephant may swim."

a. "Its stories are so simple that even a child will love them, but its statements are so profound that no philosopher can fathom them." (Erdman)

b. So, if we give diligent attention to entertainment, sports, music, or the news, how much more should we give careful attention "when a man is speaking from heaven, and utters a voice plainer than thunder?" (John Chrysostom)

B. Prologue to the Gospel of John.

This remarkable, profound portion is not merely a preface or an introduction. It is a summation of the entire book. The remainder of John's Gospel deals with the themes introduced here: the identity of the Word, life, light, regeneration, grace, truth, and the revelation of God the Father in Jesus the Son.

1. (1-2) The pre-existence of the **Word** (*Logos*).

In the beginning was the Word, and the Word was with God, and the Word was God. He was in the beginning with God.

a. **In the beginning**: This refers to the timeless eternity of Genesis 1:19 (*In the beginning, God created the heavens and earth*). John essentially wrote, "When the **beginning** began, **the Word** was already there." The idea is that **the Word** existed before creation or even time.

i. John makes it clear that **the Word** is not just the beginning, but it is the beginning of the beginning. He was there **in the beginning**, before anything was.

ii. **Was the Word**: "Had the Word a beginning? John says, 'No: for if we reach back to any beginning, there already was in existence the Word.' At once it is evident to John's vision 'The Word' is no other than God the self-existent." (Trench)

iii. "This description is given in order that we may at once grasp a continuous history which runs out of an unmeasured past, and the identity of the person who is subject of that history." (Dods)

b. **In the beginning was the Word: Word** translates the ancient Greek word *Logos*. The idea of the *logos* had deep and rich roots in both Jewish and Greek thinking.

i. Jewish rabbis often referred to God (especially in His more personal aspects) in terms of His word. They spoke of God Himself as "the word of God." For example, ancient Hebrew editions of the Old Testament change Exodus 19:17 (*Moses brought the people out of the camp to meet*

God) to "Moses brought the people out of the camp to meet the word of God." In the mind of the ancient Jews, the phrase "the word of God" could be used to refer to God Himself.

ii. The Greek philosophers saw the *logos* as the power that puts sense into the world, making the world orderly instead of chaotic. The *logos* was the power that set the world in perfect order and kept it going in perfect order. They saw the *logos* as the "Ultimate Reason" that controlled all things. (Dods, Morris, Barclay, Bruce, and others)

iii. Therefore in this opening John said to both Jews and Greeks: "For centuries you've been talking, thinking, and writing about **the Word** (the *logos*). Now I will tell you who He is." John met both Jews and Greeks where they were at, and explained Jesus in terms they already understood.

iv. "John was using a term which, with various shades of meaning, was in common use everywhere. He could reckon on all men catching his essential meaning." (Morris)

v. "The word being thus already in use and aiding thoughtful men in their efforts to conceive God's connection with the world, John takes it and uses us to denote the Revealer of the incomprehensible and invisible God." (Dods)

c. **And the Word was with God, and the Word was God**: With this brilliant statement, John 1:1 sets forth one of the most basic foundations of our faith - the Trinity. We can follow John's logic:

- There is a Being known as **the Word**.
- This Being is God, because He is eternal (**In the beginning**).
- This Being is God, because He is plainly called God (**the Word was God**).
- At the same time, this Being does not encompass all that God is. God the Father is a distinct Person from **the Word** (**the Word was *with* God**).

i. So, the Father and the Son (the Son is known here as **the Word**) are equally God, yet distinct in their Person. The Father is not the Son, and the Son is not the Father. Yet they are equally God, with God the Holy Spirit making one God in three Persons.

ii. **The Word was with God**: "This preposition implies intercourse and therefore separate personality. As Chrysostom says: 'Not in God but with God, as person with person, eternally.'" (Dods)

iii. **And the Word was God**: "This is the true form of the sentence; not '*God was the Word.*' This is absolutely required by the usage of the Greek language." (Alford)

iv. "Luther says 'the Word was God' is against Arius: 'the Word was with God' against Sabellius." (Dods)

v. **And the Word was God**: "Everything that can be said about God the Father can be said about God the Son. In Jesus dwells all the wisdom, glory, power, love, holiness, justice, goodness, and truth of the Father. In Him, God the Father is known." (Boice)

d. **In the beginning was the Word, and the Word was with God, and the Word was God**: The Watchtower (the Jehovah's Witnesses) bible, called *New World Translation*, translates this line quite differently. The Jehovah's Witness translation reads like this: "In [the] beginning the Word was, and the Word was with God, and the Word was a god." Their translation is used to deny the teaching that Jesus is God, and is a wrong and misleading translation.

i. The claim of the Watchtower defending their translation of John 1:1-2 is that because before the second time "God" is used in the passage, no article appears (it is written "God" and not "the God"). In answer to this approach to Greek grammar and translation, we can only refer to the multitude of other times in the New Testament where "God" appears without the article. If the Watchtower were honest and consistent, they would translate "God" as "god" every place it appears without the article. But it seems that this grammatical rule only applies when it suits the purpose of backing up the doctrinal beliefs of the Watchtower. The Greek text of Matthew 5:9, 6:24, Luke 1:35 and 1:75, John 1:6, 1:12, 1:13, and 1:18, Romans 1:7 and 1:17, shows how the Watchtower translates the exact same grammar for "God" as "God" instead of "god" when it suits their purpose.

ii. In the main resource the Watchtower uses to establish their claim (*The Kingdom Interlinear*), the Watchtower quotes two well-known Greek authorities to make them *appear* to agree with their translation. But they both have been misquoted, and one of them, Dr. Mantey has even written the Watchtower, and demanded that his name be removed from the book! Another "scholar" whom the Watchtower refers to in their book *The Word - Who Is He? According to John*, is Johannes Greber. Greber was actually an occult-practicing spiritist, and *not* a scholar of Biblical Greek.

iii. *Real* Greek scholars do not recognize the Jehovah's Witness translation of John 1:1-2.

- "A GROSSLY MISLEADING TRANSLATION. It is neither scholarly nor reasonable to translate John 1:1 'the Word was a god.' But of all the scholars in the world, so far as we know, none have translated this verse as Jehovah's Witnesses have done." (Dr. Julius R. Mantey)

- "Much is made by Arian amateur grammarians of the omission of the definite article with 'God' in the phrase 'And the Word was God.' Such an omission is common with nouns in a predicate construction. 'A god' would be totally indefensible." (Dr. F.F. Bruce)

- "I can assure you that the rendering which the Jehovah's Witnesses give John 1:1 is not held by any reputable Greek scholar." (Dr. Charles L. Feinberg)

- "The Jehovah's Witness people evidence an abysmal ignorance of the basic tenets of Greek grammar in their mistranslation of John 1:1." (Dr. Paul L. Kaufman)

- "The deliberate distortion of truth by this sect is seen in their New Testament translations. John 1:1 is translated: '...the Word was a god,' a translation which is **grammatically impossible**. It is abundantly clear that a sect which can translate the New Testament like that is intellectually dishonest." (Dr. William Barclay)

e. **He was in the beginning with God**: This again makes the point that the Father is distinct from the Son, and the Son distinct from the Father. They are equally God, yet they are separate Persons.

2. (3-5) The work and nature of the Word.

All things were made through Him, and without Him nothing was made that was made. In Him was life, and the life was the light of men. And the light shines in the darkness, and the darkness did not comprehend it.

a. **All things were made through Him, and without Him nothing was made that was made**: The Word created *all* things that were created. Therefore He Himself is an uncreated Being, as the Apostle Paul wrote in Colossians 1:16.

i. "In Genesis 1:1, GOD is said to have created all things: in this verse, *Christ* is said to have created all things: the same unerring Spirit spoke in *Moses* and in the *evangelists*: therefore *Christ* and the *Father* are ONE." (Clarke)

b. **In Him was life**: The Word is the source of all life - not only biological life, but the very *principle* of life. The ancient Greek word translated **life** is *zoe*, which means "the life principle," not *bios*, which is mere biological life.

> i. "That power which creates life and maintains all else in existence was in the Logos." (Dods)

c. **The life was the light of men**: This **life** is **the light of men**, speaking of spiritual light as well as natural light. It isn't that the Word "contains" life and light; He *is* **life** and **light**.

> i. Therefore, without Jesus, we are *dead* and in *darkness*. We are lost. Significantly, man has an inborn fear towards both death and darkness.

d. **And the light shines in the darkness, and the darkness did not comprehend it**: *Did not overcome it* is another way to translate the phrase, "**did not comprehend it**." The light cannot lose against the darkness; the darkness will never overcome it.

> i. **Comprehend**: "The Greek verb is not easy to translate. It contains the idea of laying hold on something so as to make it one's own. This can lead to meanings like 'lay hold with the mind', and thus 'comprehend'…[Yet] The verb we are discussing has a rarer, but sufficiently attested meaning, 'overcome'. It is that that is required here." (Morris)

> ii. "In the first creation, 'darkness was upon the face of the deep' (Genesis 1:2) until God called light into being, so the new creation involves the banishing of spiritual darkness by the light which shines in the Word." (Bruce)

3. (6-8) The forerunner of the Word.

There was a man sent from God, whose name *was* John. This man came for a witness, to bear witness of the Light, that all through him might believe. He was not that Light, but *was sent* to bear witness of that Light.

a. **There was a man sent from God**: John the Baptist bore witness of the light, **that all through him might believe**. The work of John the Baptist was deliberately focused on bringing people to faith in Jesus the Messiah.

> i. "The testimony of John is introduced not only as a historical note but in order to bring out the aggravated blindness of those who rejected Christ." (Dods)

b. **He was not that Light, but was sent to bear witness of that Light**: John the Baptist's work was remarkably well received and widely known. It was important for the John the Gospel writer to make it clear that John the

Baptist **was not that Light**, but that He pointed towards and bore witness of **that Light**.

> i. **He was not that Light**: "Possibly this was directed toward the sect that survived John and perpetuated his teaching but had not knowledge of the completion of the work of Christ (Acts 18:24-25; 19:1-7)." (Tenney)

> ii. "We know him as 'John the Baptist' but in this Gospel the references to his baptism are incidental... But there is repeated reference to his witness." (Morris)

> iii. The matter of **witness** is a serious thing, establishing truth and giving ground for faith. Yet, **witness** "does more. It commits a man. If I take my stand in the witness box and testify that such-and-such is the truth of the mater I am no longer neutral. I have committed myself. John lets us know that there are those like John the Baptist who have committed themselves by their witness to Christ." (Morris)

4. (9-11) The rejection of the Word.

That was the true Light which gives light to every man coming into the world. He was in the world, and the world was made through Him, and the world did not know Him. He came to His own, and His own did not receive Him.

a. **That was the true Light which gives light to every man coming into the world**: John did not mean that the Word gives this **light** to everyone in the ultimate, saving sense. He meant that the reason why anyone is born into a world with any love or care or goodness at all is because of the **true Light** and the light He gives to the **world**.

b. **The world did not know Him**: This is strange. God came to the same world He created, to the creatures made in His image, and yet **the world did not know Him**. This shows how deeply fallen human nature rejects God, and that many reject (**did not receive**) God word and **Light**.

> i. **He came to His own**: "We might translate the opening words, 'he came home'. It is the exact expression used of the beloved disciple when, in response to Jesus' word from the cross, he took Mary 'unto his own home' (John 19:27; *cf.* 16:32). When the Word came to this world He did not come as an alien. He came home." (Morris)

> ii. "It is said of 'His own' that they did not 'know' Him, but that they did not receive Him. And in the parable of the Wicked Husbandman our Lord represents them as killing the heir not in ignorance but because they knew him." (Dods)

iii. "This little world knew not Christ, for God had hid him under the carpenter's son; his glory was inward, his kingdom came not by observation." (Trapp)

5. (12-13) The receiving of the Word.

But as many as received Him, to them He gave the right to become children of God, to those who believe in His name: who were born, not of blood, nor of the will of the flesh, nor of the will of man, but of God.

a. **But as many as received Him, to them He gave the right to become children of God, to those who believe in His name**: Though some rejected this revelation, others received Him and thereby became children of God. They became **children of God** through a new birth, being **born... of God**.

i. "The end of the story is not the tragedy of rejection, but the *grace* of acceptance." (Morris)

ii. **As many as received Him**: The idea of "receiving Jesus" is Biblically valid. We need to embrace and receive Him unto ourselves. **As many as received Him** is just another to say **those who believe in His name**. "Faith is described as 'receiving' Jesus. It is the empty cup placed under the flowing stream; the penniless hand held out for heavenly alms." (Spurgeon)

iii. **The right to become children of God**: "The word *children* (*tekna*) is parallel to the Scottish *bairns* - 'born ones.' It emphasizes vital origin and is used as a term of endearment (cf. Luke 15:31). Believers are God's 'little ones,' related to him by birth." (Tenney)

b. **Not of blood, nor of the will of the flesh, nor of the will of man, but of God**: John reminds us of the nature of the birth. Those who received Him are born of God, but not of human effort or achievement.

i. "They are 'not of bloods'. The plural is curious...The plural here may point to the action of both parents, or it may refer to blood as made up of many drops." (Morris)

ii. This new birth is something that brings change to the life. "The man is like a watch which has a new mainspring, not a mere face and hands repaired, but new inward machinery, with freshly adjusted works, which act to a different time and tune; and whereas he went wrong before, now he goes right, because he is right within." (Spurgeon)

6. (14) The Word became flesh.

And the Word became flesh and dwelt among us, and we beheld His glory, the glory as of the only begotten of the Father, full of grace and truth.

a. **And the Word became flesh and dwelt among us**: This is John's most startling statement so far. It would have amazed both thinkers in both the Jewish and the Greek world to hear that **the Word became flesh**.

i. "The most general expression of the great truth He became *man*. He became that, of which man is in the body compounded... The simplicity of this expression is no doubt directed against the Docetae of the Apostle's time, who maintained that the Word *only apparently* took human nature." (Alford)

ii. The Greeks generally thought of God *too low*. To them John wrote: **the *Word* became flesh**. To ancient people, gods such as Zeus and Hermes were simply super-men; they were not equal to the order and reason of the Logos. John told the Greek thinkers, "The Logos you know made and ordered the universe actually **became flesh**."

iii. The Jews generally thought of God *too high*. To them John wrote: **the Word became *flesh* and *dwelt among us***. Ancient Jews had a hard time accepting that the great God revealed in the Old Testament could take on human form. John told the Jewish thinkers, "The Word of God **became flesh**."

iv. God has come close to you in Jesus Christ. You don't have to struggle to find Him; *He came to you*. Some think they go from place to place to try and find God, and continue their search. More commonly they stay at a place until God draws close to them - then they quickly move on.

v. "Christ entered into a new dimension of existence through the gateway of human birth and took up his residence among men." (Tenney)

vi. "Augustine afterwards said that in his pre-Christian days he had read and studied the great pagan philosophers and had read many things, but he had never read that the word became flesh." (Barclay)

b. **And dwelt among us**: The idea behind this phrase is more literally, *dwelt as in a tent among us*. From the sense and the context, John connected the coming of Jesus to humanity with God's coming to and living with Israel in the tent of the tabernacle. It could be stated, *and tabernacled among us*.

i. "*And tabernacled among us*: the human nature which he took of the virgin, being as the *shrine, house,* or *temple*, in which his immaculate

Deity condescended to dwell. The word is probably an allusion to the Divine Shechinah in the Jewish temple." (Clarke)

ii. "Properly the verb signifies 'to pitch one's tent'." (Morris) "The association in John's mind was…with the Divine tabernacle in the wilderness, when Jehovah pitched His tent among the shifting tents of His people." (Dods)

iii. The tabernacle was many things that Jesus is among His people:

- The center of Israel's camp.
- The place where the Law of Moses was preserved.
- The dwelling place of God.
- The place of revelation.
- The place where sacrifices were made.
- The center of Israel's worship.

iv. "If God has come to dwell among men by the Word made flesh *let us pitch our tents around: this central tabernacle*; do not let us live as if God were a long way off." (Spurgeon)

v. "The *Shechinah* means *that which dwells*; and it is the word used for the visible presence of God among men." (Barclay)

c. **We beheld His glory**: John testified to this as an eyewitness, even as John the Baptist testified. John could say, "I *saw* His glory, the glory belonging to the **only begotten of the Father**."

i. The word **beheld** is stronger than the words "saw" or "looked." John tells us that he and the other disciples *carefully studied* the glory of the Word made flesh.

ii. 'The verb 'beheld' is invariably used in John (as, for that matter, in the whole New Testament) of seeing with the bodily eye. It is not used of visions. John is speaking of that glory that was seen in the literal, physical Jesus of Nazareth." (Morris)

d. **Full of grace and truth**: The glory of Jesus wasn't primarily an adrenaline rush and certainly not a sideshow. It was **full of grace and truth**.

i. "Beloved, notice here that both these qualities in our Lord are *at the full*. He is 'full of grace.' Who could be more so? In the person of Jesus Christ the immeasurable grace of God is treasured up." (Spurgeon)

ii. "These two ideas should hold our minds and direct our lives. God is grace, and truth. Not one without the other. Not the other apart from the one. In His government there can be no lowering of the simple and severe standard of Truth; and there is no departure from the purpose and passion of Grace." (Morgan)

7. (15-18) Bearing witness to God's new order.

John bore witness of Him and cried out, saying, "This was He of whom I said, 'He who comes after me is preferred before me, for He was before me.'" And of His fullness we have all received, and grace for grace. For the law was given through Moses, *but* grace and truth came through Jesus Christ. No one has seen God at any time. The only begotten Son, who is in the bosom of the Father, He has declared *Him*.

a. **He who comes after me is preferred before me, for He was before me**: John the Baptist's testimony was rooted in his understanding of the pre-existence of Jesus. He knew that Jesus was **before** him in every sense.

i. "In antiquity it was widely held that chronological priority meant superiority. Men were humble about their own generation, and really thought that their fathers were wiser than they - incredible as this may sound to our generation!" (Morris)

b. **Of His fullness we have all received, and grace for grace**: This new order has an inexhaustible supply of grace (**grace for grace**, the figure of speech similar to *sorrows upon sorrows*) and truth, contrasting with an order of rigid laws and regulations **given through Moses**.

i. **Grace for grace**: "Literally it means 'grace instead of grace'. Clearly John intends to put some emphasis on the thought of grace. Probably also he means that as one piece of divine grace (so to speak) recedes it is replaced by another. God's grace to His people is continuous and is never exhausted. Grace knows no interruption and no limit." (Morris)

c. **For the law was given through Moses, but grace and truth came through Jesus Christ**: This describes and demonstrates the fullness of grace announced by John the Baptist and brought by Jesus Christ. God the Word, Jesus Christ, brought a different order than the one instituted by Moses.

i. **Grace and truth came through Jesus Christ**: "Here, then, as in Paul's writings, Christ displaces the law of Moses as the focus of divine revelation and the way to life." (Bruce)

d. **No one has seen God at any time**: Jesus, the Word, is the perfect declaration of the unseen God. The Father and the Son belong to the same family, and Jesus **has declared** the nature of the unseen God to man. We don't have to wonder about the nature and personality of God. Jesus has **declared** it with both His teaching and His life.

i. "The noun *God* (*theon*) has not article in the Greek text, which indicates that the author is presenting God in his nature of being rather than as a person. 'Deity' might be a more accurate rendering. The meaning is that no human has ever seen the essence of Deity." (Tenney)

ii. "The *sight of God* here meant, is not only bodily sight (though of that it is true, see Exodus 33:20; 1 Timothy 6:16), but *intuitive* and *infallible knowledge*, which enables him who has it to declare the nature and will of God." (Alford)

iii. **Who is in the bosom of the Father**: "The expression signifies, as Chrysostom observes, *Kindred and oneness of essence*: - and is derived from the fond and intimate union of children and parents." (Alford)

C. The testimony of John the Baptist.

1. (19-22) Religious leaders from Jerusalem question John the Baptist.

Now this is the testimony of John, when the Jews sent priests and Levites from Jerusalem to ask him, "Who are you?" He confessed, and did not deny, but confessed, "I am not the Christ." And they asked him, "What then? Are you Elijah?" He said, "I am not." "Are you the Prophet?" And he answered, "No." Then they said to him, "Who are you, that we may give an answer to those who sent us? What do you say about yourself?"

a. **Now this is the testimony of John**: We have already learned that John the Baptist *came for a witness* (John 1:7 and 1:15). Now we learn what his **testimony** regarding Jesus was.

i. **The Jews**: "Here for the first time we come upon the use of the term 'the Jews' in this Gospel to denote not the people as a whole but one particular group - here, the religious establishment in Jerusalem." (Bruce)

ii. "Thus the parents of the man born blind were certainly members of the Jewish nation, but they are said to fear 'the Jews' (John 9:22)." (Morris)

b. **I am not the Christ**: With emphasis, John told the Jewish leaders who he was *not*. He did not come to focus attention on himself, because he was not the Messiah. His job was to point to the Messiah.

i. "John completely rejected that claim; but he rejected it with a certain hint. In the Greek the word *I* is stressed by its position. It is as if John said: '*I* am not the Messiah, but, if you only knew, the Messiah is here.'" (Barclay)

ii. **He confessed, and did not deny**: "Sincerely and studiously; he put away that honour with both hands earnestly, as knowing the danger of wronging the jealous God." (Trapp)

iii. It was important for John the Gospel writer to make clear to his readers that John the Baptist did not claim to be more than he was. "As late as A.D. 250 the *Clementine Recognitions* tell us that 'there were some of John's disciples who preached about him as if their master was the Messiah.'" (Barclay)

c. **Are you Elijah?** It might be easy for the priests and Levites from Jerusalem to associate John with Elijah because of his personality and because of the promise that Elijah would come before the Day of the LORD (Malachi 4:5-6).

i. John was careful to never say of *himself* that he was Elijah. Yet Jesus noted that in a sense, John *was* Elijah, ministering in his office and spirit (Matthew 11:13-14 and Mark 9:11-13).

d. **Are you the Prophet?** In Deuteronomy 18:15-19 God promised that another prophet would come in due time. Based on this passage, they expected another **Prophet** to come, and wondered if John was not he.

2. (23-28) John explains his identity to the religious leaders.

He said: "I *am* 'The voice of one crying in the wilderness: "Make straight the way of the LORD,"' as the prophet Isaiah said." Now those who were sent were from the Pharisees. And they asked him, saying, "Why then do you baptize if you are not the Christ, nor Elijah, nor the Prophet?" John answered them, saying, "I baptize with water, but there stands One among you whom you do not know. It is He who, coming after me, is preferred before me, whose sandal strap I am not worthy to loose." These things were done in Bethabara beyond the Jordan, where John was baptizing.

a. **I am the voice of one crying in the wilderness**: Quoting from Isaiah 40:3, John explained his work - to prepare **the way of the LORD**. His baptism prepared people, cleansing them for the coming King. The idea was, "Get cleaned up, get ready for a royal visit."

i. "John's real function was not to teach ethics, but to point men to Jesus. 'Make straight the way of the Lord' is a call to be ready, for the coming of the Messiah is near." (Morris)

ii. The religious leaders wanted to know who John was, and he wasn't really interested in answering that question. He wanted to talk about his mission: to prepare the way for the Messiah.

b. **Why then do you baptize if you are not the Christ**: The Pharisees wondered about John's authority if he was not actually one of the prophesied ones they had in mind. Yet John's work of baptizing perfectly suited his calling, as he explained.

i. "His baptism was apparently distinctive in that he administered it personally; it was not self-administered as proselyte baptism was." (Bruce)

c. **I baptize with water**: John's baptism demonstrated the humble willingness to repent, be cleansed, and prepare for the coming Messiah. Yet John's baptism gave nothing to help someone *keep* clean. The work of Jesus and His baptism of the Holy Spirit represents more than John's baptism.

i. Jewish people in John's day practiced baptism. It was an outgrowth of ceremonial washings, but only for Gentiles who wanted to become Jews. In submitting to John's baptism, a Jew had to identify with Gentile converts. This was a genuine sign of repentance.

ii. "It is not unlikely that John's baptism followed the pattern of proselyte baptism, which required a renunciation of all evil, complete immersion in water, and then reclothing as a member of the holy communion of law-keepers." (Tenney)

iii. "The novelty in John's case and the sting behind the practice was that he applied to Jews the ceremony which was held to be appropriate in the case of Gentiles coming newly into the faith…to put *Jews* in the same class was horrifying." (Morris)

d. **There stands One among you whom you do not know. It is He who, coming after me, is preferred before me**: John explained to the religious leaders that *he* was not the focus of his work, but the **One** who was already **among** them. John's work was to prepare the way for the **One**.

e. **Who sandal strap I am not worthy to loose**: To untie the strap of a sandal (before foot washing) was duty of the lowest slave in the house.

i. Among Rabbis and their disciples, there was a teacher-student relationship that had the potential for abuse. It was entirely possible that a Rabbi might expect unreasonable service from their disciples. One of the things which was considered "too low" for a Rabbi to expect from his disciples was the untying of the Rabbi's sandal strap. John said he was *unworthy* to do even this.

ii. "'Every service which a slave performs for his master', said one rabbi, 'a disciple will perform for his teacher, except to untie his sandal-strap.'" (Bruce)

iii. **These things were done in Bethabara beyond the Jordan**: "The interview took place at Bethany (House of the ferry-boat) on the east bank of the Jordan at the spot called in Origen's time Bethabara (House of the ford) -- the traditional place of the passage of the Ark and the nation under Joshua (Joshua 3:14-17)." (Trench)

3. (29) John the Baptist's testimony: Jesus is the **Lamb of God**.

The next day John saw Jesus coming toward him, and said, "Behold! The Lamb of God who takes away the sin of the world!"

a. **The next day John saw Jesus coming toward him**: By most reckonings, this was *after* John baptized Jesus and *after* the 40 days of temptation in the wilderness. Jesus came back to see John in his baptizing work.

i. "Some weeks probably had elapsed since Jesus received baptism at John's hands; he had been away since then, but now he is back, and John draws the crowd's attention to him." (Bruce)

ii. "Since then verse 29 must be understood as happening after the baptism, it must have happened *after the Temptation* also. And in this supposition there is not the slightest difficulty." (Alford)

b. **Behold! The Lamb of God who takes away the sin of the world!** At the dawn of His ministry, Jesus was greeted with words declaring His destiny - His sacrificial agony and death on the cross for the sin of mankind. The shadow of the cross was cast over the entire ministry of Jesus.

i. John didn't present Jesus as a great moral example or a great teacher of holiness and love. He proclaimed Jesus as the sacrifice for sin. It wasn't "Behold the great example" or "Behold the great teacher" - it was **Behold, the Lamb of God who takes away the sin of the world**.

ii. "He used 'the lamb' as the symbol of sacrifice in general. Here, he says, is the reality of which all animal sacrifice was the symbol." (Dods)

c. **Behold! The Lamb of God who takes away the sin of the world!** In this one sentence, John the Baptist summarized the greatest work of Jesus: to deal with the sin problem afflicting the human race. Every word of this sentence is important.

i. **Behold!** John said this as he **saw Jesus coming toward him**. As a preacher, John first saw Jesus himself and then told all his listeners to look upon Jesus, to **behold** him.

ii. **The Lamb of God**: John used the image of the sacrificial lamb, represented many times in the Old Testament. Jesus is the perfect fulfillment of every time that image is displayed.

• He is the lamb slain before the foundation of the world.

- He is the animal slain in the Garden of Eden to cover the nakedness of the first sinners.

- He is the lamb God would Himself provide for Abraham as a substitute for Isaac.

- He is the Passover lamb for Israel.

- He is the lamb for the guilt offering in the Levitical sacrifices.

- He is Isaiah's lamb to the slaughter, ready to be shorn

- Each of these lambs fulfilled their role in their death; this was an announcement that Jesus would die, and as a sacrifice for the **sin of the world**.

iii. **Who takes away**: The sense of the original combines the words *to bear* and *to take away*. Jesus bears sin, but in the sense of bearing them upon Himself and *taking them away*. "The verb 'taketh away' conveys the notion of bearing off." (Morris)

- "John does not say 'the *sins*,' as the Litany, following an imperfect translation, makes him say. But he says, 'the *sin* of the world,' as if the whole mass of human transgression was bound together, in one black and awful bundle, and laid upon the unshrinking shoulders of this better Atlas who can bear it all, and bear it all away." (Maclaren)

iv. **The sin**: Not the plural *sins*, but the singular **sin** - with the sense that that the entire guilt of humanity was collected into one and placed upon Jesus. "Only afterwards could the Evangelist, as he looked back, have caught the Baptist's full meaning." (Trench)

v. **Of the world**: The sacrifice of this **Lamb of God** has all the capacity to forgive every sin and cleanse every sinner. It is big enough for the whole **world**. "He will give Himself as the expiatory Sacrifice not only of the sins of His people, but of the germ of all sin in Adam's descendants, the sin of the world, the apostasy in Eden: thus wide and deep is the Baptist's vision." (Trench)

4. (30-34) John the Baptist's testimony: Jesus is the **Son of God**.

"This is He of whom I said, 'After me comes a Man who is preferred before me, for He was before me.' I did not know Him; but that He should be revealed to Israel, therefore I came baptizing with water." And John bore witness, saying, "I saw the Spirit descending from heaven like a dove, and He remained upon Him. I did not know Him, but He who sent me to baptize with water said to me, 'Upon whom you see the Spirit descending, and remaining on Him, this is He who

baptizes with the Holy Spirit.' And I have seen and testified that this is the Son of God."

a. **For He was before me**: John the Baptist was actually born before Jesus - and John knew this (Luke 1). When John said **He was before me**, he spoke of the eternal pre-existence of Jesus. John knew that Jesus was eternal and that Jesus was God.

> i. **After me comes a Man**: "The Greek term *aner* is introduced here; it means 'man' with emphasis on maleness - an emphasis that is lost in the more generic *anthropos*. The use of *aner* intimates the headship of Christ over his followers in the sense of the man-woman relationship." (Tenney)

b. **Upon whom you see the Spirit descending, and remaining on Him, this is He who baptizes with the Holy Spirit**: God gave John the Baptist the sure sign to know the Messiah. He would be the one on Whom the Holy Spirit descended upon from heaven. John was a reliable witness regarding Jesus, because he had confirming evidence from God.

> i. "Jesus received nothing at His Baptism that He had not before: the Baptist merely saw that day in a visible symbol that which had actually and invisibly taken place [at the conception of Jesus]." (Trench)

> ii. "If the cleansing with water was associated with John's ministry, the bestowal of the Spirit was reserved for the one greater than John." (Bruce)

c. **I have seen and testified that this is the Son of God**: The solemn testimony of John the Baptist was that Jesus is the **Son of God**. He is the **Son of God** in the sense shown in John 1:18 - the One who perfectly declares the nature and personality of God the Father.

> i. The gospel of John emphasizes John's role as a witness, not a baptizer. Witnesses give testimony as to what they have seen and experienced, in an effort to establish the truth. Beyond that, they are unreliable and operate on hearsay - not direct evidence.

> ii. "In naming Him 'The Son of God,' the Baptist speaks with unclouded vision: he means nothing less than the full Christian doctrine that the Man Jesus is also the eternal Son of the eternal Father, co-equal, co-eternal." (Trench)

> iii. Witnesses are not neutral - they are committed to the truth of their testimony, or they are unreliable witnesses. John was a reliable witness, and knew who Jesus was because of what he saw with his own eyes.

D. The testimony of the first disciples.

1. (35-39) Two of John's disciples begin to follow Jesus.

Again, the next day, John stood with two of his disciples. And looking at Jesus as He walked, he said, "Behold the Lamb of God!" The two disciples heard him speak, and they followed Jesus. Then Jesus turned, and seeing them following, said to them, "What do you seek?" They said to Him, "Rabbi" (which is to say, when translated, Teacher), "where are You staying?" He said to them, "Come and see." They came and saw where He was staying, and remained with Him that day (now it was about the tenth hour).

a. **John stood with two of his disciples**: The Gospel writer tells us that one of these two was Andrew (John 1:40). The other of the two is not identified, but for several reasons it is reasonable to think it was John the Gospel writer himself, who appears several times in his Gospel, but is never specifically named.

i. "Who the other disciple was, is not certain: but considering (1) that the Evangelist *never names himself* in his Gospel, and (2) that this account is so minutely accurate as to specify even the hours of the day, and in all respects *bears marks of an eye-witness*, and again (3) that this other disciple, from this last circumstance, certainly *would have been named*, had not the name been suppressed *for some special reasons*, we are justified in inferring that it was *the Evangelist himself*." (Alford)

ii. **And looking at Jesus**: "*Attentively beholding*, εμβλεψας, from εν, *into*, and βλεπω, *to look*-to view with steadfastness and attention." (Clarke) "A characteristically searching look turned upon an individual." (Morris)

b. **Behold, the Lamb of God!** John already said this of Jesus in John 1:29. Perhaps by this time - after Jesus had returned from His temptations in the wilderness - John said this every time he saw Jesus. To him, it was the most important thing about Jesus.

c. **And they followed Jesus**: The text does not specifically say, but the implication is that these **two disciples** did this with John's permission and direction. John the Baptist did not care about gathering disciples after himself. He was perfectly satisfied to have these disciples leave his circle and follow Jesus. It fulfilled his ministry; it did not take away from it.

d. **What do you seek? ... Come and see**: Jesus asked these two disciples an important and logical question - and a question He continues to ask to all humanity today. For the answer, Jesus directed them to *Himself*, to live with *Him*, not to John or anyone else (**Come and see**).

i. **What do you seek?** "It was not an accident that the first words which the Master spoke in His Messianic office were this profoundly significant question, 'What seek ye?' He asks it of us all, He asks it of us to-day." (Maclaren)

ii. "He probed them to find out whether they were motivated by idle curiosity or by a real desire to know him." (Tenney)

iii. Jesus did not refer them back to John the Baptist, even though he knew a lot about Jesus. To be Jesus' disciple, they must deal with Jesus directly. So Jesus invited John and Andrew to be a part of His life. Jesus didn't live a cloistered, ultra-private life. Jesus taught and trained His twelve disciples by allowing them to live with Him.

e. **Now it was about the tenth hour**: This was such a memorable occasion for writer that he remembered the exact hour that he met Jesus. This is a subtle clue that one of the two disciples who came to Jesus from John was the apostle John himself.

2. (40-42) Andrew brings his brother, Simon Peter to Jesus.

One of the two who heard John *speak*, and followed Him, was Andrew, Simon Peter's brother. He first found his own brother Simon, and said to him, "We have found the Messiah" (which is translated, the Christ). And he brought him to Jesus. Now when Jesus looked at him, He said, "You are Simon the son of Jonah. You shall be called Cephas" (which is translated, A Stone).

a. **He first found his own brother**: Andrew met Jesus, and then wanted his brother **Simon Peter** to meet Jesus. Each time Andrew is mentioned in the Gospel of John, he is bringing someone to Jesus (also at John 6:8 and 12:22).

i. *Through the centuries, this is how most people come to faith in Jesus Christ.* A Peter has an Andrew who introduces him to Jesus. This is natural, because it is the nature of Christian experience that those who enjoy the experience desire to share their experience with others.

ii. "'Andrew finds *first* of all *his own* brother Simon': which implies that afterwards the brother of the other of the two was also found and brought to the same place and on the same day." (Trench)

b. **We have found the Messiah**: This was a simply yet great testimony. Andrew knew that Jesus was **the Messiah**, the long expected Savior of Israel and the world.

c. **You shall be called Cephas**: In giving Simon a new name (**Cephas** or Peter, meaning **A Stone**), Jesus told Andrew's brother what kind of man he would be transformed into. Before Jesus was done with Peter, he would be **a stone** of stability for Jesus Christ.

3. (43-44) Jesus calls Philip to follow Him.

The following day Jesus wanted to go to Galilee, and He found Philip and said to him, "Follow Me." Now Philip was from Bethsaida, the city of Andrew and Peter.

> a. **He found Philip and said to him, "Follow Me"**: If we only had John's Gospel we might think that this was the first time Jesus had met these men from Galilee. The other gospel accounts inform us that Jesus had met many of them before; yet this was His formal invitation to Philip.

> b. **Follow Me**: There was nothing dramatic recorded about the call of Philip. Jesus simply said to him, "**Follow Me**," and Philip did.

> > i. "The verb 'Follow' will be used here in its full sense of 'follow as a disciple'. The present tense has continuous force, 'keep on following'." (Morris)

> > ii. "Bethsaida means 'house of the fisherman' or 'Fishertown'. It lay a short distance east of the point where the Jordan enters the Lake of Galilee." (Bruce)

4. (45-51) Nathaniel overcomes prejudice to follow Jesus.

Philip found Nathanael and said to him, "We have found Him of whom Moses in the law, and also the prophets, wrote—Jesus of Nazareth, the son of Joseph." And Nathanael said to him, "Can anything good come out of Nazareth?" Philip said to him, "Come and see." Jesus saw Nathanael coming toward Him, and said of him, "Behold, an Israelite indeed, in whom is no deceit!" Nathanael said to Him, "How do You know me?" Jesus answered and said to him, "Before Philip called you, when you were under the fig tree, I saw you." Nathanael answered and said to Him, "Rabbi, You are the Son of God! You are the King of Israel!" Jesus answered and said to him, "Because I said to you, 'I saw you under the fig tree,' do you believe? You will see greater things than these." And He said to him, "Most assuredly, I say to you, hereafter you shall see heaven open, and the angels of God ascending and descending upon the Son of Man."

> a. **Him of whom Moses in the law, and also the prophets wrote**: This was Philip's testimony as a witness of Jesus Christ. He declared that He as the Messiah and the Savior predicted in the Old Testament.

i. "Nathanael is today generally understood to be the same person as Bartholomew, one of the Twelve; Nathanael being the personal name, Bartholomew (son of Tolmai) the patronymie." (Trench)

b. **Can anything good come out of Nazareth?** Nathanael responded to Philip's announcement with prejudice. Hearing that Jesus came from **Nazareth**, Nathanael thought he had no more reason to think that He might be the Messiah or anyone important.

c. **Come and see**: Instead of arguing against Nathanael's prejudice, Phillip simply invited him to meet Jesus for himself.

d. **Behold, an Israelite indeed, in whom is no deceit!** Jesus gave him a wonderful compliment. The sense is that there was nothing tricky or deceptive in Nathanael. He didn't have a mask.

i. **Deceit**: "This last word is used in early Greek writers as a 'bait' (for catching fish). Hence it comes to signify *any cunning contrivance for deceiving or catching*…It thus has the notion of 'deceit' or 'craft'. It is used in the Bible of Jacob before his change of heart (Genesis 27:35, which is the point of Temple's translation, 'an Israelite in whom there is no Jacob!'" (Morris)

ii. "He is a proper *Israelite*, a type of the man pronounced 'blessed' by the Psalmist, the man 'in whose spirit is no guile' (Psalm 32:2)." (Tasker)

e. **Under the fig tree, I saw you**: It is possible Nathanael liked to pray and meditate upon God and His Word under the shade of an actual fig tree. Yet, **under the fig tree** was a phrase Rabbis used to describe meditation on the Scriptures. We can suppose that Nathanael spent time in prayer and in meditating on the Scriptures, and Jesus told him "**I saw you**" there.

i. "It is said of Rabbi Hasa in the tract Bereshith that he and his disciples were in the habit of studying under a fig tree." (Trench)

ii. "Perhaps it was a place where Nathanael had recently sat in meditation and received some spiritual impression. It is impossible to be sure. Certainly the shady foliage of the fig tree made it a suitable tree to sit under in the heat of the day." (Bruce)

f. **You are the Son of God, the King of Israel**: This was the testimony of Nathanael regarding Jesus. **Son of God** described the unique relationship of Jesus to God the Father, and **King of Israel** described His status as Messiah and **King**.

i. **The Son of God**: "Here, as there, the article is important. It indicates that the expression is to be understood as bearing a full, not a minimal content…Here was someone who could not be described in ordinary human terms." (Morris)

g. You shall see greater things than these: Nathanael was amazed by what he already saw in Jesus, but Jesus told him that there was much, much more to see - **greater things than these**.

i. The promise to **see greater things than these** continues for the believer. "Have you known Christ as the Word? He is more; both Spirit and Life. Has He become flesh? You shall behold Him glorified with the glory He had before the worlds. Have you known Him as Alpha, before all? He is also Omega. Have you met John? You shall meet One so much greater. Do you know the baptism by water? You shall be baptized by fire. Have you beheld the Lamb on the Cross? You shall behold Him in the midst of the throne." (Meyer)

h. You shall see heaven open, and the angels of God ascending and descending upon the Son of Man: Jesus promised Nathanael a greater sign than he had seen before, even to see **heaven open**.

i. Jesus' announcement of **the angels of God ascending and descending upon the Son of Man** probably connects with the dream of Jacob in Genesis 28:12, where Jacob saw a ladder from earth to heaven, and the angels ascending and descending upon it. Jesus said that *He* was the ladder, the link, between heaven and earth. When Nathanael came to understand that Jesus is the mediator between God and man, it would be an even greater sign (**you will see greater things than these**).

ii. "He now learns that Jesus is the real ladder by which the gulf between earth and heaven is bridged." (Tasker)

iii. This seems like rather obscure reference, but it was extremely meaningful to Nathanael. Possibly it was the very portion of Scripture Nathaniel meditated on **under the fig tree**.

i. Son of Man: The idea behind this phrase is not "the perfect man" or "the ideal man" or even "the common man." Instead, it was a reference to Daniel 7:13-14, where the King of Glory who comes to judge the world was called the **Son of Man**.

i. Jesus used this title often because in His day, it was a Messianic title free from political and nationalistic sentiment. When a Jewish person of that time heard "King" or "Christ" they often thought of a political or military savior. Jesus emphasized another term, often calling Himself the **Son of Man**.

ii. "The term, 'The Son of man', then points us to Christ's conception of Himself as of heavenly origin and as the possessor of heavenly glory. At one and the same time and points us to His lowliness and His sufferings for men. The two are the same." (Morris)

iii. This section of John shows four ways of coming to Jesus:

- Andrew came to Jesus because of the preaching of John.

- Peter came to Jesus because of the witness of his brother.

- Phillip came to Jesus as a result of the direct call of Jesus.

- Nathaniel came to Jesus as he overcame personal prejudices by a personal encounter with Jesus.

iv. This section shows us four different witnesses testifying to the identity of Jesus. How much more testimony does anyone need?

- John the Baptist testified that Jesus is eternal, that He is the man uniquely anointed with the Holy Spirit, that He is the Lamb of God, and that Jesus is the unique Son of God.

- Andrew testified that Jesus is the Messiah, the Christ.

- Phillip testified that Jesus is the One prophesied in the Old Testament.

- Nathaniel testified that Jesus is the Son of God and the King of Israel.

John 2 - Conversion and Cleansing

A. Water into wine at a wedding.

1. (1-2) Jesus, His mother, and His disciples at a wedding.

On the third day there was a wedding in Cana of Galilee, and the mother of Jesus was there. Now both Jesus and His disciples were invited to the wedding.

a. **On the third day**: John continued the story from the previous chapter that noted happenings on a particular day (John 1:19-28), on *the next day* (John 1:29-34), the *next day* after that (John 1:35-42), the *following day* (John 1:43-51) and now **on the third day**.

i. "'The third day' is probably to be counted from the event last mentioned, the call of Nathanael. The reckoning is, as usual, inclusive; we should say 'two days later'." (Barclay)

b. **Jesus and His disciples were invited to the wedding**: This is the first of many stories suggesting that Jesus was always welcome among those having a good time. Jesus didn't spoil the good time, and in the Jewish culture of that day a **wedding** was the best party of all.

i. One old tradition says that this was John the Gospel writer's wedding, and he left his bride at the altar after seeing this miracle. This should be regarded as a pleasant but unlikely story.

ii. Mormons take this idea an absurd step further declaring this was *Jesus'* wedding. Of course, this is against the plain meaning of this passage and all of the gospel records of the life of Jesus.

iii. The fact that Jesus was invited to this wedding has several implications:

- The invitation of Jesus to this wedding says something about the kind of man Jesus was.

31

- The invitation of Jesus to this wedding says something about the presence of Jesus at weddings. "Jesus comes to a marriage, and gives his blessing there, that we may know that our family life is under his care." (Spurgeon)

- The invitation of Jesus to this wedding says something about what happens when we invite Jesus into the events of our life.

iv. "He was at this juncture fresh from the most disturbing personal conflict, His work awaited Him, a work full of intense strife, hazard, and pain; yet in a mind occupied with these things the marriage joy of a country couple finds a fit place." (Dods)

v. **And the mother of Jesus was there**: "There is no mention of Joseph. The explanation most probably is that by this time Joseph was dead. It would seem that Joseph died quite soon, and that the reason why Jesus spent eighteen long years in Nazareth was that he had to take upon himself the support of his mother and his family. It was only when his younger brothers and sisters were able to look after themselves that he left home." (Barclay)

2. (3-5) The wedding with no wine and a mother's request.

And when they ran out of wine, the mother of Jesus said to Him, "They have no wine." Jesus said to her, "Woman, what does your concern have to do with Me? My hour has not yet come." His mother said to the servants, "Whatever He says to you, do _it_."

a. **When they ran out of wine**: This was a major social mistake, and could shame the couple for a long time. A wedding was supposed to be the best party of all, and for a host to fail in providing adequate hospitality (partially in the form of food and drink) was a great dishonor.

i. Some believe that the presence of the disciples - thought of as uninvited guests - made the wine run out faster than expected. The text gives no evidence of this. Morris has a better idea: "This may indicate that they were poor and had made the minimum provision hoping for the best."

ii. "To fail in providing adequately for the guests would involve social disgrace. In the closely knit communities of Jesus' day such an error would never be forgotten, and would haunt the newly married couple all their lives." (Tenney)

iii. Additionally, rabbis of that day considered wine a symbol of joy. Therefore "to run out of wine would almost have been the equivalent of admitting that neither the guests nor the bride and groom were happy." (Boice)

iv. "In the ancient Near East there was a strong element of reciprocity about weddings, and that, for example, it was possible to take legal action in certain circumstances against a man who had failed to provide the appropriate wedding gift…it means that when the supply of wine failed more than social embarrassment was involved. The bridegroom as his family may well have become involved in a heavy pecuniary liability." (Morris)

b. **They have no wine**: We don't know exactly why Mary brought this problem to her son Jesus. Perhaps she eagerly anticipated the day Jesus would miraculously demonstrate that He was the Messiah. When people saw that Jesus was the Messiah it would also vindicate Mary, who lived under the shadow of a pregnancy and birth that many people questioned.

i. It wasn't wrong for Mary to sense that the time had come for her Son to enter public ministry. She knew He had been baptized by John and confirmed with a heavenly sign at His baptism. Mary knew He endured temptation in the wilderness. She knew Jesus had been publically introduced as *the Lamb of God who takes away the sin of the world* (John 1:29), and had begun to gather disciples to Himself.

c. **Woman, what does your concern have to do with Me?** Jesus spoke to His mother with a term of respect, but He did *not* call her "mother." Jesus wanted to emphasize that now, at the beginning of His public ministry, He now had a different relationship with Mary.

i. **Woman**: "So far from being a rough and discourteous way of address, it was a title of respect. We have no way of speaking in English which exactly renders it; but it is better to translate it *Lady* which gives at least the courtesy in it." (Barclay)

ii. It was not rude to say **mother**, but neither was it an expected way for a son to address a mother. "Yet we must bear in mind that it is most unusual to find it when a son addresses his mother. There appear to be no examples of this cited, other than those noticed in this Gospel." (Morris)

iii. Jesus indicated that there was a new relationship between Him and Mary. "If she sought his help now, she must not seek it on the basis of their mother-and-son relationship." (Bruce)

iv. Jesus seemed to say to Mary, "I won't do it. It's not time" - but then He went on to do it. What He really said to Mary was, "We now have a different relationship. Let me consult My heavenly Father." Jesus must have prayed and then known what to do, because He later said in this Gospel:

- *Most assuredly, I say to you, the Son can do nothing of Himself, but what He sees the Father do; for whatever He does, the Son also does in like manner.* (John 5:19)
- *I can of Myself do nothing... I do not seek My own will, but the will of the Father who sent Me.* (John 5:30)
- *I do nothing of Myself; but as My Father taught Me, I speak these things.* (John 8:28)
- *For I always do those things that please Him.* (John 8:29)

v. "He will indeed take action, as she was so very sure He would when she told the servants to do whatever He told them, but He will act in His own way, for His own reasons, and at His own time." (Tasker)

vi. "Jesus in His public ministry was not only or primarily the Son of Mary, but 'the Son of man' who was to bring the realities of heaven to men. A new relationship was established. Mary must not presume." (Morris)

vii. "With all loving respect, he yet very decidedly shuts out all interference from Mary; for his kingdom was to be according to the spirit, and not after the flesh. I delight in believing, concerning the mother of Jesus, that though she fell into a natural mistake, yet she did not for an instant persist in it; neither did she hide it from John, but probably took care to tell it to him, that no others should ever fall into similar error by thinking of her in an unfitting manner." (Spurgeon)

viii. Trench was correct when he noted, "Christendom, Catholic or Orthodox, has long seen in this His first miracle the value our Lord attaches to His mother's supplications and the pleasure He has in granting them." Yet that is to misunderstand this work entirely. Jesus made it clear that He did *not* do this on the basis of the mother-son relationship.

ix. **My hour has not yet come**: "This expression, **mine hour**, is generally used in John of the time of the *Death* of Christ. But it is only so used because His death in those passages is the subject naturally underlying the narrative. It is, *any fixed or appointed time*; -- and therefore here, the appointed time of His self-manifestation by miracles."

d. **Whatever He says to you, do it**: The recorded words of Mary are few. However, it is good to pay attention to her words that were recorded because they consistently glorify Jesus, not Mary herself. It is wise for everyone to obey Mary's direction, **whatever He says to you, do it**.

i. To deliberately go through Mary to get to Jesus is to regard Jesus as hardhearted, and Mary as tenderhearted. This concept "is totally alien from the Bible. It comes from mother-son ideas prevalent in pagan religions." (Barnhouse)

ii. "The recorded words of Mary are few; these particular words have an application beyond the immediate occasion which called them forth." (Bruce)

3. (6-7) Filling the waterpots.

Now there were set there six waterpots of stone, according to the manner of purification of the Jews, containing twenty or thirty gallons apiece. Jesus said to them, "Fill the waterpots with water." And they filled them up to the brim.

a. **Six waterpots of stone**: Jesus began this miracle by using what was at hand. He could have supplied more wine any number of ways, but He started with what was there.

b. **According to the manner of purification of the Jews**: The waterpots are connected with the system of Law, because they were used in ceremonial purification.

i. **Containing twenty or thirty gallons apiece**: Spurgeon saw significance for preachers in John's approximate number. "Let us always speak correctly; sometimes, 'almost' or 'thereabouts' will be words that will just save our truthfulness. Let us not speak positively when we do not know; and when the accuracy of a statement is necessary, and we cannot give it in terms that are definite, let us give it in words like these, 'containing two or three firkins apiece.'" (Spurgeon)

c. **Fill the waterpots with water**: The servants under the direction of Jesus were in a unique place of blessing for this miracle. Jesus wanted the cooperation of men in this miracle. He could have filled the pots Himself, or just as easily created the liquid in the pots. But He knew that if the servants shared in the work, then they also shared in the blessing.

i. The servants did not *do* the miracle. Their efforts alone were completely insufficient. But because of their obedience to Jesus, they shared in the joy of the miracle.

ii. The servants were especially blessed because they obeyed without question, and to the fullest (**they filled them up to the brim**). This means that the miracle would be fulfilled in the greatest measure possible. If they were lazy and only filled the waterpots half full, there would have only been half as much wine.

d. **They filled them up to the brim**: The waterpots were filled to the brim - with no room to add any more - because Jesus wasn't going to *add something* to the water; He was going to *transform it*.

> i. This is a pattern for our faith and obedience. "When you are bidden to believe in him, believe in him up to the brim. When you are told to love him, love him up to the brim. When you are commanded to serve him, serve him up to the brim." (Spurgeon)

4. (8-10) The water turned to wine, and the best wine.

And He said to them, "Draw *some* out now, and take *it* to the master of the feast." And they took *it*. When the master of the feast had tasted the water that was made wine, and did not know where it came from (but the servants who had drawn the water knew), the master of the feast called the bridegroom. And he said to him, "Every man at the beginning sets out the good wine, and when the *guests* have well drunk, then the inferior. You have kept the good wine until now!"

a. **Draw some out now, and take it to the master of the feast**: This took *faith* on behalf of the servants. Imagine how angry the **master of the feast** would be if they brought him *water* to taste! Yet in faith, they obeyed the word of Jesus.

> i. "The architriklinos, then, when he had tasted the water which had now become wine, and did not know whence it had been procured, and was therefore impartially judging it merely as wine among wines." (Dods)

> ii. Jesus insisted that the miracle be put to the test, and right away. He didn't command that the water made wine first be served to the guests, but to the master of the feast. Test it, by the proper authority, and do it right away.

> iii. "In order for wine to be produced, we have the growth and ripening of the grape; the crushing of it in proper vessels; the fermentation; -- but here all these are in a moment brought about by their *results*, by the same Power which made the laws of nature, and created and unfolded the capacities of man." (Alford)

b. **The servants who had drawn the water knew**: The faithful servants who did their work to the full **knew** the greatness of the miracle. The **master of the feast** only knew it was good wine; he didn't know it was a miracle. This knowledge was a special blessing for the **servants**.

> i. We are not told exactly *how* Jesus performed this miracle. We assume that the transformation took place in the waterpots, but it also could have happened in the actual serving of the wine. Yet according to the

record, Jesus did not say a word or perform a ceremony; He simply exercised His will and the miracle was done.

ii. "When Moses sweetened the bitter water it was by a tree which the Lord showed to him. When Elisha purged the springs he threw salt into the water. We have no instrumentality here." (Spurgeon)

iii. "Is this not the signature of divinity, that without means the mere forth-putting of the will is all that is wanted to mould matter as plastic to His command?" (Maclaren)

iv. In the first temptation in the wilderness, the devil asked Jesus to turn stones into bread - for Himself. In this first sign, Mary asked Jesus to turn water into wine - for others. Jesus refused the first and did the second.

v. "It is manifest that *one miracle proves the power to work every miracle.* If Christ can turn water into wine by his will, he can do anything and everything. If Jesus has once exercised a power beyond nature, we may readily believe that he can do it again: there is no limit to his power." (Spurgeon)

vi. The large quantity of wine - much more than a wedding party could consume - was deliberate. Selling the excess wine was a likely source of income for the newlyweds. Also, "It would furnish proof, after the marriage was over, that the transformation had been actual. The wedding guests had not dreamt it. There was the wine." (Dods) "No small gifts fall from so great a hand." (Trapp)

c. **You have kept the good wine until now!** The **master of the feast** paid the bridegroom a great and public compliment. Running out of wine would have meant social disgrace; the miracle of Jesus transformed that into a better wedding party than ever.

i. When Jesus made wine, it was **good wine**. It doesn't mean that it had a particularly high alcohol content, but that it was well-made wine.

ii. Some go to great lengths to show that what Jesus made here was really grape juice. While some find that line of thinking convincing, it is not the opinion of the author. **Good wine** is **good wine**, not good grape juice. It is true that wine in that day (as commonly served) was diluted (two parts wine to three parts water, according to Barclay) and had a much lower content of alcohol than modern wine; but it was still wine.

iii. "As to the wine such as is commonly used in the East, a person must drink inordinately before he would become intoxicated with it. It would be possible, for there were cases in which men were intoxicated with wine; but, as a rule, intoxication was a rare vice in the Savior's times and in the preceding ages." (Spurgeon)

iv. "Are there not many things which Jesus brought to the world, the same in *kind* as the world had always had, yet overtopping them all in worth and excellence?" There was love and joy and kindness in the world before Jesus, but it was a different kind altogether after Jesus. (Morrison)

d. **You have kept the good wine until now!** There is a principle behind these words; the principle that for the people of God, the best is always yet to come.

i. "I can conceive you, brethren, in the very last moment of your life, or rather, in the first moment of your life, saying, 'He has kept the best wine until now.' When you begin to see him face to face, when you enter into the closest fellowship, with nothing to disturb or to distract you, then shall you say 'The best wine is kept until now.'" (Spurgeon)

ii. "Without God the last is the worst…If sin conceals the worse behind tomorrow, may it not conceal the worse behind the grave?" (Morrison)

iii. "I shall bid you look within the doors of the devil's house, and you will find he is true to this rule; he brings forth first the good wine, and when men have well drunk, and their brains are muddled therewith, then he bringeth forth that which is worse." (Spurgeon)

5. (11-12) The beginning of signs.

This beginning of signs Jesus did in Cana of Galilee, and manifested His glory; and His disciples believed in Him. After this He went down to Capernaum, He, His mother, His brothers, and His disciples; and they did not stay there many days.

a. **This beginning of signs Jesus did in Cana of Galilee**: This **beginning of signs** in the Gospel of John (the first of seven) is a miracle of conversion, from the old ways of law, ceremony and purification to the new life of Jesus.

i. "But for him [John] the miracles are all 'signs'. They point beyond themselves. This particular miracle signifies that there is a transforming power associated with Jesus." (Morris)

ii. Moses turned water into blood, showing that the Law results in death (Exodus 7:17-21). But Jesus' first miracle turned water into wine, showing the gladness and joy of His new work. This acts out what John said in John 1:17: *For the law was given through Moses, but grace and truth came through Jesus Christ.*

iii. We could say that the water is like a relationship with God under the Old Covenant, and the wine is like a relationship with God under the New Covenant.

- The wine was *after* the water, and the New Covenant is *after* the Old Covenant.

- The wine was *from* the water, and the New Covenant is *from* the Old Covenant.

- The wine was and *better* than the water; and the New Covenant is *better* than the Old Covenant.

iv. This **beginning of signs** is the first of seven signs presented in the Gospel of John, each designed to bring the reader to faith in Jesus Christ. John explained this purpose in John 20:30-31: *And truly Jesus did many other signs in the presence of His disciples, which are not written in this book; but these are written that you may believe that Jesus is the Christ, the Son of God, and that believing you may have life in His name.*

v. Most reckon the seven signs in the Gospel of John as:

- John 2:1-11 - Water into wine.

- John 4:46-54 - Healing of the nobleman's son.

- John 5:1-15 - Healing at the pool of Bethesda.

- John 6:1-14 - Feeding the 5,000.

- John 6:15-21 - Jesus walks on water.

- John 9:1-12 - Healing of the man born blind.

- John 11:1-44 - Lazarus raised from the dead.

vi. The ancient Greek word *semeion* [sign] is used 74 times in the New Testament, and 23 of the 74 are in John's writings. Most of the remaining are in the other gospels, with also some in Acts and Paul's letters. "John has *semeion* in the formal sense of 'sign' or 'pointer'... The *semia* establish faith, but God is the content of the faith, not the *semeia*." (Kittel)

vii. "That the incident can be allegorised is no proof that it is only allegory and not history. All incidents and histories can be allegorised." (Dods)

viii. **Beginning of signs**: "This assertion of St. John excludes all the apocryphal miracles of the Gospel of the Infancy, and such like works, from credit." (Afford)

b. **And manifested His glory**: According to John 2:1, this miracle happened *on the third day*. John hints at the idea that Jesus showed His glory on the third day, and that His disciples believed in Him when they saw His glory.

i. The **glory** of Jesus is found in His compassion, and this was a miracle full of compassion. The wine was not an absolute necessity; no one would die drinking water. All at risk was the embarrassment, reputation, and perhaps the bank account of the bridal couple. Yet, Jesus - and His Father - counted that enough to do this first public miracle and sign.

c. **His disciples believed in Him**: Of course they believed before, but now their belief was deepened and re-expressed. This is typical in the Christian life. God does great things in our lives, and we *believe in Him* all over again.

i. "Will you that read your Greek Testament notice the expression here? Is it said, 'His disciples believed him'? No. Is it 'Believed in him'? No. 'Believed on him'? Yes. It is so in our version; but into would be more correct. The Greek is 'eis': his disciples believed into him. They so believed that they seemed to submerge themselves in Jesus." (Spurgeon)

ii. The faith of the disciples is significant, especially in comparison to the others present who benefited from the miracle, but of whom no specific belief is mentioned.

- The master of the feast didn't believe.
- The bridegroom didn't believe.
- Doesn't even say that the servants believed.
- Those who were His disciples believed.

iii. Each of the persons around Jesus shows us something significant regarding Jesus and His work.

- Mary shows us to expect Jesus to do big things, but not to tell Him *how* to do them.
- The servants show us to obey Jesus without question and to the utmost, and to enjoy being part of the miracle.
- The bridegroom shows us that Jesus loves to save the day.
- The master of the feast shows us that Jesus saves the best for last.
- The disciples show us that this was for real.

d. **After this He went down to Capernaum**: On the northern shore of the Sea of Galilee, the village of **Capernaum** was the adopted home of Jesus (Matthew 4:13).

i. "It appears that the holy family as a whole moved from Nazareth to Capernaum, where Jesus had his headquarters for the greater part of his Galilean ministry." (Bruce)

ii. "The Greek text by the form of the sentence and its use of ----- (singular) implies that this removal was owing to our Lord, and that the others named went because He went." (Trench)

iii. **His brothers**: "The expression, 'his brethren' has been variously understood. The most natural way of taking it is to understand children of Joseph and Mary... The expression occurs several times in the Synoptic Gospels, and never with any qualification such as would be expected if the words were to bear any other meaning." (Morris)

iv. "The word for cousin (*anepsios*) existed in the Greek language and could have been used if needed." (Tenney) Two other passages, in the most plain sense, tell us that Jesus had half-siblings through Mary.

- Joseph knew her not till she had brought forth a son. (Matthew 1:25)
- Jesus was Mary's firstborn son. (Luke 2:7)

B. The temple cleansed.

1. (13-17) Jesus drives out the moneychangers and sellers of sacrificial animals.

Now the Passover of the Jews was at hand, and Jesus went up to Jerusalem. And He found in the temple those who sold oxen and sheep and doves, and the moneychangers doing business. When He had made a whip of cords, He drove them all out of the temple, with the sheep and the oxen, and poured out the changers' money and overturned the tables. And He said to those who sold doves, "Take these things away! Do not make My Father's house a house of merchandise!" Then His disciples remembered that it was written, "Zeal for Your house has eaten Me up."

a. **The Passover of the Jews was at hand**: Jerusalem would be crowded with thousands of visitors coming at **Passover**. The **temple** mount would be particularly crowded, and Jesus saw many **doing business** in the outer courts of the temple.

i. "The very fact of the market being held there would produce an unseemly mixture of sacred and profane transactions, even setting aside the abuses which would be certain to be mingled with the traffic." (Alford)

ii. **The moneychangers doing business**: "Astonishing as it may sound, it is likely that as many as two and a quarter million Jews sometimes assembled in the Holy City to keep the Passover." (Barclay) According to Barclay, they all had to pay the temple tax, which was the equivalent of about two days wages for a working man - but had to be paid in the special temple coin. This is why the **moneychangers** did so much business.

iii. Many commentators say the reason why foreign coins were not allowed in temple contributions was because they bore the image of the emperor or pagan gods. But "Tyrian coinage was not only permitted, but expressly prescribed (Mishnah, *Bekh.* 8:7), and this bore heathen symbols." (Morris). It seems that the issue was not what was on the coin, but what was *in* the coin, and only coinage that had a reputation for being of good weight and content was allowed.

iv. "Being familiar it became legitimate, and no one though of any incongruity in it until this young Nazarene felt a flash of zeal for the sanctity of His Father's house consuming Him." (Maclaren)

v. **The Passover of the Jews**: "Our Evangelist repeatedly refers to festivals as festivals 'of the Jews' - not because he himself was not a Jew by birth and upbringing (he was), but because many of his readers would be Gentiles, unacquainted with the details of the Jewish sacred year." (Bruce)

b. **When He had made a whip of cords**: When Jesus drove those **doing business** out of the temple courts, He did not do it in a flash of anger. He carefully took the time to make **a whip of cords**, and thought carefully about what He would do.

i. Curiously, some commentators are confident that Jesus used the **whip of cords** only upon the animals, and others are confident that He used it upon both men and animals. Nevertheless, the sense is much more a display of Jesus' *authority* than *violence*.

c. **He drove them all out... poured out the changers' money and overturned tables**: Those **doing business** in the outer courts of the temple spoiled the only place where Gentiles could come and worship. This area (the court of the Gentiles) was made into a **house of merchandise**.

i. Remember that *cleansing* was part of the Passover celebration. Removing every speck of anything leavened (made with yeast) from the home was a symbol, a picture, of cleansing from sin.

ii. Matthew, Mark, and Luke each describe *another* cleansing of the temple performed by Jesus, towards the *end* of His earthly ministry. In both cases, the *presence* of these merchants in the temple courts spoiled the only place Gentiles could pray. In addition their *dishonesty* made their presence all the worse.

iii. "John is not correcting a supposed chronological blunder on the part of the earlier evangelists, nor deliberately altering their history in the interests of theological exposition, but, we may reasonably suppose, relating an additional 'cleansing'." (Tasker)

iv. "The evil in question was one which was likely to recur after a check. Jesus' action, though salutary, is not likely to have put a permanent end to the practice." (Morris)

d. **Zeal for Your house has eaten Me up**: The disciples remembered this line from Psalm 69:9 and connected it to the **zeal** Jesus had for the purity of God's house and worship practiced there.

i. John began with a miracle of *conversion* (changing water into wine). Then he showed Jesus performing a work of *cleansing* (the cleansing of the temple). This is always how Jesus works in His people: *conversion* first, then *cleansing*.

2. (18-22) Jesus speaks of a new temple, and its destiny.

So the Jews answered and said to Him, "What sign do You show to us, since You do these things?" Jesus answered and said to them, "Destroy this temple, and in three days I will raise it up." Then the Jews said, "It has taken forty-six years to build this temple, and will You raise it up in three days?" But He was speaking of the temple of His body. Therefore, when He had risen from the dead, His disciples remembered that He had said this to them; and they believed the Scripture and the word which Jesus had said.

a. **What sign do You show to us, since You do these things?** This wasn't necessarily a bad question. Anyone who drove the merchants out from the temple courts claimed the authority to do it. The Jews wanted to know if Jesus really had this authority. The problem is that they demanded a **sign** from Jesus to prove it.

i. "Their request for a 'sign' was misguided: what sign could have been more eloquent than that which they had just witnessed?" (Bruce)

b. **Destroy this temple, and in three days I will raise it up**: Jesus spoke here of the **temple of His body**. He probably even gestured to Himself as He said this. Jesus knew that these religious leaders would attempt to **destroy** His body, but He also knew that they would not succeed.

i. The irony is that the religious leaders themselves would be the means by which the prophecy was fulfilled. When Jesus said, "**Destroy this temple**," He knew that they would in fact do their best to **destroy** it.

ii. At the trial of Jesus, one of the charges brought against Him was that He said He would destroy the temple (Matthew 26:60-61, Mark 14:57-59). When He died on the cross, the mockers reminded Jesus of what seemed to be an impossible promise (Matthew 27:40, Mark 15:29).

iii. **Destroy this temple**: Jesus wasn't against the temple, but He certainly looked beyond it. He told the Samaritan woman that there was a day coming when people would no longer worship at a temple in Samaria or Jerusalem, but they would worship God in Spirit and in truth.

iv. The body of Jesus is still a temple. Ephesians 2:19-22 and 1 Peter 2:5 both connect the idea of the church - metaphorically called the body of Christ - with a temple built upon and built by Jesus Christ.

c. **I will raise it up**: Jesus confidently claimed the power to raise *Himself* from the dead, and He repeated the claim in John 10:18. It is interesting to note that the New Testament also claims that God the Father raised Jesus from the dead (Romans 6:4 and Galatians 1:1), and that that Holy Spirit raised Him from the dead (Romans 1:4 and 8:11). The resurrection of Jesus was a work of each Person of the Trinity, each working together.

i. No mere man could make the claim to raise *himself* from the dead, even if one had confidence that God would raise him. The claim of Jesus is remarkable, audacious, and evidence of His self-awareness of Deity.

ii. "Jesus' technique of using a paradoxical statement to bewilder his enemies, which he subsequently explained for his disciples, frequently appears in John's Gospel." (Tenney)

d. **His disciples remembered that He had said this to them; and they believed the Scripture**: It was only *after* the death and resurrection of Jesus that His disciples understood and **believed** both the Scriptures and the specific promises of Jesus.

i. The Scripture they believed was primarily Psalm 16:10, the promise that God's Holy One would not remain in the grave.

ii. **They believed the Scripture and the word which Jesus had said**: "The placing of Jesus' saying alongside Scripture is interesting and its Christological implications should not be overlooked." (Morris)

3. (23-25) Jesus does not entrust Himself to the many who believe.

Now when He was in Jerusalem at the Passover, during the feast, many believed in His name when they saw the signs which He did. But Jesus did not commit Himself to them, because He knew all *men*, and had no need that anyone should testify of man, for He knew what was in man.

a. **Many believed in His name when they saw the signs**: Jesus knew that this was thin, superficial belief. It wasn't based on anything other than an admiration of the spectacular. Knowing this, **Jesus did not commit Himself to them**.

i. "If belief is nothing more than admiration for the spectacular, it will create in multitudes applause; but the Son of God cannot commit Himself to that kind of faith." (Morgan)

ii. A light or superficial faith may be better than none at all, but no one should think that it is *enough* - and Jesus knows. "It is what Luther calls 'milk faith' and may grow into something more trustworthy." (Dods)

b. **He knew what was in man**: Knowing what was and is in humanity, Jesus *still* loves. He knew and knows the worst; yet also sees the image of God, even upon fallen men and women.

i. **Jesus did not commit Himself to them**: "Other leaders and teachers may be misled at times into giving their followers more credit for loyalty and understanding than they actually possess; not so Jesus, who could read the inmost thoughts of men and women like an open book." (Bruce)

ii. "When many came to believe on Him He did not commit Himself to them. He was not dependent on man's approval." (Morris)

iii. **He knew what was in man**: "Nothing less than *divine knowledge* is here set forth...as the text now stands, it asserts an entire knowledge of all that is in all men." (Alford)

John 3 - The New Birth

"If we were asked to read to a dying man who did not know the gospel, we should probably select this chapter as the most suitable one for such an occasion; and what is good for dying men is good for us all, for that is what we are; and how soon we may be actually at the gates of death, none of us can tell." (Spurgeon)

A. Nicodemus and the new birth.

1. (1-3) Nicodemus comes to Jesus by night.

There was a man of the Pharisees named Nicodemus, a ruler of the Jews. This man came to Jesus by night and said to Him, "Rabbi, we know that You are a teacher come from God; for no one can do these signs that You do unless God is with him." Jesus answered and said to him, "Most assuredly, I say to you, unless one is born again, he cannot see the kingdom of God."

    a. **Nicodemus, a ruler of the Jews**: Nicodemus was one of those impressed by Jesus' signs (John 2:23), and a member of the ruling Sanhedrin. He was religious (**of the Pharisees**), educated (**Nicodemus** is a Greek name), influential (**a ruler**), and earnest enough to come **by night**. Nicodemus came to Jesus as a representative of *all men* (John 2:23-25), and in a sense he represented what is highest and best in men.

    b. **This man came to Jesus by night**: Perhaps Nicodemus came **by night** because he was timid, or perhaps he wanted an uninterrupted interview with Jesus.

    c. **We know that You are a teacher come from God**: It is difficult to know if Nicodemus spoke of himself, of the Sanhedrin, or of popular opinion. "It is possible, however, that οιδαμεν, *we know*, signifies no more than, *it is known, it is generally acknowledged* and *allowed*, that thou art a teacher come from God." (Clarke)

d. **No one can do these signs that You do unless God is with him**: We understand the sense in which Nicodemus meant this, but his statement was not entirely true. The Bible tells us that deceivers and false prophets can sometimes perform remarkable signs (2 Thessalonians 2:9 and Revelation 13:13-14).

e. **Unless one is born again, he cannot see the kingdom of God**: Jesus' reply to Nicodemus shattered the Jewish assumption that their racial identity - their old birth - assured them a place in God's Kingdom. Jesus made it plain that a man's first birth does not assure him of the **kingdom**; only being **born again** gives this assurance.

> i. It was taught widely among the Jews at that time that since they descended from Abraham, they were automatically assured of heaven. In fact, some Rabbis taught that Abraham stood watch at the gate of hell, just to make sure that none of his descendants accidentally wandered in there.

> ii. Most Jews of that time looked for the Messiah to bring in a *new world*, in which Israel and the Jewish people would be pre-eminent. But Jesus came to bring *new life*, in which *He* would be preeminent.

> iii. Nicodemus addressed Jesus as a **rabbi** and **teacher**; Jesus responded to him as the one who announced new life. "Our Lord replies, It is not *learning*, but *life* that is wanted for in the Messiah's Kingdom; and *life* must begin by *birth*." (Alford)

f. **Born again**: The ancient Greek word translated **again** (*anothen*) can be also translated "from above." This is the sense in which John used this word in John 3:31 and in John 19:11 and 19:23. Either way, the meaning is essentially the same. To be born *from above* is to be born again.

> i. "The word rendered 'anew' might equally be translated by 'from above'. Both senses are true, and in the Johannine manner it is likely that we should understand both here." (Morris)

> ii. Essentially, this means to *have new life*. A theological term for this is *regeneration*. It isn't simply a moral or religious reform, but the bringing of new life. "To belong to the heavenly kingdom, one must be born into it." (Tenney)

> iii. Jesus clearly said that without this – that **unless one is born again** – he cannot enter or be part of (**see**) the **kingdom of God**. Moral or religious reform isn't enough. One must be **born again**.

> iv. This isn't something that we can do to ourselves. If Jesus had said, "Unless you are washed, you cannot see the kingdom of God" then we

might think, "I can wash myself." A man might wash himself; but he could never *birth* himself.

v. "All over the New Testament this idea of *rebirth, re-creation* occurs." (Barclay)

- 1 Peter speaks of being born anew by God's great mercy (1 Peter 1:3).

- 1 Peter speaks of being born anew from an imperishable seed (1 Peter 1:22-23).

- James speaks of God bringing us forth by the word of truth (James 1:18).

- Titus speaks to us of the washing of regeneration (Titus 3:5).

- Romans speaks of dying with Jesus and rising anew (Romans 6:1-11).

- 1 Corinthians speaks of new believers as new-born babes (1 Corinthians 3:1-2).

- 2 Corinthians speaks of us being a new creation in Jesus (2 Corinthians 5:17).

- Galatians says that in Jesus we are a new creation (Galatians 6:15).

- Ephesians says the new man is created after God in righteousness (Ephesians 4:22-24).

- Hebrews says that at the beginning of our Christian life we are like children (Hebrews 5:12-14).

2. (4) Nicodemus answers: How can this be?

Nicodemus said to Him, "How can a man be born when he is old? Can he enter a second time into his mother's womb and be born?"

a. **How can a man be born when he is old?** Nicodemus' reply may not have been out of ignorance, but from thinking that Jesus meant a moral reformation. His question may be "How can you teach an old dog new tricks?" One way or another, Nicodemus clearly did not understand Jesus or the truth about the new birth.

i. "Had our Lord said: 'Every Gentile must be born again,' he would have understood." (Dods)

b. **How can a man be born when he is old?** In His description of new birth, Jesus recalled a familiar theme from Old Testament promises of the New Covenant (Deuteronomy 30:1-6, Jeremiah 23:1-8, Jeremiah 31:31-

34, Jeremiah 32:37-41, Ezekiel 11:16-20, Ezekiel 36:16-28, Ezekiel 37:11-14, 37:21-28). These passages essentially made three promises in the New Covenant:

- The gathering of Israel.
- The cleansing and spiritual transformation of God's people.
- The reign of the Messiah over Israel and the whole world.

i. In Jesus' day, the common teaching among the Jewish people was that the first two aspects of the New Covenant had been fulfilled. They saw Israel gathered - at least in part - after the Babylonian exile. They saw strong spiritual movements like the Pharisees, which they believed fulfilled the promise of spiritual transformation. All they waited for was the reign of the Messiah.

ii. That's why Jesus' statement about the new birth was so strange to Nicodemus. He *thought* that the Jewish people already had it; they certainly weren't looking for it. They only looked for a triumphant Messiah.

3. (5-8) Jesus explains the new birth.

Jesus answered, "Most assuredly, I say to you, unless one is born of water and the Spirit, he cannot enter the kingdom of God. That which is born of the flesh is flesh, and that which is born of the Spirit is spirit. Do not marvel that I said to you, 'You must be born again.' The wind blows where it wishes, and you hear the sound of it, but cannot tell where it comes from and where it goes. So is everyone who is born of the Spirit."

a. **Most assuredly... you must be born again**: Jesus was emphatic in saying that man does not need *reformation*, but a radical conversion by the Spirit of God. We must be **born of water and the Spirit**.

i. "In verse 3 Jesus has spoken of 'seeing' the kingdom of God, whereas here He speaks of 'entering' it. There is probably no great difference of meaning." (Morris)

ii. **Most assuredly**: "The words add solemnity to and underline the truth of what follows. The modern expressions, 'In truth I tell you', 'Believe me when I say', 'I do assure you', convey the meaning." (Tasker)

iii. **Unless one is born of water and the Spirit, he cannot enter the kingdom of God**: If a nation passed a law that said no one could live there except those who were born in that nation, and someone wanted to live there who was not born there.

- It wouldn't matter if he took a name that was common in that nation.
- It wouldn't matter if he spoke the language.
- It wouldn't matter if he observed some of the customs.
- It wouldn't matter if he dressed like those in that nation.
- It wouldn't matter if he practiced some of the religious traditions of that nation.
- It wouldn't matter if his parents were born in that nation.
- It wouldn't matter if his children were born there.
- It wouldn't matter if he had many friends in that nation.
- All that would matter was if he was actually **born** there.

iv. "A man may cast away many vices, forsake many lusts in which he indulged, and conquer evil habits, but no man in the world can make himself to be born of God; though he should struggle never so much, he could never accomplish what is beyond his power. And, mark you, if he could make himself to be born again, still he would not enter heaven, because there is another point in the condition which he would have violated -- 'unless a man be born of the *Spirit*, he cannot see the kingdom of God.'" (Spurgeon)

b. **You must be born of water**: We know from John 3:10 that whatever being **born of water** was, it should have been familiar to Nicodemus from the Old Testament.

i. Some have thought **born of water** means to be baptized. Water here may represent baptism, but there is no real Old Testament foundation for this.

ii. Some have thought that **born of water** refers to our physical birth, since we come forth from a sack of water. This approach is more attractive, but doesn't it simply state the obvious? However, it does make a good parallel with the idea of *that which is born of the flesh* in John 3:6.

iii. Some have thought that **born of water** means to be born again by the Word of God. In other passages of Scripture, water represents the Word, as we are *washed by the water of the word* (Ephesians 5:26).

iv. Some have thought that **born of water** means to be regenerated by the Holy Spirit, the *living water* of John 7:38-39.

v. Some have thought that **born of water** means to receive the water of cleansing prophesied in Ezekiel 36:25-28 as part of the New Covenant.

This is the approach has the most weight (though it is a tough call), because of its firm connections to Old Testament prophecy - which Jesus says Nicodemus should have know to understand these things.

c. **That which is born of the flesh is flesh**: Without the new birth of the Spirit, the flesh taints all works of righteousness. Yet, everything that a Spirit-led man does can be pleasing to God.

i. "In this **flesh** is included *every part* of that which is born after the ordinary method of generation: even the spirit of man, which, receptive as it is of the Spirit of God, is yet in the natural birth *dead*, sunk in trespasses and sins." (Alford)

d. **Do not marvel that I said to you, "You must be born again"**: Again, Nicodemus *did* marvel at this statement, because he - like most all Jews of his time - believed they *already had* the inner transformation promised in the New Covenant. Jesus wants him to take hold of the fact that *he does not have it*, and **must be born again**.

i. We should not forget *whom* Jesus said this to. Nicodemus was a religious leader, a Pharisee, an educated man, and an earnest man. By all outward appearance, he was *already* transformed unto God - yet he was not.

ii. "These solemn words for ever exclude the possibility of salvation by human merit. Man's nature is so gripped by sin that an activity of the very Spirit of God is a necessity of he is to be associated with God's kingdom." (Morris)

e. **The wind blows where it wishes**: Jesus' idea to Nicodemus was "You don't understand everything about the wind, but you see its effects. That is just how it is with the birth of the Spirit." Jesus wanted Nicodemus to know that he didn't have to understand everything about the new birth before he experienced it.

i. Since we can't control the Spirit, "It should lead us to be very tender and jealous in our conduct towards the Holy Ghost, so that we do not grieve him and cause him to depart from us." (Spurgeon)

4. (9-13) Jesus responds to the question "**how can these things be?**"

Nicodemus answered and said to Him, "How can these things be?" Jesus answered and said to him, "Are you the teacher of Israel, and do not know these things? Most assuredly, I say to you, We speak what We know and testify what We have seen, and you do not receive Our witness. If I have told you earthly things and you do not believe, how will you believe if I tell you heavenly things? No one has ascended to

heaven but He who came down from heaven, *that is,* the Son of Man who is in heaven."

a. **How can these things be?** Nicodemus was confused. He was so set in his thinking that the new birth has already happened to him and all of faithful Israel, that he had a hard time thinking differently. Jesus had to keep explaining.

b. **Are you the teacher of Israel, and do not know these things?** Jesus chided Nicodemus for not being aware of the need and the promise of the new birth, because these were plainly laid out in the Old Testament. Nicodemus knew these passages well, but believed that they had been fulfilled in regard to the new birth. He should have known better.

i. **Are you the teacher of Israel**: "Nicodemus's exact position in the theological circles of Israel is not defined, but the language suggests that he was a very important person. Jesus implies that as the outstanding teacher of the nation, Nicodemus should have been familiar with the teaching of the new birth." (Tenney)

c. **If I have told you earthly things and you do not believe, how will you believe if I tell you heavenly things?** A simple look at **earthly things** - like the illustrations Jesus used, and even a look at his own life - should have made the point plain to Nicodemus. If he could not see that he needed this spiritual transformation, what more could Jesus tell him?

d. **No one has ascended to heaven but He who came down from heaven**: Jesus "makes it clear that He can speak authoritatively about things in heaven, though no one else can." (Morris)

i. "In short, we have here the basis in Christ's own words of the statement in the prologue that the Word was in the beginning with God, and became flesh to be a light to men." (Dods)

ii. **No one has ascended to heaven**: "This seems a figurative expression for, *No man hath known the mysteries of the kingdom of God*; as in Deuteronomy 30:12; Psalm 73:17; Proverbs 30:4; Romans 11:34. And the expression is founded upon this generally received maxim: That to be perfectly acquainted with the concerns of a place, it is necessary for a person to be on the spot." (Clarke)

5. (14-15) Jesus and the brazen serpent.

"And as Moses lifted up the serpent in the wilderness, even so must the Son of Man be lifted up, that whoever believes in Him should not perish but have eternal life."

a. **As Moses lifted up the serpent in the wilderness**: Jesus made a remarkable statement, explaining that the serpent of Numbers 21:4-9 was a picture of the Messiah and His work.

i. Serpents are often used as pictures of evil in the Bible (Genesis 3:1-5 and Revelation 12:9). However, Moses' serpent in Numbers 21 was made of bronze, and bronze is a metal associated with judgment in the Bible, because bronze is with fire, a picture of judgment.

ii. So, a *bronze* serpent does speak of sin, but of sin judged. In the same way Jesus, who knew no sin became sin for us on the cross, and our sin was judged in Him. A bronze serpent is a picture of sin judged and dealt with.

iii. We would have wanted to diminish our sense of sin, and put the image of a man up on the pole. Our image of man might represent "both good and bad" in man. But a serpent is more apparently sinful, and shows us our true nature and true need of salvation.

iv. In addition, if the serpent lay horizontally on the vertical pole, it is easy to see how this also was a *visual* representation of the cross. However, many traditions show the serpent being wrapped around the pole, and this is the source for the ancient figure of healing and medicine - a serpent, wrapped around a pole.

v. In the Numbers 21:4-9 account, the people were saved not by *doing* anything, but by simply *looking* to the bronze serpent. They had to trust that something as seemingly foolish as looking at such a thing would be sufficient to save them, and surely, some perished because they thought it too foolish to do such a thing.

vi. As it says in Isaiah 45:22: *Look to Me, and be saved, all you ends of the earth! For I am God, and there is no other.* We might be willing to do a hundred things to earn our salvation, but God commands us to only trust in Him - to *look to* Him.

b. **Even so must the Son of Man be lifted up**: Even though Jesus bore our sins, He never *became* a sinner. Even His becoming sin for us was a holy, righteous, act of love. Jesus remained the *Holy One* throughout the entire ordeal of the cross.

i. "Nicodemus had failed to grasp the teaching about the new birth when it was presented to him in terms drawn from Ezekiel's prophecy; now it is presented to him by means of an object-lesson, from a story with which he had been familiar since childhood." (Bruce)

ii. **Must be lifted up**: "He *must* die because He *would* save, and He *would* save because He *did* love." (Maclaren)

c. **Lifted up**: This is a term later used to describe both Jesus' crucifixion (John 12:32) and His ascension (Acts 2:33). Both meanings are in view, His suffering *and* exaltation. Jesus was **lifted up** in both ways.

> i. The Son of Man is to be lifted up. Yes, but not on a throne in Herod's palace. He was to be conspicuous, but as the brazen serpent had been conspicuous, hanging on a pole for the healing of the people." (Dods)

d. **Should not perish but have eternal life**: The idea behind **eternal life** means much more than a *long* or *never ending* life. **Eternal life** does not mean that this life goes on forever. Instead, **eternal life** also has the idea of a certain *quality* of life, of God's kind of life. It is the kind of life enjoyed in eternity.

> i. "The nature of the belief is implied in the illustration of Moses lifting up the serpent in the wilderness. Belief consists of accepting something, not doing something." (Tenney)

6. (16) God's gift of salvation.

"For God so loved the world that He gave His only begotten Son, that whoever believes in Him should not perish but have everlasting life."

a. **For God so loved the world**: John 3:16 has long been celebrated as a powerful, succinct, declaration of the gospel. Of the 31,373 verses in the Bible, it may be the most popular single verse used in evangelism.

> i. We learn the *object* of God's love: **For God so loved the world**. God did not wait for the world to turn to Him before He loved the world. He loved and gave His only begotten Son to the world when it was *still* the **world!**

> ii. What Jesus told Nicodemus in John 3:7 (*You must be born again*) refuted the popular Jewish idea regarding the *way* to salvation. Now Jesus refuted the popular Jewish idea regarding the *scope* of salvation: **for God so loved the *world***.

> iii. The Jews of that day rarely thought that God **loved the world**. Many of them thought that God only loved *Israel*. The universal offer of salvation and life in Jesus was revolutionary.

> iv. "The Jew was ready enough to think of God as loving Israel, but no passage appears to be cited in which any Jewish writer maintains that God loved the world. It is a distinctively Christian idea that God's love is wide enough to embrace all mankind." (Morris)

> v. Morrison suggested that there are three centers of love:

> - *God so loved the world* (John 3:16).

- *Christ also loved the church* (Ephesians 5:25).
- *The Son of God, who loved me* (Galatians 2:20).

b. **He gave His only begotten Son**: This describes both the *expression* and the *gift* of God's love. God's love didn't just *feel* for the plight of a fallen world. God *did* something about it, and He **gave** the most precious thing to give: **His only begotten Son**.

> i. **He gave his only begotten Son**: "These words seem to carry a reference to the offering of Isaac; and Nicodemus in that case would at once be reminded by them of the love *there required*, the *substitution there made*, and the *prophecy there uttered to Abraham*." (Alford)

c. **Whoever believes in Him**: This describes the *recipient* of God's love. God loves the world, but the world does not receive or benefit from that love until it **believes in** Jesus, the gift that the Father gave. **Believes in** means much more than intellectual awareness or agreement. It means to *trust in*, to *rely on*, and to *cling to*.

d. **Should not perish**: This describes the *intention* of God's love. God's love *actually saves* man from eternal destruction. God looks at fallen humanity, does not want it to **perish**, and so in His love He extends the gift of salvation in Jesus Christ.

e. **Everlasting life**: This describes the *duration* of God's love. The love we receive among people may fade or turn, but God's love will never change. He will never stop loving His people, even unto the furthest distance of eternity.

> i. We may say there are Seven Wonders in John 3:16.

God	The Almighty Authority
So loved the world	The Mightiest Motive
That He gave His only begotten Son	The Greatest Gift
That whoever	The Widest Welcome
Believes in Him	The Easiest Escape
Should not perish	The Divine Deliverance
But have everlasting life	The Priceless Possession

> ii. "If there is one sentence more than another which sums up the message of the Fourth Gospel, it is this. The love of God is limitless; it embraces all mankind. No sacrifice was too great to bring its unmeasured intensity home to men and women: the best that God had to give, he gave - his only Son, his well-beloved." (Bruce)

7. (17-21) Sin's condemnation.

"For God did not send His Son into the world to condemn the world, but that the world through Him might be saved. He who believes in Him is not condemned; but he who does not believe is condemned already, because he has not believed in the name of the only begotten Son of God. And this is the condemnation, that the light has come into the world, and men loved darkness rather than light, because their deeds were evil. For everyone practicing evil hates the light and does not come to the light, lest his deeds should be exposed. But he who does the truth comes to the light, that his deeds may be clearly seen, that they have been done in God."

a. **God did not send His Son into the world to condemn the world**: Jesus revealed the heart of God the Father in sending God the Son; to bring *salvation* - rescue, hope, healing - to the world **through Him**.

i. "Some men will, in fact, be condemned, and that as the result of Christ's coming into the world (John 3:19). But the purpose of His coming was not this." (Morris)

b. **He who does not believe is condemned already**: John 3:16 is the most gracious, wonderful offer conceivable - eternal life for all who believe. Yet the offer has inherent consequences, for any who reject, who refuse to **believe**. Their refusal makes their condemnation certain.

i. A significant issue regarding those who do **not believe** is, "What about those who never had the opportunity to believe because they never heard the good news of Jesus Christ?" This is an important but separate question, addressed best by the Apostle Paul in Romans 1 and 2. Here, the focus seems to be on those who *deliberately reject the message*, as those who heard and encountered Jesus in the first century had opportunity to do.

ii. "No explicit mention is made here of those who have never had the opportunity of believing in Christ, those on whom the light in its fullness has never shone. But John's words probably unfold the principle of their judgment too. As the eternal Word came to men and women before becoming incarnate in Christ, so it is with the light of God. If men and women are judged by their response to the light, they are judged by their response to such light as is available to them." (Bruce)

c. **This is the condemnation**: Jesus came to bring salvation, but those who reject that salvation condemn themselves. We never need to leave the *reason* for anyone's **condemnation** at God's door. The responsibility is theirs alone.

    i. "Heaven is too hot to hold unregenerate persons; no such dirty dog ever trampled on that golden pavement, it is an undefiled inheritance." (Trapp)

d. **Men loved darkness rather than light, because their deeds were evil**: Jesus explained what keeps people from faith and rescue in Him. It is because they are drawn to darkness, and love it more than the light. There is a critical *moral* dimension to unbelief that is often denied or ignored.

    i. Those who consciously reject Jesus often present themselves as heroic characters who bravely put away superstition and deal honestly with deep philosophical problems. It is far more often true that there is a *moral* compromise at the root of their rejection.

    ii. Many opponents of Christianity have a vested interested in fighting against the truth of Jesus, because they love their sin and don't want to face it, or face a God who will judge their sin.

    iii. When we think of the *love of sin* that sends people to hell, we often other think of notorious sin. But the simple demand to be lord of my own life is enough of a sin to deserve condemnation before God.

e. **Everyone practicing evil hates the light**: Some express their hatred of the truth by actively fighting against it, and others express their hatred by ignoring God's truth - by saying to Jesus "You are not worth my time." In contrast, **he who does the truth comes to the light**.

    i. **He who does the truth**: "'To do the truth' is at any rate to live up to what one knows; to live an honest, conscientious life." (Dods)

    ii. "They chose to walk in the darkness, that they might do the works of darkness-they broke the Divine law, refused the mercy offered to them, are arrested by Divine justice, convicted, condemned, and punished. Whence, then, does their damnation proceed? From THEMSELVES." (Clarke)

B. John the Baptist's final testimony about Jesus.

1. (22-24) Jesus baptizes in Judea as John continues his work of baptizing.

After these things Jesus and His disciples came into the land of Judea, and there He remained with them and baptized. Now John also was baptizing in Aenon near Salim, because there was much water there. And they came and were baptized. For John had not yet been thrown into prison.

a. **Jesus and His disciples came into the land of Judea**: John continues his account of the life of Jesus with the emphasis on what He did in **Judea**. The other Gospels focus on the work of Jesus in the Galilee region.

b. **He remained with them and baptized**: Jesus, together with His disciples, did a work of baptizing apparently similar to the work of John the Baptist. This was Jesus' humble way of recognizing the goodness and importance of John's work.

> i. Of the baptizing work of Jesus, Morris observed: "More probably it represents a continuation of the 'baptism of repentance' that was characteristic of John the Baptist." We know that when Jesus began to preach, He began with John's same message: *repent* (Matthew 3:2 and 4:17). It made sense for Jesus to also practice the symbol of repentance that John used with such great effect.

> ii. "The baptism now carried on by the disciples [of Jesus] appears to have stood very much in the same position as that of John." (Alford)

> iii. "'Tarried' [**remained**] is another word that is not very specific, but we get the impression of an unhurried period during which Jesus and His followers got to know each other better." (Morris)

> iv. The location of Jesus' work of baptizing is not reported. This may be because it happened in several places in the general area.

c. **John also was baptizing in Aenon near Salim**: There is some dispute as to the exact location of this place. The best evidence is that it was a place some seven miles (12 kilometers) south of modern Bethshan.

> i. "The name Aenon (Ainun means 'springs', which would provide the 'much water' (literally 'many waters') required by John for baptizing." (Bruce)

> ii. "The exact location of Aenon is uncertain. Two sites are possible: one south of Bethshan, where there were numerous springs; another, a short distance from Shechem. Of the two, the former seems to be the better possibility." (Tenney)

> iii. John's work of baptizing was still showing itself effective; we read: **And they came and were baptized**. "The sense of the last two verbs is continuous and we might give it the force of it as 'they kept coming and being baptized'." (Morris)

2. (25-26) John learns of the baptizing work of Jesus.

Then there arose a dispute between *some* of John's disciples and the Jews about purification. And they came to John and said to him, "Rabbi,

He who was with you beyond the Jordan, to whom you have testified—behold, He is baptizing, and all are coming to Him!"

a. **A dispute between some of John's disciples and the Jews about purification**: We don't know the precise nature of this **dispute**. John's baptism certainly had an element of personal **purification**, and perhaps some of the Jewish leaders objected to what he did or how he did it.

b. **He is baptizing, and all are coming to Him!** We don't know the details of the dispute regarding purification, but in that discussion the disciples of John learned that Jesus was baptizing, and drawing large crowds.

i. "'All men' is an indignant exaggeration, very natural in the circumstances." (Morris)

c. **All are coming to Him!** John's disciples seemed alarmed, but it didn't bother John one bit. John would not allow envy or the fickle crowds make him forget his mission: to announce that the Messiah had come, and then to step back and let the attention be focused upon the Messiah.

3. (27-30) John's answer to his worried disciples.

John answered and said, "A man can receive nothing unless it has been given to him from heaven. You yourselves bear me witness, that I said, 'I am not the Christ,' but, 'I have been sent before Him.' He who has the bride is the bridegroom; but the friend of the bridegroom, who stands and hears him, rejoices greatly because of the bridegroom's voice. Therefore this joy of mine is fulfilled. He must increase, but I *must* decrease."

a. **A man can receive nothing unless it has been given to him from heaven**: John first answered his worried disciples that everything he had - including those who responded to his ministry - were a gift from God. If they are God's gift, then they should be received gratefully.

b. **I said, "I am not the Christ," but, "I have been sent before Him"**: John then reminded his disciples that he knew who *he* was, and he also knew who *Jesus* was. Understanding that, he could keep his proper place; not too high (thinking he was the Christ) and not too low (thinking he had no call or place in God's plan).

c. **The friend of the bridegroom**: John explained to his followers that he was like the best man at a wedding; he isn't the bridegroom. He isn't to be the focus of attention, but to supervise the bringing of two people together.

i. In the Jewish wedding customs of that day, the **friend of the bridegroom** arranged many of the details of the wedding and brought the bride to the groom. Nevertheless, the **friend of the bridegroom** was never the focus of attention, and wanted it that way.

ii. The fact that the bridegroom represents Jesus is another way the Bible says Jesus is God. In the Old Testament, it was only *Yahweh* who was the husband of Israel. "The Baptist would have been well aware that in the Old Testament Israel is regarded as the bride of Jehovah." (Morris)

d. **Therefore this joy of mine is fulfilled**: John wanted his followers to know that all these arrangements **fulfilled** his **joy**. One might say that John the Baptist lost his congregation - and *he was happy about it!* John was happy because he lost his congregation to Jesus.

i. "It is not John's regret that men are attracted to Jesus: rather it is the fulfillment of his work and hope." (Dods)

ii. "John betrays no sense of envy or rivalry. It is not easy to see another's influence growing at the expense of one's own; it is even less easy to rejoice at the sight. But John found his joy completed by the news which his disciples brought." (Bruce)

e. **He must increase, but I must decrease**: John the Baptist understood it was good for him to become less visible and known, for Jesus to become more visible and known. In even larger aspects, this should be the motto of every Christian, especially leaders among God's people. Jesus should become greater and more visible, and the servant should become less and less visible.

i. Even though Jesus was baptizing men unto repentance and drawing large crowds, John understood that they did *not* have the same ministry, the same role. Jesus was uniquely the Messiah and His work must be continually exalted.

ii. John the Baptist shows us that we may be very popular and outwardly successful, and still be humble. John the Baptist had fame and crowds that modern celebrity pastors could only dream of, yet he was an example of genuine humility.

iii. John that Baptist also did not *quit* his work just because Jesus was doing a similar work and doing it for more people. He labored on, content to do what God called him to do even though Jesus gained more and more attention and John less and less.

iv. "Here ministers may learn not to be wanting to their duties, though God may stir up others about them of greater parts and better success to obscure them." (Trapp)

v. "If it is not due to your lethargy or sloth that the crowds have ebbed away, and that the tide of conversions has dropped below its former level, be at peace. These are things which the Holy Spirit worketh, dividing to each one severally even as He will." (Meyer)

4. (31-33) John's testimony about Jesus.

"He who comes from above is above all; he who is of the earth is earthly and speaks of the earth. He who comes from heaven is above all. And what He has seen and heard, that He testifies; and no one receives His testimony. He who has received His testimony has certified that God is true."

a. **He who comes from above**: John wanted everyone to know *where Jesus came from*. Jesus was different from everyone else because He came from heaven. He wasn't an exceptionally spiritual or wise or good man; He was and is God, **from heaven**.

i. There is some debate as to if John 3:31 continues the words of John the Baptist or if it begins a section where John the Evangelist comments on themes suggested by the prior words of the Baptist.

b. **He who comes from heaven is above all**: Jesus is not only different from everyone else; Jesus is also *greater* than everyone else.

i. "If we want information about a family, we will get it at first hand only from a member of that family. If we want information about a town we will get it at first hand only from someone who comes from that town. So, then, if we want information about God, we will get it only from the Son of God; and if we want information about heaven and heaven's life, we will get it only from him who comes from heaven." (Barclay)

ii. **What He has seen and heard**: "Seeing and hearing are equivalent to having direct knowledge." (Dods)

c. **No one receives His testimony**: John prophetically anticipated the rejection Jesus would endure in His ministry. He came from heaven, He testified to the truth, but relatively **no one** received **His testimony**, even though witnesses **certified** it as the truth of God.

i. "He meant that *comparatively* none received it. Compared with the crowds who came to him, compared with the nation of Israel, compared with the human race, those who received Christ's testimony were so few that his sadness made him call them none." (Spurgeon)

ii. "To accept His teaching is therefore to testify that *God is true*; on the other hand, to reject it, is in effect to make God a liar (John 3:33; cf. 1 John 1:10, 5:10)." (Tasker)

iii. **Certified**: "When you believe in Jesus, you have set your seal to the testimony of Jesus, which is the revelation of the Lord. You have certified that you believe in God as true." (Spurgeon)

5. (34-36) The price for rejecting the true testimony regarding Jesus.

"For He whom God has sent speaks the words of God, for God does not give the Spirit by measure. The Father loves the Son, and has given all things into His hand. He who believes in the Son has everlasting life; and he who does not believe the Son shall not see life, but the wrath of God abides on him."

a. **He whom God has sent speaks the words of God**: Jesus is a uniquely reliable revelation, because He has the Holy Spirit without **measure**, in contrast to the previous prophets.

b. **For God does not give the Spirit by measure**: John spoke both of Jesus (who had the Holy **Spirit** without **measure**) and prophetically of the New Covenant (which featured a true outpouring of the Holy Spirit). For those joined to the Messiah through the New Covenant, there is as much of the Spirit as needed, given without **measure**.

i. "The Rabbinical books say that the Holy Spirit was only given to the prophets by measure. This unmeasured pouring of the Spirit on Him accounts for his speaking the words of God." (Alford)

ii. **The Father loves the Son**: "Twice in this Gospel we read that 'the Father loves the Son' - here (John 3:35) and in John 5:20. The verb here is *agapao*; in the other place it is *phileo*. The alternation of those two verbs in identical statements illustrates the Evangelist's propensity for varying his choice of synonyms." (Bruce)

iii. **The Son**: "This absolute use of 'the Son' as a designation of Christ certainly suggests, if it does not prove, the proper Divinity of Christ. It is the favourite designation in this Gospel." (Dods)

c. **He who does not believe the Son shall not see life, but the wrath of God abides on him**: John explained that *because* Jesus is the man from heaven, there is a heavy price to pay for rejecting Him. If you reject the Son, then you receive the wrath.

i. **He who does not believe**: "He may think that his not believing is a very small business, but, indeed, it is a barbed shaft shot against the Deity." (Spurgeon)

ii. **The wrath of God**: "The word does not mean a sudden gust of passion or a burst of temper. Rather, it is the settled displeasure of God against sin. It is the divine allergy to moral evil, the reaction of righteousness to unrighteousness." (Tenney)

iii. To reject the Son is to reject His gift - eternal life. You can't tell Him, "I'll take the gift but reject You."

iv. "'The wrath of God' is a concept which is uncongenial to many modern students, and various devices are adopted to soften the expression or explain it away. This cannot be done, however, without doing great violence to many passages of Scripture and without distracting from God's moral character." (Morris)

v. "It is not that God sends wrath upon him; it is that he brings that wrath upon himself." (Barclay)

d. **The wrath of God abides**: It **abides** in this world, because sin's evil abides until the wrong of it is perfectly satisfied. It **abides** into the next world, because those who reject Jesus cannot offer a perfect sacrifice acceptable to God. The wrath of God **abides** until the perfect payment Jesus made on the cross satisfies the debt of evil and guilt.

i. "We may not like it but we should not ignore it. John tells us that this wrath 'abideth'. We should not expect it to fade away with the passage of time." (Morris)

ii. "Holy Whitfield, when he was preaching, would often hold up his hands, and, with tears streaming down his eyes, would exclaim, 'Oh, the wrath to come! the wrath to come!' Then would he pause because his emotions checked his utterance." (Spurgeon)

iii. Looking back over John 3, one might say that it is a *must read* chapter of the Bible. There are four prominent *musts* in John 3.

- The Sinner's must: *you must be born again* (John 3:7).
- The Savior's must: *so must the Son of Man be lifted up* (John 3:14).
- The Sovereign's must: *He must increase* (John 3:30).
- The Servant's must: *I must decrease* (John 3:30).

John 4 - A Samaritan Woman and a Nobleman Meet Jesus

A. The Samaritan woman.

1. (1-4) Jesus travels from Judea to Galilee, passing though Samaria.

Therefore, when the Lord knew that the Pharisees had heard that Jesus made and baptized more disciples than John (though Jesus Himself did not baptize, but His disciples), He left Judea and departed again to Galilee. But He needed to go through Samaria.

a. **When the Lord knew... He left Judea**: Jesus knew that because of His rising prominence and popularity, there would soon be a confrontation with the religious establishment (among whom were **the Pharisees**). Yet, Jesus knew that the time was not yet right for a confrontation in Jerusalem, so He returned to **Galilee**.

b. **Jesus made and baptized more disciples than John (though Jesus Himself did not baptize, but His disciples)**: Jesus' work of baptism was first referred to in John 3:22. Jesus considered it important to also do John's work of baptizing as a demonstration of repentance and cleansing in preparation for the Messiah. Here we learn that in the actual baptizing work, Jesus delegated that work to **His disciples**.

i. This also means that when the disciples began the practice of *Christian* baptism on Pentecost (Acts 2:41), their prior experience of baptizing was in connection with repentance, cleansing, and identification with the Messiah's work.

ii. "By baptizing, He attested the unity of His work with that of the forerunner. By not Himself baptizing, he made the superiority of His position above that of John the Baptist to be felt." (Godet, cited in Morris)

c. **He needed to go through Samaria**: Although the road through Samaria was the shortest route from Jerusalem to Galilee, pious Jews often avoided it. They did so because there was a deep distrust and dislike between many of the Jewish people and the Samaritans.

> i. When the Babylonians conquered the southern kingdom of Judah, they took almost all the population captive, exiling them to the Babylonian Empire. All they left behind were the lowest classes of society, because they didn't want these lowly regarded people in Babylonia. These ones left behind intermarried with other non-Jewish peoples who slowly came into the region, and the *Samaritans* emerged as an ethnic and religious group.

> ii. Because the Samaritans had a historical connection to the people of Israel, their faith was a combination of commands and rituals from the Law of Moses, put together with various superstitions. Most of the Jews in Jesus' time *despised* the Samaritans, disliking them even more than Gentiles - because they were, religiously speaking, "half-breeds" who had an eclectic, mongrel faith. The Samaritans built their own temple to Yahweh on Mount Gerizim, but the Jews burned it around 128 B.C. This obviously made relations between the Jews and the Samaritans even worse.

> iii. "Their route from Jerusalem to Galilee lay through the region beyond the Jordan. This was considerably longer, but it avoided contact with the Samaritans. Those who were not so strict went through Samaria." (Morris)

> iv. It says that Jesus **needed to go through Samaria**. The need wasn't because of travel arrangements or practical necessities, but because there were people there who needed to hear Him.

2. (5-9) Jesus comes to a well in Sychar of Samaria.

So He came to a city of Samaria which is called Sychar, near the plot of ground that Jacob gave to his son Joseph. Now Jacob's well was there. Jesus therefore, being wearied from *His* journey, sat thus by the well. It was about the sixth hour.

a. **Now Jacob's well was there**: The city of **Sychar** was ancient *Shechem*, and was the capital city of the Samaritans.

- This is where Abram first came when he arrived into Canaan from Babylonia. (Genesis 12:6)

- This is where God first appeared to Abram in Canaan, and renewed the promise of giving the land to him and his descendants. (Genesis 12:7)

- This is where Abram built an altar and called upon the name of the Lord. (Genesis 12:8)

- This is where Jacob came safely when he returned with his wives and children from his sojourn with Laban. (Genesis 33:18)

- This is where Jacob bought a piece of land from a Canaanite named Hamor, for 100 pieces of sliver. (Genesis 33:19)

- This is where Jacob built an altar to the Lord, and called it *El Elohe Israel* (Genesis 33:20). This established the connection between Jacob and what became known as **Jacob's well** there in Sychar.

- Sychar (Shechem) was also the place where Dinah, the daughter of Jacob, was raped – and the sons of Jacob massacred the men of the city in retaliation. (Genesis 34)

- This was **the plot of ground that Jacob gave his son Joseph**, land Jacob had conquered from the Amorites with his sword and bow in an unrecorded battle. (Genesis 48:22)

- This is where the bones of Joseph were eventually buried when they were carried up from Egypt. (Joshua 24:32)

- This is where Joshua made a covenant with Israel, renewing their commitment to the God of Israel and proclaiming, *as for me and my house, we will serve the Lord.* (Joshua 24)

  i. "Some think that Sychar, which means 'drunken,' was originally a contemptuous name applied by the Jews to Shechem." (Alford)

b. **Being wearied from His journey**: After a long day walking, Jesus was **wearied**. John has been careful to show us that Jesus *is* God, but also wanted us to know that Jesus was *not* a super-man. Jesus genuinely submitted to our human limitations.

  i. **Sat thus by the well**: "That little word *thus* seems to have a force difficult to reproduce in English. It is apparently intended to enhance the idea of utter weariness." (Maclaren)

  ii. "While our Evangelist insists that it was the divine Word that became flesh in Jesus, he insists at the same time that what the divine word became was *flesh*." (Bruce)

  iii. "This 'spring' of Jacob is beyond doubt that known to-day by Samaritan, Jew, Christian, and Moslem as the 'spring' or 'well', 'of Jacob.'" (Trench)

c. **It was about the sixth hour**: By the reckoning John used, this was about noon, during the heat of the day. Jesus, being tired and hot, would have wanted a refreshing drink.

3. (7-9) Jesus speaks with a Samaritan woman.

A woman of Samaria came to draw water. Jesus said to her, "Give Me a drink." For His disciples had gone away into the city to buy food. Then the woman of Samaria said to Him, "How is it that You, being a Jew, ask a drink from me, a Samaritan woman?" For Jews have no dealings with Samaritans.

a. **A woman of Samaria came to draw water**: This woman came for water at an unusual hour and she came alone. Typically, women came for water earlier in the day and they came in groups. Perhaps there was a sudden need, or perhaps she was a social outcast, shunned by other women in the community.

i. "Women usually came to draw water in company, and at a cooler time of the day." (Bruce)

ii. Adam Clarke extended this thought: "The Jews say that those who wished to get wives went to the wells where young women were accustomed to come and draw water; and it supposed that women of ill fame frequented such places also."

iii. All in all, this woman is a fascinating character. "She is of mature age, and has had a not altogether reputable past. She is frivolous, ready to talk with strangers, with a tongue quick to turn grave things into jests; and yet she possesses, hidden beneath masses of unclean vanities, a conscience and a yearning for something better than she has." (Maclaren)

iv. The disciples **had gone away into the city**, perhaps passing her on their way into town. "We can be certain at this stage of their lives Peter and the others would never have moved off the path for any woman, much less a Samaritan and perhaps one with loose morals at that. Perhaps she had been pushed aside or made to wait while the body of Galileans marched by." (Boice)

b. **Jesus said to her**: By tradition, a rabbi would not speak with a woman in public, not even with his own wife. It was also *very* unusual for a Jewish person of that time to ask a favor or accept a drink from a Samaritan's cup. Jesus' request genuinely surprised the woman. The disciples were also surprised that Jesus spoke to her (John 4:27).

i. "The strict Rabbis forbade a Rabbi to greet a woman in public. A Rabbi might not even speak to his own wife or daughter or sister in public. There were even Pharisees who were called 'the bruised and bleeding Pharisees' because they shut their eyes when they saw a woman on the street and so walked into walls and houses!" (Barclay)

c. **Give Me a drink**: Some people imagine that God is most glorified when human participation is most excluded. Yet Jesus did not diminish His glory one bit by asking the help and cooperation of the Samaritan woman. As it worked toward the accomplishment of the divine purpose, the Father and the Son were *most* glorified in this display of love and goodness to the woman.

i. **Give Me a drink**: "He is not unaware that the way to gain a soul is often to ask a service of it." (Godet, cited in Morris)

ii. In all this, we see many of the seeming paradoxes of Jesus' work.

- He who gives rest is weary.
- He who is Israel's Messiah speaks to a Samaritan woman.
- He who has living water asks for a drink from a well.

iii. "He felt that his miraculous power was to be used for others, and in his great work; but as for himself, his humanity must bear its own infirmity, it must support its own trials: so he keeps his hand back from relieving his own necessities." (Spurgeon)

iv. There is every reason to believe that she gave Jesus what He asked for, and she asked the question of John 4:9 as Jesus drank the water, or after Jesus drank the water from the well.

d. **How is it that You, being a Jew, ask a drink from me, a Samaritan woman?** Immediately, the woman was impressed by the friendliness of Jesus. It was unusual for her to hear a kind greeting from a Jewish man, for generally speaking, **Jews have no dealings with Samaritans**.

i. John felt this was so well understood in his day that he needed no further explanation. "The deadly hatred that subsisted between these two nations is known to all. The Jews cursed them, and believed them to be accursed. Their most merciful wish to the Samaritans was, that they might have no part in the resurrection; or, in other words, that they might be *annihilated*." (Clarke)

ii. For many reasons, this woman would have been despised by most of the religious leaders in the days of Jesus. She was a woman, a Samaritan, and a woman of questionable reputation. Yet, in the interview with Nicodemus John showed us, *Jesus has something to say to the religious establishment*. In the meeting with the Samaritan woman at the well

John showed us, *Jesus has something to say to those despised by the religious establishment.*

4. (10-12) Jesus interests the woman in living water.

Jesus answered and said to her, "If you knew the gift of God, and who it is who says to you, 'Give Me a drink,' you would have asked Him, and He would have given you living water." The woman said to Him, "Sir, You have nothing to draw with, and the well is deep. Where then do You get that living water? Are You greater than our father Jacob, who gave us the well, and drank from it himself, as well as his sons and his livestock?"

a. **If you knew the gift of God, and who it is who says to you, "Give Me a drink"**: Jesus drew the woman into conversation, making her curious about several things.

- He made her curious about the things of God (**If you knew the gift of God**).

- He made her curious about who Jesus is (**who it is who says to you**).

- He made her curious about what He could give her (**He would have given you living water**).

  i. There is a principle connected with the words **if you knew... you would have asked Him**: If you knew more, you would pray more.

  ii. There is another principle at work: Jesus often speaks to us as if we were more spiritual or understanding than we actually are. He does this on purpose.

b. **He would have given you living water**: In ancient times they called spring water **living water** because it seemed alive as it bubbled up from the ground. At first glance, it might seem that Jesus told this woman about a nearby active spring. But Jesus made a play on words with the phrase "**living water**," because He meant the spiritual water that quenches spiritual thirst and gives life.

  i. "In the Old Testament living water is sometimes associated with Jehovah. He is called 'the fountain of living waters' (Jeremiah 2:13, 17:13)." (Morris)

  ii. "The (admittedly much later) Samaritan liturgy for the Day of Atonement says of the Taheb (the Samaritan counterpart to the Jewish Messiah), 'Water shall flow from his buckets' (language borrowed from Balaam's oracle in Numbers 24:7)." (Bruce)

c. **You have nothing to draw with**: Going into town, the disciples probably took with them the leather pouch used as a bucket to draw water.

d. **Are you greater than our father Jacob**: It is hard to tell if the woman asked a sincere question, or if she was a cynical critic. All depended on the tone of her voice. The fact that she came to belief at the end of her encounter with Jesus *may* suggest it was an honest question.

5. (13-15) Jesus describes the effect of the living water He offers.

Jesus answered and said to her, "Whoever drinks of this water will thirst again, but whoever drinks of the water that I shall give him will never thirst. But the water that I shall give him will become in him a fountain of water springing up into everlasting life." The woman said to Him, "Sir, give me this water, that I may not thirst, nor come here to draw."

a. **Whoever drinks of this water will thirst again**: Jesus knew that this woman – and everyone in the village – had to come to this well daily to satisfy their natural thirst. Jesus used **thirst** as a picture of the spiritual need and longing that everyone has.

b. **Whoever drinks of the water that I shall give him will never thirst**: Jesus made an amazing offer. What he offered – to this woman and to anyone who would drink – was something to give *lasting* satisfaction. The key is to drink **of the water that *Jesus* shall give**.

i. It's common for people to try and satisfy their God-created inner thirst through many things, or through any thing except for what Jesus gives. People are *thirsty* – they want, they long, they search, they reach; but only what Jesus gives satisfies to the deepest levels of man's soul and spirit.

ii. Drinking and thirst are common pictures of God's supply and man's spiritual need. Drinking is an action, but an action of receiving - like faith, it is *doing* something, but it is not a merit-earning work in itself.

iii. "What does a thirsty man do to get rid of his thirst? He drinks. Perhaps there is no better representation of faith in all the Word of God than that. To drink is to receive-to take in the refreshing draught-and that is all. A man's face may be unwashed, but yet he can drink; he may be a very unworthy character, but yet a draught of water will remove his thirst. Drinking is such a remarkably easy thing, it is even more simple than eating." (Spurgeon, *Good News for Thirsty Souls*)

iv. Someone might object: "I drank of what Jesus offers, and I feel thirsty and empty again." The answer is simple: drink again! It isn't a one-time sip of Jesus that satisfies forever, but continual connection with Him.

c. **But the water that I shall give him will become in him a fountain of water springing up into everlasting life**: The effect of this water does much more than simply satisfy the thirst of the one who drinks it. It also *creates* something good, something life-giving in the heart of the one who drinks it. It *becomes* a **fountain of water springing up into everlasting life**.

d. **Sir, give me this water**: The response of the Samaritan woman was logical, yet not spiritual. She wanted to avoid the work of coming to the well every day. It was as if she responded, "Jesus, if you want to make my life easier and more convenient, then I'm all for it. Give it to me!"

6. (16-19) Jesus speaks of her sinful life.

Jesus said to her, "Go, call your husband, and come here." The woman answered and said, "I have no husband." Jesus said to her, "You have well said, 'I have no husband,' for you have had five husbands, and the one whom you now have is not your husband; in that you spoke truly." The woman said to Him, "Sir, I perceive that You are a prophet."

a. **Go, call your husband, and come here**: This was not a strange request. In this extended, public conversation with the woman, Jesus was straining the boundaries of cultural propriety. The conversation would be more culturally appropriate if the woman's husband were present.

b. **I have no husband...you have had five husbands**: The woman claimed to have no husband – which was technically true, but Jesus knew – supernaturally – that there was much more to the story of the woman's marriage history.

i. "Christ has different doors for entering into different people's souls. Into some, he enters by the understanding; into many, by the affections. To some, he comes by the way of fear; to another, by that of hope; and to this woman he came by way of her conscience." (Spurgeon)

c. **And the one whom you now have is not your husband**: Jesus brought up this embarrassing issue because her sinful life had to be confronted. This woman had to decide what she loved more: her sin or the Messiah.

i. When Jesus said that the man she lived with was "**not your husband**," Jesus showed that *living together* and *marriage* are not the same thing. Jesus also showed that just because someone calls a relationship *marriage*, it does not mean that Jesus considers it *marriage*.

ii. "I am persuaded that the right account is found, in viewing this command, as the *first step of granting her request, 'give me this water.'* The first work of the Spirit of God, and of Him who here spoke in the fullness of that Spirit, is, to *convince of sin*." (Alford)

d. **Sir, I perceive that You are a prophet**: This was an obvious observation from the woman. She was no doubt surprised; perhaps stunned that Jesus had supernatural knowledge of her life.

> i. "It would have been better if she had perceived that she was a sinner." (Spurgeon)

7. (20-26) The Samaritan woman and Jesus discuss worship.

"Our fathers worshiped on this mountain, and you *Jews* say that in Jerusalem is the place where one ought to worship." Jesus said to her, "Woman, believe Me, the hour is coming when you will neither on this mountain, nor in Jerusalem, worship the Father. You worship what you do not know; we know what we worship, for salvation is of the Jews. But the hour is coming, and now is, when the true worshipers will worship the Father in spirit and truth; for the Father is seeking such to worship Him. God *is* Spirit, and those who worship Him must worship in spirit and truth." The woman said to Him, "I know that Messiah is coming" (who is called Christ). "When He comes, He will tell us all things." Jesus said to her, "I who speak to you am *He*."

a. **Our fathers worshipped on this mountain**: It is possible that this was a genuine source of confusion and a stumbling block to her, but it is more likely that this simply was an evasion, trying to avoid the issue of her many prior husbands and her current non-husband.

> i. If she offered an argument about places of worship here, Jesus didn't take the bait. Jesus was more interested in winning a soul than in winning an argument.

b. **You worship what you do not know**: The Samaritans believed that Moses commissioned an altar on Mount Gerazim, the mountain of blessing - this was their justification of they system of worship on that mountain. But like all faith that tries to combine elements of different religions, they **worship what** they **do not know**.

> i. **You worship what you do not know; we know what we worship**: "Both his 'ye' and His 'we' are emphatic. He sets Jews and Samaritans in sharp contrast. And He associates Himself quite definitely with the Jews." (Morris)

> ii. The Samaritans also only accepted the first five books of the Hebrew Scripture, and rejected the rest. "The Samaritans took as much of scripture as they wished and paid no attention to the rest." (Barclay)

c. **The hour is coming when you will neither on this mountain, nor in Jerusalem, worship the Father**: Jesus pointed her to a time when worship would no longer be focused on *places* (neither Jerusalem nor Mount

Gerazim). The greater work of Jesus would bring a greater, more spiritual worship.

> i. Dods said of this promise, "One of the greatest announcements ever made by our Lord; and made to one sinful woman."

> ii. "The prophetic **ye shall worship**, though embracing in its wider sense *all mankind*, may be taken primarily as foretelling the success of the Gospel in Samaria, Acts 8:1-26." (Alford)

d. God is Spirit, and those who worship Him must worship in spirit and truth: With these words Jesus described the basis for true worship: it is not found in places and trappings, but **in spirit and in truth**.

> i. To worship **in spirit** means you are concerned with spiritual realities, not so much with places or outward sacrifices, cleansings, and trappings.

> ii. To worship **in truth** means you worship according to the whole counsel of God's word, especially in light of the New Testament revelation. It also means that you come to God **in truth**, not in pretense or a mere display of spirituality.

e. I who speak to you am He: Though this woman was a sinner, Jesus revealed Himself to her. Jesus reveals Himself to sinners.

8. (27-30) The woman tells her neighbors.

And at this *point* His disciples came, and they marveled that He talked with a woman; yet no one said, "What do You seek?" or, "Why are You talking with her?" The woman then left her waterpot, went her way into the city, and said to the men, "Come, see a Man who told me all things that I ever did. Could this be the Christ?" Then they went out of the city and came to Him.

a. The disciples came, and they marveled that He talked with a woman: The disciples were surprised that Jesus stretched the limits of cultural propriety with the extended conversation with the Samaritan woman. Yet – probably sensing that it *was right and appropriate* – they did not question Jesus about this.

> i. **Yet no one said**: "Their silence was due to reverence. They had already learned that He had reasons for His actions which might not lie on the surface." (Dods) "They had learned enough to know that, while Jesus did not always respect the conventions of the Rabbis, He had good reasons for what He did." (Morris)

b. The woman then left her waterpot, went her way into the city: Perhaps sensing the silent awkwardness of the disciples, the woman left her conversation with Jesus and went back into the city of Sychar. She left so impressed by her time with Jesus (and so certain she would return to him) that she **left her waterpot** at the well.

i. The left-behind waterpot is the kind of small point remembered by an eyewitness. As one of the disciples to see this, John remembered this event clearly.

c. **Come, see a Man who told me all the things that I ever did. Could this be the Christ?** Jesus so impressed this woman that she was compelled to tell those in her city that *they* should come to the well and meet Jesus. Jesus impressed and attracted her, *even though* He confronted her with her sin (**all the things that I ever did**).

i. The Samaritan woman was so impressed by the love of Jesus that she now sought out her fellow villagers, even when they had treated her as an outcast before. "If she had avoided the company of her fellow-citizens before, she was a changed woman now; she must seek them out and share her news with them." (Bruce)

ii. The Samaritan woman was so impressed by the love of Jesus - even as He confronted her sin - that she forgot that she would rather everyone else forget **all the things that I ever did**. "This pardonable exaggeration indicates the profound impression that Jesus' knowledge of her private life had made on her." (Morris)

iii. Jesus displayed so much love and such a sense of security that she felt safe with Him even when her sin was exposed. It's important for the followers of Jesus to give people today a safe place to confess their sin, repent, and put their trust in Jesus.

iv. The whole interaction with Jesus did not leave her with the impression, "He hates me" or "He judges me" or "He doesn't want me around." It left her with the impression that quite possibly, Jesus was who He claimed to be: the Messiah, **the Christ** (*I who speak to you am He*, John 4:26).

v. **Told me all things that I ever did**: "The Jews believed that one essential characteristic of the Messiah would be, that he should be able to tell the secrets of all hearts. This they believed was predicted, Isaiah 11:2, 3." (Clarke) It isn't unreasonable to think that some among the Samaritans believed similar things about the Messiah.

d. **Then they went out of the city and came to Him**: The woman's invitation was *effective*. The people came when she told them who Jesus was and how He had impacted her life with their brief conversation.

9. (31-34) Jesus teaches His disciples the source of His strength and satisfaction.

In the meantime His disciples urged Him, saying, "Rabbi, eat." But He said to them, "I have food to eat of which you do not know." Therefore the disciples said to one another, "Has anyone brought Him *anything* to eat?" Jesus said to them, "My food is to do the will of Him who sent Me, and to finish His work."

a. **I have food to eat of which you do not know**: The disciples went into the Samaritan village to get food, and wanted Jesus to eat what they brought to Him.

i. "It is right for the spiritual man to forget his hunger, but it is equally right for his true friends to remind him that he ought to eat for his health's sake: it is commendable for the worker to forget his weakness and press forward in holy service; but it is proper for the humane and thoughtful to interpose with a word of caution, and to remind the ardent spirit that his frame is but dust. I think the disciples did well to say, 'Master, eat.'" (Spurgeon)

ii. Jesus wasn't saying that food and drink and rest are not important. Instead, He wanted His disciples to know that life was more than those things; that man does not eat by bread alone.

iii. **I have food to eat of which you do not know**: "The pronouns are emphatic: *I* am refreshed by nourishment hidden from *you*." (Dods)

iv. "In these words our Lord revealed the secret of His strength, and that of the weakness of His disciples." (Morgan)

b. **My food is to do the will of Him who sent Me**: Jesus had a greater source of strength and satisfaction than the food He ate. Jesus explained to His disciples that His true satisfaction was **to do the will** of His God and Father.

i. Jesus did not have His focus primarily on the work, the need, the strategy, the techniques, or even the needy soul. First and foremost His focus was on doing **the will of Him who sent Me**. In contrast, Satan is the ultimate example of one who did not want the will of God, but asserted his will against God's will (Isaiah 14:12-15).

ii. "He does not even say, 'My meat is to do my Father's will.' He takes a lower position than that of sonship, and dwells chiefly upon his mission, its service, and the absorption in the will of God which it involved." (Spurgeon)

iii. The experience of countless others through the centuries has proved Jesus true in this statement. There *is* nothing more satisfying than doing the work of God, whatever that is for the particular believer. Though this is counter-intuitive and against our natural self-seeking, it is true.

iv. "The man of the world thinks that, if he could have his own way, he would be perfectly happy, and his dream of happiness in this state or in the next is comprised in this, that his own wishes will be gratified, his own longings fulfilled, his own desires granted to him. This is all a mistake. A man will never be happy in this way." (Spurgeon)

v. Jesus found great satisfaction in doing the will of God *even when He was weary*. In fact, the conscious doing of God's will refreshed the weary Jesus. "The bodily thirst (and hunger probably, from the time of day) which our Lord had felt before, had been and was forgotten in the carrying on of His divine work in the soul of this Samaritan woman." (Alford)

c. **And to finish His work**: Jesus found satisfaction in not merely starting the work of God, but *finishing* it. This completes the thought begun in the previous verse.

- Jesus was surrendered to the Master's will.
- Jesus was on a recognized commission.
- Jesus came to do.
- Jesus came to finish His work.

i. **To finish His work**: "The verb is cognate with that used on the cross, when Jesus cried 'It is finished' (John 19:30)." (Morris)

10. (35-38) Jesus teaches His disciples about the urgency of spiritual work and opportunity.

Do you not say, 'There are still four months and *then* comes the harvest'? Behold, I say to you, lift up your eyes and look at the fields, for they are already white for harvest! And he who reaps receives wages, and gathers fruit for eternal life, that both he who sows and he who reaps may rejoice together. For in this the saying is true: 'One sows and another reaps.' I sent you to reap that for which you have not labored; others have labored, and you have entered into their labors."

a. **There are still four months and then comes the harvest**: This was a proverb with the idea that there is no particular hurry for a task because things simply take time and you can't avoid the waiting. Jesus *did not* want His disciples to have this mentality; He wanted them to think and act as if the **harvest** was ready *now*.

i. "In Greek the words 'Yet four months and harvest comes' have a rhythmic form which suggests that we have to do with a popular or proverbial saying." (Bruce)

ii. "The harvest is ready. The wages are there. Let no man hang back. A harvest will not wait." (Morris)

b. **Lift up your eyes and look at the fields, for they are already white for harvest!** Jesus used the idea of food and harvest to communicate spiritual ideas. The idea of **harvest** meant that there were many people ready to be received into the Kingdom of God, and that the disciples should see themselves as workers - reapers - in that **harvest**.

i. "As he was speaking, the Samaritans were leaving the town and coming across the fields toward him. The eagerness of the people the Jews regarded as alien and rejected showed that they were like grain ready for harvesting." (Tenney)

ii. Jesus warned His disciples to not think, **there are still four months and then comes the harvest**. If they had the eyes to see it, the *harvest was ready now* - even **white for harvest**, implying that the grain was fully ripe or over ripe.

iii. We should believe, **they are already white for harvest!** "Expect a present blessing; believe that you will have it; go to work to get it, and do not be satisfied unless you do have it." (Spurgeon)

c. **He who reaps receives wages, and gathers fruit for eternal life, that both he who sows and he who reaps may rejoice together**: Jesus encouraged His disciples in their work with Him in at least three ways.

- Their work in the harvest would be rewarded (**He who reaps receives wages**).

- The good of their work would last forever (**gathers fruit for eternal life**).

- Every worker in the harvest would **rejoice together** in the work.

d. **I sent you to reap that for which you have not labored; others have labored, and you have entered into their labors**: The disciples could now reap a harvest immediately, and they reaped it from seeds they didn't sow.

i. John the Baptist and Jesus sowed the seeds, and at the moment the disciples had the opportunity to reap. Many times, this is how the work of God happens - **one sows and another reaps** (1 Corinthians 3:6-8).

11. (39-42) Many Samaritans believe on the **Savior of the world**.

And many of the Samaritans of that city believed in Him because of the word of the woman who testified, "He told me all that I *ever* did." So when the Samaritans had come to Him, they urged Him to stay with them; and He stayed there two days. And many more believed because of His own word. Then they said to the woman, "Now we believe, not because of what you said, for we ourselves have heard *Him* and we know that this is indeed the Christ, the Savior of the world."

a. **Many of the Samaritans of that city believed in Him**: At that moment they did not know enough to trust Jesus and His work on the cross; but they could most certainly **believe in Him** as the Messiah of God. They did believe, and **because of the word of the woman who testified**.

b. **He told me all that I ever did**: The woman was amazed not only that Jesus knew the facts of her life, but that *He loved her* even knowing the facts of her life. We sometimes fear that if someone knew **all that I ever did**, they could not love us, but Jesus loved this woman.

c. **He stayed there two days**: This was remarkable in light of the opinions of most of the Jewish people of Jesus' day regarding the Samaritans. They regarded Samaria and the Samaritans as a place and people to avoid if possible, and if it were necessary to go through Samaria it should be done as quickly as possible. Yet Jesus **stayed there two days**.

i. "That Samaritans should invite a Jewish teacher to stay with them, with no fear of a rebuff, shows how completely he had won their confidence." (Bruce)

ii. "During the stay His reasoning and discoursing added greatly to the number of the believers and supplemented the woman's work." (Trench)

d. **Many more believed because of His own word**: In the days Jesus spent among the Samaritans He taught them, and **many more believed**.

i. "We may wonder if this was the same 'city of Samaria' as was evangelized by Philip a few years later [Acts 8:5]." (Bruce)

e. **We know that this is indeed the Christ, the Savior of the world**: The remarkable testimony of the woman at the well connected these Samaritans of Sychar to Jesus; but in hearing Him they came to a deeper personal faith in Jesus as both Messiah (**Christ**) and **the Savior of the world**.

i. **Savior of the world**: "Not of the *Jews* only, but of the *Samaritans*, and of the whole *Gentile* world." (Clarke)

ii. "The title 'Saviour of the World' was of course prompted by the teaching of Jesus Himself during His two days' residence." (Dods)

B. Healing of the nobleman's son: the second sign.

1. (43-46a) Jesus returns to Galilee.

Now after the two days He departed from there and went to Galilee. For Jesus Himself testified that a prophet has no honor in his own country. So when He came to Galilee, the Galileans received Him, having seen all the things He did in Jerusalem at the feast; for they also had gone to the feast. So Jesus came again to Cana of Galilee where He had made the water wine.

a. **A prophet has no honor in his own country**: Galilee was Jesus' **country** - where He grew up. Because these people felt so familiar with Jesus, they did not honor Him the way they should have. In this we recognize that they *really* were not familiar with Jesus; if they were, they would have honored Him all the more.

i. There is such a thing as a *false* familiarity with Jesus; a dangerous feeling that we know all about Him. Such a dangerous feeling leads to a lack of **honor** towards Jesus.

ii. It's a little hard to know if John meant to associate the place where Jesus was not honored to be Judea or Galilee. A case can be made for either; clearly the other Gospels quoted this principle and related it to Galilee (Matthew 13:57 and Mark 6:4).

iii. "He betakes himself to Galilee therefore, to avoid fame, testifying that His own country (Galilee) was that where, as a prophet, He was least likely to be honoured." (Alford)

b. **Having seen all the things He did in Jerusalem at the feast**: It was customary for the Jews in Galilee to go to Jerusalem for the feasts (fulfilling Exodus 23:14-17). This particular time they remembered all that Jesus had done in Jerusalem.

i. Perhaps they remembered when Jesus turned the merchant's tables in the outer courts of the temple (John 2:13-27). Jesus also predicted His own resurrection (John 2:18-22) and performed many other unspecified signs when in Jerusalem (John 2:23-25).

ii. "The enthusiasm of the Galileans was not soundly based. It was dependent on the wonders arising from their sight of the signs, not on a realization that Jesus was indeed the Christ, the Saviour of the world. Their very acceptance of Him was thus in its way a rejection. They gave Him honor of a sort, but it was not the honor that was due to Him." (Morris)

2. (46b-48) The nobleman and his sick son.

And there was a certain nobleman whose son was sick at Capernaum. When he heard that Jesus had come out of Judea into Galilee, he went to Him and implored Him to come down and heal his son, for he was at the point of death. Then Jesus said to him, "Unless you *people* see signs and wonders, you will by no means believe."

a. **Whose son was sick at Capernaum**: By this time Jesus had made His home in Capernaum (Matthew 4:13 and John 2:12). Though Jesus was at Cana (John 4:46a), the nobleman travelled the 20 or so miles (32 kilometers) from **Capernaum** to Cana.

i. **A certain nobleman**: "Literally, '*a royal person*'... this man was probably an officer of Herod Antipas." (Alford)

b. **Implored Him to come down and heal his son, for he was at the point of death**: This **certain nobleman** was one of many parents who came to Jesus on behalf of an afflicted child. He obviously came with passion and urgency of a father of a sick child - and **at the point of death**.

i. "How vapid and vain was all the showy courtlife when there rang through it, in a voice he loved so well, the wild and delirious cries of raging fever!" (Morrison)

c. **Unless you people see signs and wonders, you will by no means believe**: Jesus rebuked those who depended on signs and wonders *before* they would believe. It might seem that Jesus was harsh towards this man who wanted his son healed, but He encountered many in Galilee who were interested only in His miracles - He therefore questioned this man accordingly.

i. Signs and wonders can lead a person towards belief in God, and can validate a heavenly messenger - but they can also have no effect on a person, and Satan can also use lying signs and wonders (2 Thessalonians 2:9).

ii. Signs and wonders from God are obviously good things, but they should not form the foundation of our faith. We should not depend on them to *prove* God to us. In themselves, signs and wonders cannot change the heart; Israel saw incredible signs at Mount Sinai and even heard the very voice of God (Exodus 19:16-20:1), yet a short time later they worshipped a gold calf (Exodus 32:1-6).

iii. "These words imply the contrast between the Samaritans, who believed *because of His word*, and the Jews who would not believe but *through signs and prodigies*." (Alford)

3. (49-50) Jesus declares the nobleman's son healed, and the nobleman believes the declaration.

The nobleman said to Him, "Sir, come down before my child dies!" Jesus said to him, "Go your way; your son lives." So the man believed the word that Jesus spoke to him, and he went his way.

a. **The nobleman said to Him**: This man was a **nobleman**, a man of high standing and stature. All of his standing and stature seemed to matter nothing in light of his great need. He experienced the leveling effect of affliction.

b. **Sir, come down before my child dies!** In His previous words, it *seemed* that Jesus discouraged the nobleman from asking for a miracle. Yet this request shows that the nobleman properly understood that Jesus did not intend to discourage asking Jesus for miraculous help, only to discourage a faith that seeks only the miraculous.

i. The nobleman did not appeal to Jesus on the basis of his noble status, but on the basis of his son's great need. Coming to Jesus as a great and important man would gain him nothing before Jesus.

ii. "He urged no merit, but pleaded the misery of the case. He did not plead that the boy was of noble birth — that would have been very bad pleading with Jesus; nor did he urge that he was a lovely child — that would have been a sorry argument; but he pleaded that he was at the point of death. His extremity was his reason for urgency: the child was at death's door; therefore his father begs that mercy's door may open." (Spurgeon)

c. **Go your way; your son lives**: Jesus severely tested this man's faith, forcing him to believe in Jesus' word alone and not in any outward demonstration of the miraculous. Despite the test, *the man took Jesus at His word and departed* (NIV). The nobleman demonstrated that true faith is simply taking Jesus at His word.

i. "It was worthy of His care to heal the boy; it was far more needful that He should train and lead the father to faith." (Maclaren)

ii. "Had our Lord gone with him, as he wished, his unbelief could not have been fully removed; as he would have still thought that our Lord's power could not reach from Cana to Capernaum: in order to destroy his unbelief at once, and bring him into the fulness of the faith of his supreme power, he cures him, being apparently absent, by that energy through which he fills both the heavens and the earth." (Clarke)

d. **Your son lives**: Jesus did not use any dramatic effects in this healing. Many people want to see dramatic effects in God's work; and sometimes

God provides them. Real faith may perceive and accept the outward demonstration of the miraculous, but does not require it.

4. (51-54) The nobleman discovers that his son is healed and when it happened.

And as he was now going down, his servants met him and told *him,* **saying, "Your son lives!" Then he inquired of them the hour when he got better. And they said to him, "Yesterday at the seventh hour the fever left him." So the father knew that** *it was* **at the same hour in which Jesus said to him, "Your son lives." And he himself believed, and his whole household. This again** *is* **the second sign Jesus did when He had come out of Judea into Galilee.**

a. **Your son lives!** The nobleman *believed* it before the evidence, but the evidence was clearly welcome. One may only imagine how beautiful this news was to the nobleman and to know, **it was at the same hour in which Jesus said to him, "Your son lives."**

i. The proof of this miracle was plain. When Jesus proclaimed the boy healed, he was in fact healed - and in a demonstrated way.

ii. According to his servants, this happened "**Yesterday at the seventh hour.**" This means that the nobleman took his time to return from his meeting with Jesus in Cana back to his home in Capernaum. His leisurely pace was a demonstration of faith. In fear, the nobleman *ran* from Capernaum to Cana; in faith he *walked* from Cana back to Capernaum.

iii. "The nobleman was so sure that that his child was alive and well, that he was in no violent hurry to return. He did not go home immediately, as though he must be in time to get another doctor, if Christ had not succeeded; but he went his way leisurely and calmly, confident in the truth of what Jesus had said to him." (Spurgeon)

b. **And he himself believed, and his whole household**: The miraculous power of Jesus developed greater faith in both the nobleman and his household. He believed before, but now he believed more. His faith was deepened by his personal experience of God's power.

i. "His disciples *believed on him* after the water had been turned into wine; the father and the rest of the household *believed* as the result of the healing of the boy: and in both cases the verb in the original is an inceptive aorist 'they put their faith in Him'." (Tasker)

ii. It would not "be easy at the court of Herod to profess faith in Jesus. He would have mockery and laughter to endure; and no doubt there would be those who thought that he had gone slightly mad." (Barclay)

c. **This again is the second sign**: In the Gospel of John the **signs** are given to lead the reader to faith (John 20:29-31). The relation between belief and signs is clear in John chapter 2 and chapter 4.

- The first sign persuaded His disciples.
- The second sign persuaded a Jewish nobleman and his household.
- The Samaritans believed without a sign.

  i. The first two signs in the Gospel of John took place at Cana of Galilee. The first was at the best party ever - a wedding party. The second was connected with the worst tragedy ever - the illness and soon death of a child. *Jesus is real in both aspects.*

John 5 - A Healing and a Discourse

A. Jesus heals a man at the pool of Bethesda.

1. (1-4) The pool of Bethesda.

After this there was a feast of the Jews, and Jesus went up to Jerusalem. Now there is in Jerusalem by the Sheep *Gate* a pool, which is called in Hebrew, Bethesda, having five porches. In these lay a great multitude of sick people, blind, lame, paralyzed, waiting for the moving of the water. For an angel went down at a certain time into the pool and stirred up the water; then whoever stepped in first, after the stirring of the water, was made well of whatever disease he had.

a. **A feast of the Jews**: We don't know what feast this was, but it was probably one of the major three feasts in which attendance was required.

i. The debate centers on if this was Passover, Pentecost, or Purim. If it was a Passover, then we can date four Passovers in Jesus' ministry and we know it lasted about 3½ years.

b. **A pool, which is called in Hebrew, Bethesda**: This pool has been excavated in the area just north of the temple area, and found to have **five porches**, just as John said.

i. "The expression **there is** has been thought to import that St. John wrote his Gospel *before the destruction of Jerusalem*. But this must not be pressed. He might have spoken in the present without meaning to be literally accurate with regard to the moment when he was writing." (Alford)

ii. There is a crusader-era church near the remains of this pool. "That they [the Crusaders] regarded this pool as that mentioned here is shown by their having represented on the wall of the crypt the angel troubling the water." (Dods)

c. **For an angel went down... whoever stepped in first... was made well**: Many **sick** and injured people gathered at this pool in hope of healing. Perhaps this hope of healing was real, and God honored a release of faith. Or, it may be that this was merely a hopeful legend; nevertheless, **a great multitude of sick people** believed it.

i. The words from **waiting for the moving of the water** through **was made well of whatever disease he had** are not in several old manuscripts. Nevertheless, the truth of the perception of a healing received by being first in the water is also demonstrated in the words of John 5:7.

ii. "From MSS. evidence, this verse and the last clause of verse 3 seem not to be by John, but to be a very early insertion (as least as early as Tertullian, 2nd century)." (Trench)

iii. **At a certain time**: Clarke and others believe that this **certain time** was feast time, perhaps specifically Passover. The idea is that the people gathered around the pool in expectation of healing at the Passover season or other feast seasons. "Once a year only, saith Tertullian. Others (more probably) at all their great feasts, when the people met out of all parts at Jerusalem." (Trapp)

iv. If there were people genuinely healed by the waters of the Pool of Bethesda, it was one of many unusual occasions healing in the Bible.

- Some were healed by a purified pot of stew (2 Kings 4:38-41).
- Naaman was healed by washing in the Jordan River (2 Kings 5:10-14).
- One was healed by touching the bones of Elisha (2 Kings 13:20-21).
- Some were healed when the shadow of Peter fell upon them (Acts 5:14-16).
- Some were healed when Paul's handkerchiefs were laid upon them (Acts 19:11-12).

v. God can and does do things in unexpected ways. But something isn't necessarily from God simply because it is unexpected or unusual.

2. (5-6) Jesus questions a lame man.

Now a certain man was there who had an infirmity thirty-eight years. When Jesus saw him lying there, and knew that he already had been *in that condition* **a long time, He said to him, "Do you want to be made well?"**

a. **A certain man was there who had an infirmity thirty-eight years**: This man suffered from a paralytic condition for a long time, and apparently was frequently at the Pool of Bethesda in hope of healing. It was a hope that had been long disappointed (**thirty-eight years**).

b. **When Jesus saw him lying there**: For some reason, Jesus selected this man among the *great multitude of sick people* (John 5:3). Jesus was not about to conduct a healing crusade at the Pool of Bethesda, but He was about to miraculously meet this one man's need.

i. A multitude of needy people were there, yet none of them looked to Jesus. "A blindness had come over these people at the pool; there they were, and there was Christ, who could heal them, but not a single one of them sought him. Their eyes were fixed on the water, expecting it to be troubled; they were so taken up with their own chosen way that the true way was neglected." (Spurgeon)

ii. Spurgeon pictured the multitude waiting around the waters of the Pool of Bethesda, all of them waiting - instead of looking to Jesus. He thought of how foolish this waiting is for many people.

- Some wait for a more convenient season.

- Some wait for dreams and visions.

- Some wait for signs and wonders.

- Some wait to be compelled.

- Some wait for a revival.

- Some wait for particular feelings.

- Some wait for a celebrity.

c. **Do you want to be made well?** This was a sincere question. Jesus knew that not every sick person *wants* to be healed, and that some are so discouraged that they put away all hope of being healed. Jesus dealt with a man who may have had his *heart* withered as well as his legs. Jesus therefore attempted to build the faith of this man.

i. "It certainly is possible that the man's long and apparently hopeless infirmity may have given him a look of lethargy and despondency, and the question may have arisen from this." (Alford)

ii. It is possible that Jesus asked this even as the waters were stirred and people started jumping and diving and rolling into the waters, each hoping for evidence that *they* were the favored one. The man Jesus spoke with knew that *he* was not one of the favored, and had no real hope to be healed.

iii. In this man's particular case, it was reasonable to wonder if he really wanted to be healed. "An eastern beggar often loses a good living by being cured of his disease." (Barclay) As bad as his current situation was, at least he was familiar with it.

3. (7-9) The man replies and Jesus heals him.

The sick man answered Him, "Sir, I have no man to put me into the pool when the water is stirred up; but while I am coming, another steps down before me." Jesus said to him, "Rise, take up your bed and walk." And immediately the man was made well, took up his bed, and walked. And that day was the Sabbath.

a. **Sir, I have no man to put me into the pool**: The crippled man assumed Jesus knew how things worked at the Pool of Bethesda, and he explained to Jesus why it wasn't possible for him to be healed. Quite naturally, the man couldn't think of any other way for his need to be met.

i. The man was an interesting case of hope combined with hopelessness. He had hope, or would never have come to the Pool of Bethesda. Yet once there, he had little hope to be the favored one to win the healing that day.

ii. **Another steps down before me**: "The man's answer implies the popular belief that whoever stepped in immediately after the bubbling up of the water was made whole." (Alford)

iii. "The sick man does what we nearly all do. He limits God's help to his own ideas and does not dare promise himself more that he conceives in his mind." (Calvin)

b. **Rise, take up your bed and walk**: Jesus told the man to do what he could not do. Being paralyzed, it was impossible for him to **rise** or to **take up** his bed-mat or to **walk**. At this moment, Jesus challenged the man to believe Him for the impossible.

i. The **bed** was not a full-framed bed, but a bed-mat. Morris on the ancient Greek word translated **bed**: "It is apparently Macedonian in origin and denotes a camp-bed, a pallet."

ii. It's easy to imagine that the man's first reaction was, *I can't do that - why even try?* Yet something wonderful prompted the man to say, *If this man tells me to do it, I will try.* Jesus guided the man towards a response of faith.

iii. "The man might well have said with a kind of injured resentment that for thirty-eight years his bed had been carrying him and there was not much sense in telling him to carry it." (Barclay)

iv. "He was commanded to take up his bed that he might recognise that the cure was permanent. No doubt many of the cures at the pool were merely temporary." (Dods)

c. **Immediately the man was made well**: This happened as the man responded in faith and did exactly what Jesus told him to do, though a moment before this it was impossible to do it. The fact of his healing was confirmed in that he had the strength to carry his own **bed**-mat and walk with it.

i. "Because Jesus told him, he asked no questions, but doubled up his couch, and walked. He did what he was told to do, because he believed in him who spake. Have you such faith in Jesus, poor sinner?" (Spurgeon)

ii. "He healed the man beside the pool, but without his touching the pool, to show that He could heal without the water." (Trench)

iii. This shows us that the New Testament describes many different ways people may be healed.

- The elders of the church may anoint someone with oil and pray for them, and they may be healed (James 5:14-16).

- God's people can lay hands on each other in prayer, ask God for healing, and people may be healed (Mark 16:17-18).

- God may grant someone a gift of healing - either that they are directly healed, or have the power to bring healing to another (1 Corinthians 12:9).

- God may grant healing in response to the faith of the person who desires to be healed (Matthew 9:22).

- God may grant healing in response to the faith of another on behalf of the person who is healed (Mark 2:4-5, Matthew 8:13).

- God may heal through medical treatment (1 Timothy 5:23, James 5:14 with Luke 10:34).

d. **That day was the Sabbath**: That all this was done on the Sabbath day will be the source of the controversy that follows.

B. The Sabbath controversy.

1. (10-13) The Jews ignore the miracle and take offense.

The Jews therefore said to him who was cured, "It is the Sabbath; it is not lawful for you to carry *your* bed." He answered them, "He who made me well said to me, 'Take up your bed and walk.'" Then they asked him, "Who is the Man who said to you, 'Take up your bed and

walk'?" But the one who was healed did not know who it was, for Jesus had withdrawn, a multitude being in *that* place.

a. **The Jews therefore said**: Throughout his Gospel, John uses the term **the Jews** in the sense of the Jewish leaders, not of all the Jews in Jerusalem.

> i. "Here, as regularly in the Gospel of John, it is important to mark who exactly 'the Jews' in question are: in this context they are members of the religious establishment in Jerusalem." (Bruce)

b. **It is the Sabbath; it is not lawful for you to carry your bed**: Carrying a **bed** (actually a sleeping-mat or a bedroll) was in fact a violation of the rabbis' interpretation of the commandment against doing work or business on the Sabbath. It was not a breaking of God's law of the Sabbath, but the human interpretation of God's law.

> i. "The Rabbis of Jesus' day solemnly argued that a man was sinning if he carried a needle in his robe on the Sabbath. They even argued as to whether he could wear his artificial teeth or his wooden leg." (Barclay)

> ii. "Jesus persistently maintained that it is lawful on the sabbath to do good. He ignored the mass of scribal regulations, and thus inevitably came into conflict with the authorities." (Morris)

> iii. This devotion to the rabbis' interpretation of the Sabbath law continues in modern times. An example is found in an April 1992 news item: Tenants let three apartments in an Orthodox neighborhood in Israel burn to the ground while they asked a rabbi whether a telephone call to the fire department on the Sabbath would violate Jewish law. Observant Jews are forbidden to use the phone on the Sabbath, because doing so would break an electrical current, which is considered a form of work. In the half-hour it took the rabbi to decide "yes," the fire spread to two neighboring apartments.

c. **Who is the Man who said to you, "Take up your bed and walk"?** The Jewish leaders didn't want to know who healed the crippled man. They wanted to know who told him to carry a bed-mat on the Sabbath day.

> i. This probably seemed strange, and perhaps confusing to the healed man. "I was carried to the pool today and if I were not healed I would need to be carried home. That's a lot more work than me carrying my little bed-mat. In healing me and sending me home, Jesus was saving work on the Sabbath, not making more work."

> ii. To the religious leaders Jesus was *the man who broke the Sabbath*. To the healed man Jesus was *He who made me well.*

d. **For Jesus had withdrawn, a multitude being in that place**: Jesus did not want to remain with the commotion surrounding the man's healing. Because He did not intend to heal the entire **multitude**, it was better for Him to withdraw.

> i. "Jesus spoke the healing words, and then went on among the crowd, so that no particular attention was attracted to Himself, either by the sick man or others." (Alford)

2. (14-15) Jesus warns the healed man of a greater danger.

Afterward Jesus found him in the temple, and said to him, "See, you have been made well. Sin no more, lest a worse thing come upon you." The man departed and told the Jews that it was Jesus who had made him well.

> a. **Afterward Jesus found him**: Jesus **found him** because He was concerned for his spiritual health (**sin no more lest a worse thing come upon you**), not only his physical health. Living a life of sin is worse, and will bring a worse result, than being crippled for thirty-eight years.

> > i. **See, you have been made well**: "Employs the perfect of the verb, indicating that the cure was permanent. No doubt some of the 'cures' that were reported from the pool did not last very long." (Morris)

> > ii. "The man's eight-and-thirty years of illness had apparently been brought on by dissipation. It was a sin of the flesh, avenged in the flesh, that had given him that miserable life." (Maclaren)

> b. **The man departed and told the Jews that it was Jesus**: The fact that he reported Jesus to the authorities showed how intimidated the man was by those same religious leaders.

> > i. "The man who had been healed seems to have been an unpleasant creature…as soon as he found out the identity of his Benefactor he betrayed Him to the hostile authorities." (Morris)

> > ii. In theory, the penalties for disobedience on the Sabbath were serious. Dods cites Lightfoot: "Whosoever on the Sabbath bringeth anything in, or taketh anything out from a public place to a private one, if he hath done this inadvertently, he shall sacrifice for his sin; but if willfully, he shall be cut off and shall be stoned."

3. (16-18) Jesus defends His Sabbath actions.

For this reason the Jews persecuted Jesus, and sought to kill Him, because He had done these things on the Sabbath. But Jesus answered them, "My Father has been working until now, and I have been working." Therefore the Jews sought all the more to kill Him, because

He not only broke the Sabbath, but also said that God was His Father, making Himself equal with God.

a. **For this reason the Jews persecuted Jesus, and sought to kill Him**: Remarkably, the healing seemed to make no difference to those who **persecuted** Jesus. All they could see was that their religious rule was broken, a rule that went *beyond* the command of Scripture itself.

i. "Inciting others to break the law (as they understood it) was worse than breaking it oneself. Therefore they launched a campaign against Jesus which was not relaxed until his death some eighteen months later." (Bruce)

ii. The absolute devotion to the traditions of man surrounding the Sabbath can't be understated. For example, Deuteronomy 23:12-14 tells Israel to practice good sanitation when their armies are camped. Ancient rabbis applied the same principle to the city of Jerusalem, which they regarded as "the camp of the Lord." When this was combined with Sabbath travel restrictions, it resulted in a prohibition against going to the bathroom on the Sabbath.

b. **And sought to kill Him**: The anger and hatred of the religious leaders is difficult to explain, apart from seeing that it had a spiritual root. They did not like Jesus, and therefore they did not like God the Father (**but also said that God was His Father**).

c. **My Father has been working until now, and I have been working**: Jesus did not try and explain that He had not truly worked on the Sabbath. Instead, He boldly explained to the religious leaders that His **Father** worked on the Sabbath, and therefore Jesus the Son also worked on the Sabbath.

i. "God never stops working, for as it is the property of fire to burn and of snow to be cold so of God to work." (Philo, cited in Dods)

ii. In some ways, it is strange that the God of the Bible is a *working* God. "In the old world, it was hardly an honourable thing to work. It was a think for slaves and serfs and strangers, not for freeborn men. Hence work and greatness rarely went together; and nothing could be more alien to the genius of paganism than a toiling God. It was a revolution when Jesus taught 'God loves.' But it was hardly less revolutionary when He taught 'God works.'" (Morrison)

iii. "Though he rested from creating, he never ceased from *preserving* and *governing* that which he had formed: in this respect he can keep no *sabbaths*; for nothing can continue to exist, or answer the end proposed by the Divine wisdom and goodness, without the continual *energy* of God." (Clarke)

iv. This answers the objection raised by a hostile (and ignorant) critic of Christianity. I saw this statement written in an anti-Christian tract: *Just say "no!" to a god who claims to be all powerful, but then requires a nap after only six days of creating (Genesis 2:2).* This objection betrays the lack of understanding on behalf of the writer. The Bible clearly says that God does not need sleep or rest (Psalm 121:3-4, *He who keeps Israel shall neither slumber nor sleep*). The rest of God on the seventh day was given for man's benefit, not God's, demonstrating a pattern of rest necessary for man's well being.

v. **My Father... and I**: "His explanation shows that he did not claim identity with the Father as one person, but he asserted his unity with the Father in a relationship that could be described as sonship." (Tenney)

d. **But also said that God was His Father, making Himself equal with God**: The religious leaders did not miss the fact that Jesus claimed to be **equal with God**. They knew clearly that when Jesus said that God was His Father in this unique way, He declared **Himself equal with God**.

i. "He was claiming that God was *His* Father in a special sense. He was claiming that He partook of the same nature as His Father. This involved equality." (Morris) Morris also notes that the verbs **broke** and **said** are both in continuous tenses; Jesus habitually broke their man-made Sabbath rules and habitually said He was **equal with God**.

ii. "The individual use of 'MY FATHER' by Jesus had a totally distinct, and in their view a blasphemous meaning; this latter especially, because He this made God a participator in His crime of breaking the sabbath." (Alford)

iii. "It should be carefully observed that He did not deny the accuracy of their deduction, but continued to speak as One who claimed such equality of authority." (Morgan)

iv. Augustine wisely said of this passage: "Behold, the Jews understand what the Arians do not understand." Today, Jehovah's Witnesses are among those that hold the doctrines of the Arians, denying the deity of Jesus.

C. Jesus explains His relationship to the Father.

1. (19-20) The Son does as the Father does.

Then Jesus answered and said to them, "Most assuredly, I say to you, the Son can do nothing of Himself, but what He sees the Father do; for whatever He does, the Son also does in like manner. For the Father

loves the Son, and shows Him all things that He Himself does; and He will show Him greater works than these, that you may marvel."

a. **Then Jesus answered and said to them**: In this extended discussion Jesus explained to the religious leaders some of the nature of His relationship and work with God the Father. Because of this, we have a lot of information of the relationship between God the Father and God the Son.

i. Leon Morris said of this section, "The language Jesus uses throughout is thoroughly Rabbinic."

b. **The Son can do nothing of Himself**: Jesus explained that He, as God the Son, does nothing independently. He was and is fully submitted to the Father's will. This submission comes by choice, not by coercion or by an inferior nature.

i. Relevant to the Sabbath controversy discussed in the previous verses, this was Jesus' way of telling the religious leaders that He did not tell the healed man to carry his bed on His *own* authority; He did it in complete submission to God the Father in heaven.

ii. "It is not simply that He does not act in independence of the Father, He cannot act in independence of the Father." (Morris)

c. **Whatever He does, the Son also does in like manner**: Jesus explained that His work was a perfect reflection of the work and will of God the Father. Jesus showed us exactly what the work and will of God is.

i. "The Father is not passive in the matter, merely allowing Jesus to discover what He can of the Father's will; but the Father shows Him." (Dods)

ii. "C.H. Dodd discerned an 'embedded parable' in verses 19 and 20: Jesus draws an analogy from his own boyhood experience in the carpenter's workshop, when he learned to imitate the things he saw Joseph doing, thus serving his apprenticeship." (Bruce)

iii. Some people think of a great difference - or even a small difference - between God the Father and God the Son, as if God the Father emphasized judgment and God the Son emphasized love. Sometimes they think the same way over what they call *the God of the Old Testament* and the *God of the New Testament*. This thinking is wrong; it usually comes from refusing to see the display of love in God the Father, or the display of righteousness in God the Son.

iv. "He is explaining also, by inference, the mystery of the Incarnation - that God The Son in becoming Man ceased not to be God, and that the Personality of Jesus is the Personality of God The Son." (Trench)

d. **The Father loves the Son**: The relationship between the First and Second members of the Trinity is not one of master and slave, not of employer and employee, but of **Father** and **Son**, united by love.

i. "The Father loves the Son (the tense denotes a continuing habitual love; the Father never ceases to love the Son)." (Morris)

ii. "That 'the Father loves the Son' has been affirmed already in this Gospel (John 3:35); it is immaterial that the verb here is *phileo* whereas in the earlier occurrence it is *agapao*." (Bruce)

e. **He will show Him greater works than these, that you may marvel**: The religious leaders were stunned by what Jesus told the formerly paralyzed man to do. Jesus here told them that they would see even **greater works**, ones that would make them **marvel**.

2. (21-23) The works of the Father, the works of the Son.

"For as the Father raises the dead and gives life to *them,* **even so the Son gives life to whom He will. For the Father judges no one, but has committed all judgment to the Son, that all should honor the Son just as they honor the Father. He who does not honor the Son does not honor the Father who sent Him."**

a. **As the Father raises the dead and gives life to them, even so the Son gives life to whom He will**: Jesus used the *work of resurrection* as an example of the shared work of the Father and the Son. Here the Son has the power and authority to raise the dead and give life to them just as the Father does.

i. In this Jesus appealed to *ultimate power*. It's hard to think of greater power and authority than of that to raise the dead. The religious leaders didn't want to think much about Jesus' ability to heal a paralytic; they focused on Him as a Sabbath breaker. Yet the power of Jesus went far beyond the power to heal.

ii. **The Son gives life to whom He will**: "Here our Lord points out his sovereign power and independence; he gives life according to *his own will*-not being obliged to supplicate for the power by which it was done, as the *prophets* did; his own will being absolute and sufficient in every case." (Clarke)

b. **But has committed all judgment to the Son**: Jesus used the *work of judgment* as an example of a division of labor between the Father and the Son. It is before God the Son that people will stand on the Day of Judgment. Even during His earthly ministry, Jesus was something of a judge among humanity.

i. Just being in the presence of Jesus led one to know, "I'm not like *Him*." Jesus looked at the rich young ruler, and he was judged. He looked upon Simon Peter, and he was judged. Those were not looks of anger; they were looks of love. Yet when they saw the face of Jesus they knew a love was extended to them that they were not worthy of.

ii. "Wherever Jesus was, there was the element of judgment... there was always self-reproach where Jesus was. Men were ashamed of themselves, they knew not why. His life was an unceasing act of love, and yet it was an unceasing act of judgment." (Morrison)

c. **That all should honor the Son just as they honor the Father**: God the Father gave this work of judgment to God the Son so that people would **honor** Jesus as they should, and that they should **honor** the Son **just as they honor the Father**. *Failing* to honor God the Son means that it is impossible for one to also **honor** God the Father who sent the Son.

i. This was a clear claim to deity. If Jesus - designating Himself as **the Son** - was not God, then it would be idolatry to **honor the Son *just as* they honor the Father**.

ii. "All must honour Him with equal honour to that which they pay to the Father - and whosover does not, however he may imagine that he honours or approaches God, does not honour Him at all; because *He can only be known or honoured by us as* 'THE FATHER WHO SENT HIS SON.'" (Alford)

iii. **The Father who sent Him**: "The Incarnation is every whit as much The Father's act as it is The Son's: The Father 'sent,' The Son 'came.'" (Trench)

3. (24-27) From death to life in the Son of God.

"Most assuredly, I say to you, he who hears My word and believes in Him who sent Me has everlasting life, and shall not come into judgment, but has passed from death into life. Most assuredly, I say to you, the hour is coming, and now is, when the dead will hear the voice of the Son of God; and those who hear will live. For as the Father has life in Himself, so He has granted the Son to have life in Himself, and has given Him authority to execute judgment also, because He is the Son of Man."

a. **He who hears My word and believes in Him who sent Me has everlasting life**: Jesus explained to the astonished religious leaders that those who heard his word would have **everlasting life**. They would have the life connected with eternity, and have that live now.

i. John 3:16 stated that belief in Jesus - in the sense of trusting in, relying on, and clinging to - was the path to everlasting life. Here Jesus said that hearing His word and belief in the Father (**Him who sent Me**) is the path to everlasting life. Because the Father and the Son are so united in their work, each is true of the other. True belief in the Father *is* belief in the Son, and true belief in the Son *is* belief in the Father.

ii. With these words Jesus lifted Himself far about the level of any mere man. Think of it: "Hear My word and have everlasting life." This was either the babbling of an insane man or the words of God Himself. There is no neutral ground to be found here.

iii. "It does not appear from our text that everlasting life is communicated by drops of water, or in any other ceremonial manner; but the command is, 'Hear, and your soul shall live.'" (Spurgeon)

b. **Shall not come into judgment, but has passed from death into life**: This is one aspect that is essential to everlasting life; to escape judgment for sin and to pass from the position of death to the position of life.

i. **Has passed from death into life**: "Has *changed his country*, or *place of abode*. Death is the country where every Christless soul lives. The man who knows not God lives a dying life, or a living death; but he who believes in the Son of God *passes over* from the empire of death, to the empire of life." (Clarke)

c. **The dead will hear the voice of the Son of God; and those who hear will live**: Jesus had already explained that one who lives can hear His word, believe, and have everlasting life. Now He adds that one day even **the dead will hear the voice of the Son of God**, and be raised again. These are remarkable claims to be much more than a man.

d. **He has granted the Son to have life in Himself**: Jesus further described His uniqueness to the religious leaders by claiming that He has **life in Himself**, a gift granted by God the Father. Jesus had **life in Himself**, not dependent upon other people or things.

i. None of us has life inherent in ourselves. Our life is derived from our parents, and the fragile environment around us. Jesus claimed that His life was derived from no one; it is inherent and uncreated. Theologians call this quality of self-existence *aseity* and recognize that God alone possesses it.

ii. "What a paradox it is to say that it is '*given*' to Him to have 'life in *Himself*'! And when was that gift given? In the depths of eternity." (Maclaren)

iii. As Jesus explained His nature and deity to the religious leaders in this chapter, it is evident that He did not claim identity with the Father as one person, but asserted His equality to God the Father and His relationship of love with the Father. Jesus and the Father are not the same, but they are equal, just as John 1:1 states.

iv. These words of Jesus contradict two later errors about the nature of the deity of God the Son. One is sometimes called the "Jesus Only" doctrine, confusing the Father and the Son (anciently known as *Sabellianism*, and held today by groups like Oneness Pentecostals). The other is the error that Jesus is not God, (anciently known as *Arianism*, and held today by groups like the Jehovah's Witnesses).

4. (28-30) The reality of the Son's coming judgment.

"Do not marvel at this; for the hour is coming in which all who are in the graves will hear His voice and come forth—those who have done good, to the resurrection of life, and those who have done evil, to the resurrection of condemnation. I can of Myself do nothing. As I hear, I judge; and My judgment is righteous, because I do not seek My own will but the will of the Father who sent Me."

a. **The hour is coming in which all who are in the graves will hear His voice**: Previously Jesus said that all who have everlasting life would hear His voice and live (John 5:25). He now extended the concept of resurrection to all humanity, both those who have **done good** and who have **done evil**.

i. "This does not mean that salvation is on the basis of good works, for this very Gospel makes it plain over and over again that men enter eternal life when they believe on Jesus Christ. But the lives they live form the test of the faith they profess." (Morris)

b. **The resurrection of life... the resurrection of condemnation**: Jesus explained this to the astonished religious leaders to explain who He was, the nature of His authority and deity. At the same time, it tells us something remarkable about humanity; that everyone, both those **who have done good** and **those who have done evil** will live forever, far beyond the physical and material life they know on this earth in this age. Jesus will command them to rise on that day, in bodies suited for eternity.

i. "The double resurrection assumes that both the righteous and the wicked will receive bodies in the future life and that presumably each body will express the character of the person who is resurrected." (Tenney)

c. **My judgment is righteous**: Jesus explained that He is qualified as a completely righteous judge, because His power is in submission to God the Father. He repeated the themes: **I can of Myself do nothing... I do not seek My own will but the will of the Father who sent Me.**

D. The five-fold testimony to who Jesus is.

1. (31-32) Jesus tells of testimony beyond His own regarding himself.

"If I bear witness of Myself, My witness is not true. There is another who bears witness of Me, and I know that the witness which He witnesses of Me is true."

a. **If I bear witness of Myself, My witness is not true**: Like anyone else, it was not enough for Jesus to simply claim things about Himself. There had to be outside and independent **witness** to His true identity and nature.

i. This principle is established by Deuteronomy 19:15, which says *by the mouth of two or three witnesses the matter shall be established*. Jesus explained to the religious leaders that He was God, but His testimony alone was not enough.

b. **There is another who bears witness of Me**: In the following passage, Jesus brought forth three trustworthy witnesses who will testify that He is equal to the Father. Jesus found it important to give them reason to believe beyond what He said about Himself.

2. (33-35) The testimony of John the Baptist.

"You have sent to John, and he has borne witness to the truth. Yet I do not receive testimony from man, but I say these things that you may be saved. He was the burning and shining lamp, and you were willing for a time to rejoice in his light."

a. **You have sent to John, and he has borne witness to the truth**: Jesus noted that the religious leaders knew of and heard John the Baptist for themselves. They needed to think of and believe what John said about Jesus.

b. **He was the burning and shining lamp, and you were willing for a time to rejoice in his light**: The religious leaders accepted the work of John the Baptist **for a time**. They needed to continue to believe John regarding Jesus the Messiah.

i. "The expression of *lamp* our Lord took from the ordinary custom of the Jews, who termed their eminent doctors *the lamps of Israel*." (Clarke)

ii. "He said that John was the lamp which burns and shines. That was the perfect tribute to him. (*a*) A lamp bears a borrowed light. It does not light itself; it is lit. (*b*) John had warmth, for his was not the cold message of the intellect but the burning message of the kindled heart. (*c*) John had light. The function of light is to guide, and John pointed men on the way to repentance and to God. (*d*) In the nature of things a lamp burns itself out; in giving light it consumes itself. John was to decrease while Jesus increased. The true witness burns himself out for God." (Barclay)

iii. **To rejoice**: "To *jump for joy*, as we would express it. They were exceedingly rejoiced to hear that the Messiah was come, because they expected him to deliver them out of the hands of the Romans; but when a *spiritual deliverance*, of infinitely greater moment was preached to them, they rejected both it and the light which made it manifest." (Clarke)

3. (36) The testimony of the works of Jesus.

"But I have a greater witness than John's; for the works which the Father has given Me to finish—the very works that I do—bear witness of Me, that the Father has sent Me."

a. **A greater witness than John's... the very works that I do**: Jesus claimed another witness regarding His identity and deity - **the very works** that He did. This present controversy started with a remarkable healing of a man paralyzed for 38 years. This was one of many **works** that testified to the deity of Jesus.

b. **The very works that I do; bear witness of Me**: The majority of the miraculous works of Jesus were simple acts of compassion and mercy, done for simple and needy people. In this, these **works... bear witness** to the heart of God. The Jews looked for a miraculous Messiah, but they did not look for One who would express His miraculous power in simple acts of compassion and mercy. They looked for the Messiah to use miraculous power to bring military and political deliverance to Israel.

i. Because Jesus' miraculous works didn't fit in with what they thought the Messiah would do, they didn't receive this **witness** of Jesus' works.

4. (37-38) The testimony of the Father.

"And the Father Himself, who sent Me, has testified of Me. You have neither heard His voice at any time, nor seen His form. But you do not have His word abiding in you, because whom He sent, Him you do not believe."

a. **The Father Himself, who sent Me, has testified of Me**: In virtually every work and word of Jesus, God the Father testified to Jesus status as the Son of God. But specifically, the Father testified of the Son in Old Testament prophecy and at the baptism of Jesus (Luke 3:22).

b. **But you do not have His word abiding in you**: They will not receive the testimony of the Father, because they **do not have His word abiding** in them. They can't hear God the Father audibly, or see Him, but they have His word. They are guilty because they do not abide in the word that God gave them.

5. (39) The testimony of the Scriptures.

"You search the Scriptures, for in them you think you have eternal life; and these are they which testify of Me."

a. **You search the Scriptures**: In theory the religious leaders in Jesus' day loved and valued the **Scriptures** (here used in the sense of the Old Testament). They studied and memorized and thought upon them continually, correctly thinking **eternal life** was found in God's revelation.

i. "They read them with a wooden and superstitious reverence for the letter, and never penetrated into the great truths to which they pointed." (Morris)

ii. "They read it not to search for God but to find arguments to support their own positions. They did not really love God; they loved their own ideas about him." (Barclay)

iii. **Search the Scriptures**: "The verb itself (*eraunao*) implies keen scrutiny, tracking down the message of the Scriptures. The tragedy was that these people, for all their painstaking exploration of the sacred writings, had never found the clue which would lead them to their goal." (Bruce)

b. **These are they which testify of Me**: If their study of the **Scriptures** was accurate and sincere, they would see that they spoke of the Messiah, God the Son. Their recognition of and belief upon Jesus was a measure of their true understanding of the Scriptures.

6. (40-44) The reason for their unbelief.

"But you are not willing to come to Me that you may have life. I do not receive honor from men. But I know you, that you do not have the love of God in you. I have come in My Father's name, and you do not receive Me; if another comes in his own name, him you will receive. How can you believe, who receive honor from one another, and do not seek the honor that *comes* from the only God?"

a. **But you are not willing to come to Me**: The religious leaders were **not willing**, even though they had all the testimony one could have wanted. They were concerned with man's **honor**, not the honor that comes from God (**do not seek the honor that comes from the only God**).

i. Jesus made it clear that having **life** is found in fulfilling the command "**come to Me**." "Christ is a person, a living person, full of power to save. He has not placed his salvation in sacraments, or books, or priests, but he has kept it in himself; and if you want to have it you must come to him." (Spurgeon)

ii. Their refusal to come to Jesus was *despite* their searching of the Scriptures (John 5:39). "They search the Scriptures, but they will not come to Jesus. Is it not, therefore, a good thing to search the Scriptures? Ay, that it is, and the more you search them the better; but still it is not *the* thing: it is not the saving work. You may be Bible readers and yet perish, but this can never happen if you come to Jesus by faith." (Spurgeon)

iii. "The words *Ye are not* **willing** *to come* here set forth strikingly *the freedom of the will*, on which the unbeliever's condemnation rests." (Alford)

iv. "Let me tell you, the day will come when you will wring your hands in anguish to think that you despised that life. It may be that it will be so in the throes of death, but it is certain that it will be so amid the terrors of judgment, when there shall open wide before you the gates of hell, and before you shall blaze the lake that burneth with fire and brimstone, which is the second death." (Spurgeon)

v. **I do not receive honor from men**: "I do not stand in need of you or your testimony. I act neither through self-interest nor vanity. Your salvation can add nothing to me, nor can your destruction injure me: I speak only through my love for your souls, that ye may be saved." (Clarke)

b. **That you do not have the love of God in you**: The reasons for their rejection were fundamentally reasons of the heart, not of the mind. These religious leaders could hide behind supposedly intellectual excuses, but their real lack was **love** and desire for the honor that comes from God.

c. **If another comes in his own name, him you will receive**: Jesus prophesied the coming day when the descendants of these religious leaders would embrace a false Christ, an Antichrist, who **comes in his own name**. The rejection of Jesus left them open to terrible deception.

i. "The words are perhaps spoken primarily of the false or Idol-Messiah, the Antichrist, who shall appear in the latter days (2 Thessalonians 2:8-12); whose appearance shall be *according to the working of Satan* (their *father*, John 8:44), *shewing himself that he is God*, 2 Thessalonians 2:4." (Alford)

ii. Though this will ultimately be fulfilled in the very end times, there were lesser fulfillments through history. "An outstanding fulfillment of this prediction came about in AD 132, when one Simeon ban Kosebah claimed to be the Messiah of David's line, and led a revolt against Rome...Simeon's messianic pretensions involved himself, his supporters and the people of Judea in the most fearful ruin." (Bruce)

e. **How can you believe, who receive honor from one another, and do not seek the honor that comes from the only God?** The fatal error of the religious leaders of Jesus' day - and ever since - is *pride*. They longed for prestige and **honor from one another** and were willing to sacrifice the honor that comes from God alone for the sake of man's honor.

i. Charles Spurgeon preached a message on John 5:44 (*Why Men Cannot Believe in Christ*) and in one remarkable section of that sermon he examined of how fame, honor, and celebrity hinder true faith (**how can you believe, who receive honor from one another**). Following are some lines from that sermon:

- "The mere fact of receiving honor, even if that honor be rightly rendered, may make faith in Christ a difficulty."

- "When a man gets to feel that he ought to be honored, he is in extreme danger."

- "Always receiving this undeserved honor, they deceived themselves into believing that they deserved it."

- "Dear friends, it is very difficult to receive honor and to expect it, and yet to keep your eyesight; for men's eyes gradually grow dull through the smoke of the incense which is burned before them."

- "Once more, the praise of men generally *turns the receivers of it into great cowards*."

- "But, oh, how many live on the breath of their fellow men; to be approved — to be applauded — that is their heaven; but to be despised, to be sneered at, to be called fool, to have some nickname applied to them; oh no, they would sooner go to hell than bear that."

ii. "The grand obstacle to the salvation of the scribes and Pharisees was their *pride, vanity*, and *self-love*. They lived on each other's praise. If they had acknowledged Christ as the *only teacher*, they must have given up the good opinion of the multitude; and they chose rather to lose their souls than to forfeit their reputation among *men*!" (Clarke)

iii. "Seeking credit as religious men from one another, they necessarily habituated themselves to current ideas, and blotted out Divine glory from their mind." (Dods)

iv. "They had accused Jesus of acting independently of God; He now accuses them of displaying that independence. The motive of their actions is not love for God but the approval of their fellows." (Tasker)

7. (45-47) The testimony of Moses.

"Do not think that I shall accuse you to the Father; there is *one* who accuses you—Moses, in whom you trust. For if you believed Moses, you would believe Me; for he wrote about Me. But if you do not believe his writings, how will you believe My words?"

a. **If you believed Moses, you would believe Me:** These religious leaders rejected Jesus because they rejected God's word through Moses. **Moses** accuses them, because Moses wrote about Jesus and they would not receive the testimony of Moses.

b. **For he wrote about Me:** Jesus said of the Scriptures that they *testify of Me* (John 5:39). The words and writings of Moses fulfill this, prophetically speaking of the Messiah in many places.

i. *The LORD your God will raise up for you a Prophet like me from your midst, from your brethren. Him you shall hear.* (Deuteronomy 18:15)

ii. *Then the LORD said to Moses, "Make a fiery serpent, and set it on a pole; and it shall be that everyone who is bitten, when he looks at it, shall live." So Moses made a bronze serpent, and put it on a pole; and so it was, if a serpent had bitten anyone, when he looked at the bronze serpent, he lived.* (Numbers 21:8-9)

iii. Jesus was typified in the rock that gave Israel water in the wilderness (Numbers 20:8-12 and 1 Corinthians 10:4).

iv. The ministry of Jesus was shown in almost every aspect of the seven different kinds of offering that God commanded Israel to bring (Leviticus 1-7).

v. Jesus and His ministry were shown in the Tabernacle and its service. One place where the New Testament makes this connection is with the word *propitiation* in Romans 3:25, which speaks of the mercy seat on the Ark of the Covenant.

vi. The law of the bondservant speaks of Jesus (Exodus 21:5-6 and Psalm 40:6-8).

vii. No wonder Jesus could say *Behold, I come; in the scroll of the Book it is written of Me* (Psalm 40:7). He could teach a Bible study where *beginning at Moses and all the Prophets, He expounded to them in all the Scriptures the things concerning Himself* (Luke 24:27).

viii. "Thus the writings of Moses were prophetic. In them nothing was completed. They pointed on to other things, which came to pass when He came. Thus in this word we find at once the authority and limitation of Moses." (Morgan)

ix. "This is an important testimony by the Lord to the *subject* of the whole Pentateuch; it is *concerning Him*. It is also a testimony to *the fact*, of Moses *having written those books*, which were then, and are still, known by his name." (Alford)

c. **But if you do not believe his writings, how will you believe My words?** Jesus did not call these religious leaders to a *new* or a *different* faith. He called them to believe what Moses, what the Scriptures, what His works, what John the Baptist each testified about Jesus: that He is the Messiah, the Son of God and God the Son. If they refused to believe this overwhelming testimony, it was unlikely they would believe Jesus' own **words**.

John 6 - The Bread from Heaven

A. Preparation for the miracle.

1. (1-4) A crowd gathers to Jesus near the Sea of Galilee.

After these things Jesus went over the Sea of Galilee, which is *the Sea of Tiberias*. Then a great multitude followed Him, because they saw His signs which He performed on those who were diseased. And Jesus went up on the mountain, and there He sat with His disciples. Now the Passover, a feast of the Jews, was near.

a. **After these things Jesus went over the Sea of Galilee**: John now records some of the acts and words of Jesus in the **Galilee** region, north of Judea. John mainly recorded things that Jesus did and said in Judea and Jerusalem, but sometimes included material that the other gospel writers also wrote of, mainly in the Galilee region.

b. **Then a great multitude followed Him**: This miracle is also recorded in the other three Gospel accounts. Luke mentioned that on this occasion Jesus went out to a deserted place to be alone (Luke 9:10), yet the crowds **followed Him** there. In spite of this imposition, Jesus still served the multitude with great compassion.

c. **They saw His signs which He performed on those who were diseased**: Luke 9:11 tells us that Jesus *also* taught this multitude, something that John doesn't specifically mention.

> i. Morris gives the sense of the Greek verbs of John 6:2: "The multitude 'kept following' Jesus because they 'continually saw' the signs that He 'habitually did' on the sick." (Morris)

d. **The Passover, a feast of the Jews, was near**: John is the only one of the four Gospel writers who told us this took place near the time of the Passover. Perhaps this **great multitude** was made up of Galilean pilgrims on their way to Jerusalem.

i. Passover is associated with the Exodus and God's sustenance of Israel in the wilderness. Jesus would soon sustain this multitude in their small "wilderness" with bread from heaven - both literally and spiritually.

ii. **Went up on the mountain**: "The 'high ground' is the sharply rising terrain east of the lake, well known today as the Golan heights. From there one overlooks the level plain east of the river and the lake." (Bruce)

2. (5-7) Jesus asks Philip a question.

Then Jesus lifted up *His* eyes, and seeing a great multitude coming toward Him, He said to Philip, "Where shall we buy bread, that these may eat?" But this He said to test him, for He Himself knew what He would do. Philip answered Him, "Two hundred denarii worth of bread is not sufficient for them, that every one of them may have a little."

a. **Where shall we buy bread, that these may eat?** Perhaps Jesus asked **Philip** this question because he was from Bethsaida (John 1:44) and this was near where this miracle took place (Luke 9:10).

i. "John does not say, as Mark does (Mark 6:34 f.), that the crowd had been listening to Jesus' teaching all day, but this explains his concern about feeding them." (Bruce)

b. **He said this to test him, for He Himself knew what He would do**: Jesus knew what miracle He was about to perform, but wanted to use the opportunity to teach His disciples. For Jesus this wasn't only about getting a job done (feeding the multitude), but also about teaching His disciples along the way.

i. Philip had already seen Jesus do many miracles; there should have been no question to him about the divine resources Jesus had.

c. **Two hundred denarii worth of bread is not sufficient**: Their problem was in at least two parts. First, they didn't have the resources to buy bread and to feed the multitude. Second, even if they had the money it would be impossible to purchase enough bread to feed them all.

i. With greater faith and knowledge, Philip might have said: "Master, I don't know where the food is to feed this crowd but You are greater than Moses whom God used to feed a multitude everyday in the wilderness, and God can certainly do a lesser work through a Greater Servant. You are greater than Elisha, whom God used to feed many sons of the prophets through little food. What is more, the Scriptures say that *man shall not live by bread alone*, and You are great enough to fill this multitude from the words of your mouth."

d. **Two hundred denarii worth of bread is not sufficient for them**: Philip's knowledge of the situation was accurate and impressive (**two hundred denarii** is more than six month's wages), but his knowledge was useless in getting the problem solved.

i. Philip thought in terms of money; and how much money it would take to carry out God's work in a *small* way (**every one of them may have a little**). We often limit God the same way, looking for how God's work can be done in the smallest way. Jesus wanted to use a completely different approach and provide in a big way.

ii. "He was a man of figures; he believed in what could be put into tables and statistics. Yes; and like a great man other people of his sort, he left out one small element in his calculation, and that was Jesus Christ, and so his answer went creeping along the low levels." (Maclaren)

iii. "Philip was apparently a matter-of-fact person (John 14:8), a quick reckoner and good man of business, and therefore more ready to rely on his own shrewd calculations than on unseen resources." (Dods)

3. (8-9) Andrew's help.

One of His disciples, Andrew, Simon Peter's brother, said to Him, "There is a lad here who has five barley loaves and two small fish, but what are they among so many?"

a. **Andrew, Simon Peter's brother said to Him, "There is a lad here"**: Andrew once again introduced someone to Jesus. First it was his **brother** Peter (John 1:40-42). Now it was **a lad** with some **barley loaves and two small fish**.

i. "The word for 'lad' is a double diminutive, probably meaning 'little boy'." (Morris)

b. **Five barley loaves**: Barley was always regarded as simple food, more often fit for animals than for people. This means it is likely that the young boy came from a poor family.

i. In the Talmud, there is a passage where one man said, "There is a fine crop of barley" and another man answered, "Tell it to the horses and donkeys."

ii. "Barley scarcely bore one-third of the value of wheat in the east: see Revelation 6:6. That it was a very *mean* fare appears from Ezekiel 13:19, where the false prophetesses are said *to pollute the* name of God *for handfuls of barley*, i.e. for the meanest reward." (Clarke)

iii. **Two small fish**: "While the other Evangelists use the ordinary word for fish (*ichthys*), John calls them *osparia*, indicating that they were two small (perhaps salted) fish to be eaten as a relish along with the cakes of barley." (Bruce)

c. **What are they among so many?** There wasn't much to work with, but God doesn't need much. In fact, God doesn't *need* any help - but He often deliberately restrains His work until He has our participation.

i. "Small things are not always contemptible. It all depends on the hands in which they are." (Taylor)

B. The five thousand are fed.

1. (10) Jesus commands the group to sit down.

Then Jesus said, "Make the people sit down." Now there was much grass in the place. So the men sat down, in number about five thousand.

a. **Make the people sit down**: Jesus was in no panic or hurry. He had a huge catering job to fulfill, but went about His work in an orderly way, making them **sit down** upon the **grass**.

i. One might say that Jesus here fulfilled the role of the loving Shepherd in Psalm 23:1-2. *He makes me to lie down in green pastures.* That Psalm also gave the picture of the Lord as a host, serving a meal to His servant as a guest: *you prepare a table for me...you anoint my head with oil; my cup runs over...I will dwell in the house of the LORD forever* (Psalm 23:5-6).

b. **The men sat down, in number about five thousand**: Jesus administered everything in an orderly way. Yet, they had to come under Jesus' order to receive Jesus' miraculous provision. The ones who came under Jesus' order would soon be filled to the full.

i. "Our blessed Master has glorious leisure, because he is always punctual. Late people are in a hurry; but he, being never late, never hurries." (Spurgeon)

2. (11) The five thousand are fed.

And Jesus took the loaves, and when He had given thanks He distributed *them* to the disciples, and the disciples to those sitting down; and likewise of the fish, as much as they wanted.

a. **When He had given thanks**: Jesus only had a few loaves of bread and a few fish, but He was determined to give His Father **thanks** for what He did have.

i. "For five little cakes and two sprats Christ gave thanks to the Father; apparently a meagre cause for praise, but Jesus knew what he could make of them, and therefore gave thanks for what they would presently accomplish. 'God loves us,' says Augustine, 'for what we are becoming.' Christ gave thanks for these trifles because he saw whereunto they would grow." (Spurgeon)

b. **Jesus took the loaves... He distributed them to the disciples**: The miracle resided in the hands of Jesus, not in the distribution. Little is much in His hands.

i. "A moment ago, they belonged to this lad, but now they belong to Christ. 'Jesus took the loaves.' He has taken possession of them; they are his property." (Spurgeon)

ii. "The multiplication of the food was obviously not done with great fanfare." (Tenney) This is so true that we aren't told specifically *where* the multiplication happened. It seems to have happened as Jesus broke the bread and fish and **distributed them to the disciples**. "It was not the integral loaves or integral fishes that were multiplied, but the broken portions of them." (Trench)

- Most everyone ate and was filled, but had no idea that a miracle was happening.
- The disciples did not do the miracle; they simply distributed the miraculous work of Jesus.

iii. Bread comes from grain, which has the power of multiplication and reproduction within itself. But when it is made into bread, the grain is crushed, making it "dead" - no one ever multiplied wheat by planting flour. Yet Jesus can bring life from death; He multiplied loaves of bread made from dead, crushed grain and from dead fish.

iv. "These five loaves (by a strange kind of arithmetic) were multiplied by division, and augmented by subtraction." (Trapp)

c. **He distributed them to the disciples**: Jesus relied on the labor of the disciples in this great miracle. He could have created bread and fish in the pocket or bag of every person, but He didn't. Jesus deliberately chose a method that brought the **disciples** into the work.

i. Jesus refused to miraculously make bread to feed Himself in the wilderness temptations; but He did *for* others and *with* others what He would not do for Himself.

d. **As much as they wanted**: God's supply was extravagant, as much as any of them **wanted**. All ate until they were completely satisfied.

i. "For the significance of this story we must bear in mind that the figure of eating and drinking is widely used in the Old Testament. It is a figure of prosperity... and it is often used of the blessings the people of God would enjoy in the Promised Land." (Morris)

ii. **As much as they wanted** also included the little boy who gave the five loves and two fish. The boy himself ended up with more than he started with. It certainly was an adequate lunch for himself; but he gave it to Jesus and He it turned into an all-you-can-eat buffet for *the boy* as well.

3. (12-13) Gathering up the fragments of the feast.

So when they were filled, He said to His disciples, "Gather up the fragments that remain, so that nothing is lost." Therefore they gathered *them* up, and filled twelve baskets with the fragments of the five barley loaves which were left over by those who had eaten.

a. **When they were filled**: Jesus was generous, giving everyone as much as they wanted. This was a remarkable miracle, and some think that the disciples should have (or could have) anticipated that Jesus would do such a thing.

i. Old Testament passages warn against doubting God's provision: *Yes, they spoke against God: They said, "Can God prepare a table in the wilderness?"* (Psalm 78:19) 2 Kings 4:38-34 is an example of God multiplying barley loaves, though this miracle of Jesus was on a much greater scale.

ii. Though the disciples did not understand or anticipate the miracle, Jesus invited them to participate in it. They distributed the miraculously multiplied bread and fish. Without their work, no one would have been fed.

iii. Jesus demonstrated to them the giving character of God - the same character God desires to build within us. Proverbs 11:24 says, *There is one who scatters, yet increases more; and there is one who withholds more than is right, but it leads to poverty.* This bread was multiplied as it was "scattered."

b. **Gather up the fragments that remain, so that nothing is lost**: Jesus was generous, but never wasteful. Jesus wanted to make good use of everything.

i. "The *fragments* are not the half-eaten morsels and crumbs which might well be left for birds and beasts, but the broken portions which He had handed for distribution." (Trench)

ii. "The term used for 'basket' (*kophinos*) usually denotes a large basket, such as might be used for fish or bulky objects." (Tenney)

C. The reaction to the miracle.

1. (14) Jesus as the Prophet predicted by Moses.

Then those men, when they had seen the sign that Jesus did, said, "This is truly the Prophet who is to come into the world."

a. **When they had seen the sign that Jesus did**: The way Jesus provided bread for a multitude in the open air (something of a wilderness) reminded **those men** of how God worked through Moses to feed Israel with manna in the wilderness.

b. **Truly this is the Prophet**: Moses predicted the coming of the **Prophet** they expected: *The LORD your God will raise up for you a Prophet like me from your midst, from your brethren. Him you shall hear.* (Deuteronomy 18:15) If the coming **Prophet** was to be like Moses, it made sense that he would also feed the people miraculously as Moses did.

i. This crowd was willing to support Jesus so long as He gave them what they wanted - bread. It's easy to criticize how the crowd loved for Jesus for the bread He gave them, but we often only love Jesus for what He give us. We must also love and obey Him simply for *who He is* - Lord and God.

ii. "A rabbi of a later date is credited with the observation that 'as the first redeemer caused manna to descend, …. so will the last redeemer cause manna to descend', and the general idea seems to have been current in the first century." (Bruce)

2. (15) The people attempt to make Jesus their earthly king.

Therefore when Jesus perceived that they were about to come and take Him by force to make Him king, He departed again to the mountain by Himself alone.

a. **They were about to come and take Him by force to make Him king**:

King was a *political* title. The crowd was willing to support Jesus because they wanted to *use* Him to throw off Roman oppression either directly in Judea or indirectly through Herod Antipas in Galilee.

i. "Suddenly there was this unusual man Jesus. He had miraculous power. So they must have said something like this to themselves, 'Wouldn't it be wonderful if we could get Him on our side and get Him to help us drive out the Romans?'" (Boice)

ii. "If the Galileans did not live directly under Roman control, as their brethren in Judea did, their ruler Herod Antipas was a creature of Rome, and they experienced no feelings of patriotic pride as they contemplated the Herodian dynasty." (Bruce)

b. **He departed again to a mountain by Himself alone**: Jesus wasn't impressed or seduced by a crowd that wanted to make Him king. He turned His back on the crowd and went to pray because Jesus was more interested in being with His Father in heaven than in hearing the applause of the crowd.

i. "But to Jesus the prospect of an earthly kingdom was nothing else than a temptation of the devil, and He decisively rejected it." (Morris)

ii. "He saw the crowds were in great excitement and were meaning to come and violently carry Him off and declare Him their king and Messiah in opposition to the civil power; perhaps already He saw His disciples beginning to be caught in that wild enthusiasm." (Trench)

iii. "He who is already King has come to open His kingdom to men; but in their blindness men try to force Him to be the kind of king they want; thus they fail to get the king they want, and also lose the Kingdom He offers." (Morris)

D. Jesus walks on the water.

1. (16-17) The disciples go out on the Sea of Galilee.

Now when evening came, His disciples went down to the sea, got into the boat, and went over the sea toward Capernaum. And it was already dark, and Jesus had not come to them.

a. **His disciples went down to the sea, got into the boat**: Matthew and Mark tell us that Jesus *made His disciples get into the boat* (Mark 6:45). They set off across the Sea of Galilee because Jesus told them to do it.

i. "According to Mark 6:45, Jesus 'compelled' (*anankazo*) his disciples to embark and go back across the lake; perhaps he saw that they were being infected with the crowd's excitement." (Bruce)

b. **It was already dark**: Several of the disciples were fishermen, all accustomed to fishing on this very lake. When they got into the boat, the thought of rowing across the lake at night did not concern them.

c. **Jesus had not come to them**: This actually was the *second* time Jesus dealt with His disciples on a stormy Sea of Galilee. In the first storm (Matthew 8:24), Jesus was present with them in the boat and He rebuked and calmed the storm. In this storm Jesus asked His disciples to trust His *unseen* care and concern for them.

2. (18) The wind disrupts their efforts to cross the Sea.

Then the sea arose because a great wind was blowing.

a. **Then the sea arose**: The wind alone was bad enough, but the wind also whipped up the waters, making for troublesome seas.

b. **A great wind was blowing**: The Sea of Galilee was and is well known for its sudden, violent wind storms that quickly make the lake dangerous.

i. "The Sea of Galilee is six hundred feet below sea level, in a cuplike depression among the hills. When the sun sets, the air cools; and as the cooler air from the west rushes down over the hillside, the resultant wind churns the lake. Since the disciples were rowing toward Capernaum, they were heading into the wind; consequently, they made little progress." (Tenney)

3. (19) Jesus comes to His disciples, walking on the water.

So when they had rowed about three or four miles, they saw Jesus walking on the sea and drawing near the boat; and they were afraid.

a. **When they had rowed about three or four miles**: In the first storm upon the Sea of Galilee the disciples were terrified (Matthew 8:25-26). In the beginning of the second storm they were more *frustrated* than afraid. Jesus told them to row across the lake and despite their hard work, they seemed to make little progress.

i. Matthew 14:25 this this happened *in the fourth watch of the night*, sometime between three and six in the morning. So, they rowed hard for perhaps six to eight hours, and had only come a little more than half way across the lake (**three or four miles**).

ii. They were in this place of frustration *at the will of Jesus*, doing exactly what He told them to do. Additionally, Mark 6:48 says that Jesus watched the disciples as they rowed across the lake. His eye was on them all the time. They were in the will of Jesus and watched by Jesus, yet working hard in frustration all the time.

iii. "Up on the hillside Jesus had prayed and communed with God; as he set out the silver moon had made the scene almost like the daylight; and down on the lake he could see the boat with the rowers toiling at the oars...He had not forgotten. He was not too busy with God to think of them." (Barclay)

iv. "He is on the mountain while we are on the sea. The stable eternity of the Heavens holds Him; we are tossed on the restless mutability of time, over which we toil at His command." (Maclaren)

b. **They saw Jesus walking on the sea... and they were afraid**: Mark 6:49-50 says the disciples were afraid because they thought Jesus, walking on the water, was a ghost or a spirit.

i. Mark "adds the remarkable detail that Jesus 'meant to pass-by them' *i.e.* overtaking, as though He had wished that the mere vision of Himself should prove sufficient support and assurance to them." (Trench)

ii. The disciples were not ready for any kind of supernatural help. They knew what Jesus commanded them to do and they set out to do it - but without any direct help from Jesus. So they were surprised and afraid to see supernatural help coming to them.

iii. Jesus also gave them reasons and reminders to trust His supernatural help. Undoubtedly, they took with them at least some of the twelve baskets of leftover bread (John 6:13), yet they were still shocked when the supernatural help came to them on the sea.

4. (20) The calming words of Jesus.

But He said to them, "It is I; do not be afraid."

a. **It is I**: For Jesus, it was enough to announce His presence. He was with His disciples and would meet them in their frustration and fear.

i. "There are places in this Gospel where the words *ego eimi* have the nature of a divine designation (as we shall see on 8:24, 28), but here they simply mean 'It is I'." (Bruce)

b. **Do not be afraid**: Jesus came to bring supernatural help and comfort to His disciples. His presence gave them what they needed, even though He came in an unexpected way.

i. We know from Matthew 14:28-32 that after this Peter asked Jesus if he could come out and walk on the water and Peter did walk on the water - for short time.

5. (21) Jesus brings them to their destination.

Then they willingly received Him into the boat, and immediately the boat was at the land where they were going.

a. **Then they willingly received Him into the boat**: The implication was that Jesus would not come *unless* He was **willingly received**. Even walking on the Sea of Galilee, Jesus waited to be welcomed by His disciples.

b. **Immediately the boat was at the land where they were going**: When they *had* **willingly received Him into the boat**, the miraculous happened. *This was a remarkable miracle*. The work that was so frustrating a few moments before suddenly was divinely accomplished.

i. "From this detail given by John it is inferred that the ship seemed to move automatically, without sail or oar, in obedience to His will: so that without effort of the disciples or crew it quickly passed over the remaining distance (two miles or so) and came to shore." (Trench)

ii. One could say that Jesus rescued His disciples from frustration and futility. Jesus wants us to work hard; but He never wants us to work in futility. Their work had not been a waste, but it waited for the touch of divine power and presence.

c. **Immediately the boat was at the land where they were going**: Such a remarkable miracle was helpful for the disciples, especially because Jesus had just refused an offer to be recognized as a King Messiah. This assured them that He was full of divine power even though He did not claim a throne according to popular expectation and opinion.

i. "How far they were from the place at which they landed, when our Lord came to them, we know not. But the evangelist seems to speak of their *sudden* arrival there as extraordinary and miraculous." (Clarke)

ii. "A dying saint hath no sooner taken death into his bosom, but he is immediately landed at the quay of Canaan, at the kingdom of heaven." (Trapp)

E. Jesus, the bread of life.

1. (22-24) The crowd follows Jesus and His disciples to Capernaum.

On the following day, when the people who were standing on the other side of the sea saw that there was no other boat there, except that one which His disciples had entered, and that Jesus had not entered the boat with His disciples, but His disciples had gone away alone—however, other boats came from Tiberias, near the place where they ate bread after the Lord had given thanks—when the people therefore saw that Jesus was not there, nor His disciples, they also got into boats and came to Capernaum, seeking Jesus.

a. **On the following day**: The day after the miraculous feeding of the 5,000 and the night crossing of the Seal of Galilee, many of the crowd that was fed by Jesus and the disciples wondered where they went. They saw the disciples (without Jesus) leave in a boat, and now they noted that **Jesus was not there** with them.

i. **Other boats came from Tiberias**: "The fact parenthetically introduced, verse 23, that boats from Tiberias had put in on the east shore, is an incidental confirmation of the truth that a gale had been blowing the night before." (Dods)

b. **They also got into boats and came to Capernaum, seeking Jesus**: These people were from the same crowd that Jesus fed and the same crowd that wanted to force Jesus to be recognized as an earthly king (John 6:14-15).

> i. "The crowd, then, made sure that Jesus was nowhere in the vicinity, and that there was no sign of the disciples returning to fetch him, so they crossed to the west side to look for him." (Bruce)

> ii. "That is, as many of them as could get accommodated with boats took them and thus got to Capernaum; but many others doubtless went thither on foot, as it is not at all likely that five or six thousand persons could get boats enow to carry them." (Clarke)

2. (25-27) Jesus responds to their first question: **Rabbi, when did You come here?**

And when they found Him on the other side of the sea, they said to Him, "Rabbi, when did You come here?" Jesus answered them and said, "Most assuredly, I say to you, you seek Me, not because you saw the signs, but because you ate of the loaves and were filled. Do not labor for the food which perishes, but for the food which endures to everlasting life, which the Son of Man will give you, because God the Father has set His seal on Him."

a. **When did You come here?** Jesus did not answer this question. The answer would have been, "I walked over the Sea of Galilee in the night time to help My disciples, then I miraculously transported our boat across the remaining distance of the Sea. That's when and how I came here."

> i. Later in this chapter, John tells us that this took place at the synagogue in Capernaum at a Sabbath service (John 6:59). Also, according to Matthew 15, Jewish leaders from Jerusalem came to Capernaum to question Jesus. They were also part of this crowd.

b. **You seek Me, not because you saw the signs, but because you ate of the loaves and were filled**: Instead of telling them when and why He came, Jesus told them why *they* came - because they wanted more food miraculously provided by Jesus.

> i. Often we can learn more from understanding the reason *we* ask God a question than from the answer to the question itself. This was the case with those who followed Jesus around the Galilee and asked the question.

> ii. They wanted the bread, but more than just the bread; they also wanted the *display of the miraculous* and a *miracle king* to lead them against their Roman oppressors.

iii. "The were quite unaffected by the wisdom of His words and the beauty of His deeds, but a miracle that found food precisely met their wants, and so there was an excited but impure enthusiasm, very unwelcome to Jesus." (Maclaren)

c. **Do not labor for the food which perishes, but for the food which endures for everlasting life**: Those asking this question of Jesus went to a lot of trouble to follow and find Him. Yet their work was for **the food which perishes** - things that fill a stomach and rule and earthly kingdoms. Jesus wanted to them **labor** for **the food which endures for everlasting life**.

i. Jesus made a contrast between *material* things and *spiritual* things. It is almost universally true that people are more attracted to material things than spiritual things. A sign that says *free money and free food* will get a bigger crowd than one that says *spiritual fulfillment and eternal life*.

ii. "He struck at the root of the materialistic aspirations of these carnally-minded Galilaeans." (Tasker)

d. **Which the Son of Man will give you**: They were rightly impressed at the miracle of bread worked through Jesus; but He wanted them to be *more* impressed for the *spiritual* food He brings by a miracle.

i. **Son of Man**: "He avoids using the term 'Messiah' or any other which would have appealed to his hearers' militant aspirations. The designation 'the Son of Man' suited his purpose well enough; it was not current coin in their religious or political vocabulary and could therefore bear whatever meaning he chose to put on it." (Bruce)

e. **Because God the Father has set His seal on Him**: A seal was a mark of ownership and a guarantee of the contents. They should have confidence in Jesus because God the Father has "guaranteed" Him.

i. "If the aorist tense of the verb 'sealed' (Gk. *esphragisen*) suggests that we identify the sealing with one particular event, we should probably think of our Lord's baptism (cf. John 1:32-34)." (Bruce)

ii. "**Sealed**, by *undoubted testimony*, as at His baptism; and since, *by His miracles*." (Alford)

iii. "As a person who wishes to communicate his mind to another who is at a distance writes a letter, seals it with his own seal, and sends it directed to the person for whom it was written, so Christ, who lay in the bosom of the Father, came to *interpret* the Divine will to man, bearing the image, superscription, and seal of God, in the immaculate holiness of his nature, unsullied truth of his doctrine, and in the astonishing evidence of his miracles." (Clarke)

3. (28-29) Jesus answers their second question: **What shall we do, that we may work the works of God?**

Then they said to Him, "What shall we do, that we may work the works of God?" Jesus answered and said to them, "This is the work of God, that you believe in Him whom He sent."

a. **What shall we do, that we may work the works of God?** Jesus told them, *Do not labor for the food which perishes* (John 6:27). In reply, they used the same word Jesus used and asked, "How shall we labor for this?"

i. The sense behind their question seemed to be, "Just tell us what to do so we can get what we want from You. We want Your miracle bread and for You to be our Miracle King; tell us what to do to get it."

ii. Those who questioned Jesus seemed sure that if only Jesus told them what to do, they could please God by their works of God. For these people, as with many people today, pleasing God is found in the right formula for performing works that will please God.

b. **This is the work of God, that you believe in Him whom He sent**: Jesus first and foremost commanded them (and us) not to *do*, but to *trust*. If we want to do the **work of God**, it begins with trusting Jesus.

i. A parent does not *only* want obedience from their child; a relationship of trust and love is even more important to the parent. The hope is that obedience grows out of that relationship of trust and love. God wants the same pattern in our relationship with Him.

ii. The first work is to **believe in Him whom He sent**, yet God is also concerned about our obedience. In this sense our faith in Him is not a substitute for works; our faith is the foundation for works that truly please God.

iii. Maclaren on the contrast between **works** and **work**: "They thought of a great variety of observances and deeds. He gathers them all up into one."

iv. "The priest says, 'Rites and ceremonies.' The thinker says, 'Culture, education.' The moralist says, 'Do this, that, and the other thing,' and enumerates a whole series of separate acts. Jesus Christ says, 'One thing is needful...This is the work of God.'" (Maclaren)

v. "This is a most important saying of our Lord, as containing the germ of that teaching afterwards so fully expanded in the writings of St. Paul." (Alford)

4. (30-33) Jesus answers their third question: **What sign will You perform then, that we may see it and believe You? What work will You do?**

Therefore they said to Him, "What sign will You perform then, that we may see it and believe You? What work will You do? Our fathers ate the manna in the desert; as it is written, 'He gave them bread from heaven to eat.'" Then Jesus said to them, "Most assuredly, I say to you, Moses did not give you the bread from heaven, but My Father gives you the true bread from heaven. For the bread of God is He who comes down from heaven and gives life to the world."

a. **What sign will You perform then**: The crowd that heard Jesus at the synagogue in Capernaum followed Him from the feeding of the 5,000. Yet there were also among them Jewish leaders from Jerusalem (Matthew 15:1, John 6:41). These heard the excited talk of the miraculous feeding, but wanted to see it again. As well, those who ate wanted to eat again!

i. "They have again come under the influence of the Scribes from Jerusalem who have come up (Matthew 15:1: Mark 7:1) to Capernaum to counteract Him and drive Him away." (Trench)

b. **Our fathers ate the manna in the desert**: Jesus' questioners hoped to manipulate Him into providing daily bread for them, just as Israel had from God during the Exodus. They even knew how to quote Scripture in the attempt (**"He gave them bread from heaven to eat"**, Psalm 105:40).

c. **My Father gives you the true bread from heaven**: We might paraphrase the reply of Jesus like this: "What other work will I do? This is the work: to give you the Word of God and eternal life in and through Me. This is the spiritual bread you must feast on to have life."

i. "Our Lord does not here *deny*, but *asserts* the miraculous character of the manna." (Alford)

d. **For the bread of God is He who comes down from heaven**: Jesus tried to lift their minds above earthly things and on to heavenly realities; to an understanding that He is necessary for spiritual life just as bread is necessary for physical survival.

i. "The bread of God was he who came down from heaven and gave men not simply satisfaction from physical hunger, but life. Jesus was claiming that the only real satisfaction was in him." (Barclay)

5. (34-40) Jesus answers their fourth request: **Lord, give us this bread always.**

Then they said to Him, "Lord, give us this bread always." And Jesus said to them, "I am the bread of life. He who comes to Me shall never hunger, and he who believes in Me shall never thirst. But I said to you

that you have seen Me and yet do not believe. All that the Father gives Me will come to Me, and the one who comes to Me I will by no means cast out. For I have come down from heaven, not to do My own will, but the will of Him who sent Me. This is the will of the Father who sent Me, that of all He has given Me I should lose nothing, but should raise it up at the last day. And this is the will of Him who sent Me, that everyone who sees the Son and believes in Him may have everlasting life; and I will raise him up at the last day."

a. **Give us this bread always**: We wonder if those who travelled across the Sea of Galilee to find and meet Jesus were hungry when they had this conversation with Jesus. They wanted the material **bread** Jesus miraculously provided, and they wanted it **always**.

i. When we are hungry, we feel as though food will answer all our problems. It's the same way with almost all other practical difficulties we find ourselves in. Just as Jesus tried to lift their understanding above their material, physical needs, so we need to have our minds lifted.

ii. "What they wanted, he would not give; what he offered, they would not receive." (Bruce)

iii. **Lord, give us this bread always**: "*Kurie* should probably be translated *Sir* in this verse rather than *Lord*, as it is clear from verse 36 that these Galilaeans did not believe in Jesus." (Tasker)

b. **I am the bread of life**: In Jesus' answer, He hoped to lift up their eyes from material bread and earthly kingdoms, and on to spiritual realities. They needed to put their confidence in Jesus instead of in material bread.

i. "This is the first of the distinctive 'I am' sayings of this Gospel (where Jesus uses *ego eimi* with a predicate)." (Bruce)

c. **He who comes to Me shall never hunger**: Jesus explained that the one who comes to Him - that is, receives Him, believes upon Him - will find his spiritual hunger satisfied in Jesus.

i. "The coming here meant is performed by desire, prayer, assent, consent, trust, obedience." (Spurgeon)

ii. "This verse should not be regarded as an abstract statement. It constitutes an appeal. Since Jesus is the bread of life men are invited to come to Him, and to believe on Him." (Morris)

iii. "Faith in Christ is simply and truly described as coming to him. It is not an acrobatic feat; it is simply a coming to Christ. It is not an exercise of profound mental faculties; it is coming to Christ. A child comes to his mother, a blind man comes to his home, even an animal comes to his master. Coming is a very simple action indeed; it seems to have only two things about it, one is, to come away from something, and the other is, to come to something." (Spurgeon)

d. **All that the Father gives Me will come to Me, and the one who comes to Me I will by no means cast out**: Jesus made it clear that coming to Jesus *begins* with the work of the Father, and He will receive all who come to Him.

> i. **All that the Father gives Me**: "'All' is neuter, which makes it very general, 'everything', although persons are certainly meant." (Morris)

> ii. **I will by no means cast out**: "Our blessed Lord alludes to the case of a person in deep distress and poverty, who comes to a nobleman's house, in order to get relief: the person appears; and the owner, far from treating the poor man with asperity, welcomes, receives him kindly, and supplies his wants. So does Jesus." (Clarke)

> iii. "I will not not, cast out out. A powerful speech, and a most comfortable consideration. Who would not come to Jesus Christ upon such sweetest encouragement?" (Trapp)

e. **Not to do My own will, but the will of Him who sent Me**: As Jesus invited them to come to Him, He also reminded them that He was *safe* to come unto. He wasn't interested in His own agenda, but in His Father's will.

f. **All He has given Me I should lose nothing**: This was another compelling reason to come unto the Son - all who are **given** of the Father and come to Him, He keeps safe.

g. **Everyone who sees the Son and believes in Him may have everlasting life**: This is the wonderful *destiny* of all who are **given** of the Father and come to Jesus.

> i. In all this, Jesus had in mind *both* the broad community of believers (**All that the Father gives Me will come to Me...should raise it up**) *and* the individual believer (**the one who comes to Me...will raise him up**).

> ii. **Everyone who sees the Son**: "In this 'gazes upon' the Son there is certainly a reference to the bronze serpent that was lifted up by Moses in the wilderness upon a pole (shaped like a cross, as Rabbinical tradition says), and everyone who looked on it was healed." (Trench)

6. (41-46) Jesus explains why they reject Him.

The Jews then complained about Him, because He said, "I am the bread which came down from heaven." And they said, "Is not this Jesus, the

son of Joseph, whose father and mother we know? How is it then that He says, 'I have come down from heaven'?" Jesus therefore answered and said to them, "Do not murmur among yourselves. No one can come to Me unless the Father who sent Me draws him; and I will raise him up at the last day. It is written in the prophets, 'And they shall all be taught by God.' Therefore everyone who has heard and learned from the Father comes to Me. Not that anyone has seen the Father, except He who is from God; He has seen the Father."

a. **Is this not Jesus, the son of Joseph, whose father and mother we know?** The people **complained** about Jesus, thinking what He said about Himself was too big, too exalted (**How is it then that He says, "I have come down from heaven?"**)

i. "Six times in this immediate context Jesus says that he 'came down from heaven' (6:33, 38, 41, 50, 51, 58). His claim to heavenly origin is unmistakable." (Tenney)

ii. "This was one of the real difficulties of the contemporaries of Jesus. The Messiah was to come 'in the clouds,' suddenly to appear; but Jesus had quietly grown up among them." (Dods)

iii. **The Jews then complained**: "'The Jews,' not as we might expect, 'the Galileans,' probably because John identifies this unbelieving crowd with the characteristically unbelieving Jews." (Dods)

b. **Do not murmur among yourselves**: As Jesus spoke to the crowd at the synagogue, they murmured and commented among themselves.

i. "'Murmured' indicates discontent. It is the confused sound that runs through a crowd when they are angry and in opposition." (Morris)

c. **No one can come to Me unless the Father who sent Me draws him**: The Jews thought that they were all chosen by God by virtue of their physical, natural birth. Jesus made it clear that God must draw them before they can come to God. Everyone who responds to the Father will respond to the Son.

i. "Unless God thus draw, no man will ever come to Christ; because none could, without this drawing, ever feel the need of a Saviour." (Clarke)

ii. We often like to feel as though we "lead" in our relationship with God. In truth, He calls and we come. This understanding of God's initiative in salvation should makes us *more* confident in evangelism, knowing that God *is* drawing people, and we can expect to see those whom the Father draws come to Him.

iii. "The word which John uses for *to draw* is *helkuein*. The word used in the Greek translation of the Hebrew when Jeremiah hears God say as the Authorized Version has it: 'With loving-kindness have I drawn thee' (Jeremiah 31:3)." (Barclay)

iv. "That this 'drawing' is not *irresistible grace*, is confessed even by Augustine himself, the great upholder of the doctrines of grace. 'If a man is drawn, says an objector, he comes against his will. (We answer) if he comes unwillingly, he does not believe: if he does not believe, he does not come. For we do not run to Christ on our feet, but by faith; not with the movement of the body, but with the free will of the heart…Think not that thou are drawn against thy will; the mind can be drawn by love.'" (Alford)

v. "*Drawing*, or *alluring*, not *dragging* is here to be understood. 'He,' say the rabbins, 'who desires to cleave to the holy and blessed God, God lays hold of him, and will not cast him off.' *Synops. Sohar.* p. 87. The best Greek writers use the verb in the same sense of *alluring, inciting*, &c." (Clarke)

vi. "Chrysostom says, 'This expression does not remove our part in the coming, but rather shews that we want help to come.'" (Alford)

vii. **Draws** "has the same latitude of meaning as 'draw.' It is used of towing a ship, dragging a cart, or pulling on a rope to set sails. But it is also used, John 12:32, of a gentle but powerful moral attraction." (Dods)

d. **And I will raise him up at the last day**: All those who *do* come to Jesus drawn by the Father will receive eternal life and will be resurrected **at the last day**.

e. **And they shall all be taught by God**: Jesus quoted from Isaiah 54:13, which may have been part of the synagogue reading for that Sabbath. The idea is that all those who belong to God are **taught by God**, being drawn to Him (**everyone who has heard and learned from the Father comes to Me**).

i. "God will teach His people Himself, *i.e.* He will teach then within their hearts. Only those who are taught in this fashion will come to Jesus." (Morris)

ii. "This was as much as to say, 'The Father has never taught you. You have learned nothing from him, or you would come to me; but in your rejection of me you prove that you are strangers to the grace of God.'" (Spurgeon)

f. **Everyone who has heard and learned from the Father comes to Me**: Those who *have* a revelation from God the Father will come to His Son and Perfect Representative. To hear and learn from the Son is to hear and learn from the Father.

i. "But whether it is also true that every one whom God teaches comes is not here stated; the καὶ μαψων introduces a doubtful element." (Dods)

ii. "If, as some believe, Isaiah 54 as included in the appointed synagogue lessons for this period of the year, then the words quoted by Jesus may have been fresh in the minds of many of his hearers." (Bruce)

g. **He has seen the Father**: Jesus here again insisted on His *unique* relationship to God the Father. He claimed a relationship and connection with God the Father that no one else had.

i. "Their unbelief does not alter the fact, nor weaken His assurance of the fact." (Dods)

ii. "He is teaching the theologians about the Godhead, how that the Unity of God is not the final word of revelation concerning the one God. So long as it is thought that there is but one Person in the Godhead, the Incarnation and the whole scheme of Redemption cannot possibly be understood." (Trench)

7. (47-51) The true bread from heaven.

"Most assuredly, I say to you, he who believes in Me has everlasting life. I am the bread of life. Your fathers ate the manna in the wilderness, and are dead. This is the bread which comes down from heaven, that one may eat of it and not die. I am the living bread which came down from heaven. If anyone eats of this bread, he will live forever; and the bread that I shall give is My flesh, which I shall give for the life of the world."

a. **He who believes in Me has everlasting life**: We read this staggering statement with two main thoughts in mind. First, *what it means to "believe" in the sense Jesus meant*; that is, to trust in, rely on, and cling to. It is a *trusting love*. Second, we think of *the astounding nature of this claim*. No other prophet or holy man of the Bible ever said such a thing; "Believe **in me** and find **everlasting life**."

b. **I am the bread of life**: Jesus repeated and continued the use of this metaphor. As bread is necessary for physical life, so Jesus is necessary for spiritual and eternal life.

i. "Every man feeds on something or other. You see, one man getting his Sunday newspaper; how he will feed on that! Another goes to frivolous amusements, and he feeds on them. Another man feeds upon his business, and upon the thought of his many cares! But all that is poor food; it is only ashes and husks. If you did but possess true spiritual life, you would know the deep necessity there is of feeding upon Christ." (Spurgeon)

c. **Your fathers ate the manna in the wilderness, and are dead**: The spiritual bread Jesus offers is even greater than the manna Israel ate in the wilderness. What they ate only gave them temporal life; what Jesus offers brings eternal life.

d. **I am the living bread which came down from heaven. If anyone eats of this bread, he will live forever**: Jesus spoke in a figure of speech. The metaphor of eating and drinking was common in Jesus' day, and pointed to a taking within one's innermost being.

> i. "When a man once takes it ('eat' is in the aorist tense, of the once-for-all action of receiving Christ) he will not die." (Morris)

> ii. Some mistakenly take this passage as speaking of the Christian practice of communion, the Lord's Table as instituted by Jesus on the night before His crucifixion (Luke 22:14-23), celebrated among early Christians (Acts 2:42) and taught on in Paul's letters (1 Corinthians 11:23-26). They mistakenly think that receiving the bread and cup of the Lord's Table is essential for salvation, and that all who do are guaranteed salvation.

> iii. What Jesus spoke of here is *not* communion, the Lord's Table - yet the concept is *related* to that of communion. "Our Lord in this discourse is not indeed speaking directly of the Lord's Supper, but he does expound the truth which the Lord's Supper conveys." (Bruce)

> iv. "Many commentators speak as though the word 'flesh' self-evidently marked a reference to Holy Communion. It, of course, does nothing of the sort. It is not found in the narratives of the institution, nor in 1 Corinthians 10, nor in 1 Corinthians 11 in connexion with the sacrament. Nor is it common in the Fathers in this sense." (Morris)

> v. "The Fathers commonly expounded this part of our Saviour's sermon as spoken of the sacrament of the Lord's supper; and so fell into that error, that none but communicants could be saved; wherefore they also gave the sacrament to infants, and put it into the mouths of dead men." (Trapp)

> vi. "He is saying: 'You must stop thinking of me as a subject for theological debate; you must take me into you, and you must come into me; and then you will have real life.'" (Barclay)

vii. "*Crede et manducasti*, said Augustine, 'believe' - or, rather, *trust* - 'and thou hast eaten.'" (Maclaren)

e. The bread that I shall give is My flesh, which I shall give for the life of the world: Jesus plainly explained what He meant by **bread** in this context. That bread was His **flesh**, given **for the life of the world**. It was His soon-coming work on the cross when He gave His life as a sacrifice pleasing to God the Father and as a substitute for guilty sinners.

i. Morris on the use of **flesh**: "It is a strong word and one bound to attract attention. Its almost crude forcefulness rivets attention on the historical fact that Christ did give Himself for man."

ii. "To give one's flesh can scarcely mean anything other than death, and the wording here points to a death which is both voluntary ('I will give') and vicarious ('for the life of the world')." (Bruce)

iii. "The words, then, are a cryptic allusion to the atoning death that Christ would die, together with a challenge to enter the closest and most intimate relation with Him." (Morris)

iv. "Now, brothers and sisters, the food of your faith is to be found in the death of the Lord Jesus for you; and, oh, what blessed food it is!" (Spurgeon)

v. "Here our Lord plainly declares that his death was to be a *vicarious sacrifice* and *atonement* for the sin of the world; and that, as no human life could be preserved unless there was *bread* (proper nourishment) received, so no soul could be saved but by the merit of his death." (Clarke)

vi. Jesus explained that receiving Him as *bread* was not receiving Him as a great moral teacher, example, or prophet. It was not receiving Him as a good or great man or noble martyr. It was receiving Him in light of what He did on the cross, His ultimate act of love for lost humanity.

8. (52-59) Receiving Jesus in the fullest sense.

The Jews therefore quarreled among themselves, saying, "How can this *Man* give us *His* flesh to eat?" Then Jesus said to them, "Most assuredly, I say to you, unless you eat the flesh of the Son of Man and drink His blood, you have no life in you. Whoever eats My flesh and drinks My blood has eternal life, and I will raise him up at the last day. For My flesh is food indeed, and My blood is drink indeed. He who eats My flesh and drinks My blood abides in Me, and I in him. As the living Father sent Me, and I live because of the Father, so he who feeds on Me will live because of Me. This is the bread which came down from heaven—not as your fathers ate the manna, and are dead. He who eats this bread

will live forever." These things He said in the synagogue as He taught in Capernaum.

a. **How can this Man give us His flesh to eat?** It's probable that the Jewish leaders *willfully* misunderstood Jesus at this point. He just explained that the bread was His body that would be given as a sacrifice *for the life of the world* (John 6:51). They willfully twisted His words to imply a bizarre cannibalism.

i. This was the result of their quarreling (**The Jews therefore quarreled among themselves**). "They differed in their judgment of Him. Some impatiently denounced Him as insane; others suggesting that there was truth in His words." (Dods)

ii. "Our Savior was, however, led to make these remarks from the fact that the ignorant Jews, when he talked about eating his flesh, and drinking his blood, really thought that he meant that they were to turn cannibals, and eat him up. You may well smile at so ridiculous an idea; yet you know that the idea is still prevalent in the Church of Rome. The Romish priest solemnly assures us that the people who eat the bread and drink the wine, or the stuff he calls bread and wine, do actually act the part of cannibals, and eat the body of Christ, and drink his blood." (Spurgeon)

b. **Unless you eat the flesh of the Son of Man and drink His blood, you have no life in you:** Jesus responded to their willful misunderstanding by speaking even more boldly, amplifying the point made at John 6:51 - His "**flesh**" was His laid-down life.

i. *Bread of life* is a metaphor. *Bread from heaven* is a metaphor. *Living bread* is a metaphor. *Bread of God* is a metaphor. It doesn't surprise that Jesus extends the bread metaphor to His actual, soon-to-come sacrifice on the cross.

ii. "He gave them a further statement which they, doctors of the Law well versed in the theory of Sacrifices, would not fail to understand. The 'eating of the flesh and drinking of the blood' was a plain allusion to the *Sacrificial* idea." (Trench)

iii. The crucified and risen Jesus must be received and internalized - metaphorically eating - or there is no true spiritual **life**, no **eternal life**.

iv. "Eating Christ's flesh and drinking His blood point to that central saving act described otherwise in, say, John 3:16. Christ's death opens the way to life. Men enter that way by faith... Eating the flesh and drinking the blood represent a striking way of saying this." (Morris)

v. "Our Lord went further still, and spoke in mystic language of the necessity for drinking His blood. The figure was suggestive of a way into life through death and sacrifice." (Morgan)

vi. "In verse 54 it is the person who eats the flesh of the Son of Man and drinks his blood that will be raised up by him at the last day; in verse 40 the same promise is held out to 'every one who sees the Son and believes in him'." (Bruce)

c. **My flesh is food indeed, and My blood is drink indeed**: The sacrificed life of Jesus *is* **food** and **drink** for the hungry and thirsty soul. When we receive and internalize Jesus Christ and Him crucified for us, we truly abide in Jesus, and He in us (**abides in Me, and I in him**).

i. Such radical statements offend many; in part this was Jesus' intent. In response to those who twisted His words and meaning, He made the metaphors *stronger*, not weaker. He refused to back down from the truth: *I am the bread of life*, and the substance of that bread is His sacrifice on the cross, the giving of His flesh and blood. What He gave at the cross, we must receive.

ii. "The actual flesh and blood, the human life of Christ, was given for men; and men eat His flesh and drink His blood, when they use for their own advantage His sacrifice, when they assimilate to their own being all the virtue that was in Him." (Dods)

iii. **Abides in Me, and I in him**: "He lives in them, and they in him; for they are made partakers of the Divine nature: 2 Peter 1:4." (Clarke)

d. **He who feeds on Me will live because of Me**: Those who *do* come to Jesus, believe upon Him, *feed* upon Him will find life. They **will live**, but *not* because they have found or earned the answer, but because Jesus has freely given what He won at the cross - **because of Me**.

i. **He who feeds on Me**: "That is, that partaketh of my person, merits, passions, privileges; he that receiveth me in all mine offices and efficacies." (Trapp)

ii. "In eating and drinking, a man is not a producer, but a consumer; he is not a doer or a giver forth; he simply takes in. If a queen should eat, if an empress should eat, she would become as completely a receiver as the pauper in the workhouse. Eating is an act of reception in every case. So it is with faith: you have not to do, to be, or to feel, but only to receive." (Spurgeon)

e. **He who eats this bread will live forever**: Jesus offers us heavenly bread for eternal life, but we must *eat* it. Faith in Jesus is not compared with *tasting* or *admiring*, but with *eating*. Jesus says that we must have Him within us, and we must partake of Him.

- Seeing a loaf of bread on a plate will not satisfy our hunger.
- Knowing the ingredients in the bread will not satisfy our hunger.
- Taking pictures of the bread will not satisfy our hunger.
- Telling other people about the bread will not satisfy our hunger.
- Selling the bread will not satisfy our hunger.
- Playing catch with the bread will not satisfy our hunger.
- Nothing will satisfy our hunger and bring us life except actually eating the bread. **He who eats this bread will live forever**.

f. **These things He said in the synagogue as He taught in Capernaum**: This remarkable discourse of Jesus, starting at John 6:26 and including the back and forth with His listeners happened during a synagogue service. Jesus likely was given the freedom of the synagogue, the opportunity to speak to the congregation.

i. "'These things He spoke in a synagogue, teaching in Capernaum,' and no doubt *on a Sabbath*, as several MSS. add." (Trench)

F. Reacting to the Radical Statements of Jesus.

1. (60-64) Many disciples turn away.

Therefore many of His disciples, when they heard *this,* said, "This is a hard saying; who can understand it?" When Jesus knew in Himself that His disciples complained about this, He said to them, "Does this offend you? *What* then if you should see the Son of Man ascend where He was before? It is the Spirit who gives life; the flesh profits nothing. The words that I speak to you are spirit, and *they* are life. But there are some of you who do not believe." For Jesus knew from the beginning who they were who did not believe, and who would betray Him.

a. **This is a hard saying**: This refers to that which is **hard** to accept, not to what is hard to understand. No doubt, these disciples (disciples in the broad sense, not the narrower sense) found Jesus' words somewhat mysterious, but it was the parts they *did* understand that were really disturbing.

i. "It is little wonder that the disciples found the discourse of Jesus hard. The Greek word is *skleros*, which means not *hard to understand*, but *hard to accept*." (Barclay)

b. **Does this offend you?** Jesus understood the offence many of His listeners took at His teaching, yet He didn't change the teaching or feel it was His fault. Jesus didn't preach just to please His audience. If that was

His concern, He would have instantly taken back what was just said, seeing His audience was offended. Jesus didn't take it back. He challenged and confronted them even more.

i. "The events of this chapter had made it all too clear that following Him meant something different from anything they had anticipated. Nothing is said to give us a clear idea of their views, but the probability is that they were interested in a messianic kingdom in line with the general expectation." (Morris)

c. **What then if you should see the Son of Man ascend where He was before?** Jesus essentially said, "If all this has offended you, what will you think when you see Me in glory, and have to answer to Me in judgment?" Better to be offended now and to get over it, than to be offended on that day.

d. **It is the Spirit who gives life; the flesh profits nothing**: This could well be the theme statement for this whole discourse of Jesus. He continually called them and us to put heart and focus on spiritual realities, not material things.

i. "The Spirit imparts life to the believer; it is not transmitted by the process of physical eating." (Tenney)

e. **Jesus knew from the beginning who they were who did not believe**: Because Jesus is God, He had the divine prerogative to know the heart of man. Yet it is entirely possible that Jesus knew this simply as a Man submitted to the Father and gifted by the Holy Spirit. He was never deceived by a false faith, nor by the one **who would betray Him**.

2. (65-66) The spiritual reason why many walked away.

And He said, "Therefore I have said to you that no one can come to Me unless it has been granted to him by My Father." From that *time* many of His disciples went back and walked with Him no more.

a. **Therefore I have said to you that no one can come to Me unless it has been granted to him by My Father**: Jesus rebuked their own material and earthly motivations for following Him. If they did not seek Him by the Spirit instead of seeking Him for food and a kingdom, then they had not come to Him at all.

i. Perhaps they followed Him halfway around the Sea of Galilee, but they did not truly **come to** Jesus until they came in the sense of believing in Him, trusting Him, loving Him (John 6:35).

b. **From that time many of His disciples went back and walked with Him no more**: Once Jesus effectively discouraged every material and earthly motive for following Him, many stopped following. They were also discouraged and perhaps confused by the deliberate controversy (John 6:52) introduced by the religious leaders visiting from Jerusalem (Matthew 15:1).

> i. **From that time**: "'From this time' is a possible translation of *ek toutou*. It could also mean 'Because of this [utterance].' The latter makes good sense because it was not simply the chronology that changed the disciples' attitude." (Tenney)

> ii. *When so many left, it looked like the enemies of Jesus won.* "It is the crisis of the first great apostasy in His Ministry. His enemies, 'the Jews,' have to all appearances carried the day." (Trench) Jesus was left with only the 12, and perhaps they would also leave. Yet the battle was not yet over. Many who left would come back, but the loss of those who followed Jesus for material or impure motives was painful - one wished they remained to hear and receive the work of the Spirit. Their leaving didn't prove Jesus and those who kept with Him to be false.

> iii. "Churches have summers, like our gardens, and then all things are full; but then come their winters, and, alas, what emptyings are seen!" (Spurgeon)

> iv. It's important to do as Jesus did, and to *not* encourage others to follow Jesus for material and temporal motives, promoting Jesus simply something to add to make a better life. Of those who come in such ways, it may be revealed that it was never been **granted to him by My Father** to follow after Jesus.

3. (67-69) The disciples stand as examples of willingness to follow even if they don't understand it all.

Then Jesus said to the twelve, "Do you also want to go away?" But Simon Peter answered Him, "Lord, to whom shall we go? You have the words of eternal life. Also we have come to believe and know that You are the Christ, the Son of the living God."

> a. **Do you also want to go away?** What a scene! Scores of would-be followers of Jesus left Him, and He asked the twelve if they would also go. Jesus searched the motives of *all* that follow Him, including the twelve. As the synagogue emptied, Jesus asked this question that assumed a "No" answer.

> > i. "As John phrases our Lord's question in Greek, he implies that it was not asked in a mood of despair; the use of the Greek negative *me* in a question indicates that the answer 'No' is expected. '*You* don't want to go away too, do you?'" (Bruce)

b. **Lord, to whom shall we go? You have the words of eternal life**: Speaking for the twelve, Simon Peter gave a wonderful statement of faith.

- He recognized Jesus as **Lord**.

- He recognized Jesus as the preferred alternative, despite the difficulties.

- He recognized the value of spiritual things, more than the material and earthly desires of those who walked away (**the words of eternal life**).

- He recognized Jesus as Messiah (**the Christ**) and God (**Son of the living God**).

4. (70-71) Jesus' knowledge of His own disciples.

Jesus answered them, "Did I not choose you, the twelve, and one of you is a devil?" He spoke of Judas Iscariot, *the son* of Simon, for it was he who would betray Him, being one of the twelve.

a. **Did I not choose you**: Jesus did in fact, choose the twelve disciples. Yet one among whom He chose was like **a devil** - and **would betray Him**.

i. "One of them was a *diabolos* - the Greek word means a 'slanderer' or 'calumniator' or 'false accuser', but it is probably used here as the counterpart to the Hebrew *satan*, 'adversary'." (Bruce)

ii. "In the dark act here prophesied, Judas was under the immediate instigation of and yielded himself up to Satan." (Alford)

iii. "There are Judases among the apparent followers of the Lord in our day. They are in our pews, even in our pulpits, and they are sometimes undetected. They betray the Lord and the gospel by both their words and their actions." (Boice)

b. **He spoke of Judas**: The simple, spiritual devotion of the disciples to Jesus made the contrast of Judas' apostasy that much more horrible. Though many walk away and some may even betray Jesus, it should not change the faith or the walk of the true follower of Jesus Christ.

i. **Judas Iscariot, the son of Simon**: "Not only was Judas's father from Karioth, but Judas himself was from Karioth, as we learn from all four gospel. For all call him Iscariot, which means 'a man of Karioth.'" (Trench)

ii. "Kerioth was a city in the southern part of Judah (Joshua 15:25), south of Hebron in the dry Negeb." (Tenney)

John 7 - At the Feast of Tabernacles

A. Jesus goes up to Jerusalem in secret.

1. (1-2) In Galilee as the Feast of Tabernacles approaches.

After these things Jesus walked in Galilee; for He did not want to walk in Judea, because the Jews sought to kill Him. Now the Jews' Feast of Tabernacles was at hand.

a. **He did not want to walk in Judea, because the Jews sought to kill Him**: It was not a lack of courage that made Jesus stay in Galilee, but an awareness of the Father's perfect timing - and it was not time yet for Him to be arrested and delivered to the Gentiles.

b. **Feast of Tabernacles**: This was a joyful, weeklong celebration in September or October when families camped out in temporary shelters to remember God's faithfulness to Israel in the wilderness on the way from Egypt to Canaan under Moses.

i. "The Hebrews called it the festival of booths (*sukkoth*), because for the full week that it lasted people lived in makeshift booths of branches and leaves (cf. Leviticus 23:40-43); town-dwellers erected them in their courtyards or on their flat housetops." (Bruce)

2. (3-5) The unbelief and opposition of the brothers of Jesus against Him.

His brothers therefore said to Him, "Depart from here and go into Judea, that Your disciples also may see the works that You are doing. For no one does anything in secret while he himself seeks to be known openly. If You do these things, show Yourself to the world." For even His brothers did not believe in Him.

a. **His brothers therefore said to Him**: Some are surprised to read that the Bible says Jesus had brothers, but this is one plain reference. John already mentioned the brothers of Jesus at John 2:12, and Matthew wrote of the brothers of Jesus at Matthew 12:46-47. In Matthew 13:55-56, the *sisters* of Jesus were described.

i. "Our blessed Lord, it is true, was her *first born*, while she was yet a *virgin*; but no man can prove that he was her *last*. It is an article of faith, in the Popish Church, to believe in the *perpetual virginity* of Mary; and in this respect, without any reason, several *Protestants* seem to be *Papists*." (Clarke)

b. **Go into Judea, that Your disciples also may see the works that you are doing... If You do these things, show Yourself to the world**: Jesus' brothers told Him to prove Himself the Messiah on a bigger platform, Jerusalem - the center of Judaism.

i. The people of Jerusalem often looked down on the Jews of Galilee. Since Jesus did most of His miraculous works there, it gave the religious leaders in Jerusalem another reason to say that Jesus wasn't the Messiah, because He didn't do most of His work in front of the right audience.

ii. "It was widely believed that when the Messiah came he would make himself publically known in some spectacular way." (Bruce) The Living Bible gives a good sense of this: *You can't be famous when you hide like this! If you're so great, prove it to the world!*

iii. "They imagined His glory to be limited to demonstrations of His miraculous powers, whereas in reality it could only be supremely displayed by His crucifixion." (Tasker)

iv. "His brethren were thinking that His success depended on the world's attitude to Him: in other words, they believed in the world rather than in Him." (Trench)

c. **For even His brothers did not believe in Him**: Remarkably, the brothers of Jesus never seemed to be supportive of His ministry before His death and resurrection, (see also Mark 3:21). *After* His resurrection the brothers of Jesus were numbered among the disciples (Acts 1:14).

i. "This does not mean that they did not believe He wrought miracles, but that they had not submitted to His claim to be Messiah." (Dods)

ii. "Many a man faced with cruel opposition in public life has been sustained by the faith and faithfulness of his kith and kin. Jesus was denied this solace." (Morris)

iii. "The emphatic expression, **for even his brethren**, &c., is a strong corroboration of the view that they were really and literally *brethren*." (Alford)

3. (6-9) Jesus' reply: we are of different worlds.

Then Jesus said to them, "My time has not yet come, but your time is always ready. The world cannot hate you, but it hates Me because I testify of it that its works are evil. You go up to this feast. I am not yet going up to this feast, for My time has not yet fully come." When He had said these things to them, He remained in Galilee.

a. **My time has not yet come, but your time is always ready**: Because Jesus was completely submitted to the will of the Father, the timing of God the Father was important. The brothers of Jesus were not submitted to God's will in the same way, so *any* time was fine with them.

i. **My time**: "In this passage the word is *kairos*, which characteristically means an *opportunity*; that is, the best time to do something, the moment when circumstances are most suitable." (Barclay)

ii. As Jesus obeyed His Father, He lived out the truth that God's *timing* is an important expression of His *will*. Something may be in God's will but not yet in His timing.

b. **The world cannot hate you, but it hates Me because I testify of it that its works are evil**: The brothers of Jesus agreed with the common opinions of their day about good and evil - therefore the world could not hate them. Jesus boldly confronted the sins of His age, and was therefore the target of much hatred.

i. **The world cannot hate you**: "There is no danger of your incurring the world's hatred by anything you do or say; because your wishes and actions are in the world's own spirit." (Dods)

c. **I am not yet going up to the feast**: Some compare this statement with what it says in John 7:10 (*He also went up to the feast, not openly, but as it were in secret*) as if they caught Jesus in a lie. Schopenhauer, the German philosopher of pessimism, pompously wrote: "Jesus Christ of set purpose did utter a falsehood." (Barclay) But Christians have observed for centuries that if Jesus said He would not go *publicly* as to attract attention (as His brothers wanted), but that did not preclude Him from going up *privately*.

4. (10-13) Jesus goes up to Jerusalem, where many secretly discuss Him.

But when His brothers had gone up, then He also went up to the feast, not openly, but as it were in secret. Then the Jews sought Him at the feast, and said, "Where is He?" And there was much complaining among the people concerning Him. Some said, "He is good"; others said, "No, on the contrary, He deceives the people." However, no one spoke openly of Him for fear of the Jews.

a. **When His brothers had gone up, then he also went up to the feast, not openly, but as it were in secret**: Jesus did *not* go with His brothers in one of the large processions of travelers from Galilee to Jerusalem at feast time. He went after them, traveling alone - almost (**as it were**) in **secret**.

> i. **Not openly**: "Not in the usual caravan-company, nor probably by the usual way." (Alford) "That is to say, He went up, but not at His brothers' instigation, nor with the publicity they had recommended." (Dods)

> ii. "The secret departure for Jerusalem was not an act of deception. It was an attempt to avoid unwelcome publicity. Jesus' enemies were watching for him, obviously for the purpose of arresting him." (Tenney)

b. **There was much complaining among the people concerning Him**: They complained because they wanted Jesus to fulfill *their* wishes for the Messiah, and to fulfill them *now* - when they wanted them.

c. **Some said, "He is good"; others said, "No, on the contrary, He deceives the people"**: Then as well as now, Jesus divides people. Those who heard Him and knew Him couldn't remain neutral. They decided one way or another regarding who Jesus was, either **good** or a deceiver.

d. **However, no one spoke openly of Him**: They religious leaders did not want people to talk about Jesus at all. The common people feared some penalty of problem from the religious leaders if they were heard speaking **openly** of Jesus.

> i. "Whether they approved of disapproved of him, they did not voice their opinions too loudly or too publicly. The authorities did not wish him to be discussed at all, and any one who disregarded their wishes was liable to feel their displeasure." (Bruce)

B. Jesus answers objections and teaches.

1. (14-18) The religious leaders object that Jesus isn't educated.

Now about the middle of the feast Jesus went up into the temple and taught. And the Jews marveled, saying, "How does this Man know letters, having never studied?" Jesus answered them and said, "My doctrine is not Mine, but His who sent Me. If anyone wants to do His will, he shall know concerning the doctrine, whether it is from God or *whether* I speak on My own *authority*. He who speaks from himself seeks his own glory; but He who seeks the glory of the One who sent Him is true, and no unrighteousness is in Him."

a. **Jesus went up into the temple and taught**: Though Jesus avoided a grand entrance, when He came to Jerusalem in His Father's timing, He taught boldly. He never shrank back from proclaiming the truth.

b. **How does this Man know letters, having never studied**: The Jewish leaders knew that Jesus had not studied or been a disciple under a prominent rabbi (as Paul studied under Gamaliel, Acts 22:3). Jesus did not follow the normal and expected course of education for a teacher.

> i. The sense of **know letters** is "Particularly, **scripture-learning** - perhaps because this was *all the literature* of the Jews. Probably His teaching consisted in *exposition of the Scripture*." (Alford) "His skill in interpreting Scripture and His knowledge of it is what is referred to." (Dods)

> ii. If they could have condemned Jesus on some false doctrine or wrong understanding of Scripture, they would have. Since they could not, the attack the credentials of Jesus. "These words are spoken in the true bigotry and prejudice of so-called 'learning.'" (Alford)

c. **My doctrine is not Mine, but His who sent Me**: Jesus didn't point to His credentials, but to His **doctrine**. It was as if He said, "I don't have a seminary degree, but judge Me by **My doctrine**." If the Jewish leaders listened carefully to the **doctrine** of Jesus, they would know that it was all rooted in the Old Testament Scriptures, and that it was **from God**.

> i. "Our blessed Lord, in the character of Messiah, might as well say, *My doctrine is not mine*, as an ambassador might say, I speak not my own words, but his who sent me: and he speaks these words to draw the attention of the Jews from the teaching of man to the teaching of God." (Clarke)

d. **My doctrine is not Mine, but His who sent Me**: Jesus was an eloquent, gifted teacher, but He was not self taught; Jesus was God taught. His authority was not from any man, but from His Father.

> i. Jesus didn't claim to be self-taught; He claimed to be God-taught, practically inviting His listeners to examine His teachings according to the Scriptures.

> ii. There is a great spiritual principle behind the words, **If anyone wills to do His will, he shall know concerning the doctrine**. "Spiritual understanding is not produced solely by learning facts or procedures, but rather it depends on obedience to known truth." (Tenney)

e. **He who seeks the glory of the One who sent Him is true, and no unrighteousness is in Him**: Jesus contrasted Himself with the one who **speaks from himself** and who **seeks his own glory**. Jesus was different.

- Jesus sought the **glory** of God.

- Jesus **is true**.
- Jesus has **no unrighteousness** in Him.

   i. In a sense, Jesus gave us two measures of a true teacher.

   - Does the teaching come from God? That is, is it according to the revealed Word of God?
   - Does the work give glory to God?

2. (19-24) The people object that Jesus is crazy, and has a demon.

"Did not Moses give you the law, yet none of you keeps the law? Why do you seek to kill Me?" The people answered and said, "You have a demon. Who is seeking to kill You?" Jesus answered and said to them, "I did one work, and you all marvel. Moses therefore gave you circumcision (not that it is from Moses, but from the fathers), and you circumcise a man on the Sabbath. If a man receives circumcision on the Sabbath, so that the law of Moses should not be broken, are you angry with Me because I made a man completely well on the Sabbath? Do not judge according to appearance, but judge with righteous judgment."

a. **None of you keeps the law**: Jesus just stated that He was absolutely sinless and true, always seeking the glory of God in heaven (John 7:18). In contrast to Jesus, the religious leaders did not keep the law. They had the law (**Did not Moses give you the law**), but did not keep it.

b. **Why do you seek to kill Me?** In following the thought of Jesus, He said something like this: "I am sinless and none of you keep the law. Why then do you **seek to kill Me?** You are the ones guilty under the law, not I."

c. **You have a demon. Who is seeking to kill You?** The people didn't know that the rulers wanted to kill Jesus because He healed a man on the Sabbath (John 5:16). They thought Jesus was crazy and perhaps paranoid.

d. **If a man receives circumcision on the Sabbath, so that the law of Moses should not be broken**: It was permitted - even commanded - to do a negative work on the Sabbath, such as cutting away the flesh in circumcision (Leviticus 12:3). It was even more right to make **a man completely well on the Sabbath**, as Jesus did (John 5:8-9).

   i. "If you may wound a man on the sabbath-day, may not I heal one?" (Trapp)

e. **Do not judge according to appearance, but judge with righteous judgment**: They decided that Jesus appeared to be a sinner, and they appeared to be righteous. They were wrong each time, and they needed to **judge with righteous judgment** instead of only by appearances.

i. "No righteous judgment can be come to if appearances decide." (Dods) The iconic figure of *Justice* has a blindfold for this reason.

ii. "We should ever bear in mind that that 'appearance' may be deceitful, and therefore with the love that hopeth all things, we should be ready to give men the benefit of any doubt or any uncertainty that is in our minds." (Morgan)

3. (25-29) The people of Jerusalem object that Jesus could not be the Messiah because they know where He came from.

Now some of them from Jerusalem said, "Is this not He whom they seek to kill? But look! He speaks boldly, and they say nothing to Him. Do the rulers know indeed that this is truly the Christ? However, we know where this Man is from; but when the Christ comes, no one knows where He is from." Then Jesus cried out, as He taught in the temple, saying, "You both know Me, and you know where I am from; and I have not come of Myself, but He who sent Me is true, whom you do not know. But I know Him, for I am from Him, and He sent Me."

a. **Is this not He whom they seek to kill?** The people **from Jerusalem** knew that the religious leaders wanted to kill Jesus. The crowd that came for the feast did not know it (John 7:20), but those from Jerusalem did. Yet they were amazed that the **rulers** would not and could not stop Jesus from teaching.

b. **He speaks boldly, and they say nothing to Him**: Jesus was never afraid or intimidated by the threats against Him. He still spoke **boldly**, and with such boldness that no one could make Him stop.

c. **We know where this Man is from; but when the Christ comes, no one knows where He is from**: Many (but not all) of the Jews of that time believed the Messiah would appear suddenly, as if out of nowhere.

i. Malachi 3:1 says that God's messenger will come *suddenly to the temple*. This was the kind of saying that made them think the Messiah would come out of nowhere to show Himself to Israel.

ii. Popular belief "held that the Messiah would *appear*. The idea was that he was waiting concealed and some day would burst suddenly upon the world and no one would know where he had come from." (Barclay)

iii. **We know where this Man is from**: We don't know if the people thought, *this Man comes from Bethlehem* or *this Man comes from Nazareth*. They probably associated Jesus with Nazareth (Jesus of Nazareth).

d. **You both know Me, and you know where I am from**: This first sentence of Jesus' reply may well have been sarcastic. They *thought* they knew where He was from, but they were unaware of His heavenly origin.

i. "He agrees that they know Him and that they know where he came from, but this is almost certainly ironical: 'So you know me and my origin!'" (Morris)

e. **I am from Him, and He sent Me**: The crowds were perhaps confused about where the Messiah would come from, but Jesus knew exactly where He came from. Jesus was not a confused man, wondering if He was really the Son of God.

i. "The language is simple and unambiguous; the claim is august. Jesus asserts afresh his unique relation to the Father, and his hearers cannot miss the implication of his words." (Bruce)

4. (30-36) The officers try to arrest Jesus as many believe in Him.

Therefore they sought to take Him; but no one laid a hand on Him, because His hour had not yet come. And many of the people believed in Him, and said, "When the Christ comes, will He do more signs than these which this *Man* has done?" The Pharisees heard the crowd murmuring these things concerning Him, and the Pharisees and the chief priests sent officers to take Him. Then Jesus said to them, "I shall be with you a little while longer, and *then* I go to Him who sent Me. You will seek Me and not find *Me,* and where I am you cannot come." Then the Jews said among themselves, "Where does He intend to go that we shall not find Him? Does He intend to go to the Dispersion among the Greeks and teach the Greeks? What is this thing that He said, 'You will seek Me and not find Me, and where I am you cannot come'?"

a. **No one laid a hand on Him, because His hour had not yet come**: Until the time was right, no one could lay a hand on Jesus. There would come a time when Jesus would say that His hour had come (John 12:23). Until that **hour**, Jesus was protected.

i. The arresting officers *wanted* **to take Him**, but they couldn't. It just wouldn't happen. When the officers returned to the religious leaders empty handed - no arrested Jesus with them - their bosses wanted to know why. They answered, *no man ever spoke like this Man!* (John 7:46)

b. **Many of the people believed in Him**: As Jesus spoke to the people, they were drawn to faith in Him. It didn't matter that many opposed Him or even wanted to kill Him. Jesus made public was Jesus believed upon, and they marveled at the many **signs** that He did.

i. They spoke with clear logic when they asked, "**When the Christ comes, will He do more signs than these which this Man has done?**" It is fair to ask, who has done more than Jesus?

ii. If Jesus isn't the Messiah, then when Messiah comes, will he...

- Do more miracles than Jesus?
- Teach with more insight and authority than Jesus?
- Love more remarkably than Jesus?
- Suffer with more courage than Jesus?
- Atone for more sinners than Jesus?
- Raise from the dead with more triumph than Jesus?
- Ascend to heaven in greater glory than Jesus?
- Present a greater Gospel than Jesus?
- Change more lives than Jesus?
- Free more addictions than Jesus?
- Comfort more grief-stricken hearts than Jesus?
- Heal more broken hearts than Jesus?
- Restore more marriages than Jesus?
- Triumph over more tyrants than Jesus?
- Gain more followers than Jesus?

iii. *None of this is possible.* No one can do more than Jesus did, and He deserves all our confidence, life, and faith as Messiah.

c. **I shall be with you a little while longer**: As the religious leaders **sent officers to take Him**, Jesus assured the officers that He *would* go away, but only at the appointed time - at His ascension (**I go to Him who sent Me**). They would not take Him away at the present time.

i. "To the officers the saying is an exhibition of His triumphant confidence that their malice is impotent and their arms paralysed; that when He wills He will *go*, not be dragged by them or any man." (Maclaren)

d. **Does He intend to go to the Dispersion among the Greeks**: Jesus spoke of His coming ascension to heaven, but they didn't understand. Willfully misunderstanding, they asked if He would go away to the Jewish communities outside the Promised Land.

i. "The Jews understood not *his death* to be meant, but some journey which He would take in the event of their rejecting Him." (Alford)

ii. "Little did the speakers know that, while Jesus was not to go in person among the Greeks, his followers would be numbered in the tens of thousands in the Greek lands in a few years' time." (Bruce)

e. **You will seek Me and not find Me**: Remarkably, they exactly repeated what Jesus previously said. This statement troubled them, and they wanted to know what Jesus meant. He meant that He would not be found by the hostile examiner, those intending to arrest, silence, or kill Him.

5. (37-39) The great invitation: **If anyone thirsts, let him come to Me and drink.**

On the last day, that great *day* of the feast, Jesus stood and cried out, saying, "If anyone thirsts, let him come to Me and drink. He who believes in Me, as the Scripture has said, out of his heart will flow rivers of living water." But this He spoke concerning the Spirit, whom those believing in Him would receive; for the Holy Spirit was not yet *given*, because Jesus was not yet glorified.

a. **On the last day, that great day of the feast**: The Feast of Tabernacles lasted eight days. All through the first seven days water from the Pool of Siloam was carried in a golden pitcher and poured out at the altar to remind everyone of the water God miraculously provided for a thirsty Israel in the wilderness. It seems that on the eighth day there was *no* pouring of water - only prayers for water - to remind them that they came into the Promised Land.

i. "But the eighth day was not properly one of the *feast days*; the people ceased to dwell in the tabernacles on the seventh day. Philo says of it that it was *the solemn conclusion, not of that feast alone, but of all the feasts in the year*." (Alford)

ii. This was the last feast-time Jesus would spend in Jerusalem *before* the Passover of His death. This was the last day of the last feast; the last time He would speak to many of them before His crucifixion.

b. **Jesus stood and cried out**: What Jesus was about to say was of great importance.

- Important because of *where* He said it (standing in the temple courts, right outside the temple itself).

- Important because of *when* He said it (at the last day of Tabernacles, after water had been poured out on the previous days).

- Important because of *how* He said it (crying out, even shouting - in contrast to the general tone of His ministry, according to Isaiah 42:2:

He will not cry out, nor raise His voice, nor cause His voice to be heard in the street).

c. **If anyone thirsts, let him come to Me and drink**: The celebration of the Feast of Tabernacles emphasized how God provided water to Israel in the wilderness on their way to Canaan. Jesus boldly called people to *Himself* to drink and satisfy their deepest thirst, their spiritual thirst.

i. The invitation was broad because it said, **if anyone**. Intelligence, race, class, nationality, or political party don't limit it. The invitation was narrow because it said, **if anyone thirsts**. One must see their need. Thirst is not anything in itself; it is a *lack* of something. It is an emptiness, a crying need.

ii. There is dispute among commentators as to if Jesus said this *as water was being poured out*, or if He did it on the day when *no water was poured out*. It is perhaps impossible to be certain, but John's emphasis on **the last day** probably indicates that Jesus meant to show a contrast. "There's no more water at the temple and in the rituals we love. *I* have the water you're looking for."

iii. "On the eighth day no water was poured, and this would make Jesus' claim all the more impressive." (Morris)

iv. "On the eighth day, which commemorated their entrance into 'a land of springs of water,' this ceremony was discontinued. But the deeper spirits must have viewed with some misgiving all this ritual, feeling still in themselves a thirst which none of these symbolic forms quenched." (Dods)

d. **He who believes in Me**: Jesus explained what He meant by the metaphor of *drinking*. To **come to** Jesus and to **drink** was essentially to put one's faith into Him; to trust in, rely on, and cling to Jesus for both time and eternity.

i. "Then thou art told to *drink*. That is not a difficult action. Any fool can drink: in fact, many are great fools because they drink too much of poisonous liquors. Drinking is peculiarly the common-place act of sinners." (Spurgeon)

e. **Out of his heart will flow rivers of living water**: For the one who *does* believe in Him, Jesus offered a perpetual river of **living water** out of His innermost being. Tabernacles also looked forward to the prophecies of water flowing from the throne and from Jerusalem where Messiah would be enthroned. Essentially Jesus said, "Put your loving trust in Me, enthrone Me in your heart, and life and abundance will flow out."

i. "The Greek is, 'out of his belly', *i.e.* 'from his innermost being'." (Morris)

ii. Jesus did not only speak of something coming *into* a person, but something flowing *out of* them as well. It was not only a blessing received, but also becoming a source of blessing to others.

iii. "He was able to satisfy thirst, and, moreover, that those who received such satisfaction from Him should become channels through whom the overflowing rivers should pass." (Morgan)

iv. **As the Scripture has said**: "Though no specific passage of Scripture is quoted, this would in fact be a fulfillment of such prophecies as that of Zechariah that one day a fountain would be open to the house of David, and living waters would go out from Jerusalem (Zechariah 13:1, 14:8); and of Isaiah that God would pour water upon the thirsty (Isaiah 44:3, 55:1)." (Tasker)

f. **This He spoke concerning the Spirit, whom those believing in Him would receive**: This outflowing life and abundance comes in and through the presence of **the Spirit** in the life of the believer. This speaks of an *experience* that belongs to **those believing in Him**. The nature of that experience may differ among believers, but there is some aspect of it that is promised to all who will receive it by faith.

i. "The Jerusalem Talmud connects the ceremonies and this scripture with the Holy Spirit: 'Why is the name of it called, The drawing out of water? Because of the pouring out of the Holy Spirit, according to what is said: "With joy shall ye draw water out of the wells of salvation.""" (Morris)

ii. "It is a blessed thing to preach the work of Jesus Christ, but it is an evil thing to omit the work of the Holy Ghost; for the work of the Lord Jesus itself is no blessing to that man who does not know the work of the Holy Spirit." (Spurgeon)

g. **For the Holy Spirit was not yet given**: This outflowing life and abundance could not come yet, **because Jesus was not yet glorified** - that is, glorified on the cross and through resurrection. This giving of the Holy Spirit for the people of God could not happen until Jesus completed His work at the cross and the empty tomb.

i. Translators have added the word **given**. More literally it is *"for it was not yet Spirit."* John tells us that it was not yet Pentecost and the days of the Spirit. "The word implied is not exactly *'given,'* but rather *'working,'* or some similar word... *the dispensation of the Spirit was not yet."* (Alford)

ii. "It is a point repeated in this Gospel that the Spirit could not come during the time of Christ's earthly ministry. But when the work was consummated the Spirit was given." (Morris)

C. The crowd questions, the religious leaders reject.

1. (40-43) Jesus brings division among the crowd.

Therefore many from the crowd, when they heard this saying, said, "Truly this is the Prophet." Others said, "This is the Christ." But some said, "Will the Christ come out of Galilee? Has not the Scripture said that the Christ comes from the seed of David and from the town of Bethlehem, where David was?" So there was a division among the people because of Him.

a. **This is the Prophet... This is the Christ**: Some said one thing, others said something else about who Jesus was; but everyone had an opinion. They could not be confronted with Jesus and remain truly neutral. If someone pretended to be neutral, they were really against Him.

i. **This is the Prophet**: "Some no doubt knew that by the prophet, the Messiah was meant; but others seem to have thought that one of the ancient prophets should be raised from the dead, and precede the appearing of the Messiah." (Clarke)

b. **Will the Christ come out of Galilee?** Some rejected Jesus because they were ignorant, not knowing the truth about Him. These ones did not know that Jesus was really born in Bethlehem, even though they knew the prophecies about Jesus being born in **Bethlehem**.

i. "The preposition rendered 'out of' refers to birth and origin, not to residence." (Trench)

ii. "The very passage that convinced his critics that he could not be the Messiah was one of the strongest to prove that he was." (Tenney)

iii. "Are you the one who has been rejecting Jesus Christ on a quibble? Do you refuse to come because you cannot understand where Cain got his wife? Or how God can punish sinners? Or why we are to believe in a virgin birth or a resurrection?" (Boice)

c. **So there was a division among the people because of Him**: During the days of His earthly work, Jesus divided people. People could not truly be of two opinions about Jesus, so some would be for Him while others would be against Him.

i. "The word rendered **division** implies a *violent dissension* - some taking up His cause, some wishing to lay hands on Him." (Alford)

ii. The division didn't come because Jesus spoke foolishly, or because He spoke on a theologically controversial topic. He spoke about Himself, the Messiah - and He spoke clearly, not in dark mysterious sayings.

iii. Jesus repeated this idea in Matthew 10:34-36: *Do not think that I came to bring peace on earth. I did not come to bring peace but a sword. For I have come to "set a man against his father, a daughter against her mother, and a daughter-in-law against her mother-in-law"; and "a man's enemies will be those of his own household."*

iv. Such division should never exist among the followers of Jesus. "We can sometimes even fight with one another for what we believe to be the truth, and rebuke each other to the face if we think there is an error; but when it comes to Christ and his dear cross, give me thy hand, brother. You are washed in the blood, and so am I. You are resting in Christ, and so am I. You have put all your hope in Jesus; and that is where all my hope is, and therefore we are one. Yes, there is no real division among the true people of God because of Christ." (Spurgeon)

2. (44-49) The failure of an attempted arrest of Jesus.

Now some of them wanted to take Him, but no one laid hands on Him. Then the officers came to the chief priests and Pharisees, who said to them, "Why have you not brought Him?" The officers answered, "No man ever spoke like this Man!" Then the Pharisees answered them, "Are you also deceived? Have any of the rulers or the Pharisees believed in Him? But this crowd that does not know the law is accursed."

a. **Some of them wanted to take Him, but no one laid hands on Him**: The arrest was unsuccessful, but it wasn't because the arresting officers were incompetent. It was because the time wasn't right yet, and it was impossible for Jesus to be stopped until it was right in the Father's timing.

b. **No man ever spoke like this Man!** These **officers** of the temple had heard many rabbis teach, but they *never* heard someone speak like Jesus. They were so impressed by the message of Jesus that they found it impossible to do their assigned work of arresting and silencing Him.

i. "'Never did any *man* talk in this fashion.' In the Greek the word 'man' (*anthropos*) occurs in the emphatic position at the end of the sentence and implies by contrast that he must be more than an ordinary human being." (Tenney)

ii. "Their testimony was expressed in few and simple words, but it has stood the test of nineteen centuries." (Bruce)

c. **Are you also deceived? Have any of the rulers or the Pharisees believed in Him? But this crowd that does not know the law is accursed**: The pride of the religious leaders was plain, as was their despising of the common people. They hoped to shame and intimidate the officers who didn't arrest Jesus with the idea *all the smart and spiritual people don't follow Jesus - neither should you.*

> i. "The religious snobbishness of the rulers was revealed in their contemptuous dismissal of the guards' testimony." (Tenney)

> ii. "The Pharisees had a phrase by which they described the ordinary, simple people who did not observe the thousands of regulations of the ceremonial law. They called them *the People of the Land*; to them they were beneath contempt." (Barclay)

> iii. "Even the liberal Rabbi Hillel, of the generation before Christ, summed up this attitude when he said, 'No member of the common people is pious.'" (Bruce)

3. (50-52) The reaction to Nicodemus' small stand for Jesus.

Nicodemus (he who came to Jesus by night, being one of them) said to them, "Does our law judge a man before it hears him and knows what he is doing?" They answered and said to him, "Are you also from Galilee? Search and look, for no prophet has arisen out of Galilee."

a. **Does our law judge a man before it hears him and knows what he is doing**: Nicodemus tried to reason with the religious leaders, warning them against judging Jesus hastily.

b. **Are you also from Galilee**: The religious leaders who lived in Jerusalem and Judea despised the people of **Galilee**, and often mocked them. To these religious leaders from Judea, nothing good could come from Galilee.

c. **Search and look, for no prophet has arisen out of Galilee**: They were wrong. In fact, a prophet *had* risen from Galilee. Jonah (who was a picture of Jesus Christ) came from Gath Hepher, which was three miles north of Nazareth in Lower Galilee (2 Kings 14:25).

> i. "The way the question is introduced in the original conveys a marked note of surprise; 'Why surely the Christ is not going to come from Galilee?'" (Tasker)

> ii. "It was *not historically true*; - for two prophets at least had arisen from Galilee: Jonah of Gathhepher, and the greatest of the prophets, Elijah of Thisbe; and perhaps also Nahum and Hosea. Their contempt for Galilee made them lose sight of historical accuracy." (Alford)

John 8 - The Light of the World

A. A woman caught in adultery is brought to Jesus for judgment.

1. (7:53-8:2) Jesus teaches at the temple.

And everyone went to his *own* house. But Jesus went to the Mount of Olives. Now early in the morning He came again into the temple, and all the people came to Him; and He sat down and taught them.

a. **Everyone went to his own house**: The sense in the text as we have it is that Jesus confounded His opponents as He preached at the temple and then they went their own ways. Jesus went **to the Mount of Olives** to sleep.

i. As a matter of the original text, this is a section (John 7:53-8:11) of some debate and controversy. From manuscript current evidence, it seems unlikely that this portion was part of the original text of John's gospel, or at least in this place.

- Most of the earliest ancient Greek manuscripts omit this section.

- Many later manuscripts mark this section with asterisks.

- One group of manuscripts inserts this section after Luke 21:38.

- A few manuscripts have this section after John 21:24, and one has it after John 7:36.

- "All this evidence suggests that scribes were often ignorant of its exact position, though anxious to retain it as part of the four Gospels." (Tasker) They knew it belonged, but they didn't exactly know where.

ii. Some ancient Christians (such as Augustine and Ambrose) omitted this story, not so much because of the textual evidence but because they thought it made Jesus appear to approve of sexual immorality, or at least not regard it as serious.

iii. At the same time, the character of the story makes it seem obvious that it is genuine, and many scholars note that it is historical and factual. Early Christian writers mention this account as soon as the early second century (A.D. 100). We have good reason to believe that this actually happened, and that John really wrote this. There is some debate as to *where* it belongs in the Gospel accounts, but there is good reason to believe it belongs.

iv. "If not John's it was a very early interpolation: it may possibly have had the sanction of Simeon or Jude (early 2nd century), the second and third bishops of Jerusalem, 'brethren' of our Lord, the last survivors of the Apostolic age. These two seem to have been connected with the editing of this gospel, for they are probably the 'we' of John 21:24 and the two unnamed disciples of John 21:2." (Trench)

v. "If we cannot feel that this is part of John's Gospel we can feel that the story is true to the character of Jesus." (Morris)

b. **He came again into the temple, and all the people came to Him; and He sat down and taught them**: If we take the chronology of the Gospel of John in its current composition, Jesus remained in Jerusalem for a few days after the Feast of Tabernacles (John 7:37). Though the religious authorities wanted to silence and arrest Him, He still boldly taught large crowds in the most public place in Jerusalem - **the temple**.

2. (3-5) The woman is brought to Jesus, caught in the act of adultery.

Then the scribes and Pharisees brought to Him a woman caught in adultery. And when they had set her in the midst, they said to Him, "Teacher, this woman was caught in adultery, in the very act. Now Moses, in the law, commanded us that such should be stoned. But what do You say?"

a. **Brought to Him a woman caught in adultery**: They did this as Jesus publically taught in the temple courts. They wanted to make this as public as possible, to embarrass both the woman and Jesus.

i. "All the indications are that her accusers had some special vindictiveness against her. This is shown also in the fact that they brought the woman along publicly…There was no need for this. She might have been kept in custody while the case was referred to Jesus." (Morris)

ii. The verb **caught** is in the perfect tense. "The perfect indicates a meaning like 'taken with her shame upon her'. It points to her continuing character as an adulteress." (Morris)

b. **This woman was caught in adultery, in the very act**: The religious leaders brought this woman to Jesus in shame-filled, humiliating circumstances. She was held against her will, a prisoner under the custody of the religious police who caught her involved with a man not her husband, **in the very act** of adultery.

i. To mention the obvious, there was also a man involved in this **very act** of **adultery** - yet the guilty man was *not* brought before Jesus for judgment. It also meant that there were pre-arranged spies sent to witness this affair, and they carefully noted the sordid details.

ii. Morris points out that legally speaking, the standard of evidence was very high for this crime. There had to be two witnesses and they had to agree perfectly. They had to see the sexual act take place; it wasn't enough to see the pair leaving the same room together or even lying on the same bed together. "The actual physical movements of the couple must have been capable of no other explanation.... conditions were so stringent that they could have been met only on rare occasions." (Morris)

iii. "Under these conditions the obtaining of evidence in adultery would be almost impossible were the situation not a setup." (Boice)

c. **Moses, in the law, commanded us that such should be stoned**: It is true that adultery was a capital offense under Jewish law, but the rules for evidence in capital cases were extremely strict. The actual act had to be observed by multiple witnesses who agreed exactly in their testimony. As a practical matter, virtually no one was executed for adultery, since this was a relatively private sin.

i. "It appears that by the first century AD the full rigour of the law was no longer applied as a general rule, in urban communities at any rate." (Bruce)

ii. "From the reference to the law in verse 5 it might seem that she was liable to this particular punishment because she had sinned during the period of betrothal, fornication during that time being regarded as adultery." (Tasker)

d. **But what do You say?** They set a trap for Jesus. If Jesus said, "Let her go," then He would seem to break the Law of Moses. If He said, "Execute her for the crime of adultery," then Jesus would seem harsh and perhaps cruel. Also, He would break Roman law, because the Romans had taken the right of official execution for religious offenses away from the Jews.

i. This was a similar dilemma as posed by the question to Jesus about paying taxes to Caesar (Matthew 22:15-22).

3. (6) Jesus ignores the accusers, as if He never heard them.

This they said, testing Him, that they might have *something* of which to accuse Him. But Jesus stooped down and wrote on the ground with *His* finger, as though He did not hear.

a. **This they said, testing Him, that they might have something of which to accuse Him**: The religious leaders - wretched men as they were - used this woman as a weapon against Jesus. They presented her as a sinner before Jesus, but ignored their own sin in the matter.

i. They cared nothing for true righteousness, for it was evident that they carefully arranged both the adulterous act and her arrest. They claimed that **this woman was caught in adultery, in the very act** - yet they did not bring the guilty *man* before Jesus. It's possible that the man was one of them, and they simply used the woman as a weapon or pawn in their conflict against Jesus.

ii. "Adultery is not the kind of offence that can be committed by one person in solitude; if she was caught red-handed, how was her guilty partner allowed to escape?" (Bruce)

iii. "They were not looking on this woman as a person at all; they were looking on her only as a thing, an instrument whereby they could formulate a charge against Jesus." (Barclay)

b. **Jesus stooped down and wrote on the ground with His finger**: This was a careful and deliberate response from Jesus. Instead of making an immediate verbal response He **stooped down**. Then He **wrote on the ground with His finger**, presumably in the dirt on the ground.

i. **Stooped down** indicates humility. Jesus didn't react with anger or immediate outrage. He didn't scream at the woman or those who brought the woman. Jesus paused and **stooped down**.

ii. **Stooped down** is a low posture, identifying with the humiliation of the woman. Jesus did what He could to identify with, care for, and ease the embarrassment of this woman. One may say this story illustrates the great problem: how can God show love and grace to the sinner without being unjust, without breaking His own law? He does it by first identifying with the sinner in their low condition.

iii. **Wrote on the ground** means that Jesus could write, and that He wrote in the presence of the woman and these men. *What Jesus wrote* has been an endless source of speculation for teachers, preachers, and commentators.

- Some think that Jesus simply doodled in the dirt. The verb translated **wrote** could also mean, "to draw." (Morris)

- Some think Jesus simply stalled for time.

- Some think that Jesus wrote the passage in the law that condemned the adulterous woman.

- Some think Jesus wrote out a passage like Exodus 23:1: *Do not put your hand with the wicked to be an unrighteous witness.*

- Some think that Jesus wrote the names of the accusers.

- Some think that Jesus the sins of the accusers.

- Some think that Jesus followed Roman judicial practice and wrote out His sentence before He said it.

iv. "The normal Greek word for *to write* is *graphein*; but here the word used is *katagrapheini*, which can mean *to write down a record against someone*." (Barclay)

c. **As though He did not hear**: As Jesus stooped down and wrote, He acted as if He did not even hear the accusation against the woman. Perhaps Jesus ignored them because He despised their wicked work. Perhaps Jesus ignored them because He was embarrassed for the woman's sake.

i. Paul made reference to *the meekness and gentleness of Christ* (2 Corinthians 10:1) - this is what we see on display here.

4. (7-8) Jesus passes sentence upon the accusers.

So when they continued asking Him, He raised Himself up and said to them, "He who is without sin among you, let him throw a stone at her first." And again He stooped down and wrote on the ground.

a. **So when they continued asking Him**: Jesus stooped down, wrote on the ground, and acted as if He did not hear the accusers of the woman taken in adultery. The men who brought the woman didn't stop asking Jesus what should be done with her - **they continued asking Him**.

b. **He raised Himself up and said to them**: Jesus said this directly to the accusers of the woman, standing up to make eye contact with them.

c. **He who is without sin among you, let him throw a stone at her first**: In Jewish law, witnesses to the capital crime began the stoning. Jesus really said, "We may execute her, but we must do it correctly. One of the witnesses must begin her execution. So who among you is the one who witnessed this crime, and only brought to Me the woman, not the man? Who designed the humiliation of this poor woman?"

i. Instead of passing a sentence upon the woman, Jesus passed a sentence upon His accusers. He didn't say, "Don't execute her." He simply demanded that justice be fairly and righteously applied.

ii. **Without sin among you**: It wasn't that these men had sinned once or twice before, and so had no right to be concerned about the woman's sin. It's that they orchestrated and plotted her sin, her shame, using her as a weapon against Jesus. *In this direct incident* they had a greater sin and a greater guilt.

iii. In this Jesus exposed a common sin: a desire to punish the sins of others, while ignoring our own sin. King David was an example of this when Nathan the Prophet told him the story of a man who stole and killed the pet lamb of another man (2 Samuel 12:1-10).

iv. *If we must look at the sins of others, we must be aware that we have also sinned.* There is still a place for exposing and rebuking and directly dealing with the sins of others in God's family, but it must always be done with a heart that recognizes itself as a forgiven sinner. When done right, confronting sin is done more often with tears and a broken heart than with anger and condemnation.

d. **Again He stooped down and wrote on the ground**: Jesus seemed to do everything He could to calm the excitement and tension at the scene, probably out of concern for the woman's dignity and safety. Again, Jesus **wrote on the ground**.

i. He didn't stare down the accusing men in an act of intimidation. Jesus did everything in this situation to make things less tense, not more tense. He did not try to change them through intimidation.

ii. Jesus continued to care about the shame of the woman and did what He could to ease it. Shame may serve a helpful purpose, but God never intended it to be a permanent condition.

5. (9) The accusers respond by leaving.

Then those who heard *it*, being convicted by *their* conscience, went out one by one, beginning with the oldest *even* to the last. And Jesus was left alone, and the woman standing in the midst.

a. **Being convicted by their conscience**: They were **convicted** by what they **heard** from Jesus. Seemingly it wasn't what Jesus wrote (though that may have had something to do with it). More so, it was what Jesus *said* that **convicted** their **conscience**.

i. It spoke well of these men that their conscience was not dead or burned over. They still could be **convicted by their conscience**. They were now more aware of their own sin than the sin of the woman.

b. **Went out one by one, beginning with the oldest even to the last**: We understand why they left; they were **convicted by their conscience**. It's not immediately clear why they left in order; **the oldest even to the last**. Perhaps the oldest left first because they most easily understood that Jesus was talking about them.

i. "The continuous tense in this last verb gives the thought of something like a procession. They kept on going out." (Morris)

ii. Some speculate that Jesus wrote on the ground an account of their own sins, beginning from the oldest to the youngest - explaining the order of their departure.

c. **The woman standing in the midst**: This is the only reference in the account to the physical posture of the woman. It is possible that the religious leaders who brought her to Jesus forced her to stand through the ordeal. Yet human nature and the repeated stooping posture of Jesus suggests that the woman, for all or some of this ordeal, was in a low posture on the ground.

i. The ancient Greek word translated **standing** (*hestimi*) often means "to stand," but is sometimes understood in a figurative sense - such as to set or to place, as in Matthew 4:5 and 18:2. The phrase **standing in the midst** doesn't demand that the woman was actually standing upon her feet.

ii. Trench says of a later use of *hestimi* in John 18:18 and 18:25: "Luke is quite definite that they and Peter were *sitting*: so too Matthew as to Peter. John seems to speak of them and Peter as *standing*: but these words used by John are so frequently idiomatic to mean merely 'to be stationary,' 'to continue,' 'to be there,' 'to be,' exactly like the Italian *stare*, that the *standing* cannot be pressed -- no more here than *e.g.* in the other nineteen places where they occur in John's gospel." (Trench)

6. (10-11) Jesus challenges the woman to sin no more.

When Jesus had raised Himself up and saw no one but the woman, He said to her, "Woman, where are those accusers of yours? Has no one condemned you?" She said, "No one, Lord." And Jesus said to her, "Neither do I condemn you; go and sin no more."

a. **When Jesus had raised Himself up and saw no one but the woman**: The accusers left as Jesus was bowed down to the ground, writing in the dirt.

b. **Where are those accusers of yours? Has no one condemned you?** With her accusers gone, there was no one left to **condemn** the woman, and Jesus Himself did not **condemn** her.

c. **She said, "No one, Lord"**: The woman - guilty of sin, and a great sin - knew the goodness of having no condemnation. She passed from sin and a death sentence to forgiveness and life.

d. **Neither do I condemn you**: In a sense, *Jesus took her guilt upon Himself,* especially as He so demonstrably stooped down. He alone was *without sin among* them. Knowing all things, He had the right to cast the first stone - but He did not. The woman found refuge in connection to Jesus.

> i. "They knew the thrill of exercising power to condemn; Jesus knew the thrill of exercising the power to forgive." (Barclay)

> ii. In a sense, Jesus here modeled the great truth of Romans 8:1: That there is no condemnation for those who are in Christ Jesus.

e. **Go and sin no more**: Jesus sent her away with a call to stop her sin, and to *continue* stopped in regard to that sin. He sent her away without ever approving of or accepting her sin.

> i. "The form of the command implies a ceasing to commit an action already started: 'Stop your sinful habit'. And the 'no more' points to the thought of no return." (Morris)

> ii. Jesus did several things with these powerful words.

> - He recognized that what the woman had done was **sin**, because He told her to *stop* sinning.

> - He told her to repent, and to not continue her sin.

> - He gave her hope that her life could go on in freedom from sexual sin.

> - He gave her a word of hope to speak against the shame that would later likely threaten to overwhelm her life.

> iii. The woman needed hope because the consequences of her sin would be severe enough. After this she would likely be shunned by her community, and rejected by her husband, perhaps even divorced (assuming she was married or betrothed).

B. The Light of the World answers opposition at the temple.

1. (12) Jesus, the light of the world.

Then Jesus spoke to them again, saying, "I am the light of the world. He who follows Me shall not walk in darkness, but have the light of life."

a. **Jesus spoke to them again**: If we take the arrangement of the Gospel of John as it is in the common text, the incident of the woman caught in adultery interrupted Jesus as He taught at the temple courts in the days immediately following the Feast of Tabernacles. Now, He resumed His teaching.

b. **I am the light of the world**: Light was an important symbol in the Feast of Tabernacles. During the feast, many emblems and ceremonies remembered the pillar of fire that gave light to Israel during the Exodus. Now, Jesus took this important symbol and simply applied it to Himself: **I am the light of the world**.

> i. Barclay and several others connects the **light of the world** sayings with a ceremony associated with the Feast of Tabernacles known as *The Illumination of the Temple*. "It was the custom during the first night, if not during every night, of the feast of tabernacles, to light up two large golden chandeliers in the court of the women, the light of which illuminated all Jerusalem. All that nigh they held a festal dance by the light." (Alford)

> ii. This was a strong and eloquent contrast to the darkness of those opposing Jesus, those who just brought to Him the woman caught in adultery.

> iii. "'I am' is emphatic. It is the very style of deity which we have seen employed before in this Gospel." (Morris)

c. **He who follows Me shall not walk in darkness**: Jesus, being the **light of the world**, brings light to those who follow Him. When we follow Him, we stay in the light and do not **walk in darkness**.

> i. **He who follows Me**: "If a man could travel so fast as always to follow the sun, of course he would always be in the light. If the day should ever come when the speed of the railway shall be equal to the speed of the world's motion, then a man may so live as to never lose the light. Now he that follows Christ shall never walk in darkness." (Spurgeon)

> ii. The Hebrew Scriptures often spoke of God's Word as light.

> > • *Your word is a lamp to my feet and a light to my path* (Psalm 119:105).

> > • *Oh, send out Your light and Your truth! Let them lead me* (Psalm 43:3).

> iii. Since Jesus is the *Word* (John 1:1), it makes perfect sense that He is also the **light**.

2. (13-16) The first witness to Jesus: Jesus Himself.

The Pharisees therefore said to Him, "You bear witness of Yourself; Your witness is not true." Jesus answered and said to them, "Even if I bear witness of Myself, My witness is true, for I know where I came from and where I am going; but you do not know where I come from and where I am going. You judge according to the flesh; I judge no one. And yet if I do judge, My judgment is true; for I am not alone, but I *am* with the Father who sent Me.

a. **You bear witness of Yourself; Your witness is not true**: Jesus just proclaimed that He was the light of the world, but the Pharisees couldn't see it. They couldn't see His light, but it was because they were blind, not because the light of Jesus failed to shine.

i. A seeing man doesn't need someone to *prove* the light; he simply sees it. "Light establishes its claim. It does so, not by arguments, but by shining. Light must always be accepted for itself, and that notwithstanding the objections of the blind." (Morris)

ii. The Pharisees couldn't prove that Jesus was not the Messiah that He claimed to be. They hoped to change the argument, saying that Jesus couldn't *prove* Himself to be Messiah and God, that He didn't have the witnesses to prove the claim.

iii. If they couldn't kill Jesus the witness, they hoped to intimidate Him. If they couldn't intimidate Him, they hoped to show that He was an unreliable, untrustworthy witness.

b. **Even if I bear witness of Myself, My witness is true**: Jesus would agree that under normal circumstances, a man's testimony regarding Himself could not be established as true. Nevertheless, Jesus pointed out the He was qualified to give testimony about Himself.

i. Jesus can testify about Himself because He (and not they) had a view of eternity: **I know where I came from and where I am going**.

ii. Jesus can testify about Himself because He (and not they) judged righteously: **You judge according to the flesh; I judge no one**. "They had constituted themselves His judges, and the decided against Him, because 'according to the flesh' He was born in Galilee." (Dods)

iii. Jesus can testify about Himself because His testimony was fully supported by God the Father: **My judgment is true; for I am not alone, but I am with the Father who sent Me**.

iv. "He *must* give witness about Himself: no one else is qualified to give witness about His nature and about His essential work." (Trench)

c. **I am with the Father who sent Me**: Though the religious leaders protested, Jesus was absolutely settled and secure in His identity, despite all the voices that told Him otherwise. This place of being settled and secure in one's identity is a wonderful pattern for believers today.

3. (17-18) The second witness to Jesus: God the Father.

It is also written in your law that the testimony of two men is true. I am One who bears witness of Myself, and the Father who sent Me bears witness of Me."

a. **It is also written in your law that the testimony of two men is true**: Jesus believed that His testimony was enough. Yet to accommodate them, He also brought another testimony.

i. "If the Jews then demand *two* witnesses in order to satisfy the Jewish law of evidence, those two witness exist; they are Jesus and His Father." (Tasker)

b. **I am One who bears witness of Myself, and the Father who sent Me bears witness of Me**: God the Father also testified that Jesus was the Messiah, the Son of God and God the Son.

i. "Our Lord speaks here exactly in the character of an ambassador. Such a person does not bring a *second* with him to vouch his truth; his *credentials* from his king ascertain his character: he represents the king's person. So our Lord represents the Father as bearing witness with him." (Clarke)

4. (19-20) Jesus knows His Father; the Pharisees did not.

Then they said to Him, "Where is Your Father?" Jesus answered, "You know neither Me nor My Father. If you had known Me, you would have known My Father also." These words Jesus spoke in the treasury, as He taught in the temple; and no one laid hands on Him, for His hour had not yet come.

a. **Where is Your father?** The Pharisees probably intended this as a deeply cutting insult to Jesus. They referred to the controversy around His virgin birth, and to the rumors that it was not a miraculous conception, but an impure one.

i. "In the East, to question a man's paternity is definite slur on his legitimacy." (Tenney)

b. **You know neither Me nor My Father**: In referring to Jesus' parentage, the Pharisees thought they had some damaging or scandalous information on Him. They must have thought, "Watch how He reacts when we reveal what we know about Him." In response, Jesus made it clear that they did not know anything about Him or His Father.

i. "They prided themselves on their knowledge of their God. Jesus tells them that they have no knowledge of Him at all." (Morris)

c. **These words He spoke in the treasury**: John reminds us that Jesus had this debate with His opponents in the most public place in Jerusalem - right on the temple mount. Still, **no one laid hands on Him, for His hour had not yet come**.

5. (21-22) Jesus tells of His coming departure; the religious leaders insult Him.

Then Jesus said to them again, "I am going away, and you will seek Me, and will die in your sin. Where I go you cannot come." So the Jews said, "Will He kill Himself, because He says, 'Where I go you cannot come'?"

a. **I am going away... Where I go you cannot come**: Jesus knew He was going to heaven. Because of their hatred against Him, Jesus could say that His accusers were not going to heaven. Where He was going, they could not follow.

i. If we follow Jesus on earth, we will follow Him to heaven. If we express no desire to follow Him on earth, what would make us think we would follow Him to heaven?

b. **Will He kill Himself?** This was another insult against Jesus. The Jews of Jesus' time taught that the lowest levels of Hades were for those who committed suicide. Here the Pharisees tried to twist Jesus' words to imply that He will commit suicide and therefore be damned.

i. "According to Jewish thought, the depths of hell were reserved for those who took their own lives." (Barclay)

6. (23-24) Two destinies: Jesus will go to glory; on their present course they will die in their sins.

And He said to them, "You are from beneath; I am from above. You are of this world; I am not of this world. Therefore I said to you that you will die in your sins; for if you do not believe that I am *He,* you will die in your sins."

a. **You are from beneath; I am from above. You are of this world; I am not of this world**: The Pharisees opposing Jesus implied that He would go to hell as a suicide (according to their teaching). Jesus answered that they did have different destinies, just not as they thought.

b. **If you do not believe that I am, you will die in your sins**: These men were religious leaders, yet lived in darkness that filled their mind and their deeds. The darkness remained because they rejected (**do not believe**) the light. Jesus gave them a serious warning; the day of grace would not last forever. Death would make their sinful darkness permanent.

i. People are born in sin (Psalm 51:5), and if we hold on to our sin, and do not deal with it, we will die in our sins. Since all sin must be dealt with, those who die in their sins will have to pay for their sins in hell. But if we have our sins dealt with now, on this side of death, by trusting in whom Jesus is and what He did to save us, we can avoid dying in our sins.

ii. "The plural 'sins' is used in verse 24, as against the singular 'sin' in verse 21; if the singular expresses the root sin of unbelief, the plural expresses those particular attitudes, words and actions which make up its fruit." (Bruce)

c. **If you do not believe that I am He, you will die in your sins**: Jesus called them to **believe that I am**. The "**He**" is rightly in italics and added by the translators. The title "**I am**" is a claim to deity, and if the Pharisees will be saved from dying in their sins, they must believe in Jesus and in who He really is - God the Son.

i. "We should probably understand it along the lines of the similar expression in LXX, which is the style of deity …The same Greek expression occurs in 6:20, 18:6, neither of which is difficult to understand." (Morris)

7. (25-27) Jesus tells of His dependence on God the Father for all He said.

Then they said to Him, "Who are You?" And Jesus said to them, "Just what I have been saying to you from the beginning. I have many things to say and to judge concerning you, but He who sent Me is true; and I speak to the world those things which I heard from Him." They did not understand that He spoke to them of the Father.

a. **Who are You?** This is a wonderful question to ask with a sincere heart. Yet this question of the Pharisees came from a combination of willful confusion and contempt. Though Jesus told them again and again who He was, they continued to ask, always hoping for an answer they could use to trap and condemn Him.

i. Some questions aren't used to discover the truth; they are used to resist the truth and justify a refusal to believe. The religious leaders asked many hostile questions:

- *Where is Your Father?* (John 8:19)
- *Will He kill Himself?* (John 8:22)
- *Who are You?* (John 8:25)

ii. "The question 'Who are you, anyway?' shows the Pharisees' exasperation with Jesus' hints and seeming extravagant claims." (Tenney)

b. **Just what I have been saying to you from the beginning**: Jesus didn't have a new answer for them. He would repeat the truths and themes He spoke to them many times before.

i. **I have many things to say and to judge concerning you**: "I could speedily expose all your iniquities-your pride and ambition, your hypocrisy and irreligion, your hatred to the light, and your malice against the truth, together with the present obstinate unbelief of your hearts, and show that these are the reasons why I say you will die in your sins." (Clarke)

c. **I speak to the world those things which I heard from Him**: Jesus emphasized the point again, that His words were from God the Father. Therefore if the Pharisees opposed Jesus, they really opposed God the Father.

8. (28-30) Jesus tells of His dependence on God the Father for all He does.

Then Jesus said to them, "When you lift up the Son of Man, then you will know that I am *He,* and *that* I do nothing of Myself; but as My Father taught Me, I speak these things. And He who sent Me is with Me. The Father has not left Me alone, for I always do those things that please Him." As He spoke these words, many believed in Him.

c. **When you lift up the Son of Man**: The "lifting up" Jesus described had nothing to do with "exalting" Jesus in ways we normally think. It wasn't about getting Him applause and celebrity. Instead, it had to do with "lifting up" Jesus off the ground on a cross. When Jesus was crucified, they would see the perfect obedience of the Son to the Father. They would see that truly, **I do nothing of Myself**.

i. "His 'lifting up' would be his vindication: then it would be manifest that he had acted and spoken throughout by the Father's authority." (Bruce)

b. **The Father has not left Me alone**: The unity between the Father and the Son continued and will continue. Despite the accusations of the Pharisees, Jesus was as close to His Father as ever.

c. **I always to the things that please Him**: Jesus was bold enough to say these words to His adversaries - essentially challenging His enemies to find some thing the He did or does that is not pleasing to God the Father. In response, *His enemies were silent*. This was a remarkable testimony to the sinlessness of Jesus.

i. **I always do those things that please Him**: It is easy to *say*, "I always do the will of the Father" when you only debate theological points. It is another thing entirely to "always do the will of the Father" when it means going to the cross. The cross would prove the perfect obedience of Jesus.

d. **As He spoke these words, many believed in Him**: When the Pharisees heard Jesus speak they became more opposed to Him. Yet there were **many** who heard the same words and **believed in Him**. They believed despite the evident opposition of the religious leaders.

i. Jesus' message of His unity with the Father was so well received by some because His life was consistent with the message. Unlike the Pharisees, one could see that Jesus was close to God. The Pharisees cultivated an image of intimacy with God, but it was evident they were not actually close to God.

9. (31-32) Jesus offers discipleship and freedom to those believing in Him.

Then Jesus said to those Jews who believed Him, "If you abide in My word, you are My disciples indeed. And you shall know the truth, and the truth shall make you free."

a. **Jesus said to those Jews who believed Him**: The previous verse tells us that *many believed in Him* (John 8:30). Jesus spoke to those who had that beginning of belief, telling them what they needed to continue in belief.

i. "This section of the discourse is addressed to those who believe, and yet do not believe. Clearly they were inclined to think that what Jesus said was true. But they were not prepared to yield Him the far-reaching allegiance that real trust in Him implies. This is a most dangerous spiritual state." (Morris)

b. **If you abide in My word, you are My disciples indeed**: If we will be Jesus' disciples, we *must* abide in His word. There is no other way. To be a follower of Jesus - the Word made flesh - is to **abide** (to live in, to dwell in, to make your home in) His **word**.

i. **If you abide in My word**: "To those who have just been described as believing on Him Jesus went on to say, 'If you' - emphasized in distinction from those who had not believed - 'abide in my word' - not content with making the first step towards faith and obedience - 'then' - but not till then - 'are ye really my disciples.'" (Dods)

ii. Tasker described what it means to **abide** in His **word**: "Welcoming it, being at home with it, and living with it so continuously that it becomes part of the believer's life, a permanent influence and stimulus in every fresh advance in goodness and holiness." (Tasker)

iii. This too is another statement reflecting the unity between the Father and the Son. Jesus called men to abide in *His* word. In the mouth of anyone other than Jesus, these words would be absurd.

iv. "Our treatment of our Lord's words discriminates us: He that hath my commandments, and keepeth them, is he that loveth Me." (Meyer)

c. **You shall know the truth, and the truth shall make you free**: This is the result of abiding in the word of Jesus. We prove ourselves to be His disciples and we **know the truth**, and God works His freedom in our life through His **truth**. The freedom Jesus spoke of doesn't come from just an academic pursuit of truth in general; but from abiding in His word and being His disciple.

i. There is nothing like the freedom we can have in Jesus. No money can buy it, no status can obtain it, no works can earn it, and nothing can match it. It is tragic that not every Christian experiences this freedom, which can never be found except by abiding in God's word and being Jesus' disciple.

10. (33-36) Jesus answers their protest that they are already free.

They answered Him, "We are Abraham's descendants, and have never been in bondage to anyone. How *can* you say, 'You will be made free'?" Jesus answered them, "Most assuredly, I say to you, whoever commits sin is a slave of sin. And a slave does not abide in the house forever, *but* a son abides forever. Therefore if the Son makes you free, you shall be free indeed."

a. **We are Abraham's descendants, and have never been in bondage to anyone**: The reaction of the religious leaders wasn't, "That's wonderful! Tell us more about what it means to be free by trusting in Your word." Instead they reacted, *we don't need this. We're good.*

i. This was a remarkable and unthinking statement. They Jewish people had been in bondage under Egypt and the Philistines; under Babylon, Persia, Syria, and Rome. "Was there not a Roman garrison looking down from the castle into the very Temple courts where this boastful falsehood was uttered?" (Maclaren)

ii. Yet, many Jewish people of that time had a strong sense of their own independence. "Josephus writes of the followers of Judas in Galilee who led a famous revolt against the Romans: 'They have an inviolable attachment to liberty, and they say that God is to be their only Ruler and Lord' (Josephus, *Antiquities of the Jews*, 18:1,6)." (Barclay)

iii. "The power of self-deception in the unconverted man is infinite." (Ryle)

b. **Whoever commits sin is a slave of sin**: **Sin** in this passage is in a verb tense indicating a habitual, continual action. The person in habitual sin is a slave of sin.

i. "The participial construction 'everyone who sins' is in the present tense, which implies a continual habit of sinning rather than an occasional lapse." (Tenney)

ii. "There is another kind of slavery than social or economic slavery. Sin is a slave-master, and it is possible even for people who think of themselves as free to be enslaved in sin." (Bruce)

iii. "It is far commoner for man never to have done some given evil, never to have got drunk, never to have stolen, or the like, than to have done it only once." (Maclaren)

iv. "We should not minimize the force of 'bondservant'. It does not mean a person who is paid wages and who has a considerable area of freedom. It means a slave." (Morris)

c. **A slave does not abide in the house forever, but a son abides forever**: Slavery to sin is the worst kind of slavery, because there is no escape from our self. A Son must set us free, and the Son of God sets us free and brings us into the household of God.

i. "The slave has no permanent footing in the house; he may be dismissed or sold." (Dods)

d. **If the Son makes you free, you shall be free indeed**: If we are set free from our slavery to sin - set free by a Son, and set free by abiding in Jesus' word and being His disciple - then we are **free indeed**, having a true freedom that contrasts to the "freedom" the Pharisees blindly claimed in John 8:33.

i. **The Son makes you free**: "So the slave of sin cannot by himself change his status. He cannot convert himself, nor can he be converted by any fellow-sinner... The liberator from our bondage must come from outside the ranks of enslaved humanity." (Tasker)

ii. "If we are slaves of Sin, then we may be transferred from its household and brought into our true home in our Father's house. Here, then, is the blessed hope for us all." (Maclaren)

iii. An 82 year-old Christian woman from Hong Kong told of her life in China, but still used much of the vocabulary that the Communists used in describing their revolution - they called it "the liberation." She was asked, "When you were back in China, were you free to gather together with other Christians to worship?" "Oh no," she answered. "Since the liberation no one is permitted to gather together for Christian services." "But surely you were able to get together in small groups and discuss the Christian faith?" "No, we were not," the woman replied. "Since the liberation all such meeting are forbidden." "Were you free to read the Bible?" "Since the liberation, no one is free to read the Bible."

iv. The point is clear: freedom does not consist in the word "freedom," or in words, but in relationship to Jesus Christ, through abiding in His Word, and being His disciple.

11. (37-41a) They prove themselves to be unlike their father Abraham.

"I know that you are Abraham's descendants, but you seek to kill Me, because My word has no place in you. I speak what I have seen with My Father, and you do what you have seen with your father." They answered and said to Him, "Abraham is our father." Jesus said to them, "If you were Abraham's children, you would do the works of Abraham. But now you seek to kill Me, a Man who has told you the truth which I heard from God. Abraham did not do this. You do the deeds of your father."

a. **I know that you are Abraham's descendants**: Jesus would admit that they are **Abraham's descendants** in a genetic sense, but Abraham was not their **father** in a *spiritual* sense. When messengers from heaven came to Abraham, he received them (Genesis 18); but these genetic descendants of Abraham rejected and sought to **kill** the One sent from heaven.

i. "To cherish murderous intentions against someone who has imparted the truth of God to them is not the mark of the children of Abraham." (Bruce)

b. **Because My word has no place in you**: Their rejection of the word of Jesus and Jesus the Word proved that they were not like Abraham, and that they did not have the freedom that comes from abiding in His word.

i. Spurgeon considered several ways that God's word should have a **place** in the believer.

- The word of God ought to have an *inward place*.
- The word of God ought to have a *place of high honor*.
- The word of God ought to have a *place of trust*.
- The word of God ought to have a *place of rule*.
- The word of God ought to have a *place of love*.
- The word of God ought to have a *permanent place*.

c. **I speak what I have seen with My Father**: Jesus reminded them that what He did was consistent with His Father, and what they did was consistent with their father (**you do what you have seen with your father**). Jesus would soon clearly tell them who their father was.

d. **Abraham is our father**: The religious leaders protested that Abraham was their true father. This was true in a genetic sense, but not in a spiritual sense. Jesus agreed they were **descendants** (John 8:37) of Abraham, but not **children** of Abraham because they sought to kill Jesus, when Abraham embraced Him. They were doing **the deeds of** their **father**.

i. Jesus exposed the inconsistency in their life. They said they were children of Abraham, but didn't act like it at all. "If their origin could be wholly traced to Abraham, then their conduct would resemble his." (Dods)

ii. Jesus' point was important. Our spiritual parentage is what determines our nature and our destiny. If we are born again, and have God as our Father, it will show in our nature and destiny. But if our father is Satan or Adam, it will also show in our nature and destiny - just as it shows in these adversaries of Jesus.

12. (41b-43) The religious leaders again question the parentage of Jesus.

Then they said to Him, "We were not born of fornication; we have one Father—God." Jesus said to them, "If God were your Father, you would love Me, for I proceeded forth and came from God; nor have I come of Myself, but He sent Me. Why do you not understand My speech? Because you are not able to listen to My word."

a. **We were not born of fornication**: As previously in John 8:19, they again insulted the parentage of Jesus, calling Him an illegitimate child. The implication was, "*We* **were not born of fornication**, but we don't know about *You*, Jesus."

i. "While John does not speak directly of the virgin birth, there may be hints that he knew of it and that some of the people knew that there was a mystery surrounding Jesus' origin." (Tenney)

b. **If God were your Father, you would love Me**: Jesus again made the remarkable claim that He and His Father were and are so close in nature that if one truly lives as if God is their **Father**, they would also **love** Jesus. There is no room left for the person who says, "I love God but reject Jesus."

c. **For I proceeded forth and came from God**: Jesus here described His unity of nature and purpose and will with God the Father.

i. "**Am come** conveys the result of **proceeded forth**, which must be taken in its deeper theological meaning, of the proceeding forth of the Eternal Son from the essence of the Father." (Alford)

ii. **I proceeded forth and came from God**: "That points to His earthly life as being the permanent result of an initial act, which was voluntary and His own, and behind which stretched on an indefinite existence." (Maclaren)

iii. "So long as the Jews thought there was but One Person in the Godhead, it was impossible for them to believe aright in our Lord: hence His insistence to their theologians that He has a Father; that He is not The Father, but is The Son; that The Son, though He is not The Father, is for all that God." (Trench)

d. **Why do you not understand My speech? Because you are not able to listen to My word**: Jesus explained that the problem with their lack of understanding was rooted in their failure - even inability - to **listen** to His **word**. This reminds is that the ability to listen to His word is a gift that one should be grateful for.

i. "The impossibility was spiritual. Prejudices, jealousies, and antagonisms made the real Christ inaudible to them though His every syllable fell upon the ear." (Morrison)

13. (44-47) Jesus reveals the identity of their true father.

"You are of *your* father the devil, and the desires of your father you want to do. He was a murderer from the beginning, and *does not* stand in the truth, because there is no truth in him. When he speaks a lie, he speaks from his own *resources,* for he is a liar and the father of it. But because I tell the truth, you do not believe Me. Which of you convicts Me of sin? And if I tell the truth, why do you not believe Me? He who is of God hears God's words; therefore you do not hear, because you are not of God."

a. **You are of your father the devil, and the desires of your father you want to do**: The religious leaders brought up the issue of parentage by insulting Jesus in John 8:41. Jesus replied by explaining *their* spiritual parentage - they were the spiritual children of the devil. This was evident in that their desires matched the devil's desires: the desire to kill and deceive.

i. "This verse is one of the most decisive testimonies for the *objective personality* of the devil. It is quite impossible to suppose an accommodation to Jewish views, or a metaphorical form of speech, in so solemn and direct an assertion as this." (Alford)

ii. **He was a murderer from the beginning**: "Cyril and some others think it is the first murder, that of Abel, that is in view (1 John 3:15), but far more probably it is the introduction of death through the first sin." (Dods)

b. **When he speaks a lie, he speaks from his own resources**: Jesus gives us some insight into the character of Satan. The **lie** is core to the devil's character, and he is the deceiver most dangerous of all - the deceiver who has deceived himself.

c. **But because I tell you the truth, you do not believe Me**: They rejected Jesus because He told them truth they did not want to hear. It was not because He spoke lies.

d. **Which of you convicts Me of sin?** Again, Jesus gave His enemies - who hated Him so badly they wanted to kill Him - an opportunity to declare some sin in Him - and they could not. This was another remarkable testimony to the sinlessness of Jesus Christ.

i. "We are often so interested in the fact that they found no charge to ay that we overlook that other fact that the really striking thing is the making of the challenge. It betokens a clear and serene conscience. Only one who was in the closest and most intimate communion with the Father could have spoken such words." (Morris)

e. **You do not hear, because you are not of God**: Jesus pressed home the point of spiritual parentage, which was evident by their actions - notably their rejection of Jesus and His word.

14. (48-50) Jesus answers the charge that He is demon possessed.

Then the Jews answered and said to Him, "Do we not say rightly that You are a Samaritan and have a demon?" Jesus answered, "I do not have a demon; but I honor My Father, and you dishonor Me. And I do not seek My *own* glory; there is One who seeks and judges."

a. **Do we not say rightly that You are a Samaritan and have a demon?** The enemies of Jesus were frustrated and exasperated. They were unable to make Jesus look bad, and even more had believed on Him (John 8:30). So they launched their last attack: name-calling.

- **You are a Samaritan** (one of the most despised races to the Jews).
- **And have a demon** (saying that Jesus was demon possessed).

b. **I do not have a demon; but I honor My Father**: Jesus' desire to honor God and His personal humility disproved any charge of demonic possession. Since those who have Satan as their spiritual parent will have some of the characteristics of Satan, they will have an evident pride and self-seeking - things that were and are absent in Jesus.

> i. "No man can be said to have a devil who honors God; for the evil spirit from the beginning has been the enemy of all that glorifies the Father." (Spurgeon)

15. (51-53) The great promise to those who accept Jesus and keep His word.

"Most assuredly, I say to you, if anyone keeps My word he shall never see death." Then the Jews said to Him, "Now we know that You have a demon! Abraham is dead, and the prophets; and You say, 'If anyone keeps My word he shall never taste death.' Are You greater than our father Abraham, who is dead? And the prophets are dead. Whom do You make Yourself out to be?"

> a. **If anyone keeps My word he shall never see death**: This is another remarkable claim that only makes sense if Jesus is God, and is one with God the Father. Jesus promises eternal life to those who keep *His* word.

> > i. "**To keep my word**, as, '*to continue in my word*,' verse 31, is not only outward obedience, but the endurance in, and obedience of faith." (Alford)

> > ii. **Never see death**: "*Our face is turned away from death*...The Greek is not fully interpreted by the word 'see': it is an intenser word. According to Westcott, the sight here mentioned is that of 'a long, steady, exhaustive vision, whereby we become slowly acquainted with the nature of the object to which it is directed.'...While unforgiven, I cannot help gazing upon it, and foreseeing it as my doom. When the gospel of the Lord Jesus comes to my soul, and I keep his saying by faith, I am turned completely round. My back is upon death, and my face is towards life eternal." (Spurgeon)

> b. **Now we know that You have a demon! Abraham is dead**: The great claim of Jesus delighted the religious leaders; they believed they finally caught Him in a clearly blasphemous claim. They denied the claim Jesus made to grant eternal life.

> > i. We note that the religious leaders slightly twisted the words of Jesus. He said that the one who keeps His word would never stare death face to face; they claimed He said that this one would never **taste death**. The believer will indeed taste death, but is not terrorized by this defeated foe.

> c. **Are you greater than our father Abraham**: They put the question plainly to Jesus. Hoping Jesus would be further caught in a trap, they asked **"Whom do You make Yourself out to be?"**

16. (54-55) The claim of Jesus to know God contrasted with the claim of the religious leaders.

Jesus answered, "If I honor Myself, My honor is nothing. It is My Father who honors Me, of whom you say that He is your God. Yet you have not known Him, but I know Him. And if I say, 'I do not know Him,' I shall be a liar like you; but I do know Him and keep His word."

a. **If I honor Myself, My honor is nothing**: Before Jesus answered their question in John 8:53 He came back to the matter of spiritual parentage. Jesus was secure in knowing that God was His Father and **it is My Father who honors Me**.

i. "It is not difficult to honour oneself; it is easy enough - in fact, fatally easy - to bask in the sunshine of one's own approval." (Barclay)

b. **Yet you have not known Him, but I know Him**: The religious leaders *claimed* that the Father in heaven was their **God**, but it was not a true claim. In truth, they did not know God, but Jesus did.

c. **I do know Him and keep His word**: Jesus could not lie and deny His true knowledge of God the Father, demonstrated by a life of obedience to God's **word**.

17. (56-59) Jesus makes the great declaration, I AM.

"Your father Abraham rejoiced to see My day, and he saw *it* and was glad." Then the Jews said to Him, "You are not yet fifty years old, and have You seen Abraham?" Jesus said to them, "Most assuredly, I say to you, before Abraham was, I AM." Then they took up stones to throw at Him; but Jesus hid Himself and went out of the temple, going through the midst of them, and so passed by.

a. **Your father Abraham rejoiced to see My day, and he saw it and was glad**: Jesus made another remarkable claim, answering their questions in John 8:53. Jesus claimed that not only was He greater than Abraham, but Abraham himself also acknowledged this.

i. "But when did he 'exult' to see the day of Christ? Perhaps when he said to Isaac on their way to the place of sacrifice, 'God will provide himself with a lamb for the burnt-offering' (Genesis 22:8)." (Bruce)

ii. "It is interesting also that the Hebrew expression in Genesis 24:1, which stated that Abraham 'went into the days' (an expression translated in our Bible 'was well-stricken in age') was taken by some Rabbis to mean that he saw into the distant future." (Tasker)

b. **You are not yet fifty years old, and have You seen Abraham?** The remarkable statement that Abraham saw and acknowledged the greatness of Jesus was more than they could understand. They asked, "How could you know Abraham rejoiced in You? Were You there?"

i. "Perhaps the tensions of his life had aged him prematurely, yet he was obviously less than fifty years of age." (Tenney)

ii. "'Fifty years' may be used as a round number, sufficiently exact for their purpose and with no intention to determine the age of Jesus." (Dods)

iii. "Why fifty? That was the age at which the Levites retired from their service (Numbers 4:3). The Jews were saying to Jesus: 'You are a young man, still in the prime of life, not even old enough to retire from service. How can you possibly have seen Abraham?'" (Barclay)

c. **Before Abraham was, I AM**: With this dramatic phrase Jesus told them that He was the eternal God, existing not only during the time of Abraham but before unto eternity past. Jesus claimed to be the great **I AM**, the voice of the covenant God of Israel revealed at the burning bush (Exodus 3:13-14).

i. **I AM**: This is the third time in this chapter Jesus uses the phrase **I AM** (John 8:24, 8:28), and here in John 8:58. The ancient Greek phrase is *ego emi*, which was the same term used in the Greek translation of the Old Testament in Jesus' day to describe the Voice from the burning bush. "All the previous lightning flashes pale into significance before the blaze of this passage." (Barclay)

ii. In using the phrase **I AM** (John 8:24, 8:58, 13:19) Jesus used a clear divine title belonging to Yahweh alone (Exodus 3:13-14, Deuteronomy 32:39, Isaiah 43:10) and was interpreted as such by Jesus' listeners (John 8:58-59). "I AM was recognized by the Jews as a title of deity." (Tenney)

iii. "Before Abraham came into existence I am, eternally existent... No stronger affirmation of pre-existence occurs." (Dods)

iv. "If Jesus' claim was not well founded, then his words were openly blasphemous: he was using language that only God could use." (Bruce)

d. **Then they took up stones to throw at Him**: This demonstrates that the religious leaders understood perfectly what Jesus meant. He claimed to be eternal God, and they regarded that as blasphemy. They felt He was worthy of death and intended to carry it out at the moment.

i. "Their passions were aroused. They were incensed. So they took the law into their own hands." (Morris)

ii. "The stones they picked up they would have found in the Court of the Gentiles: for the Temple (viz. its courts) was still building." (Trench)

iii. "A stoning in the temple is mentioned by Josephus, *Antiquities*, 17.9,3." (Dods)

e. **Jesus hid Himself and went out of the temple, going through the midst of them**: They *wanted* to kill Jesus but could not because *His hour had not yet come* (John 7:30).

i. "There does not appear to be any *miraculous* escape intended here, although certainly the assumption of one is natural under the circumstances." (Alford)

ii. Adam Clarke had an imaginative perspective on the escape of Jesus: "In all probability he rendered himself invisible-though some will have it that he conveyed himself away from those Jews who were his enemies, by mixing himself with the many who believed on him." (Clarke)

John 9 - Jesus Gives Sight to A Man Born Blind

A. The man is healed.

1. (1-2) The disciples ask a question.

Now as *Jesus* passed by, He saw a man who was blind from birth. And His disciples asked Him, saying, "Rabbi, who sinned, this man or his parents, that he was born blind?"

a. **As Jesus passed by**: The previous chapter ending as Jesus *passed by* those who wanted to stone Him, considering Jesus guilty of blasphemy. John continues the account, noting now Jesus **passed by** a man **who was blind from birth**.

i. The sense of the flow of the text is that Jesus was not shaken or disturbed by the almost deadly confrontation with the religious leaders that just happened. "We find Him calm and self-possessed, acting with a profound disregard of His enemies and their hatred." (Boice)

ii. Jesus was often reviled, but never ruffled. "One of the things worthy to be noticed in our Lord's character is his wonderful quiet of spirit, especially his marvelous calmness in the presence of those who misjudged, and insulted, and slandered him." (Spurgeon)

iii. "The blind man was sitting begging (John 9:8), possibly proclaiming the fact of his having been so born; for otherwise the disciples could hardly have asked the following question." (Alford)

b. **Rabbi, who sinned, this man or his parents, that he was born blind?** The disciples regarded this man as an unsolved riddle. They showed no interest in *helping* the man, but in discussing the cause for his condition.

i. Jesus will soon show a different way. He won't dwell on the theological puzzle, but on actually helping the man. "It is ours, not to speculate, but to perform acts of mercy and love, according to the tenor of the gospel. Let us then be less inquisitive and more practical,

173

less for cracking doctrinal nuts, and more for bringing forth the bread of life to the starving multitudes." (Spurgeon)

ii. We often suspect that where there is a more than ordinary sufferer, there is a more than ordinary sinner. The disciples believed this so much so that they wondered if this man had actually sinned before he was born, causing his blind condition. "In their thinking about divine retribution they had not advanced far beyond the position of Job's friends." (Bruce)

iii. "It was widely held that suffering, and especially such a disaster as blindness, was due to sin. The general principle was laid down by Rabbi Ammi: 'There is no death without sin, and there is no suffering without iniquity.'" (Morris)

iv. Dods suggested five possible reasons behind their question.

- Some of the Jews of that time believed in the pre-existence of souls, and the possibility that those pre-existent souls could sin.

- Some of the Jews at that time believed in some kind of reincarnation, and perhaps the man sinned in a previous existence.

- Some of the Jews at that time believed that a baby might sin in the womb.

- They thought the punishment was for a sin the man would later commit.

- They were so bewildered that they threw out a wild possibility without thinking it through.

2. (3-5) Jesus responds to the question, without answering it.

Jesus answered, "Neither this man nor his parents sinned, but that the works of God should be revealed in him. I must work the works of Him who sent Me while it is day; *the* night is coming when no one can work. As long as I am in the world, I am the light of the world."

a. **Neither this man nor his parents sinned**: First, Jesus said that the man's blindness - essentially a birth defect - was not caused by some specific sin on the part of the **man** or **his parents**.

i. Birth defects and other such tragedies are sometimes due to sinful behavior of the parents. Yet far more often - and in the case Jesus spoke of here - it is due simply to sin and our fallen condition in general, not due to any specific sin. The sin of Adam set the principle of death and its associated destruction in the world and we have had to deal with it ever since.

b. **But that the works of God should be revealed in him**: Speaking to this man's situation, Jesus told them that even his blindness was in the plan of God so that **the works of God should be revealed in him**.

i. Think of all the times the little blind boy asked his mother, "Why am I blind?" Perhaps she never felt she had a good answer. Jesus explained, *it is because God wants to work in and through even this*. Jesus pointed the question away from *why* and on to the idea, *what can God do in this?*

ii. In this man's case the specific work of God would soon be revealed: to heal him of his blindness. God may reveal His works in other lives other ways, such as joy and endurance in the midst of the difficulty.

iii. "In the economy of God's Providence, his suffering had its place and aim, and this was to bring out the **works of God** in his being healed by the Redeemer." (Alford)

iv. "Evil furthers the work of God in the world. It is in conquering and abolishing evil that He is manifested. The question for us is not where suffering has come from, but what are we to do with it." (Dods)

v. "This does not mean that God deliberately caused the child to be born blind in order that, after many years, his glory should be displayed in the removal of the blindness; to think so would again be aspersion on the character of God. It does mean that God overruled the disaster of the child's blindness so that, when the child grew to manhood, he might, by the recovering of his sight, see the glory of God in the face of Christ, and others, seeing the work of God, might turn to the true Light of the World." (Bruce)

vi. "We must suppose that every sufferer will in the long run be made aware of his share in promoting that advance; though to-day he suffer blindly, little conscious of his privilege." (Trench)

c. **I must work the works of Him who sent Me while it is day**: Instead of focusing on the man as a theology problem, Jesus saw him as an opportunity to **work the works** of God. Jesus sensed an *urgency* to do this while it was still **day** - the time of His earthly ministry.

i. **I must work** is a marvelous statement of Jesus. The Worker is "a well-earned title to the Lord Jesus Christ. He is the worker, the chief worker, and the example to all workers." (Spurgeon)

ii. "He worked under the limitations of mortality, and recognized in the brevity of life another call to eager and continuous service." (Maclaren)

iii. "Whenever you see a man in sorrow and trouble, the way to look at it is, not to blame him and inquire how he came there, but to say, 'Here is an opening for God's almighty love. Here is an occasion for the display of the grace and goodness of the Lord.'" (Spurgeon)

d. **The night is coming when no one can work**: Jesus understood that opportunities for service and doing good don't last forever. Jesus knew that healing this man on the Sabbath would bring greater opposition from the religious leaders who already wanted to silence and kill Him. Yet His compassion for the man drove Him to do it anyway.

i. "Our Lord as a man here on earth had a day. It was only a day-a short period, and not very long; he could not make it longer, for it was settled by the great Lord." (Spurgeon)

3. (6-7) The man is healed.

When He had said these things, He spat on the ground and made clay with the saliva; and He anointed the eyes of the blind man with the clay. And He said to him, "Go, wash in the pool of Siloam" (which is translated, Sent). So he went and washed, and came back seeing.

a. **He spat on the ground and made clay with the saliva**: Jesus used what was undoubtedly one of His more unusual methods leading to a miracle. We can suppose that Jesus wanted to emphasize at least two things.

- Just as God used the dust of the ground and clay to do a work of creation in Genesis, so Jesus did a work of creation with dust and clay for this man.

- Jesus found it important to change His methods of healing so one could never make a formula of the methods. The power was in God, not in a method.

    i. "The emphasis of John seems to be on compassion rather than creation. The touch of a friendly hand would be reassuring. The weight of the clay would serve as an indicator to the blind man that something had been done to him, and it would be an inducement to obey Jesus' command." (Tenney)

    ii. "In His ministry to the souls of men Jesus adopted no stereotyped approach. He dealt with each man as his particular need required." (Morris)

    iii. Several commentators note that what seems so strange to us - using saliva as a medicine upon the eyes - was not so strange in the ancient world.

- "Spittle, and especially the spittle of some distinguished persons, was believed to possess certain curative qualities." (Barclay)

- "The virtue of the *fasting* saliva, in the cases of disorders of the eye, was well known to antiquity." (Alford)

iv. Mark recorded two other healings that Jesus performed with the use of His saliva (Mark 7:33 and 8:23).

b. **Go, wash in the pool of Siloam**: In this miracle, Jesus took all the initiative. Jesus came to the blind man; the blind man did not come to Him. Even so, He expected the blind man to respond with faith-filled action. The healing would not happen unless the man responded with those faith-filled, obedient actions.

i. Not many people would appreciate having mud made with spit rubbed in their eyes. Some would look at how Jesus did this miracle and object, saying that it was *offensive, inadequate,* or even *harmful* to rub mud made with spit in a man's eyes.

- In the same way, some feel that the gospel is *offensive*. It is true that it offends man's pride and human wisdom, but *it pleased God through the foolishness of the message preached to save those who believe.* (1 Corinthians 1:21)

- In the same way, some feel that the gospel is *inadequate*. But have all the psychiatric and political and social programs in the world done more good that the life-changing gospel of Jesus Christ?

- In the same way, some feel that the gospel is *harmful,* that the free offer of grace in Jesus will cause people to sin that grace may abound. But the gospel changes our life for the good and the pure, not unto wickedness.

ii. The water for the **pool of Siloam** came through Hezekiah's tunnel, a remarkable engineering feat built in Old Testament times. "It was called *Siloam,* which, it was said, meant *sent,* because the water in it had been *sent* through the conduit into the city." (Barclay)

iii. "It was from the Siloam stream that was drawn the water which was poured over the great altar at the Feast of Tabernacles just past, which pouring out was regarded by the Rabbis (and is still) as typical of the pouring out of The Spirit in the 'latter days'." (Trench)

iv. **Which is translated, Sent**: "Again and again John refers to Jesus as having been 'sent' by the Father. So now blindness is removed with reference to and with the aid of the 'sent'." (Morris)

c. **So he went and washed**: This took faith, even when Jesus did not even *promise* the blind man sight in the doing of this. It was surely implied; but the man acted on faith even in the implied promise of Jesus.

i. Still as a blind man he had to find his way down to pool of Siloam and down its steps to the pool itself. He likely could think of a dozen reasons why this was a fool's errand, but **he went and washed** in faith and obedience, because Jesus told him to (and because there was mud in his eyes).

d. **And came back seeing**: This is the first time in the Biblical record a person born blind was healed of their blindness. From Genesis to John, no prophet, priest, or apostle ever gave sight to eyes born blind.

i. Since healing blind eyes is the work of the Lord, Yahweh, Jehovah, it shows that Jesus is God: *The LORD opens the eyes of the blind.* (Psalm 146:8)

ii. Opening the eyes of the blind was prophesied to be a work of the Messiah: *The eyes of the blind shall be opened.* (Isaiah 35:5)

iii. **Came back seeing**: "The word rendered *received sight* is literally, **recovered sight**. Sight being natural to men, the depravation of it is regarded as a *loss*, and the reception of it, though never enjoyed before, as a *recovery*." (Alford)

iv. "As the impotent man of chapter 5, cured after his thirty-eight years of sickness, may be viewed as a type of the Jews who are yet to be healed: so may this man of chapter 9, blind from birth, be viewed as a type of the Gentiles whose healing was about to begin and who were about to believe into Jesus as Him who was 'the Sent' from God." (Trench)

B. The controversy surrounding the healing.

1. (8-12) The neighbors react to the healed man.

Therefore the neighbors and those who previously had seen that he was blind said, "Is not this he who sat and begged?" Some said, "This is he." Others *said*, "He is like him." He said, "I am *he*." Therefore they said to him, "How were your eyes opened?" He answered and said, "A Man called Jesus made clay and anointed my eyes and said to me, 'Go to the pool of Siloam and wash.' So I went and washed, and I received sight." Then they said to him, "Where is He?" He said, "I do not know."

a. **Others said, "He is like him." He said, "I am he"**: It seemed too amazing to believe, but the man convinced them that he was in fact healed from congenital blindness. The transformation in his life was so significant that many found it hard to believe he was the same man.

b. **A Man called Jesus**: At this point, the man knew very little about Jesus. He didn't seem to know that Jesus was from Nazareth, or was the Messiah, or claimed to be God, or the light of the world. He didn't even know where Jesus was. The man seemed to know nothing about Jesus except His name and that Jesus was the Man who healed him.

i. The blind man never even *saw* Jesus until later in the story. His first dealings with Jesus were while he was still blind, and Jesus was not there when he washed his eyes at the Pool of Siloam and could see.

2. (13-16) The healed man is brought to the Pharisees.

They brought him who formerly was blind to the Pharisees. Now it was a Sabbath when Jesus made the clay and opened his eyes. Then the Pharisees also asked him again how he had received his sight. He said to them, "He put clay on my eyes, and I washed, and I see." Therefore some of the Pharisees said, "This Man is not from God, because He does not keep the Sabbath." Others said, "How can a man who is a sinner do such signs?" And there was a division among them.

a. **Now it was a Sabbath when Jesus made the clay and opened his eyes**: Jesus took the initiative in this miracle, and could have done it on any day He chose. Jesus chose to do this miracle on the Sabbath to challenge the petty traditions of the religious leaders, traditions that they lifted to the place of binding laws.

i. "One of the categories of work specifically forbidden on the Sabbath in the tradition interpretation of the law was kneading, and the making of mud or clay with such simple ingredients as earth and saliva was construed as a form of kneading." (Bruce)

ii. "Works of *necessity* and *mercy* never could be forbidden on that day by him whose *name* is *mercy*, and whose *nature* is *love*; for the Sabbath was made for man, and not man for the Sabbath; were it *otherwise*, the Sabbath would be rather a *curse* than a *blessing*." (Clarke)

b. **Therefore some of the Pharisees said, "This Man is not from God, because He does not keep the Sabbath"**: To the Pharisees, Jesus could not be from God because He did not line up with their traditions and prejudices.

i. **This Man**: "*This man* is contemptuous; 'This fellow'." (Tasker)

c. **There was a division among them**: Instead of uniting everyone, Jesus often divided men. They were divided between those who accepted Him and trusted Him, and those who did not.

i. In choosing, they took one of two sides regarding Jesus.

- Jesus is a sinner and should be rejected.

- Our understanding and application of the Sabbath law is wrong.

ii. There was far for evidence for the second proposition than for the first, yet it seems that far more of them adopted the second position. They did this *in spite of* the evidence, not because of it.

iii. "The group speaking tentatively in favor of Jesus must have been a small one. We do not hear of them again after this verse, and throughout the rest of the chapter the narrative proceeds a though the other group were the only one to be considered." (Morris)

iv. "The minority's question, 'How can a sinner do such miraculous signs?' sounds much like Nicodemus's opening words to Jesus: "No one could perform the miraculous sings you are doing if God were not with him' (John 3:2)." (Tenney)

3. (17-18) The religious leaders question the man born blind.

They said to the blind man again, "What do you say about Him because He opened your eyes?" He said, "He is a prophet." But the Jews did not believe concerning him, that he had been blind and received his sight, until they called the parents of him who had received his sight.

a. **What do you say about Him because He opened your eyes?** Most of the religious leaders had made up their mind about Jesus - saying that He was not of God, yet some disagreed (John 9:16). They thought they would get the opinion of the man born blind regarding Jesus.

i. "It is a measure of their perplexity and division that they ask the man what he thinks of Jesus. Normally they would not have dreamed of putting a question on a religious issue to such a man." (Morris)

b. **He is a prophet**: Jesus did not specifically *say* to this man that he would be healed if he washed in the Pool of Siloam (John 9:7), but it was implied in the action. Though Jesus was not present when the man actually gained his sight, one could say that Jesus prophesied that he would gain his sight if he did what Jesus told him to do.

i. In John 9:11, all the man knew about Jesus was His name. Here, the healed man proclaimed that Jesus was **a prophet**. He grew in his understanding and proclamation about Jesus.

ii. "Now, according to a Jewish maxim, *a prophet might dispense with the observation of the Sabbath.* See *Grotius.* If they allow that Jesus was a *prophet*, then, even in their sense, he might break the law of the Sabbath, and be guiltless." (Clarke)

c. **But the Jews did not believe concerning him, that he had been blind**: It was easier for the religious leaders to believe that the man was never really blind than to believe that Jesus healed the man.

i. "Unable to explain this unprecedented phenomenon of a man born blind being enabled to see, they will not admit that it has really happened." (Tasker)

4. (19-23) The Pharisees question the parents of the man born blind.

And they asked them, saying, "Is this your son, who you say was born blind? How then does he now see?" His parents answered them and said, "We know that this is our son, and that he was born blind; but by what means he now sees we do not know, or who opened his eyes we do not know. He is of age; ask him. He will speak for himself." His parents said these *things* because they feared the Jews, for the Jews had agreed already that if anyone confessed *that* He *was* Christ, he would be put out of the synagogue. Therefore his parents said, "He is of age; ask him."

a. **Is this your son, who you say was born blind?** The religious leaders asked the parents to verify that the man was truly born blind. The tone of their question implies that they wondered if the parents were part of the same imagined conspiracy. Yet, the parents verified, "**this is our son, and that he was born blind**."

i. This should have persuaded the religious leaders that a remarkable man from God was in their midst. It did not persuade them and they continued their hostile interrogation.

b. **By what means he now sees we do not know, or who opened his eyes we do not know**: The parents could identify their son and that he was born blind. They would not speak to the question of how he was healed because of the threat of excommunication (**the Jews had agreed already that if anyone confessed that He was Christ, he would be put out of the synagogue**).

i. Ezra 10:8 is an Old Testament example of excommunication.

ii. Dods wrote of the practice in the ancient Jewish world: "Of excommunication there were three degrees: the first lasted for thirty days; then followed 'a second admonition,' and if impenitent the culprit was punished for thirty days more; and if still impenitent he was laid under the *Cherem* or ban, which was of indefinite duration, and which entirely cut him off from intercourse with others. He was treated as if he were a leper." (Dods)

iii. Many of the rulers in Jerusalem really believed in Jesus, but were afraid to say it because they didn't want to be cast out of the synagogue (John 12:42).

iv. In the modern western world the idea of excommunication means little, because it is easy for the excommunicated one to simply go to another church and pretend that nothing happened. More common today is what one might call *self-excommunication*, where believers separate themselves from church worship and life with no good reason.

c. **He is of age, ask him**: It is instinctive and normal for parents to protect their children, even when the children are adults. The parents were so frightened by the threat of excommunication that they did all they could to put the attention back upon their son and away from them.

i. "It is plain that they discerned danger, and had no intention of being caught up in it with their son." (Morris)

ii. They *emphatically* turned the focus back upon their son. "The pronouns in the latter part of the verse are emphatic: *who hath opened* **his** *eyes* **we** *know not: ask* **him**: *he is of age,* **he** *shall speak for* **himself**." (Alford)

C. The religious leaders interrogate the man born blind, now healed by Jesus.

1. (24-25) The simple testimony of the man born blind.

So they again called the man who was blind, and said to him, "Give God the glory! We know that this Man is a sinner." He answered and said, "Whether He is a sinner *or not* I do not know. One thing I know: that though I was blind, now I see."

a. **Give God the glory**: This command to the healed man may be an admonition to tell the truth (as in Joshua 7:19), or it may be a command to deny any credit to Jesus in the healing.

i. "The words are a form of *adjuration* (see Joshua 7:19), *to tell the truth*, q.d. 'Remember that you are in God's presence, and speak as unto Him.'" (Alford)

ii. "The man is being told that he has not been completely frank up till now. He has held back something which would show Jesus to be a sinner." (Morris)

b. **We know this Man is a sinner**: They said this not because Jesus broke the law of God in the Hebrew Scriptures; they said this because Jesus did not obey their man-made traditions around the law. They said this *despite* the evidence, not because of it.

c. **One thing I know: that though I was blind, now I see**: The man born blind didn't know everything about Jesus, but he did know how Jesus had touched his life. At that moment, it was an irrefutable argument. They could not argue against what Jesus did in this man's life.

i. "They take their stand on their preconceived ideas, he on the simple facts that he knows" (Morris)

ii. "It was frustrating for his interrogators that neither of those statements could be refuted: the former statement was confirmed by the evidence of the parents; the truth of the latter they could see for themselves. Why not admit the conclusion to which these two facts pointed?" (Bruce)

iii. From time to time Christians are confronted with questions meant to embarrass or mock, questions about some science or social issue or another. One doesn't have to be an expert in all those things, though the more one knows the better. More than anything, we may simply say: "I don't know about all that; but this I know: Once I was blind, now I see."

iv. We don't base our faith on our personal experience; we base it upon God's truth, revealed to us in the Bible. Yet our experience of God's work in our life is an important and persuasive *additional* support for our faith and the faith of others. To be able to truly claim, "**though I was blind, now I see**" is a powerful argument.

2. (26-27) The man born blind reacts to the intense questioning.

Then they said to him again, "What did He do to you? How did He open your eyes?" He answered them, "I told you already, and you did not listen. Why do you want to hear *it* again? Do you also want to become His disciples?"

a. **They said to him again**: The tone implies a harsh, intense interrogation. They demanded answers from this man who now could see.

b. **I told you already, and you did not listen**: The man born blind showed a simple and profound wisdom in his back-and-forth with the esteemed and educated religious leaders. If they kept asking the same question, they would keep hearing the same answer.

i. "As the *mercy* of God had given him his *sight*, so the *wisdom* of God taught him how to escape the snares laid for his ruin." (Clarke)

c. **Do you also want to become His disciples?** Intending to or not, the healed man mocked both their prejudiced rejection of Jesus and proclaimed himself to be a disciple of Jesus (**do you also**).

> i. "He now displays a hitherto unsuspected capacity for ironical repartee." (Bruce)

> ii. "The man did not really expect that these men who were so plainly opposed to Jesus were changing their minds. But he was quite ready to bait them." (Morris)

3. (28-34) After wisely answering the religious leaders, the man is excommunicated.

Then they reviled him and said, "You are His disciple, but we are Moses' disciples. "We know that God spoke to Moses; *as for* this *fellow,* we do not know where He is from." The man answered and said to them, "Why, this is a marvelous thing, that you do not know where He is from; yet He has opened my eyes! Now we know that God does not hear sinners; but if anyone is a worshiper of God and does His will, He hears him. Since the world began it has been unheard of that anyone opened the eyes of one who was born blind. If this Man were not from God, He could do nothing." They answered and said to him, "You were completely born in sins, and are you teaching us?" And they cast him out.

a. **We know that God spoke to Moses; as for this fellow, we do not know where He is from**: The religious leaders could not keep from displaying their own proud arrogance and their prejudiced contempt of Jesus (**this fellow**).

b. **Why, this is a marvelous thing**: The healed man said this about their unbelief, not about the miracle of Jesus. It was if he told the religious leaders, "Your unbelief and ignorance in the face of the evidence is more of a miracle than my cure."

> i. **That you do not know where He is from**: "His 'ye' is emphatic and may carry some sly irony: 'You, the religious experts, cannot work out a simple thing like this?'" (Morris)

c. **We know that God does not hear sinners**: Isaiah 1:15 and Psalm 66:18 say that God is not obligated to hear the prayer of a sinner. With knowledge of the Scriptures and valid application, the simple man born blind proved that their claim "**we know this man is a sinner**" was false.

> i. "As a well-brought-up Jew the man regards it as axiomatic that a miracle wrought in answer to prayer is proof that its worker is no sinner. No divine help is available for impenitent sinners." (Tasker)

ii. The man's statement was in one sense true and in another sense false. God is certainly under no *obligation* to hear the prayer of the man or woman in rebellion against Him. Yet in His mercy and for His ultimate wise purpose, He *may* hear the unrepentant sinner.

iii. Yet the man's statement was completely true in this sense: "*If Christ had been an impostor, it is not possible to conceive that God would have listened to his prayer,* and given him the power to open the blind man's eyes." (Spurgeon)

d. **You were completely born in sins, and are you teaching us?** These religious leaders *despised* the common people, and this man in particular. They were especially angry because *he was right and they were wrong,*

i. "A mortified man will yield to learn of anybody; 'a little child shall lead him,'." (Trapp)

e. **And they cast him out**: The excommunication of the blind man - difficult as it was - turned out to be a good thing, because he would shortly be far more connected to Jesus.

i. "The casting out of this man meant his excommunication from his religious rights in Temple and synagogue." (Morgan)

ii. The religious leaders treated this man terribly.

- They abused him (**they reviled him**).
- They insulted him (**You were completely born in sins**).
- They rejected him (**they cast him out**).

iii. "They have had since many followers in their crimes. A false religion, supported by the state, has, by *fire* and *sword* silenced those whose *truth* in the end annihilated the system of their opponents." (Clarke)

4. (35-38) The man born blind and then healed believes on Jesus.

Jesus heard that they had cast him out; and when He had found him, He said to him, "Do you believe in the Son of God?" He answered and said, "Who is He, Lord, that I may believe in Him?" And Jesus said to him, "You have both seen Him and it is He who is talking with you." Then he said, "Lord, I believe!" And he worshiped Him.

a. **When He had found him**: The religious leaders rejected the man whom Jesus healed. Jesus then made it a point to meet him and receive him. It hurts to be rejected by others, but God has consolation for us in Jesus Christ.

i. "If He finds and receives, what does it matter who rejects?" (Morgan)

ii. "He that enjoys the favor of the Son of God will not tremble at the frown of the Sanhedrim." (Spurgeon)

b. **Do you believe in the Son of God?** Jesus called on the healed man to fully believe, and he did (**Lord, I believe**). When the healed man declared his loyalty to Jesus by not denying Him before the hostile religious leaders, he was rewarded when Jesus revealed more of Himself to him (**You have both seen Him and it is He who is talking with you**).

i. "The question 'Do you believe in the Son of Man?' is a summons to commitment. The Greek pronoun *su* ('you') used with the verb makes the inquiry doubly emphatic. It demanded a personal decision in the face of opposition or rejection." (Tenney)

ii. Jesus dealt with this man differently than most. He met his physical need first, then allowed him to endure persecution, then called him to a specific belief. It's good to remember that God may work differently in different lives.

iii. Some manuscripts have *Son of Man* instead of **Son of God**. Both terms point to God's Messiah, the One who should be believed and trusted.

c. **And he worshipped Him**: The religious leaders said, "You can't worship with us at the temple." Jesus said, "I will receive your worship."

i. When the man worshipped Jesus, Jesus received the worship. This is something that no man or angel in the Bible does. The fact that Jesus accepted this worship is another proof that Jesus was and is God, and that He knew Himself to be God.

ii. The formerly blind man showed an increasing awareness of Jesus.

- Jesus is a man (John 9:11).
- Jesus is a prophet (John 9:17).
- Jesus is my master, I am His disciple (John 9:27).
- Jesus is from God (John 9:33).
- Jesus is the Son of God (John 9:35-38).
- Jesus is who I trust (John 9:38).
- Jesus is who I worship (John 9:38).

5. (39-41) Jesus distinguishes between the blind and the seeing.

And Jesus said, "For judgment I have come into this world, that those who do not see may see, and that those who see may be made blind." Then *some* of the Pharisees who were with Him heard these words, and said to Him, "Are we blind also?" Jesus said to them, "If you were

blind, you would have no sin; but now you say, 'We see.' Therefore your sin remains.

a. **For judgment I have come into this world**: John recorded these words of Jesus as part of a larger theme in his Gospel - that men were divided over Jesus, with some accepting and some rejecting. This is one way Jesus brought **judgment...into this world**, by being a dividing line.

i. In this sense, Jesus is like the Continental Divide in the Rocky Mountains; a single place where an entire path is decided. Jesus is "the pivot on which human destiny turns." (Tenney)

ii. "His statement that He had come to judge the world meant that He would be the separating One, the One through whom God would judge." (Morgan)

b. **That those who do not see may see**: Those who admit their spiritual blindness can find sight in Jesus. But **those who see may be made blind** - that is, those who falsely claim to have spiritual sight will be **made blind**.

i. "*They which see not* means 'they who have no spiritual vision by are conscious of their need of it'; and *they which see* means 'they who wrongly suppose that they already possess spiritual vision'." (Tasker)

ii. **Those who do not see may see**: "Those who are conscious of their blindness and grieved on account of it may be relieved; while those who are content with the light they have lose even that." (Dods)

iii. "We ought not to suffer any person to perish for lack of knowing the gospel. We cannot give men eyes, but we can give them light." (Spurgeon)

iv. In saying **those who do not see**, Jesus used blindness in a spiritual, metaphorical sense - of those who cannot see the light and truth of God, especially as it is revealed in Jesus Christ. One may say that this entire chapter paints a picture of how Jesus heals blind souls.

- We are all spiritually blind from birth.
- Jesus takes the initiative in healing us from blindness.
- Jesus does a work of *creation* in us, not reformation.
- In this work, we must be obedient to what Jesus commands.
- Jesus commands us to be washed in the water of baptism.
- We become a mystery to our former associates, not even seeming to be the same person.

- We display loyalty to Jesus when we are persecuted, boldly and plainly testifying of His work in our lives and confounding others.

- We pass from little knowledge to greater knowledge, and this brings us to greater worship and adoration.

- We never know the name of this man born blind. Jesus is the important One; a true disciple is content to remain anonymous if his Lord gets the glory.

c. **Are we blind also?** The Pharisees sneered at Jesus, confident in their own spiritual sight - which was blindness, because they could not see the Son of God right in front of them.

i. "Take a homely illustration from myself: I used to be very backward in using spectacles for some time, because I could almost see without them, and I did not wish to be an old gentleman too soon. But now that I cannot read my notes at all without wearing spectacles, I put them on without a moment's hesitation, and I do not care whether you think me old or not. So when a man comes to feel thoroughly guilty, he does not mind depending upon God." (Spurgeon)

d. **If you were blind, you would have no sin**: If the Pharisees would admit to their spiritual blindness, they could be forgiven and set free - but because they say "**we see**," their **sin remains**.

i. There is a great difference between the one who is blind and knows it, and the one who simply shuts his eyes.

ii. "To be so self-deceived as to shut one's eyes to the light is a desperate state to be in: the light is there, but if people refuse to avail themselves of it but rather deliberately reject it, how can they be enlightened? As Jesus said, their sin remains." (Bruce)

John 10 - The Good Shepherd

A. Contrast between the Good Shepherd and the false shepherds of Israel.

1. (1-2) Jesus is the true, legitimate shepherd, who enters in the way that is proper and prepared.

"Most assuredly, I say to you, he who does not enter the sheepfold by the door, but climbs up some other way, the same is a thief and a robber. But he who enters by the door is the shepherd of the sheep."

a. **Most assuredly, I say to you**: This follows - at least thematically - in John's gospel after the great conflict with the religious leaders regarding the man born blind. The religious leaders had shown themselves to be so unhelpful and cruel to the man, his parents, and the common people in general that Jesus felt it necessary to talk about the contrast between His heart and work as a leader to God's people and the heart and work of many of the religious leaders of His day.

i. **Most assuredly**: "This is a phrase peculiar to the fourth Gospel, and it generally introduces a solemn asseveration about Jesus or his mission." (Tenney)

b. **He who does not enter the sheepfold by the door, but climbs up some other say, the same is a thief and a robber**: Political and spiritual leaders were often called *shepherds* in the ancient world (Isaiah 56:11, Jeremiah 3:15). Jesus explained that not everyone among the sheep is a true shepherd; some are like thieves and robbers. One mark of their being **a thief and a robber** is *how they gain entry among the sheep*.

i. The idea is that there is a **door**, a proper way to gain entry. Not everyone who stands among the sheep comes that way. Some climb **up some other way**.

ii. The religious leaders gained their place among God's people - the **sheep** spoken of here - through personal and political connections, through formal education, through ambition, manipulation, and corruption.

c. **He who enters by the door is the shepherd of the sheep**: A true shepherd comes in the legitimate and designed way: through love, calling, care, and sacrificial service.

> i. God always intended that His people be led, fed, and protected by those who come in the legitimate, intended way. The **door** is there for a reason. Some will always climb over the barriers, but God has the barriers and the door there for a reason.

> ii. "Whoever, therefore, enters not by Jesus Christ into the pastoral office, is no other than a thief and a robber in the sheepfold. And he enters not by Jesus Christ who *enters* with a prospect of any other interest besides that of Christ and his people. Ambition, avarice, love of ease, a desire to enjoy the conveniences of life, to be distinguished from the crowd, to promote the interests of one's family, and even the sole design of providing against want-these are all ways by which *thieves and robbers enter into the Church*. And whoever enters by any of these ways, or by simony, craft, solicitation, &c. deserves no better name." (Clarke)

2. (3-6) The sheep and their shepherd.

"To him the doorkeeper opens, and the sheep hear his voice; and he calls his own sheep by name and leads them out. And when he brings out his own sheep, he goes before them; and the sheep follow him, for they know his voice. Yet they will by no means follow a stranger, but will flee from him, for they do not know the voice of strangers." Jesus used this illustration, but they did not understand the things which He spoke to them.

a. **To him the doorkeeper opens**: In the spiritual picture Jesus spoke of, the door for the sheep pen had a **doorkeeper** - one who watched who came in and who went out. The **doorkeeper** knows the true shepherd and appropriately grants him access.

> i. In towns of that time, sheep from many flocks were kept for the night in a common sheepfold, overseen by one **doorkeeper** who regulated which shepherds brought and took which sheep.

b. **He calls his own sheep by name and leads them out**: The shepherd calls the **sheep by name**, showing that the shepherd has a personal connection with the sheep. The shepherd **leads them**, providing direction and leadership - without *driving* the sheep.

i. "As we have names for horses, dogs, cows, so the Eastern shepherds for their sheep." (Dods)

ii. "In my youth some shepherds in the Scottish Highlands not only called their individual sheep by name, but claimed that an individual sheep would recognize its own name and respond to it." (Bruce)

iii. "In this Gospel, Jesus calls the following 'sheep' by name, Philip, Mary of Magdala, Thomas, and Simon Peter; and on each occasion it is a turning-point in the disciple's life." (Tasker)

iv. **And leads them out**: "It was the custom in the eastern countries for the shepherd to go at the head of his sheep, and they *followed* him from pasture to pasture." (Clarke)

c. **For they know his voice**: In the common sheepfolds of ancient times, the shepherd merely gave his distinctive call and his sheep came out from the others, following him out of the sheepfold. Sheep are experts at discerning their shepherd's **voice**.

i. "There is a story of a Scotch traveller who changed clothes with a Jerusalem shepherd and tried to lead the sheep: but the sheep followed the shepherds voice and not his clothes." (Dods)

ii. During World War I, some soldiers tried to steal a flock of sheep from a hillside near Jerusalem. The sleeping shepherd awoke to find his flock being driven off. He couldn't recapture them by force, so he called out to his flock with his distinctive call. The sheep listened, and returned to their rightful owner. The soldiers couldn't stop the sheep from returning to their shepherd's voice.

d. **Jesus used this illustration**: This is a picture both of the work of Jesus among His sheep and of what those who seek to serve among the sheep of Jesus should focus upon. Adam Clarke described six marks of the true and legitimate minister of God in these first six verses of John 10:

- He has a proper entrance into the ministry.

- He sees the Holy Spirit open his way as a doorkeeper to God's sheep.

- He sees that the sheep respond to his voice in teaching and leadership.

- He is well acquainted with his flock.

- He leads the flock and does not drive them or lord it over them.

- He goes before the sheep as an example.

3. (7-10) The true shepherd protects and promotes life; the false shepherds take away life.

Then Jesus said to them again, "Most assuredly, I say to you, I am the door of the sheep. All who *ever* came before Me are thieves and robbers, but the sheep did not hear them. I am the door. If anyone enters by Me, he will be saved, and will go in and out and find pasture. The thief does not come except to steal, and to kill, and to destroy. I have come that they may have life, and that they may have *it* more abundantly."

a. **I am the door of the sheep**: Jesus used another picture from sheep farming in His time. Out in the pasturelands for sheep, pens were made with only one entrance. The door for those sheep pens was the shepherd himself. He laid his body across the entrance, to keep the sheep in and to keep out the wolves. The shepherd was in fact the **door**.

i. "Primarily uttered for the excommunicated man, these words conveyed the assurance that instead of being outcast by his attachment to Jesus he had gained admittance to the fellowship of God and all good men." (Dods)

b. **All who ever came before Me are thieves and robbers**: *Thief* implies deception and trickery; *robber* implies violence and destruction. These take away life but Jesus gives life and He gives it **abundantly**. These are the con men and muggers of the spiritual world.

i. Alford sees the **all who have come before** basically to be those religious leaders who were actually tools in Satan's hand - as Jesus told some of these religious leaders that their father was actually the devil. "Because the Pharisees are blind leaders, they are also bogus shepherds, and come under the category of those designated in John 10:8 *thieves and robbers*." (Tasker)

ii. "Jesus does not say that they 'were' but that they 'are' thieves and robbers. The emphasis is on His own day." (Morris)

iii. "Manes (that made heretic) made an argument from this text against Moses and the prophets, as going before Christ. But Austin answereth, Moses and the prophets came not before Christ, but with Christ." (Trapp)

iv. "κλεπτης [*kleptes*], and ληστης [*lestes*], the thief and the robber, should be properly distinguished; one takes by *cunning* and *stealth*; the other *openly* and by *violence*. It would not be difficult to find bad ministers who answer to both these characters." (Clarke)

c. **But the sheep did not hear them**: Jesus seems to say that *His* sheep are evident because they will not **hear** (follow after) the voice of the thieves and robbers who come after the sheep.

i. "They no doubt assumed authority over the people of God and compelled obedience, but the true children of God did not find in their voice that which attracted and led them to pasture." (Dods)

d. **He will be saved, and will go in and out and find pasture**: Jesus described the settled, satisfied life enjoyed by His sheep, those over whom He exercises a shepherd's care.

i. **Go in and out**: "This phrase, in the style of the Hebrews, points out all the actions of a man's life, and the liberty he has of acting, or not acting." (Clarke)

ii. "To 'go out and in' is the common O.T. expression to denote the free activity of daily life. Jeremiah 37:4, Psalm 121:8, Deuteronomy 28:6." (Dods)

e. **I have come that they may have life, and they may have it more abundantly**: Jesus said this to contrast His shepherd-like care with unfaithful and illegitimate leaders. They come to **steal, and to kill, and to destroy**. Jesus comes to bring **life** to His people.

i. "The Greek word for 'abundance,' *perissos*, has a mathematical meaning and generally denotes a surplus…The abundant life is above all the contented life, in which our contentment is based upon the fact that God is equal to every emergency and is able to supply all our needs according to His riches and glory in Christ Jesus." (Boice)

- Abundant life isn't an especially long life.

- Abundant life isn't an easy, comfortable life.

- Abundant life is a life of satisfaction and contentment in Jesus.

ii. "Life is a matter of degrees. Some have life, but it flickers like a dying candle, and is indistinct as the fire in the smoking flax; others are full of life, and are bright and vehement." (Spurgeon)

- Someone with a lot of life has *stamina*.

- Someone with a lot of life has *increased energy*.

- Someone with a lot of life has *a large sphere of living*.

- Someone with a lot of life has *the ability to do things*.

- Someone with a lot of life has *an overflow of enjoyment*.

- Someone with a lot of life has *what it takes to win*.

iii. Abundant life sheep give honor to the shepherd. They are a credit to him.

4. (11-15) The good shepherd will lay down his life for the flock.

"I am the good shepherd. The good shepherd gives His life for the sheep. But a hireling, *he who is* **not the shepherd, one who does not own the sheep, sees the wolf coming and leaves the sheep and flees; and the wolf catches the sheep and scatters them. The hireling flees because he is a hireling and does not care about the sheep. I am the good shepherd; and I know My** *sheep,* **and am known by My own. As the Father knows Me, even so I know the Father; and I lay down My life for the sheep."**

a. **I am the good shepherd**: Jesus said it so plainly there could be no mistake what He meant. He fulfills the ideal of shepherd-like care for the people of God as illustrated in the Old Testament and in that culture.

i. Jesus announced "Himself as THE GOOD SHEPHERD - the great antagonist of *the robber* - the pattern and Head of all good shepherds, as *he* of all thieves and robbers: the Messiah, in His best known and most loving office." (Alford)

ii. What Jesus described as a **good shepherd** is actually a very remarkable shepherd. Shepherds may take risks for the safety of the sheep, but it is probably rare to find one who would willingly die for their sheep.

iii. "In the Latin tongue the word for money is akin to the word 'sheep,' because, to many of the first Romans, wool was their wealth, and their fortunes lay in their flocks. The Lord Jesus is our Shepherd: we are his wealth." (Spurgeon)

iv. **Gives His life for the sheep**: "*He is giving his life still.* The life that is in the man Christ Jesus he is always giving for us. It is for us he lives, and because he lives we live also. He lives to plead for us. He lives to represent us in heaven. He lives to rule providence for us." (Spurgeon)

b. **Sees the wolf coming**: It was assumed that wild animals (**the wolf**) or bandits (the *thieves and robbers* previously mentioned) would threaten the sheep. The question was, "How will the shepherd respond?"

i. "The purposes of this **wolf** are the same as those of the thief in verse 10, and in the allegory he is the same; - *the great Foe of the sheep of Christ.*" (Alford)

c. **The good shepherd gives His life for the sheep**: The bad shepherd (**a hireling**) will not defend the sheep and thinks the flock exists for his benefit, but the **good shepherd** lives and dies for the good of the sheep.

• The good shepherd sacrifices for the sheep (**gives His life**).

- The good shepherd knows his sheep (**I know My sheep**). We think of sheep as being all the same. The shepherd knows they are individuals with their own personalities and characteristics.

- The good shepherd is known by the sheep (**and am known by My own**).

    i. "There is a mutually reciprocal knowledge between Jesus and His sheep. And the existence of this knowledge is the proof that He is the Shepherd." (Dods)

    ii. The faithful pastor will, as an under-shepherd, display the same characteristics as the Good Shepherd. He will sacrifice for the sheep, know the sheep, and be known by them. He will be a **shepherd** and not a **hireling** who **does not care about the sheep**. He can never hope to display these characteristics to the same extent as Jesus, but they should reflect his heart and his goal.

    iii. "How many there are of whom we have reason to fear that they must be hirelings, because, when they see false doctrine and error abroad, they do not oppose it! They are willing to put up with anything for the sake of peace and quietness." (Spurgeon)

    iv. The title *pastor* translates the same ancient Greek word used here for **shepherd**. It is a title that is only rightfully earned, not granted or assumed.

    d. **As the Father knows Me, even so I know the Father**: The work of Jesus as the **Good Shepherd** was rooted in His close relationship with His God and Father.

5. (16) Jesus speaks of other sheep.

"And other sheep I have which are not of this fold; them also I must bring, and they will hear My voice; and there will be one flock *and* one shepherd."

    a. **Other sheep I have which are not of this fold**: These **other sheep** are Gentile believers, not of the fold of Israel. Jesus said that He **must bring** these sheep also, who would also **hear** His **voice**.

    i. "Do not imagine that I shall lay down my life for the Jews, *exclusively* of all other people; no: I shall die also for the Gentiles; for *by the grace*, the merciful design and loving purpose *of God, I am to taste death for every man*, Hebrew 2:9; and, though they are not of *this fold* now, those among them that believe shall be *united* with the believing Jews, and made one fold under one shepherd, Ephesians 2:13-17." (Clarke)

b. **There will be one flock**: A **fold** of sheep is a part of the flock in its own structure or enclosure. A shepherd might separate the sheep into different groups to care for them better. There is **one flock** and **one shepherd**; but Jesus calls His sheep from more than one **fold** (group or structure of people).

i. "Nothing is said of unity of organisation. There may be various folds, though one flock." (Dods)

ii. "What was to hold this enlarged flock together and supply the necessary protection from external enemies? Not enclosing walls by the person and power of the shepherd. The unity and safety of the people of Christ depend on their proximity to him." (Bruce)

iii. "The unity comes from the fact, not that all the sheep are forced into one fold, but that they all hear, answer and obey one shepherd. It is not ecclesiastical unity; it is a unity of loyalty to Jesus Christ." (Barclay)

iv. "All who are one with Christ have a certain family feeling, a higher form of clannishness, and they cannot shake it off. I have found myself reading a gracious book which has drawn nine near to God, and though I have known that it was written by a man with whose opinions I had little agreement, I have not therefore refused to be edified by him in points which are unquestionably revealed. No, but I have blessed the Lord that, within all his blunders, he knew so much of precious vital truth, and lived so near his Lord." (Spurgeon)

v. The early Christian Bible translator Jerome, when translating his influential Latin version mistakenly translated *one fold* instead of **one flock** in this verse. His Latin Vulgate reading is the erroneous foundation for a doctrine of Roman Catholic exclusiveness.

vi. "In Jerome's version, Jesus seems to be saying that thee is only one organization, and the obvious deduction was that there could therefore be no salvation outside the formal organization of the Roman Church. This became official Roman teaching." (Boice)

6. (17-18) Jesus claims to have power over life and death.

"Therefore My Father loves Me, because I lay down My life that I may take it again. No one takes it from Me, but I lay it down of Myself. I have power to lay it down, and I have power to take it again. This command I have received from My Father."

a. **Therefore My Father loves Me**: God the Father saw the beauty of character and self-sacrifice in God the Son, and He loved the Son all the more because of it.

b. **That I may take it again... I have power to take it again**: In this sense, we can say that Jesus "raised Himself" from the dead. He had the power to lay down His life, and He had the power to take it up again.

i. "When any ordinary man dies he only pays 'the debt of nature.' If he were even to die for his friend, he would simply pay a little earlier that debt which he must pay ultimately, but the Christ was immortal, and he needed not to die except that he had put himself under covenant bonds to suffer for his sheep." (Spurgeon)

ii. Anyone can lay down his life; only Jesus could take His life up again. Because Jesus has the power to take up His own life, it is evidence of His unique relationship with His **Father**.

iii. It doesn't surprise us that Jehovah's Witnesses deny that Jesus could take His own life up again. Yet many others (such as Kenneth Copeland, Kenneth Hagin, Fred Price and others) teach that Jesus was a helpless victim in hell, saved only by the intervention of God the Father.

c. **This command I have received from My Father**: The death of Jesus was completely voluntary, but it was not an indirect suicide in any sense. It was part of a plan to submit to death and then to emerge from it victoriously alive, according to the **command... received from** God the Father.

7. (19-21) Jesus is accused of being demon-possessed and insane.

Therefore there was a division again among the Jews because of these sayings. And many of them said, "He has a demon and is mad. Why do you listen to Him?" Others said, "These are not the words of one who has a demon. Can a demon open the eyes of the blind?"

a. **Therefore there was a division again among the Jews because of these sayings**: Once again, Jesus is shown as the dividing line of humanity. Humanity divides between accepting or rejecting Jesus.

b. **He has a demon and is mad**: Jesus made such radical claims about Himself that people divided over Him. Some believe He was who He said He was. Others believed that anyone who claimed to be God as Jesus claimed must either have a **demon** or be **mad**.

i. William Barclay was right when wrote, "Either Jesus was a megalomaniac madman, or he was the Son of God." By what we know of Jesus, is if fair to say that He was a madman?

- The *words* of Jesus were not the words of a madman; instead, they are supreme sanity.

- The *deeds* of Jesus were not the deeds of a megalomaniac; instead, they were utterly unselfish.

- The *effect* of Jesus wasn't the effect of a madman; instead, He has changed millions for the good.

ii. "It was a wonder if the heavens did not sweat, the earth melt, and hell gape at the hearing of these horrid blasphemies." (Trapp)

iii. "And what was he doing to merit all this? Why, he was instructing the ignorant, and telling the wretched that he was just going to die to save their souls! Amazing love of God, and ingratitude and obduracy of men!" (Barclay)

c. **These are not the words of one who has a demon. Can a demon open the eyes of the blind?** Miraculous works like opening the eyes of the blind *can* be a valid testimony, but only in concert with faithfulness to the word of God. These people were right in looking at *both* the works and the words of Jesus.

B. Jesus at the Feast of Dedication.

1. (22-23) The Feast of Dedication in wintertime.

Now it was the Feast of Dedication in Jerusalem, and it was winter. And Jesus walked in the temple, in Solomon's porch.

a. **The Feast of Dedication**: This feast (also known as Hanukkah) celebrated the cleansing and re-dedication of the temple after three years of desecration by Antiochus Epiphanes, king of Syria (in 164 or 165 B.C.).

i. After Antiochus attacked Jerusalem, he instituted a reign of terror upon the Jews of the city. Barclay notes:

- Antiochus stole millions in gold and silver from the temple treasury.

- Antiochus said that possessing a copy of the law was punishable by death.

- Antiochus said that circumcising a child was punishable by death.

- Under Antiochus mothers who did circumcise their children were to be crucified with their children hanging around their necks.

- Under Antiochus the temple was turned into a house of prostitution.

- Under Antiochus the great altar of burnt offering was turned into an altar unto the Greek god Zeus.

- Under Antiochus pigs were sacrificed upon the great altar.

- Under Antiochus 80,000 Jews were killed and an equal number were sold as slaves.

ii. The rise of the Maccabees ended these horrors. "It was told that when the Temple had been purified and the great sevenbranched candlestick re-lit, only one little cruse of unpolluted oil could be found. That cruse was still intact, and still sealed with the impress of the ring of the High Priest. By all normal measures, there was only oil enough in that cruse to light the lamps for one single day. But by a miracle it lasted for eight days, until new oil had been prepared according to the correct formula and had been consecrated for its sacred use." (Barclay)

iii. **It was winter:** "χειμων ην, or, it was *stormy* or *rainy weather.*" (Clarke) "His meaning must be, 'it was stormy weather,' or 'there was a storm blowing'." (Trench)

b. **Jesus walked in the temple**: This is another confrontation between Jesus and the religious leaders **in the temple** courts. However, Jesus does not seem to be teaching when this confrontation began.

i. **Solomon's porch**: "Solomon's colonnade was the name given to the portico which ran along the east side of the outer court of Herod's temple. It is mentioned in Acts as the place where Peter addressed the crowd the congregated to see the man who had been cured of his lifelong lameness at the Beautiful Gate, and again as the place where the Jerusalem believers regularly gathered for their public witness to Jesus as the Christ (Acts 3:11; 5:12)." (Bruce)

ii. "It appears to have been a very old structure, and was popularly thought to have been part of Solomon's temple, though this belief, of course, was not well founded." (Morris)

2. (24-25) Jesus responds to the hostile question from the religious leaders.

Then the Jews surrounded Him and said to Him, "How long do You keep us in doubt? If You are the Christ, tell us plainly." Jesus answered them, "I told you, and you do not believe. The works that I do in My Father's name, they bear witness of Me."

a. **Then the Jews surrounded Him**: It isn't said that Jesus was at the temple teaching, merely that He *walked in the temple* (John 10:23). The sense is that this was a hostile ambush as Jesus simply walked.

i. "Here the Jews 'ringed Him round,' preventing His escape wand with hostile purpose." (Dods)

b. **How long do You keep us in doubt? If You are the Christ, tell us plainly**: The religious leaders (once again described as **the Jews**) refused to listen to or believe in Jesus. They hoped to blame Jesus for their unbelief (**How long do You keep us in doubt?**).

> i. This was like telling the traffic cop that they should put up a speed limit sign every 100 yards - *then* you would keep the speed limit.

> ii. "The Jews asked this question through extreme perfidiousness: they wished to get him to declare himself king of the Jews, that they might accuse him to the Roman governor; and by it they insolently insinuated that all the proofs he had hitherto given them of his Divine mission were good for nothing." (Clarke)

c. **I told you, and you do not believe**: Jesus did not often specifically refer to Himself among the Jews as the Christ, the Messiah. He did this because *messiah* was a word with political and even military implications that Jesus wished to avoid. Yet Jesus could rightly say that in many ways, **I told you and you do not believe**.

- **I told you**, I am the one who came from heaven (John 3:13, 6:38).
- **I told you**, whoever believes on Me has eternal life (John 3:15).
- **I told you**, I am the unique Son of God (John 5:19-23).
- **I told you**, I will judge all humanity (John 5:19-23).
- **I told you**, all should honor Me just as the honor God the Father (John 5:19-23).
- **I told you**, the Hebrew Scriptures all speak of Me (John 5:39).
- **I told you**, I perfectly reveal God the Father (John 7:28-29).
- **I told you**, I always please God and never sin (John 8:29, 8:46).
- **I told you**, I am uniquely sent from God (John 8:42).
- **I told you**, before Abraham was, I Am (John 8:58).
- **I told you**, I am the Son of Man, prophesied by Daniel (John 9:37).
- **I told you**, I will raise Myself from the dead (John 10:17-18).
- **I told you**, I am the Bread of Life (John 6:48).
- **I told you**, I am the Light of the World (John 8:12).
- **I told you**, I am the Door (John 10:9).
- **I told you**, I am the Good Shepherd (John 10:11).

i. The problem wasn't that Jesus was unclear about who He was and where He came from. The problem was that the religious leaders had hearts of unbelief that they wanted to blame on Jesus.

ii. "Notice His 'ye believe not'. It denotes a present attitude, and not simply a past state, and it indicates the root trouble." (Morris)

iii. Jesus more specifically revealed Himself as Messiah to those *not* part of the Jewish community, such as the Samaritan woman of John 4:1-26. With these there was less chance of misunderstanding whom Jesus was and what He came to do.

d. **The works that I do in My Father's name, they bear witness of Me**: Jesus had told them by His words who He was. Yet, the works Jesus also demonstrated that He was from God, and that He was true to His word.

i. "These works tell you what I am. They are works done in my Father's name, that is, wholly as His representative. These show what kind of Christ He sends you and that I am He." (Dods)

3. (26-29) Jesus speaks plainly to the religious leaders about their condition.

"But you do not believe, because you are not of My sheep, as I said to you. My sheep hear My voice, and I know them, and they follow Me. And I give them eternal life, and they shall never perish; neither shall anyone snatch them out of My hand. My Father, who has given *them* to Me, is greater than all; and no one is able to snatch *them* out of My Father's hand."

a. **You do not believe, because you are not My sheep**: The religious leaders wanted Jesus to speak plainly, and here He spoke more plainly than they probably wanted. Jesus previously told them they were not true shepherds (John 10:5, 10:8, 10:10, 10:12-13). Here Jesus told them they were not even true **sheep**, because the Messiah's sheep **believe** and hear His **voice**.

i. "They are not only untrustworthy shepherds of God's people, but are showing that they ought no longer to be classed among the sheep that pay attention to His voice." (Tasker)

ii. "Your unbelief is just an evidence that you were not chosen, that you have not been called by the Spirit of God, and that you are still in your sins." (Spurgeon)

iii. "Any person who reads without prejudice may easily see, that our Lord does not at all insinuate that these persons *could not* believe, because God had made it *impossible* to them; but simply because they *did not hear and follow Christ*, which the whole of our blessed Lord's discourse proves that *they might have done*." (Clarke)

b. **I give them eternal life, and they shall never perish**: Jesus described the benefits and blessings that come to His sheep. They have **eternal life**, given by Jesus. This **eternal life** begins now, but is greater than physical life.

> i. "We should not overlook the point that in fact eternal life does not end. It is this aspect that is prominent here." (Morris)

> ii. "Physical life may be destroyed, but those who are united by faith to the Son of God, those who belong to the flock of the true Shepherd, can never lose real life, for he keeps it secure." (Bruce)

> iii. "The one way by which a soul is saved is by that soul's abiding in Christ; if it did not abide in Christ, it would be cast forth as a branch and be withered. But, then, we know that they who are grafted into Christ will abide in Christ." (Spurgeon)

c. **Neither shall anyone snatch them out of My hand**: It is to be expected that the Good Shepherd would take good care of His sheep. The sheep are safe and secure in **hand** of the Good Shepherd.

d. **No one is able to snatch them out of My Father's hand**: God's sheep find safety in the both the hand of the Good Shepherd and God the Father. It's comforting to know that the hands that created the world hold on to the believer.

> i. **My Father is greater than all**: "More powerful than all the united energies of men and demons. He who loves God must be happy; and he who fears him need fear nothing on this side eternity." (Clarke)

4. (30-33) Jesus declares His unity with the Father.

"I and *My* Father are one." Then the Jews took up stones again to stone Him. Jesus answered them, "Many good works I have shown you from My Father. For which of those works do you stone Me?" The Jews answered Him, saying, "For a good work we do not stone You, but for blasphemy, and because You, being a Man, make Yourself God."

a. **I and My Father are one**: This is an important statement regarding the deity of Jesus and the nature of the Godhead. **I and My Father** means that the Father and the Son are not the same *Person*, refuting the "Jesus Only" doctrine (anciently known as Sabelianism). **Are one** means that the Father and the Son are equal in nature, in essence, what they really *are* - refuting the teaching that Jesus isn't God (anciently known as Arianism).

> i. "One in *essence* primarily, but therefore also one in *working*, and POWER, and in *will*." (Alford)

ii. "Notice, **one** is *neuter* in gender, not masculine: the Father and the Son are not *personally* one, but *essentially*." (Alford) "In the sentence, 'I and the Father are One,' the word 'One' is neuter, and means one Essence: it is not masculine, which would have been one Person." (Trench)

iii. Opponents of the deity of Jesus say that the oneness Jesus had with the Father was nothing more than a unity of *purpose* and *mission* - even as a husband and wife or father and son may have a unity of purpose of mission, yet still they are not the same person. This however misses the point. First, we never argue that the Bible teaches that the Father and the Son are the same Person - they are one God, but distinct in their Persons. Second, it misses the most obvious point: that even true unity of purpose and mission between a husband and wife or father and son exist only because they are each equally and totally *human*. The Father and the Son have this unique unity because they are equally and totally *God* - that is, Divine Being.

iv. Jesus wanted us to be one as He and the Father are one (John 17:11, 17:21). Such oneness cannot exist without an equality of essence, and all believers have this equality (Galatians 3:26-28), even as the Father and Son have this equality.

v. **Many good works I have shown you from My Father**: "All his works were done by the Father's direction (John 5:19); they were 'good works' (*erge kala*, 'beautiful works') not only because they were acts of obedience to the Father but also because they were acts of blessing to men." (Bruce)

b. **The Jews took up stones again to stone Him**: The fact that the religious leaders considered the statement "**I and the Father are one**" to be blasphemy proves that Jesus spoke of much more than a unity of purpose and will. They were wrong in their response, but they understood what Jesus said.

i. "The Greek really means that they went and fetched stones to fling at him." (Barclay)

ii. It's clear that they lost the argument. They could point to nothing in the words or works of Jesus that showed He was *not* the Messiah.

iii. "It was laid down in the Law that blasphemy was to be punished by stoning (Leviticus 24:16). But these men were not allowing the due processes of law to take their course." (Morris)

iv. "If they cannot answer holy arguments with fair reasonings, they can give hard answers with stones. If you cannot destroy the reasoning, you may, perhaps, destroy the reasoner." (Spurgeon)

c. **Because You, being a Man, make Yourself God**: The Jews of Jesus' day clearly understood what the Jehovah's Witnesses and others seem to miss - that Jesus *clearly* claimed to be God.

i. "He is not 'making himself God'; he is not 'making himself' anything, but in word and work he is showing himself to be what he truly is - the Son sent by the Father to bring life and light to mankind." (Bruce)

ii. "It was blasphemy for a man to claim to be God. And it is noteworthy that Jesus never manifests indignation when charged with making Himself God; yet were He a mere man no one could view this sin with stronger abhorrence." (Dods)

5. (34-39) Jesus reasons from Psalm 82, and from His works.

Jesus answered them, "Is it not written in your law, 'I said, "You are gods"'? If He called them gods, to whom the word of God came (and the Scripture cannot be broken), do you say of Him whom the Father sanctified and sent into the world, 'You are blaspheming,' because I said, 'I am the Son of God'? If I do not do the works of My Father, do not believe Me; but if I do, though you do not believe Me, believe the works, that you may know and believe that the Father *is* in Me, and I in Him." Therefore they sought again to seize Him, but He escaped out of their hand.

a. **Jesus answered them**: The religious leaders surrounded Jesus (John 10:24) and now held rocks to stone Him to death (John 10:31). Jesus didn't panic and didn't run; He stopped them with the power of His word. He answered them as an educated rabbi would speak to other educated rabbis.

i. "Jesus rebuts their charge of blasphemy by means of an argument from scripture, of a kind with which they themselves were quite familiar...His question would have made an interesting issue for a rabbinical debate." (Bruce)

b. **Is it not written in your law, "I said, 'You are gods'"**: The judges of Psalm 82 were called "**gods**" because in their office they determined the fate of other men. Also, in Exodus 21:6 and 22:8-9, God called earthly judges "**gods**."

i. "The word **law** here is in its widest acceptation, - the whole Old Testament, as [John] chapter 12:34; 15:25." (Alford)

ii. "They were entitled to be so designated, for they represented, however imperfectly, the divine will in so far as they were called upon to administer God's word." (Tasker)

c. **If He called them gods, to whom the word of God came**: Jesus reasoned, "If God gave these unjust judges the title 'gods' because of their office, why do you consider it blasphemy that I call Myself the 'Son of God' in light of the testimony of Me and My works?"

i. "The argument is *from the greater to the less*. If in any sense *they* could be called **gods** - how much more properly *He*." (Alford)

ii. Jesus did *not* take the statement "**you are gods**" in Psalm 82 and apply it to all humanity or to all believers. The use of **gods** in Psalm 82 was a metaphor. Jesus spoke of that metaphor to expose both the ignorance and inconsistency of His accusers.

iii. "The deeper aim of this argument is, to show them that the idea of *man and God being one*, was not alien from their Old Testament spirit, but set forth there in types and shadows of Him, the real God-Man." (Alford)

d. **And the Scripture cannot be broken**: This is a general rule for all Scripture, but Jesus applied it here to a fairly obscure passage where the essential point rested on *one word* God used to refer to human judges. It is a remarkable demonstration that the specific words of Scripture are inspired, not only the broad themes and ideas.

i. "It means that Scripture cannot be emptied of its force by being shown to be erroneous." (Morris)

ii. "'Scripture cannot be annulled' or 'made void' (Mark 7:13); it cannot be set aside when its teaching is inconvenient. What is written remains written." (Bruce)

iii. "Notice that he says this, not in connection with some declaration which might be regarded as among the key declarations of the Old Testament, but of what we might perhaps call without disrespect a rather run-of-the-mill passage." (Morris)

iv. The word of God can't be broken; it breaks whatever opposes it.

e. **Him whom the Father sanctified and sent into the world**: This was a wonderful way for Jesus to speak of Himself. He is the One whom the Father sanctified, and the One whom the Father sent **into the world**.

i. "The judges as well as the lawgivers and prophets of the old dispensation, as it is pointed out in verse 35, were those *unto whom the word of God came*, while Jesus is *Himself* sent by God, the very Word of God made flesh." (Tasker)

ii. **That you may know and believe**: "The former of these is the introductory act, the latter the abiding state, of the knowledge spoken of." (Alford)

f. **Therefore they sought again to seize Him, but He escaped out of their hand**: Once again, the enemies of Jesus were unable to carry out their violent plan against Jesus.

i. "He went forth out of that closing circle - the power that emanated from Him preventing their laying hands on Him: it was the same power that he allowed to issue from Him on the night of His arrest." (Trench)

6. (40-42) Jesus goes across the Jordan and any believe.

And He went away again beyond the Jordan to the place where John was baptizing at first, and there He stayed. Then many came to Him and said, "John performed no sign, but all the things that John spoke about this Man were true." And many believed in Him there.

a. **He went away again beyond the Jordan**: Jesus did not remain in Jerusalem among the hostile religious leaders. Knowing the time was short but not yet for His arrest and crucifixion, Jesus went **beyond the Jordan**.

i. "Perea was the domain of Herod Antipas, where the rulers in Jerusalem had no authority. Jesus would be safe from harassment there - at least temporarily." (Tenney)

ii. "In the place where one might have thought He would be welcomed men tried to stone Him. Now in despised Perea men believed on Him." (Morris)

iii. "If, my dear brother, speaking in Christ's name, you find that you have no place in such and such a town, it may be the Spirit's will that you should remove to a people who will receive you. Possibly in a place which promises less you may gain more. Bethabara may yield converts when Jerusalem only yields persecutors." (Spurgeon)

iv. "He always armed himself to meet me by first meeting God. That is why he retired to the other side of the Jordan. He was not running away: he was preparing himself for the final contest." (Barclay)

b. **John performed no sign**: It is of both interest and significance that as remarkable as the ministry of John the Baptist was, it was popularly known that he performed no miracles. Yet, *everything he said about Jesus was true* (**all the things that John spoke about this Man were true**).

i. "'And they kept saying (implied), "*John* (strongly emphatic in the Greek) did no sign,"' implying that Jesus did many here." (Trench)

ii. This shows us something about the place of miracles in the normal Christian life.

- John didn't do any miracles, but he had a high character.
- John didn't do any miracles, but he had special work to do.
- John didn't do any miracles, but he had a deep and lasting influence.
- John didn't do any miracles, but he won the highest praise of Jesus.

iii. "We are so apt to think that special service is only given to very special people, that great tasks are not for common folk but for men of wonder-working gifts." (Morrison)

c. **Then many came to Him... many believed in Him there**: Jesus still faced great opposition from the religious leaders in Jerusalem, and their greatest act of opposition was just about to begin. Yet many people still came to Jesus. God's work went on, despite the opposition of man.

John 11 - Jesus Raises Lazarus from the Dead

A. The death of Lazarus.

1. (1-3) A request is brought to Jesus.

Now a certain *man* was sick, Lazarus of Bethany, the town of Mary and her sister Martha. It was *that* Mary who anointed the Lord with fragrant oil and wiped His feet with her hair, whose brother Lazarus was sick. Therefore the sisters sent to Him, saying, "Lord, behold, he whom You love is sick."

a. **Now a certain man was sick**: This begins perhaps the most remarkable miracle Jesus performed. One might say that it is foolish to think one miracle is more difficult than another, but this seventh sign of John's gospel is unique.

i. "There is no parallel whatever for the raising of a man who had been dead for four days and whose body had begun to putrefy." (Barclay)

ii. "It is surprising that the other evangelists have omitted so remarkable an account as this is, in which some of the finest traits in our Lord's character are exhibited. The conjecture of *Grotius* has a good deal of weight. He thinks that the other three evangelists wrote their histories during the life of Lazarus; and that they did not mention him for fear of exciting the malice of the Jews against him." (Clarke)

iii. Morris suggested another reason the Synoptic Gospels did not include the account of the raising of Lazarus is that Peter was not present; in these months he was in Galilee while Jesus was in Perea and Bethany. Many think that the Synoptic Gospels are centered on Peter's account of Jesus' teaching and ministry.

iv. **Lazarus of Bethany**: "'Lazarus,' the Greek form of Eleazar = God is my Help." (Dods)

b. **Lazarus... Mary and her sister Martha**: Jesus had a close relationship with this family. When **Lazarus was sick** it was natural for them to bring their need to Jesus. It was expected that if He miraculously met the needs of so many others, He would meet their need also.

c. **Lord, behold, he whom You love is sick**: Mary and Martha did not specifically ask Jesus to come and heal Lazarus. They felt they did not need to, that it was enough to simply tell Jesus what the problem was.

> i. "The love of Jesus does not separate us from the common necessities and infirmities of human life. Men of God are still men." (Spurgeon)

2. (4-6) Jesus responds with a delay.

When Jesus heard *that*, He said, "This sickness is not unto death, but for the glory of God, that the Son of God may be glorified through it." Now Jesus loved Martha and her sister and Lazarus. So, when He heard that he was sick, He stayed two more days in the place where He was.

a. **This sickness is not unto death**: Lazarus was already dead when Jesus said this, but He knew the end result would be **the glory of God**, not death. Jesus also knew that the events recorded in this chapter would set the religious leaders in determination to kill Jesus. This meant the end result would be **that the Son of God may be glorified** in His death and resurrection.

> i. "The only right understanding of this answer, and our Lord's whole proceeding here is, -- that *He knew and foresaw all from the first*." (Alford)

> ii. "We should have said that the sickness was unto death, but, ultimately, to the glory of God. But he who sees the end from the beginning streaks with a grandeur of style which could not be imitated by us. So the Lord speaks of things, not as they seem to be, nor even as they are in the present moment, but as they shall be in the long run." (Spurgeon)

b. **Now Jesus loved Martha and her sister and Lazarus**: John reminds us that Jesus did genuinely love these sisters and their brother. It was an important reminder, showing that a testing of their faith was not a denial of His love.

> i. "The separate mention of the three persons is probably meant to put some stress on Jesus' affection for each one individually. He did not simply love the family. He loved Martha and He loved Mary and He loved Lazarus." (Morris)

ii. The *individual* love of Jesus towards these three is especially significant when we think of how they were different, both in their temperament and in their situations of life.

iii. "That disciple whom Jesus loved is not at all backward to record that Jesus loved Lazarus too: there are no jealousies among those who are chosen by the Well-beloved." (Spurgeon)

c. **He stayed two more days**: It seems strange that Jesus did not immediately act upon this great need. The delay was probably mystifying to the disciples and agonizing to Mary and Martha.

i. It is clear that Jesus prolonged the sorrow of Mary and Martha. These were **two more days** of agonized grief for them. Yet, "Sorrow is prolonged for the same reason as it was sent. It is of little use to send it for a little while." (Maclaren)

ii. Jesus deliberately waited to bring Lazarus back from the dead until he had been in the tomb four days. "Lightfoot quotes a remarkable tradition of Ben Kaphra: 'Grief reaches its height on the third day. For three days the spirit hovers about the tomb, if perchance it may return to the body. But when it sees the fashion of the countenance changed, it retires and abandons the body.'" (Dods)

iii. In John's Gospel there are three times when someone dear to Jesus asked Him to do something (John 2:1-11 and 7:1-10)). In each of these three cases, Jesus responded in the same way.

- Jesus first refused to grant their request and then He fulfilled it after showing that He does things according to the timing and will of God, not man.

- Through His actions Jesus demonstrated that His delays were not denials. They would bring greater glory to God.

3. (7-10) Jesus courageously decides to go to Judea and Jerusalem.

Then after this He said to *the* disciples, "Let us go to Judea again." *The* disciples said to Him, "Rabbi, lately the Jews sought to stone You, and are You going there again?" Jesus answered, "Are there not twelve hours in the day? If anyone walks in the day, he does not stumble, because he sees the light of this world. But if one walks in the night, he stumbles, because the light is not in him."

a. **Let us go to Judea again**: Jesus *could* have raised Lazarus from a distance. Because of the opposition from the religious leaders, Judea was a dangerous place for Jesus. Nevertheless, Jesus was willing **to go to Judea again** - despite the warnings from His disciples.

b. **Are there not twelve hours in the day?** Jesus' disciples were shocked that He would return to the region of Judea when He was a wanted man there. Jesus responded with by saying that He still had work to do. The **twelve hours** were a figurative way to speak of the time allotted by God the Father for the earthly work of Jesus.

i. There are many practical applications of this wise statement.

- Nothing can shorten our time.
- There is enough time for everything that needs to be done.
- We only have that time, so it must not be wasted.

ii. "Jesus is saying that a man must finish the day's work within the day, for the night comes when work is ended." (Barclay)

iii. "There are but twelve hours in the day, and it will be sunset before you dream of it. Get done what God has sent you here to do." (Morrison)

c. **If anyone walks in the day, he does not stumble**: During these **hours** no harm could come to Jesus and the disciples. They had to work before the **night** of Jesus' passion.

i. "I have a fixed time during which to work, appointed me by my Father; during that time I feel no danger, I walk in His light, even as the traveller in the light of this world by day." (Alford)

4. (11-15) Jesus tells them plainly of Lazarus' death.

These things He said, and after that He said to them, "Our friend Lazarus sleeps, but I go that I may wake him up." Then His disciples said, "Lord, if he sleeps he will get well." However, Jesus spoke of his death, but they thought that He was speaking about taking rest in sleep. Then Jesus said to them plainly, "Lazarus is dead. And I am glad for your sakes that I was not there, that you may believe. Nevertheless let us go to him."

a. **Our friend Lazarus sleeps, but I go that I may wake him up**: Jesus used the familiar metaphor of *sleep* to describe the death of Lazarus. The figure of speech was especially meaningful because Jesus would soon **wake him up** - bring Lazarus back from death.

i. Jesus said of Jarius' daughter that she was asleep (Matthew 9:24). At the end of Stephen's martyrdom we are told that he fell asleep (Acts 7:60).

b. **Lazarus is dead. And I am glad**: Jesus could be **glad**, even in the death of a dear friend, because He was certain of the outcome. We see at the end of the events of this chapter that grief was comforted, life was restored, many more believed, and the necessary death of Jesus was set in motion. All of these were reasons to be **glad**.

> i. "So we may learn that He often permits us to pass into profounder darkness, and deeper mysteries of pain, in order that we may prove more perfectly His power." (Morgan)

> ii. **Nevertheless let us go to him**: "Our Lord probably left *Bethabara* the day, or the day after, Lazarus died. He came to *Bethany* three days after; and it appears that Lazarus had been buried about four days, and consequently that he had been put in the grave the day or day after he died." (Clarke)

5. (16) Thomas' bold faith.

Then Thomas, who is called the Twin, said to his fellow disciples, "Let us also go, that we may die with Him."

a. **Thomas, who is called the Twin**: Church tradition says that Thomas was called **the Twin** because he looked like Jesus, putting him at special risk. If any among the disciples of Jesus were potential targets of persecution it would be the one who *looked* like Jesus.

> i. All Jews in those days had two names - one a Hebrew name by which a man was known in his own circle, the other a Greek name by which he was known in a wider circle. *Thomas* is the *Hebrew* and *Didymus* the *Greek* for a *twin*." (Barclay)

b. **Let us also go, that we may die with Him**: Thomas was willing to go with Jesus even if it meant dying with Him. He made this commitment without much understanding of a promise of resurrection.

> i. "Thomas utters a cry of loyal despair." (Tasker)

> ii. "He is the pessimist among the disciples, and now take the gloomy, and, as it is proved, the correct view of the result of this return to Judaea, but his affectionate loyalty forbids the thought of allowing Jesus to go alone." (Dods)

B. Jesus meets with Martha and Mary.

1. (17-22) Martha greets Jesus as He comes to Bethany.

So when Jesus came, He found that he had already been in the tomb four days. Now Bethany was near Jerusalem, about two miles away. And many of the Jews had joined the women around Martha and Mary, to comfort them concerning their brother. Then Martha, as soon as she heard that Jesus was coming, went and met Him, but Mary was sitting in the house. Then Martha said to Jesus, "Lord, if You had been here,

my brother would not have died. But even now I know that whatever You ask of God, God will give You."

a. **He had already been in the tomb four days**: Jesus waited **four days** because He knew the Jewish superstition of that day that said a soul stayed *near* the grave for three days, hoping to return to the body. Therefore, it was accepted that after **four days** there was absolutely no hope of resuscitation.

b. **Many of the Jews had joined the women around Mary and Martha**: This was a large crowd, still present four days after Lazarus was buried. It was considered an important obligation to join with those who mourned the death of a near relative.

i. "A procession composed of relatives, friends, and sometimes hired mourners accompanied a body to the grave; and mourning usually lasted for several days afterward." (Tenney)

ii. **Mary was sitting in the house**: "It is likely that by this circumstance the evangelist intended to convey the idea of her sorrow and distress; because anciently afflicted persons were accustomed to put themselves in this posture, as expressive of their distress; their grief having rendered them as it were immovable." (Clarke)

c. **Lord, if You had been here, my brother would not have died**: Martha honestly stated her disappointment in Jesus' late arrival. She believed that Jesus was able to heal her brother while he was sick yet still alive. It's possible that she didn't even consider that Jesus was able to raise Lazarus from the dead *now*.

i. "Death was no stronger in His presence than disease, but these did not realize this. They would think of Death as the unconquerable. With disease men may grapple, and fight, and often overcome. But in the presence of death they are helpless." (Morgan)

d. **Even now I know that whatever You ask of God, God will give You**: Martha was not confident that Jesus would raise her brother. Instead, she said that she would still trust Jesus *despite* this disappointment. This was a remarkable demonstration of faith, one that should be taken as an example.

i. "Some prayers would be all the better if they were shorter -- all the better if they did not so much declare our own will as declare our confidence in the good will of Christ. I like the omissions of Martha's and Mary's prayer." (Spurgeon)

ii. There can be great power in "**even now**" prayers.

- Your loved one can be as dead and smelly as Lazarus - do you believe Jesus for them, **even now**?

- You own situation can be as far gone as Lazarus was - do you believe Jesus for yourself, **even now**?

2. (23-27) I am the resurrection and the life.

Jesus said to her, "Your brother will rise again." Martha said to Him, "I know that he will rise again in the resurrection at the last day." Jesus said to her, "I am the resurrection and the life. He who believes in Me, though he may die, he shall live. And whoever lives and believes in Me shall never die. Do you believe this?" She said to Him, "Yes, Lord, I believe that You are the Christ, the Son of God, who is to come into the world."

a. **Your brother will rise again**: Martha understood that her brother Lazarus would **rise again** with all the righteous on the **last day**. She did not even consider that Jesus might immediately bring Lazarus from the dead.

i. We may comfort a grieving person by saying, "You will see him again." We sincerely mean it and sincerely mean the comfort, but we don't mean "You will see him again right now." Jesus meant that Lazarus would **rise again** *right now*.

ii. "That resurrection in the last day shall be only *by my Power*, and therefore I can raise now as well." (Alford)

iii. **I know that he will rise again in the resurrection at the last day**: "Thanks to the influence of the Pharisees and those who followed their line, this was now the general belief among Jews, in spite of the Sadducean resistance to it." (Bruce)

iv. "It is clear that she derived very little consolation from the fact of a distant and general resurrection: she needed resurrection and life to come nearer home, and to become more a present fact to her." (Spurgeon)

b. **I am the resurrection and the life**: Jesus did not claim to *have* resurrection and life, or *understand secrets* about resurrection and life. Instead Jesus dramatically said that He *is* **the resurrection and the life**. To know Jesus is to know resurrection and life; to have Jesus is to have resurrection and life.

i. "She looked upon the resurrection and the life as things that were to be in some dim and misty future. 'No,' says Christ, 'I am the resurrection and the life. Not only do I get these things by prayer from God, but I am these things.'" (Spurgeon)

ii. "Apart from Him there was neither resurrection nor life." (Dods)

iii. "Thou sayest that thy brother shall rise again in the resurrection at the last day; but by whom shall he arise if not by ME, who am the author of the resurrection, and the source of life? And is it not as easy for me to raise him *now* as to raise him *then?*" (Clarke)

c. **He who believes in Me, though he may die, he shall live:** Jesus boldly challenged Martha to trust that He was the source of eternal life. Jesus presented Himself as the champion over death. While humanity in general fears death, the Christian can only fear dying. The believer will never die, but simply make an instant transition from an old life to a new life.

i. "Those that believe in Jesus Christ appear to die, but yet they live. They are not in the grave, they are for ever with the Lord. They are not unconscious they are with their Lord in Paradise. Death cannot kill a believer, it can only usher him into a freer form of life." (Spurgeon)

ii. "Jesus does not of course man that the believer will not die physically. Lazarus was dead even then, and millions of Jesus' followers have died since. But He means that he will not die in the sense in which death has eternal significance." (Morris)

iii. "Death comes to the ungodly man as a penal infliction, but to the righteous as a summons to his Father's palace: to the sinner it is an execution, to the saint an undressing. Death to the wicked is the King of terrors: death to the saint is the end of terrors, the commencement of glory." (Spurgeon)

iv. "In the primitive Church, when they repeated that article of the creed, 'I believe in the resurrection of the flesh,' they would point to their bodies and say, *etiam hujus carnis,* even of this very flesh." (Trapp)

v. Jesus made an enormous claim: *I am* **the resurrection and the life. He who believes *in Me*, though he may die, he shall live.** Only God could say such things in truth.

d. **Do you believe this?** Jesus challenged Martha not to debate or intellectual assent, but to *belief*. She must believe Jesus was who He said He was and that He could do what He said He could do.

i. "He saith not, Understandest thou this?" (Trapp)

ii. "Does that mean that He would not raise her brother unless she believed? No; for He had determined to 'awake him out of sleep' before He left Perea." (Maclaren)

e. **Yes, Lord, I believe that You are the Christ, the Son of God, who is to come into the world:** Martha answered correctly. Jesus was and is indeed the Messiah (**the Christ**). Jesus was and is God in human form among us (**the Son of God**).

> i. **I believe**: "Here 'I' is emphatic. Whatever may be the case with others she has put her trust in Jesus." (Morris)

> ii. Boice called these words of Martha *faith's foothold* - they were a sure support from which she could climb higher.

3. (28-32) Mary's regret.

And when she had said these things, she went her way and secretly called Mary her sister, saying, "The Teacher has come and is calling for you." As soon as she heard *that*, she arose quickly and came to Him. Now Jesus had not yet come into the town, but was in the place where Martha met Him. Then the Jews who were with her in the house, and comforting her, when they saw that Mary rose up quickly and went out, followed her, saying, "She is going to the tomb to weep there." Then, when Mary came where Jesus was, and saw Him, she fell down at His feet, saying to Him, "Lord, if You had been here, my brother would not have died."

> a. **She went her way and secretly called Mary her sister**: We aren't told exactly *why* Martha did this secretly. It's fair to guess that she did it to help Mary have a few uninterrupted moments with Jesus before the crowd of other mourners surrounded them.

> > i. **The Teacher has come**: "She speaks of Jesus as 'The Teacher' and the article is probably important. Among His followers Jesus was designated primarily by His teaching activities. But He is recognized as incomparable. He is '*the* Teacher'." (Morris)

> > ii. **The Teacher**: "It is important to notice this use of the term by a woman. The Rabbis refused to instruct women, but Jesus took a very different view." (Morris)

> > iii. **As soon as she heard that, she arose quickly and came to Him**: "Martha told Mary that Jesus was asking for her. To Mary, this was equivalent to a command to come. Mary wasted no time in going to Jesus." (Tenne)

> b. **Lord, if You had been here, my brother would not have died**: Lazarus had two sisters, Mary and Martha. Martha has already spoken to Jesus regarding the death of Lazarus, then Mary spoke. Her words are remarkably similar to what Martha told Jesus (John 11:21).

> > i. "It is likely that they had said this to each other several times since Lazarus died." (Bruce)

c. **My brother would not have died**: This is one of the places in the Bible where we wish we could hear the tone of voice and see the expressions on the face. This could have been a noble statement of faith, saying that if Jesus was there they have no doubt at all that He would have healed Lazarus. On the other hand, it could also be seen as a criticism of what seemed to be the tardiness of Jesus.

C. Lazarus is raised.

1. (33-38) A deeply moved Jesus comes to the tomb.

Therefore, when Jesus saw her weeping, and the Jews who came with her weeping, He groaned in the spirit and was troubled. And He said, "Where have you laid him?" They said to Him, "Lord, come and see." Jesus wept. Then the Jews said, "See how He loved him!" And some of them said, "Could not this Man, who opened the eyes of the blind, also have kept this man from dying?" Then Jesus, again groaning in Himself, came to the tomb. It was a cave, and a stone lay against it.

a. **When Jesus saw her weeping**: The grief and tears of Mary and Martha moved Jesus. God sees the tears of the grief stricken and is moved with compassion.

- God sees our tears.
- God is touched by our tears.
- God remembers our tears.
- God acts to dry our tears.

b. **And the Jews who came with her weeping**: The Jews of that time and place were not reserved in their expressions of sorrow or grief.

i. "We must remember that this would be no gentle shedding of tears. It would be almost hysterical wailing and shrieking, for it was the Jewish point of view that the more unrestrained the weeping, the honour it paid to the dead." (Barclay)

ii. **Jesus saw her weeping... Jesus wept**: There is an important contrast between the tears of Mary and the tears of Jesus. **Weeping** (the word used for Mary in John 11:33) is a word that describes loud wailing. **Wept** (the word to describe Jesus' expression of grief in John 11:35) is another word that indicates a quiet weeping. Jesus *was* greatly moved, but *not* out of control.

iii. Morris on **Jesus wept**: "That used here (and here only in the New Testament) points rather to a quiet weeping. Jesus did not wail loudly but He was deeply grieved."

c. **He groaned in the spirit and was troubled**: Coming to the scene of Lazarus' tomb, Jesus intensely **groaned in the spirit**. In the ancient Greek, this phrase literally means, *to snort like a horse* - implying anger and indignation.

i. "The verb rendered 'groaned' is an unusual one. It signifies a loud inarticulate noise, and its proper use appears to be for the snorting of horses. When used of men it usually denotes anger." (Morris)

ii. According to Trench, the sense of **was troubled** is "'And troubled Himself.' The phrase is remarkable: deliberately summoned up in Himself the feelings of indignation at the havoc wrought by the evil one, and of tenderness for the mourners."

iii. "In ordinary classical Greek the usual usage of *embrimasthai* is of a horse *snorting*. Here it must mean that such deep emotion seized Jesus that an involuntary groan was wrung from his heart." (Barclay)

iv. It means that Jesus wasn't so much *sad* at the scene surrounding the tomb of Lazarus. It's more accurate to say that Jesus was *angry*. Jesus was angry and troubled at the destruction and power of the great enemy of humanity: death. Jesus would soon break the dominating power of death.

v. "Christ does not come to the sepulcher as an idle spectator, but like a wrestler preparing for the contest. Therefore no wonder that He groans again, for the violent tyranny of death which He had to overcome stands before His eyes." (Calvin)

d. **Jesus wept**: Jesus shared in the grief of those who mourn. Yet unlike any other, God the Son was able to *do* something about their grief. Jesus allowed this sympathetic passion to uniquely do for Lazarus what He will one day do for all the righteous dead.

i. **Jesus wept**: There are many aspects to these two words.

- Jesus was truly a man.
- There may be no sin or shame in tears.
- Jesus was acquainted with grief.
- Jesus was not ashamed of His humanity.
- Jesus identified with others in their sorrow.
- Jesus loves people.

ii. "Jesus had *humanity* in its perfection, and humanity unadulterated is *generous* and *sympathetic*." (Clarke) "He suffered all the innocent infirmities of our nature." (Spurgeon)

iii. Jesus dignified the tears of others in the Bible who wept, and all who weep.

- Abraham wept when he buried Sarah.
- Jacob wept when he wrestled the Angel.
- David and Jonathan wept together.
- Hezekiah wept over his sickness.
- Josiah wept over the sin of his nation.
- Jeremiah was the weeping prophet.

iv. "Sometimes we are told that if we really believed that our friends would rise again, and that they are safe and happy even now, we could not weep. Why not? Jesus did. There cannot be any error in following where Jesus leads the way." (Spurgeon)

v. Barclay explains that to the mind of the ancient Greek the primary characteristic of God was *apatheia*: the total inability to feel any emotion whatsoever. The Greeks believed in an isolated, passionless, and compassionless God. That isn't the God of the Bible. That isn't the God who is really there.

vi. **Again groaning in Himself:** "The repetition of 'deeply moved' (*embrimomenos*), the present participle of the verb, shows that Jesus was still under the same emotional tension that his first contact with the mourners had aroused." (Tenney)

vii. **See how He loved him!** "And when *we* see him pouring out his blood and life upon the cross for mankind, we may with exultation and joy cry out, *Behold how he hath loved US!*" (Clarke)

e. **And some of them said, "Could not this Man, who opened the eyes of the blind, also have kept this man from dying?"** These seem to be words of genuine sorrow and sympathy. They thought it truly sad that even Jesus, in all His greatness, could do nothing for Lazarus at this point.

i. "There is no reason for thinking of the words as spoken in mockery." (Morris)

ii. Yet, these words were not helpful to anyone. Spurgeon noted that all this "what if" talking is vain, of no use. "Perhaps the bitterest griefs that men know come not from facts, but from things which might have been, as they imagine; that is to say, they dig wells of supposition, and drink the brackish waters of regret." (Spurgeon)

iii. "Suppose that Jesus is willing to open the eyes of the blind, and does open them; is he therefore bound to raise this particular dead man? If he does not see fit to do so, does that prove that he has not the power? If he lets Lazarus die, is it proven therefore that he could not have saved his life? May there not be some other reason? Does Omnipotence always exert its power? Does it ever exert all its power?" (Spurgeon)

2. (39-40) Jesus commands the stone to be removed.

Jesus said, "Take away the stone." Martha, the sister of him who was dead, said to Him, "Lord, by this time there is a stench, for he has been *dead* four days." Jesus said to her, "Did I not say to you that if you would believe you would see the glory of God?"

a. **Take away the stone**: Everybody thought this was a strange thing for Jesus to ask. After all, Martha knew *Lord, by this time he stinketh* (King James Version). People probably thought that Jesus was so taken with grief that He wanted one last look at His dear friend Lazarus.

b. **By this time there is a stench**: In any case, the condition of the body was an irrefutable confirmation of Lazarus' death.

i. "The Greek word οζω signifies simply *to smell*, whether the scent be *good* or *bad*; but the circumstances of the case sufficiently show that the latter is its meaning here." (Clarke)

c. **If you would believe you would see the glory of God**: Jesus was fully capable of this miracle without the faith of Martha or Mary. But if they would *not* believe, then *they* would never **see the glory of God**. They could see the end result and be happy in that, but they would miss the **glory** of working together with God in the fulfillment of His plan.

3. (41-42) Jesus prays at the tomb of Lazarus.

Then they took away the stone *from the place* where the dead man was lying. And Jesus lifted up *His* eyes and said, "Father, I thank You that You have heard Me. And I know that You always hear Me, but because of the people who are standing by I said *this*, that they may believe that You sent Me."

a. **Then they took away the stone from the place where the dead man was lying**: This was a definite and remarkable step of faith. Jesus compelled Martha and Mary to act on their faith and they did by obeying Jesus and His unusual request.

i. We see that Jesus dealt with Martha according to steps deliberately intended to stretch and build her faith.

• Jesus gave her a promise.

• Jesus drew attention to Himself.

- Jesus called upon her to confess her faith.
- Jesus called her to act on her faith.

b. **Jesus lifted up His eyes and said**: Jesus likely had the traditional posture of prayer - hands raised, eyes open upwards as if looking towards heaven.

c. **Father, I thank You that You have heard Me**: Jesus was confident in His relationship with God the Father. The *public* nature of the prayer was for the sake of Mary, Martha, and **the people who are standing by**. The *power* of the prayer was rooted in the private prayer times of Jesus.

i. "No pomp of incantation, no wrestling in prayer even; but simple words of thanksgiving, as if Lazarus had already returned." (Dods)

ii. "During His humiliation on earth, these acts of power were done by Him, not by that glory of His own which He had laid aside, but by the mighty working of the Father in *Him*, and in answer to His prayer." (Alford)

4. (43-44) Jesus raises Lazarus from the dead.

Now when He had said these things, He cried with a loud voice, "Lazarus, come forth!" And he who had died came out bound hand and foot with graveclothes, and his face was wrapped with a cloth. Jesus said to them, "Loose him, and let him go."

a. **He cried with a loud voice, "Lazarus, come forth!"** Jesus simply called Lazarus out of the tomb. Others whom God used to raise dead bodies in the Scriptures often used far more elaborate procedures

i. **Cried with a loud voice**: "Means with John the loud decisive tone of authority." (Trench)

ii. "The loud voice was not, of course, because a loud voice was needed to make the dead hear. Probably it was in part at least, so that the crowd could know that this was no work of magic, but the very power of God. Wizards mutter their incantations and spells (*cf.* Isaiah 8:19). Not so the Son of God." (Morris)

iii. "Jesus had said on a previous occasion that a time would come when all who were in their graves would hear his voice (John 5:28). This occasion was a single demonstration of that authority." (Tenney)

b. **Lazarus, come forth!** Jesus spoke to a dead body as if Lazarus were alive because He is *God, who gives life to the dead and calls those things which do not exist as though they did* (Romans 4:17).

i. "The words spoken were brief, direct, and imperative and can be paraphrased, 'Lazarus! This way out!' as if Jesus were directing someone lost in a gloomy dungeon." (Tenney)

ii. "If this voice of Christ had been directed to all the dead, they had presently risen." (Trapp)

c. **And he who had died came out**: Jesus fought death at Lazarus' tomb, and plundered the grave. Jesus told death the He would soon completely conquer it completely.

d. **His face was wrapped with a cloth**: Lazarus was not resurrected, but resuscitated. He arose bound in grave-clothes, for he would need them again; Jesus left His grave-clothes behind in His tomb, never again having need of them.

i. "How he moved I do not know. Some of the old writers thought that he glided, as it were, through the air, and that this was part of the miracle. I think he may have been so bound that though he could not freely walk yet he could shuffle along like a man in a sack." (Spurgeon)

e. **Jesus said to them, "Loose him, and let him go"**: Jesus did not miraculously remove the grave-clothes from Lazarus, but He asked attendants to do so. Jesus did what only God could do, and then He looked for man's cooperation for the completion of Lazarus' deliverance.

i. "The man was wholly raised, but not wholly freed. See, here is *a living man in the garments of death!*" (Spurgeon)

ii. "What a man can do for himself God will not do for him, and what Christian people can do for sinners they must not expect the Lord to do, they must work themselves according to the ability God has given them up to the point of possibility, and then they may look for divine interposition." (Spurgeon)

D. Two reactions.

1. (45) The reaction of faith: **many of the Jews... believed in Him**.

Then many of the Jews who had come to Mary, and had seen the things Jesus did, believed in Him.

a. **Many of the Jews who had come to Mary**: Those who came to join in the sorrow of the grieving sisters did not expect that their reason for grief would be taken away.

b. **Had seen the things Jesus did, believe in him**: This was undeniably an impressive work of God, and for many it helped them put their trust in who Jesus said He was by seeing what He did.

2. (46-48) The worry of the religious leaders.

But some of them went away to the Pharisees and told them the things Jesus did. Then the chief priests and the Pharisees gathered a council and said, "What shall we do? For this Man works many signs. If we let Him alone like this, everyone will believe in Him, and the Romans will come and take away both our place and nation."

a. **But some of them went away to the Pharisees**: John continues his persistent theme - that the words and works of Jesus divide humanity between those who believe and those who reject. There were **some** who saw both the power and sympathy of Jesus yet responded by working against Him.

> i. "Astonishing! Some that had seen even this miracle steeled their hearts against it; and not only so, but conspired the destruction of this most humane, amiable, and glorious Saviour!" (Clarke)

> ii. Spurgeon called the reporting of this to the Pharisees, "some of the meanest conduct that has ever been recorded in human history."

> iii. **Gathered a council**: Though unofficial, "It was a meeting of the Sanhedrin. John's authority for the account of what passed here would be Joseph of Arimathaea or Nicodemus or some other member of the Sanhedrin who later became a Christian." (Trench)

b. **For this Man works many signs**: The religious leaders privately admitted that Jesus performed signs that authenticated His claim to be Messiah and God. As Jesus claimed, His works did bear witness of Him (John 10:25).

> i. Their opposition changed. First they opposed Jesus because they weren't convinced He was the Messiah. Now they opposed Jesus because they were convinced that He was the Messiah. They admitted the miracles, but look how they treated the Miracle-worker:

> - They denied Him.
> - The opposed Him.
> - They were afraid of His influence over the people.

c. **If we let Him alone like this, everyone will believe in Him**: The religious leaders knew the logical response to the witness of the works of Jesus was to **believe in Him**. They feared more and more would do so.

> i. There is a wonderful thought suggested by this phrase, **if we let Him alone like this, everyone will believe in Him** - simply that left alone, Jesus shows forth His glory.

ii. However, in the sense that the Pharisees meant this, they were wrong. "Historically, and in the sovereign will of God, it is just because the Pharisees did not let Christ alone that we believe and worship Him." (Morrison)

d. **The Romans will come and take away both our place and nation**: As Jesus attracted more and more followers, the religious leaders feared that the Romans would regard it as a significant threat. Wanting especially to keep their power and prestige, they wondered how to deal with the problem of Jesus.

i. Most commentators believe that **our place** refers to *the temple*. The religious leaders had made such an idol of the temple that they were willing to kill Jesus to preserve it.

ii. "'Our place' which, they feared, would be taken away was the temple ('this holy place' of Acts 6:13f.; 21:28)." (Bruce)

iii. It is telling that the religious leaders thought of the temple as **our place**, as if it belonged to them. Many church leaders today do the same, truly thinking of the church as *our church* instead of really understanding that it belongs to Jesus.

iv. In tragic fact, this rejection of Jesus resulted in the political ruin and ultimate destruction of the nation. "By the time this Gospel was written, the catastrophe which they dreaded had taken place, but not because of the presence and activity of Jesus." (Bruce)

3. (49-52) The counsel of Caiaphas.

And one of them, Caiaphas, being high priest that year, said to them, "You know nothing at all, nor do you consider that it is expedient for us that one man should die for the people, and not that the whole nation should perish." Now this he did not say on his own *authority*; but being high priest that year he prophesied that Jesus would die for the nation, and not for that nation only, but also that He would gather together in one the children of God who were scattered abroad.

a. **It is expedient for us that one man should die for the people, and not that the whole nation should perish**: Caiaphas thought logically but nor morally. It was logical that **one man should die for the people**, but it was not moral to reject the Messiah and seek the death of an innocent Man.

i. **Being high priest that year**: "He was High Priest during the whole Procuratorship of Pontius Pilate, eleven years. In the words **that year**, there is no intimation conveyed that the High Priesthood was changed every year, which it *was not*, but we must understand the words as directing attention to '*that (remarkable) year*'." (Alford)

ii. **You know nothing at all**: "According to Josephus, Sadducees had a reputation for rudeness, even among one another." (Bruce)

iii. **Nor do you consider**: "A word used of reckoning up accounts and the like. He is saying that they cannot even calculate, cannot even work it out that such and such a course of action is the expedient one." (Morris)

b. **He prophesied that Jesus would die for the nation**: Caiaphas gave an unconscious and involuntary prophecy. John was careful to give the credit to the *office*, not to the *man* (**being high priest that year he prophesied**).

i. "He is urging them to put Jesus to death: but the form of words he uses is unconsciously prophetic." (Trench)

ii. "Wholesome sugar may be found in a poisoned cane, a precious stone in a toad's head, a flaming torch in a blind man's hand." (Trapp)

c. **Also that He would gather together in one the children of God who were scattered abroad**: John explained that the unconscious prophecy of Caiaphas was greater than he could have ever imagined. The death of Jesus would also **gather together in one** the sheep of another fold Jesus had previously spoken of (John 10:16).

i. "Caiaphas's words are not big enough. John has a world-wide vision." (Morris)

4. (53-54) The plot to put Jesus to death

Then, from that day on, they plotted to put Him to death. Therefore Jesus no longer walked openly among the Jews, but went from there into the country near the wilderness, to a city called Ephraim, and there remained with His disciples.

a. **Then from that day on they plotted to put Him to death**: Before it was mostly lesser religious officials who wanted Jesus dead. At this point the men with real political power decided to murder Jesus. The time was now short until the death of Jesus.

i. Maclaren expressed the thinking of the council: "Never mind about His miracles, or His teaching, or the beauty of His character. His life is a perpetual danger to our prerogatives. I vote for death!"

ii. "This last sign raised the opposition of His foes to definite activity." (Morgan)

b. **Therefore Jesus no longer walked openly among the Jews**: Again, Jesus did not do this out of fear, but because *His hour had not yet come* (as in John 7:30). The hour had not yet come, but it was soon to come.

i. **A city called Ephraim**: This was north of Jerusalem, close to Samaria. "This city Ephraim is the Ephrain of 2 Chronicles 13:19 = the Ophrah of Joshua 18:23: it had repeatedly changed hands, between Benjamin and Ephraim, in the old wars." (Trench)

5. (55-57) Looking for Jesus at the Passover feast.

And the Passover of the Jews was near, and many went from the country up to Jerusalem before the Passover, to purify themselves. Then they sought Jesus, and spoke among themselves as they stood in the temple, "What do you think—that He will not come to the feast?" Now both the chief priests and the Pharisees had given a command, that if anyone knew where He was, he should report *it*, that they might seize Him.

a. **Before the Passover, to purify themselves**: This means that it was the last few days before the coming Passover - at which Jesus would be betrayed, arrested, condemned, and crucified.

i. "Some purifications required a week, others consisted only of shaving the head and washing the clothes." (Dods)

ii. **That He will not come to the feast?** "The second of their questions seems to show that they expected as answer 'No'...They considered it unlikely that in view of circumstances He would be so foolhardy as to put in an appearance." (Morris)

b. **Both the chief priests at the Pharisees had given a command**: Most of the **chief priests** were Sadducees and normally uncooperative with the **Pharisees**. They found common cause in their opposition to Jesus.

John 12 - The Hour Has Come

A. A dinner at Bethany.

1. (1-2) Lazarus eats and Martha serves.

Then, six days before the Passover, Jesus came to Bethany, where Lazarus was who had been dead, whom He had raised from the dead. There they made Him a supper; and Martha served, but Lazarus was one of those who sat at the table with Him.

a. **Six days before the Passover**: John gave a time marker, telling us that this was the last week before the death and burial of Jesus. Almost one-half of John's Gospel is given to this last week. Matthew used more than 33% of his Gospel to cover that week, Mark nearly 40% and Luke over 25% - to *seven days* of Jesus' entire life.

b. **There they made Him a supper**: Less than a week before His crucifixion, Jesus attended a dinner in **Bethany**, probably to celebrate the raising of Lazarus **from the dead**. With all Jesus had on His mind, knowing His fate as He came to Jerusalem for Passover, it is remarkable that He attended this dinner at all. Most would not feel like socializing.

> i. "He would not pain His hosts by self-absorbed aloofness at the table. The reason for the feast is obviously the raising of Lazarus, as is suggested by his being twice mentioned in verses 1 and 2." (Maclaren)

> ii. **There they made Him**: "The 'therefore' (which the A.V. omits) points to the gratitude for Lazarus' restoration, which that household now showed by entertaining Him at supper." (Trench)

c. **Martha served**: It seems that this dinner was at the home of Simon the Leper (Matthew 26:6 and Mark 14:3). His friends Martha, Lazarus, and Mary were also in attendance. Because **Martha** seems to be the hostess, some think Simon the Leper was related to Mary, Martha, and Lazarus or even that he was Martha's husband. If common customs were followed, this dinner was for the men of the village and Martha and the other women **served**.

> i. It's easy to see Martha in our imagination bringing the best dishes first to Jesus, pressing Him to eat more and more. She was so grateful and so happy to serve Jesus. Her service was appreciated and valued.

> ii. "John does not state, as do Mark and Matthew, that the host at Bethany was Simon the leper. In the story of Luke 7 the host, Simon the Pharisee, is almost certainly a different Simon from the one mentioned in Mark. Simon was a very common Jewish name." (Tasker)

> iii. "The only discrepancy of any consequence being that the Synoptists seem to place the feast only two days before the Passover. But they introduce the feast parenthetically to present the immediate motive of Judas' action, and accordingly disregard strict chronology." (Dods)

2. (3) Mary anoints the feet of Jesus.

Then Mary took a pound of very costly oil of spikenard, anointed the feet of Jesus, and wiped His feet with her hair. And the house was filled with the fragrance of the oil.

a. **Mary took a pound of very costly oil of spikenard, anointed the feet of Jesus**: In the midst of the supper, Mary gave a remarkable gift to Jesus. It wasn't unusual to wash the feet of a guest, but it was unusual to do it during the meal itself, to use **very costly oil of spikenard** to do it, and to **wipe the feet with her hair**, using the hair as a kind of towel.

- Mary's gift was remarkably *humble*. When a guest entered the home, usually the guest's feet were washed with water and the guest's head was anointed with a dab of oil or perfume. Here, Mary used this precious ointment and **anointed the feet of Jesus**. She considered her precious ointment only good enough for His feet. "To attend to the feet was the task of the most lowly slave. Thus Mary's action denoted great humility as well as great devotion." (Morris)

- Mary's gift was remarkably *extreme*. She used a lot (**a pound**) of a **very costly oil of spikenard**. Spices and ointments were often used as an investment because they were small, portable, and could be easily sold. Judas believed this oil was worth *300 denarii* (John 12:5), which was worth a year's wages for a workingman.

- Mary's gift was remarkably *unselfconscious*. Not only did she give the gift of the expensive oil, she also **wiped His feet with her hair**. This means that she let down her hair in public, something a Jewish woman would rarely do.

i. **Oil of spikenard:** "Both John and Mark describe it by the adjective *pistikos* (Mark 14:3). Oddly enough, no one really knows what that word means. There are four possibilities. It may come from the adjective *pistos* which means *faithful* or *reliable*, and so may mean *genuine*. It may come from the verb *pinein* which means *to drink*, and so may mean *liquid*. It may be a kind of trade name, and may have to be translated simply *pistic nard*. It may come from a word meaning the *pistachio nut*, and be a special kind of essence extracted from it. In any event it was a specially valuable kind of perfume." (Barclay)

ii. "It was very costly, but it had not cost a penny too much now that it could be used upon *him*. There was a pound of it, but there was none too much for *him*. It was very sweet, but none too sweet for *him*." (Spurgeon)

iii. "The act is all the more striking in that a Jewish lady never unbound her hair in public. That apparently was a mark of loose morals. But Mary did not stop to calculate public reaction. Her heart went out to her Lord and she gave expression to something of her feelings in this beautiful and touching act." (Morris)

iv. In all of this, Mary is a study of devotion to Jesus. "The life of Mary is painted for us, in three memorable pictures, in each of which she is at the feet of Jesus." (Eerdman)

- Luke 10:39: Mary sat at Jesus' feet and *learned.*
- John 11:32: Mary fell at Jesus' feet and *surrendered.*
- John 12:3: Mary anointed Jesus' feet and *honored* Jesus.

v. "You must sit at his feet, or you will never anoint them; he must pour his divine teaching into you, or you will never pour out a precious ointment upon him." (Spurgeon)

b. **The house was filled with the fragrance of the oil:** The sense of smell makes for long-lasting memories and John remembered how Mary's essential oils made the whole house smell good.

3. (4-6) Judas objects to Mary's rich gift.

Then one of His disciples, Judas Iscariot, Simon's *son,* who would betray Him, said, "Why was this fragrant oil not sold for three hundred denarii and given to the poor?" This he said, not that he cared for the poor, but because he was a thief, and had the money box; and he used to take what was put in it.

a. **Judas Iscariot, Simon's son, who would betray Him:** In a short time Judas would betray Jesus. His betrayal was so much darker when contrasted with the brightness of Mary's devotion to Jesus. Judas probably objected to Mary's gift because he was shamed by her simple and powerful display of love.

i. This is the only place in the New Testament where Judas is mentioned as doing something evil *other* than his betrayal of Jesus, and even this was done in secret. Judas successfully hid the darkness of his heart from everyone except Jesus. Outward appearances often deceive. Many people have a religious facade that hides secret sin.

ii. "He would sell his very Saviour. And a fair match he made: for, as Austin saith, Judas sold his salvation, and the Pharisees bought their damnation." (Trapp)

b. **Why was this fragrant oil not sold for three hundred, denarii**: This was an awkward scene. Then Judas broke the embarrassed silence with his sharp sense of financial values - but no appreciation of what God valued. He thought this was *too much* love and devotion to show to Jesus.

i. "Judas, blinded in self-interest, criticized her action, and so revealed himself as utterly opposed to the very spirit of the Lord Himself." (Morgan)

ii. The *isn't this all a little much* attitude of Judas was contagious. Matthew 26:8 shows Judas was not alone in this objection. Others seem to have felt that Judas made some sense. "The shock of what they had seen must have caused a brief embarrassed silence, which was broken by one voice giving expression to the sentiments of many." (Bruce)

iii. Sometimes this thinking is twisted into a justification for all kinds of opulence and luxury, claiming that nothing is too good for Jesus - and in the twisting, for those who claim to serve Him. We notice that this was done *directly* for Jesus, not for any of the disciples. We also notice that it was *poured out in a single act*, and not something like a work of art that could be sold for the benefit of the poor or the extension of the kingdom of Jesus.

c. **This he said, not that he cared for the poor, but because he was a thief, and had the money box; and he used to take what was put in it**: We rightly suppose that John did not know at that time that Judas was **a thief**; this was hidden to the disciples. Yet we also rightly suppose that Jesus did know that Judas was **a thief** yet He still appointed Him to be treasurer.

i. Luke 8:2-3 tells us that generous women provided some of the financial needs of Jesus and His disciples. That money would be kept and managed by Judas.

ii. "When a man has gone so far in selfish greed that he has left common honesty behind him, no wonder if the sight of utterly self-surrendering love looks to him folly." (Maclaren)

iii. "The Greek word translated *bare* [**take**] (*bastazo*) means both 'carry' and 'carry off'. Judas did both!" (Tasker) "That *ebastazen* can bear the sense of 'take away' or 'make away with' is beyond dispute." (Dods)

iv. "The verb 'bare' [**take**] is in the imperfect tense, showing that he habitually carried it", and habitually carried from it. (Trench)

v. It was probably through greed and discontent the devil gained a foothold in Judas' life. "Take heed of discontent. It was the devil's sin that threw him out of heaven. Ever since which this restless spirit loves to fish in troubled waters." (Trapp)

vi. By some chronologies Judas went out *the next day* and made his bargain with the religious leaders to betray Jesus for 30 pieces of silver (Matthew 26:14-16, Mark 14:10-11). "The impression left is that Judas, seeing one source of personal enrichment lost, hastened to create another." (Morris)

4. (7-8) Jesus defends Mary and explains what she did.

But Jesus said, "Let her alone; she has kept this for the day of My burial. For the poor you have with you always, but Me you do not have always."

a. **Let her alone**: If we are extreme in our love for Jesus, *He* will not criticize us; that was what Judas did. It is much better to be like Mary (extreme in our love for Jesus) than to be like Judas (criticizing others who show such great love for Jesus).

b. **She has done this for the day of My burial**: In the same way that it would be rude to loudly object to funeral expenses at the service for the deceased, so it was inappropriate for Judas or anyone else to put a price on Mary's love and devotion to Jesus while He was still alive.

i. "Unusual expense at a funeral was not regarded as unseemly; why should anyone object if the ointment which would otherwise have been used to anoint his dead body in due course was poured over him while he was still alive and able to appreciate the love which prompted the action?" (Bruce)

ii. Mark 14:9 says, *Assuredly, I say to you, wherever this gospel is preached in the whole world, what this woman has done will also be told as a memorial to her.* "The Evangelist who records that promise does not mention Mary's name; John, who does mention the name, does not record the promise. It matters little whether our names are remembered, so long as Jesus bears them graven on His heart." (Maclaren)

iii. What John wrote about the fragrance of the oil filling the house may have been his way of saying what Mark 14:9 said. "There is a rabbinic saying '(The scent of) good oil is diffused from the bed-chamber to the dining-hall while a good name is diffused from one end of the world to the other.'" (Morris)

5. (9-11) The plot to kill both Jesus and Lazarus.

Now a great many of the Jews knew that He was there; and they came, not for Jesus' sake only, but that they might also see Lazarus, whom He had raised from the dead. But the chief priests plotted to put Lazarus to death also, because on account of him many of the Jews went away and believed in Jesus.

a. **The chief priests plotted to put Lazarus to death also**: The **chief priests** were mostly Sadducees, and the Sadducees didn't believe in the resurrection. Lazarus was a living example of life after death, and having him around was an embarrassment to their theological system. For them, there was only one solution to this embarrassing problem - **to put Lazarus to death also**.

i. "What a giant like madness was this, to take up arms against heaven itself! to seek to kill a man, only because God had made him alive!" (Trapp) "In this devilish proposal the obduracy of unbelief is exhibited in its extreme form." (Dods)

ii. "When men hate Christ, they also hate those whom he has blessed, and will go to any lengths in seeking to silence their testimony." (Spurgeon)

iii. "How blind were these men not to perceive that he who had raised him, after he had been dead four days, could raise him again though they had slain him a thousand times?" (Clarke)

b. **On account of him many of the Jews went away and believed in Jesus**: This made the problem of the chief priests worse. The miracle of raising Lazarus from the dead drew **many** people to Jesus. Therefore, in the opinion of these religious leaders, Lazarus also had to be stopped.

i. **Went away and believed**: "The expression 'were going and believing in Jesus' may be Semitism, meaning 'were increasingly believing in Jesus'." (Bruce)

B. The triumphal entry.

1. (12-16) The crowd greets Jesus as a coming King.

The next day a great multitude that had come to the feast, when they heard that Jesus was coming to Jerusalem, took branches of palm trees and went out to meet Him, and cried out:

"Hosanna!
'Blessed *is* He who comes in the name of the Lord!'
The King of Israel!"

Then Jesus, when He had found a young donkey, sat on it; as it is written:

"Fear not, daughter of Zion;
Behold, your King is coming,
Sitting on a donkey's colt."

His disciples did not understand these things at first; but when Jesus was glorified, then they remembered that these things were written about Him and *that* they had done these things to Him.

a. **The next day a great multitude that had come to the feast**: This was the large crowd that came for the greatest holidays of Judaism - Passover. Many of them came from Galilee. When they came, they came with *lambs*. Jewish law required that the Passover lamb live with the family for at least three days before sacrifice (Exodus 12:3-6). When Jesus came and went into Jerusalem, lambs for sacrifice would surround him and everyone else.

i. "Josephus, the Jewish historian, tells us that one year a census was taken of the number of lambs slain for Passover and that figure was 256,500. In other words, with numbers this large, lambs must literally be driven up to Jerusalem throughout the entire day. Consequently, whenever Jesus entered the city He must have done so surrounded by lambs, Himself being the greatest of lambs." (Boice)

b. **Took branches of palm trees**: The many people (**a great multitude**) gathered for something that was like a patriotic parade. Palm branches were a symbol of Jewish nationalism since the time of the Maccabees. The crowd looked to Jesus as a political and national savior, but not so much as a spiritual savior.

i. "They greeted Jesus as a king, though ignorant of the nature of His kingship. It would seem that they looked upon Him as a potential nationalist leader, with whose help they might be able to become wholly independent of foreign powers." (Tasker)

ii. "From the time of the Maccabees palms or palm-branches had been used as a national symbol. Palm-branches figured in the procession which celebrated the rededication of the temple in 164 BC (2 Maccabees 10:7) and again when the winning of full political independence was celebrated under Simon in 141 BC (1 Maccabees 13:51). Later, palms appeared as national symbols on the coins struck by the Judean insurgents during the first and second revolts against Rome (AD 66-70 and 132-135)." (Bruce)

c. **Hosanna! "Blessed is He who comes in the name of the LORD!"** This large, enthusiastic crowd greeted Jesus with words from the Messianic Psalm 118:25-26. The cry **Hosanna** meant "save now," and on this day the crowd received Jesus as a triumphant Messiah.

d. **Jesus, when He had found a young donkey, sat on it**: Jesus did this both as a deliberate fulfillment of prophecy (Zechariah 9:9) and as a demonstration of the character of His kingdom. It was a spiritual kingdom, not a military kingdom. He came in peace, not war.

> i. "The ass was not normally used by a warlike person. It was the animal of a man of peace, a priest, a merchant or the like. It might also be used by a person of importance but in connection with peaceable purposes. A conqueror would ride into the city on a war horse, or perhaps march in on foot at the head of his troops. The ass speaks of peace." (Morris)

> ii. "He did not come as a conqueror but as a messenger of peace. He rode on a donkey, not the steed of royalty, but that of a commoner on a business trip." (Tenney)

e. **The King of Israel**: This shows that the crowd, in shouting "*save now!*" had in mind political salvation from the oppression of the Romans. Yet the Romans probably felt they had little to fear from a so-called king who came without armies or the accepted symbols of power.

> i. "'Daughter of Zion' is a personification of the city of Jerusalem; it occurs frequently in the Old Testament, especially in the later prophets." (Tenney)

2. (17-19) The crowds come after Jesus, to the dismay of the leaders.

Therefore the people, who were with Him when He called Lazarus out of his tomb and raised him from the dead, bore witness. For this reason the people also met Him, because they heard that He had done this sign. The Pharisees therefore said among themselves, "You see that you are accomplishing nothing. Look, the world has gone after Him!"

a. **For this reason the people also met Him, because they heard that He had done this sign**: The crowds adored Jesus because they believed that the raising of Lazarus from the dead proved that Jesus could be the conquering Messiah they longed for.

i. "One who could summon a dead man back to life would certainly be able to deliver the holy city from the yoke of Caesar." (Bruce)

b. **Look, the world has gone after Him!** The popularity of Jesus was offensive to His enemies. It made them feel that they were **accomplishing nothing**. It makes us happy to see the enemies of Jesus frustrated.

i. "The Pharisees were of course exaggerating, but the words *the world is gone after him* (John 12:19), like the words of Caiaphas in John 11:50, were unconsciously prophetic." (Tasker)

ii. "They are concerned that a few Judeans were being influenced. But their words express John's conviction that He was conquering the world." (Morris)

C. The hour has come.

1. (20-23) Greeks come to meet Jesus.

Now there were certain Greeks among those who came up to worship at the feast. Then they came to Philip, who was from Bethsaida of Galilee, and asked him, saying, "Sir, we wish to see Jesus." Philip came and told Andrew, and in turn Andrew and Philip told Jesus. But Jesus answered them, saying, "The hour has come that the Son of Man should be glorified."

a. **Now there were certain Greeks among those who came up to worship at the feast**: We are not told the background of these **certain Greeks**. They may have been Greek converts to Judaism. They may have been Greek God-fearers, those who had great respect for Judaism but didn't convert and become circumcised. The may have simply been Greek travelers, known for their curiosity.

i. "We have heard much concerning him, and we wish to see the person of whom we have heard such strange things. The final salvation of the soul often originates, under God, in a principle of simple *curiosity*. Many have only wished to se or hear a man who speaks much of Jesus, his miracles, and his mercies; and in hearing have felt the powers of the world to come, and have become genuine converts to the truths of the Gospel." (Clarke)

ii. "On this occasion the Greek's curiosity about Jesus may have been stirred simply because everyone was talking about him. But there could have been a more special reason. Between verses 19 and 20 a day or two had elapsed: Jesus was no longer on the road to Jerusalem, but teaching daily in the temple precincts. And in the meantime, according to Mark 11:15-17, he had expelled the traders and moneychangers from the precincts -- that is, more precisely, from the outer court -- in order that the place might fulfill its divinely ordained purpose of being 'a house of prayer *for all the nations*' (Isaiah 56:7). Did these Greeks recognize this action as having been undertaken in the interests of Gentiles like themselves who, when they came up to worship the true God, had to confine themselves to the outer court?" (Bruce)

b. **Sir, we wish to see Jesus**: These Greeks had heard of Jesus, perhaps of His reputation as a teacher and worker of miracles. What they *did* know of Jesus made them want to know *more* about Him, so they came to **Philip** (the one disciple with a Greek name) asking **to see Jesus**.

> i. "These men from the West at the end of the Life of Jesus, set forth the same as the Magi from the East at its beginning: -- but they come to the *Cross* of the King, as those to His *cradle*." (Stier, cited in Alford)

c. **The hour has come**: At least twice before Jesus said that the time was not ready (John 2:4 and 7:6). He took this seeking interest of Gentiles as the signal that now **the hour has come that the Son of Man should be glorified**.

> i. "In this Gospel we see Jesus as the world's Saviour, and evidently John means us to understand that this contact with the Greeks ushered in the climax... Jesus sees it as evidence that His mission has reached its climax and that he is now to die for the world, Greeks included." (Morris)

> ii. The fact that His hour had not yet come had delivered Him from violence before (John 7:30, 8:20). Now that **the hour has come**, it was time for Jesus to make the final sacrifice.

> iii. Jesus never really responded to these Gentile seekers, but He would on the other side of the cross. If humanity was to receive new life in God the Son, then Jesus must die (**be glorified**) first.

d. **The hour has come that the Son of Man should be glorified**: Jesus didn't mean that He would be **glorified** in the eyes of men. That just happened at the triumphal entry. The glorification Jesus pointed to here was being **glorified** on the cross. Something the world could only see as disgraceful humiliation, Jesus saw as being **glorified**.

> i. **The hour has come**: "The verb 'is come' is in the perfect tense, 'the hour has come and stays with us'. There is no going back on it." (Morris)

2. (24-26) Jesus explains why He is willing to face death.

"Most assuredly, I say to you, unless a grain of wheat falls into the ground and dies, it remains alone; but if it dies, it produces much grain.

He who loves his life will lose it, and he who hates his life in this world will keep it for eternal life. If anyone serves Me, let him follow Me; and where I am, there My servant will be also. If anyone serves Me, him *My Father will honor*."

a. **Unless a grain of wheat falls to the ground and dies**: Just as a seed will never become a plant unless it **dies** and is buried so the death and burial of Jesus was necessary to His glorification. Before there can be resurrection power and fruitfulness, there must be death.

i. "The principle stated in verse 24 is of wide application; in particular, if it is true of Jesus, it must be true of his followers." (Bruce)

b. **He who loves his live will lose it, and he who hates his life in this world will keep it**: We are called to *hate* our life not in the sense that we disregard it, but in the sense that we freely give it up for God. Our life is precious to us, especially because it is something we can give to Jesus.

i. Jesus focused our hatred of life when He said **hates his life in this world**. We are to disregard our life in this world, seeing instead that we are mere pilgrims and sojourners, with our home in heaven instead of earth (Hebrews 11:13-16).

ii. "The man whose priorities are right has such an attitude of love for the things of God that it makes all interest in the affairs of this life appear by comparison as hatred." (Morris)

c. **If anyone serves Me, let him follow Me**: To be a Christian is to serve Jesus, to follow Him. It doesn't mean that you stop working your job or caring for your family or studying at school. It means you do all that as a servant of Jesus, a follower of Jesus.

i. "All of you who would have Christ as your Savior, that you must be willing *to* serve him. We are not saved *by* service, but we are saved to service." (Spurgeon)

ii. **Serves Me**: "*Diakonos* is especially a servant *in attendance*, at table or elsewhere; a *doulos* may serve at a distance: hence the appropriateness of *diakonos* in this verse. The office of *diakonos* may seem a humble and painful one, but to be valued or honoured by the Father crowns life." (Dods)

iii. It would be easy for the disciples to think, "Jesus is going to the cross. Thank heaven I don't have to do that." Then Jesus says, "**Follow Me**."

iv. "Think of one Man standing up before all mankind, and coolly and deliberately saying to them, 'I am the realized Ideal of human conduct;

I am Incarnate Perfection; and all of you, in all the infinite variety of condition, culture, and character, are to take Me for your pattern and your guide.'" (Maclaren)

d. **Where I am, there My servant will be also**: Jesus described the **servant** as one who *wanted to be where Jesus is*. This isn't forced slavery where the servant wants to be free from the master. This is a chosen, willing service that simply wants to be close to the Master.

> i. **Where I am**: "The word refers, not to the place of our Lord at that moment, but to His essential, true place, i.e. (John 17:24) in the glory of the Father." (Alford)

e. **If anyone serves Me, him My Father will honor**: This is a remarkable promise. The reward for serving Jesus is to receive honor from God the **Father**. This **honor** is both *reward* and *recognition*.

3. (27-28a) At the crucial hour, Jesus expresses His resolve.

"Now My soul is troubled, and what shall I say? 'Father, save Me from this hour'? But for this purpose I came to this hour. Father, glorify Your name."

a. **My soul is troubled**: Jesus received this crucial hour, yet it troubled Him because He knew what the agonies of the cross would involve. John doesn't tell us about the prayer of Jesus in Gethsemane, but the *idea* behind that prayer of Jesus is expressed in John 12:27-28.

> ii. "As a man he was *troubled* at the prospect of a *violent* death. Nature *abhors death*: God has implanted that abhorrence in nature, that it might become a principle of self preservation; and it is to this that we owe all that *prudence* and *caution* by which we avoid danger." (Clarke)

b. **And what shall I say? "Father, save Me from this hour?"** Knowing this was the crucial hour Jesus could not ask to escape the hour, because He knew that **for this purpose I came to this hour**. The cross, which had cast a shadow over the entire life and ministry of Jesus, would now become a reality in the experience of Jesus.

> i. "It seems clear that the words represent a rhetorical question, a hypothetical prayer at which Jesus looks, but which He refuses to pray." (Morris)

> ii. "The very object of His Incarnation, the reason of this His Coming into the world and of His continuance to this hour was to meet this Suffering." (Trench)

c. **Father, glorify Your name**: As Jesus thought of the cross just a few days away, His main concern was to **glorify** the **name** and character of God the Father.

4. (28b-30) The Father testifies to Jesus in a voice from heaven.

Then a voice came from heaven, *saying,* **"I have both glorified** *it* **and will glorify** *it* **again." Therefore the people who stood by and heard** *it* **said that it had thundered. Others said, "An angel has spoken to Him." Jesus answered and said, "This voice did not come because of Me, but for your sake.**

a. **Then a voice came from heaven**: This was the third audible Divine testimony to Jesus' status as the Son of God, after the Divine voice heard at His baptism and His transfiguration.

b. **I have both glorified it and will glorify it again**: This was assurance from God the Father. Approaching the cross, the great concern of Jesus was to glorify the Father, and He was assured that He already had and would continue to do so.

i. **And will glorify it**: "Christ was glorified: 1st. By the prodigies which happened at his *death*. 2. In his *resurrection*. 3. In his *ascension*, and sitting at the right hand of God. 4. In the *descent* of the *Holy Ghost* on the apostles. and 5. In the astonishing *success* with which the Gospel was accompanied, and by which the kingdom of Christ has been established in the world." (Clarke)

ii. **And will glorify it again**: "The word **again** here implies no mere repetition, but an intensification, of the glorification a **yet once more**: and this time fully and finally." (Alford)

c. **This voice did not come because of Me, but for your sake**: To some, the voice of God sounded like thunder. Others thought it sounded like some kind of angelic speech. For those who could discern it, it gave them confidence in Jesus before these critical days.

i. "So in Acts 9:7, 22:9, Saul's companions heard the physical reverberations, but not so as to understand the Voice, for it was not meant for them." (Trench)

5. (31-33) Jesus plainly proclaims His death.

"Now is the judgment of this world; now the ruler of this world will be cast out. And I, if I am lifted up from the earth, will draw all *peoples* **to Myself." This He said, signifying by what death He would die.**

a. **Now is the judgment of this world**: The spirit of **this world** was judged by the way it treated Jesus at the cross. The cross not only judged the world it also defeated Satan (**now the ruler of this world will be cast out**). The defeat of the world (culture in opposition to Jesus) and Satan was God's victory and the victory of the people of God.

> i. We could define **this world** in the sense Jesus spoke of as *culture in opposition to Jesus*. This culture has a leader, a **ruler of this world** - Satan, the great adversary to God (John 14:30, 16:11; 2 Corinthians 4:4, Ephesians 2:2, 6:12).

b. **Now the ruler of this world will be cast out**: Satan, the great adversary, was in some sense **cast out** by what Jesus accomplished at the cross. Satan was **cast out** of any rightful authority over God's people.

> i. "But the world's judgment on Jesus, directed by the sinister spirit-ruler (*archon*) of the present order, would be overruled in a higher court; that spirit-ruler himself would be dislodged." (Bruce)

> ii. "It was because of disobedience that man was driven by God out of the Garden of Eden for having submitted to *the prince of this world* (John 12:31); now by the perfect obedience of Jesus on the cross the prince of this world will be deposed from his present ascendancy." (Tasker)

> iii. Colossians 2:14-15 vividly described the defeat of Satan at the cross: *having wiped out the handwriting of requirements that was against us, which was contrary to us. And He has taken it out of the way, having nailed it to the cross. Having disarmed principalities and powers, He made a public spectacle of them, triumphing over them in it.*

c. **If I am lifted up from the earth**: The verb used for **lifted** has a deliberate double meaning. It means both a literal *elevation* (as in being raised up on a cross) and *exaltation* (being raised in rank or honor). Jesus promised that when He was **lifted** (elevated, exalted) on the cross He would **draw all peoples to** Himself.

> i. "In *hypsotho* [**lifted**] therefore, although the direct reference is to His elevation on the cross, there is a sub-suggestion of being elevated to a throne... It was the cross which was to become His throne and by which He was to draw men to Him as His subjects." (Dods)

> ii. **If I am lifted up**: "*If*, as often, has the force of 'when'. There is no doubt in Jesus' mind that He will be crucified." (Tasker)

> iii. Jesus knew that the benefit of His work on the cross would go far beyond blessing and salvation to the Jewish people. He would **draw all peoples to** Himself.

iv. **Draw all peoples**: "The Cross is the magnet of Christianity. Jesus Christ draws men, but it is by His Cross mainly...You demagnetize Christianity, as all history shows, if you strike out the death on the Cross for a world's sin. What is left is not a magnet, but a bit of scrap iron." (Maclaren)

v. **All peoples**: "There is no exclusion of any class or creature from the mercy of God in Christ Jesus. 'I, if I be lifted up, will draw all men unto me'; and the history of the church proves how true this is: the muster-roll of the converted includes princes and paupers, peers and potmen." (Spurgeon)

d. **This He said, signifying by what death He would die**: Jesus did not only know that He would die, but also that He would die on a cross, **lifted up** from the earth. Jesus knew the painful and humiliating manner of His death, but still obeyed God's will.

6. (34-36) Will the Messiah live forever?

The people answered Him, "We have heard from the law that the Christ remains forever; and how *can* You say, 'The Son of Man must be lifted up'? Who is this Son of Man?" Then Jesus said to them, "A little while longer the light is with you. Walk while you have the light, lest darkness overtake you; he who walks in darkness does not know where he is going. While you have the light, believe in the light, that you may become sons of light." These things Jesus spoke, and departed, and was hidden from them.

a. **We have heard from the law that the Christ remains forever**: The people had been taught only the passages from **the law** (the Old Testament) which spoke of the triumph of the Messiah. They were mostly unaware of the passages that spoke of His suffering (such as Psalm 22 and Isaiah 53). It made them wonder if Jesus was really the Messiah, the **Son of Man**.

i. "There were several passages that spoke of the *perpetuity* of his reign, as Isa 9:7; Eze 37:25; Da 7:14, they probably confounded the one with the other, and thus drew the conclusion, The Messiah cannot die; for the Scripture hath said, his throne, kingdom, and reign shall be eternal." (Clarke)

ii. This crowd that enthusiastically greeted a political conqueror didn't want to consider His sacrificial death. It didn't fit in with their idea of what a Messiah should be.

iii. **Son of Man**: "This among other passages shows that the 'Son of Man' was a title suggestive of Messiahship, but not quite definite in its meaning and not quite identical with 'Messiah'." (Dods)

b. **A little while longer the light is with you...While you have the light, believe in the light**: Jesus assured them that He would be with them only a short time longer. The light of His earthly ministry was about to go out.

i. We must believe on Jesus while the light is there, because it won't last forever. God's Spirit will not always strive with man (Genesis 6:3), and we must answer His call while it rings to us.

ii. **Sons of light**: "The Semitic idiom 'sons of' describes men who possess the characteristics of what is said to be their 'father'. In our idiom, we should probably say 'men of light', cf. our expression 'a man of integrity'." (Tasker)

7. (37-41) John explains their unbelief in light of Old Testament prophecy.

But although He had done so many signs before them, they did not believe in Him, that the word of Isaiah the prophet might be fulfilled, which he spoke:

"Lord, who has believed our report?
And to whom has the arm of the LORD been revealed?"

Therefore they could not believe, because Isaiah said again:

"He has blinded their eyes and hardened their hearts,
Lest they should see with *their* eyes,
Lest they should understand with *their* hearts and turn,
S that I should heal them."

These things Isaiah said when he saw His glory and spoke of Him.

a. **Although He had done so many signs before them, they did not believe in Him**: Throughout his Gospel, John told us of many signs that Jesus performed that should cause us to **believe in Him** (John 2:11, 4:54, 6:14). Yet many **did not believe in Him**. Using two quotations from Isaiah (Isaiah 53:1 and 6:9-10), John explained that this was prophesied.

i. "After centuries of Christian history, during which the church has been almost exclusively Gentile, we have come to accept that it is quite normal that there should be very few Jews in it. But this was not the way it seemed to the men of the New Testament." (Morris)

b. **To whom has the arm of the LORD been revealed**: In quoting from Isaiah 53:1 John emphasized that if someone believes, it is because God has **revealed** Himself and His truth to them. Jesus had revealed Himself to them through the many signs and through His teaching.

c. **He has blinded their eyes and hardened their heart**: In quoting from Isaiah 6:9-10 John emphasized that unbelief was because God acted in judgment upon those who refused to see His truth and turn to Him. God would strengthen them in their decision, either for Jesus or against Him. In light of this principle, **they could not believe**, as Isaiah described.

i. "Not one of them was fated to be incapable of belief; it is made plain below (John 12:42) that some did in fact believe. But the OT prediction had to be fulfilled, and fulfilled it was in those who, as matter of fact, did not believe." (Bruce)

ii. "He does not mean that the blinding takes place without the will or against the will of these people. So with the hardening of their heart. These men chose evil. It was their own deliberate choice, their own fault." (Morris)

d. **These things Isaiah said when he saw His glory and spoke of Him**: As the prophecy is recorded in Isaiah 6, the Prophet Isaiah *saw the Lord*, Yahweh (Isaiah 6:1-13). John properly understood that Isaiah saw the glory of Jesus before His incarnation and that Jesus *is* Yahweh.

i. "The vision of Isaiah recorded in Isaiah 6 is interpreted by John as a vision of the Godhead as a whole. The prophet saw Christ's glory as well as the Father's glory." (Tasker)

8. (42-43) Some of the rulers have a weak belief in Jesus.

Nevertheless even among the rulers many believed in Him, but because of the Pharisees they did not confess *Him*, lest they should be put out of the synagogue; for they loved the praise of men more than the praise of God.

a. **Nevertheless even among the rulers many believed in Him, but because of the Pharisees they did not confess Him**: At this point in Jesus' ministry there were many who believed on Him secretly. They saw the signs and heard His teaching, yet because they were afraid of what others would think and do against them they would not openly declare (**confess**) their allegiance to and trust in Jesus.

i. "Secret discipleship is a contradiction in terms for, 'either the secrecy kills the discipleship, or the discipleship kills the secrecy.'" (Barclay)

ii. Bishop Trench was more sympathetic: "The commentators are hard on these timid ones. Are all Christians heroic? Is there no smoking flax?" (Trench)

b. **They loved the praise of men more than the praise of God**: Jesus just explained that if anyone served Him, they would receive *honor* from God (John 12:26). Yet there were many who **loved** the honor that comes from other men more than the **praise** that comes from God.

i. **Loved the praise of men**: "Which what is it else but a little stinking breath? These have their reward." (Trapp)

9. (44-50) A final appeal to belief: Jesus makes a last, passionate appeal to the multitude.

Then Jesus cried out and said, "He who believes in Me, believes not in Me but in Him who sent Me. And he who sees Me sees Him who sent Me. I have come *as* a light into the world, that whoever believes in Me should not abide in darkness. And if anyone hears My words and does not believe, I do not judge him; for I did not come to judge the world but to save the world. He who rejects Me, and does not receive My words, has that which judges him—the word that I have spoken will judge him in the last day. For I have not spoken on My own *authority*; but the Father who sent Me gave Me a command, what I should say and what I should speak. And I know that His command is everlasting life. Therefore, whatever I speak, just as the Father has told Me, so I speak."

a. **Then Jesus cried out and said**: These are the last words in John's gospel from Jesus to the public. In this last speech to the multitude, Jesus emphasized the themes of all His previous preaching in John. It included a reminder of His teaching, a challenge to decide, a warning to those who decided against Him and a promise to those who decided for Him.

i. **Cried out**: "The imperfect tense in the original signifies that the shouting was persistent." (Tasker)

ii. "As a rule our Saviour did not cry [shout]. He did not cry nor lift up His voice in the streets. But now and then, in some exalted hour, the Gospels tell us that He cried (John 7:37)." (Morrison)

b. **He who sees Me sees Him who sent Me**: Jesus emphasized His unity with God the Father. To **believe in** Jesus was to put faith in **Him who sent** Jesus, even more than it was to put faith in Jesus Himself.

i. "Though it was for asserting this (his oneness with God) that they were going to crucify him, yet he retracts nothing of what he had spoken, but strongly reasserts it, in the very jaws of death!" (Clarke)

c. **I have come as light into the world**: Jesus stressed His own truthfulness, and the *need* man has to follow Jesus - or else live in **darkness**.

d. **I did not come to judge the world but to save the world**: The incarnation wasn't necessary if Jesus came only to judge. He didn't need to add humanity to His deity to do that, but He did need to do it to rescue humanity. Yet, **the word that I have spoken will judge Him** - there are inescapable consequences for rejecting Jesus.

i. "His last word is not one of condemnation. It is one of tender appeal." (Morris)

ii. "Always in the Fourth Gospel there is this essential paradox; Jesus came in love, yet his coming is a judgment." (Barclay)

e. **I have not spoken on My own authority**: Jesus stressed His own submission to God the Father. His authority was connected to His submission to God the Father.

i. **What I should say and what I should speak**: "The former designates the doctrine according to its *contents*, the latter the varying manner of delivery." (Dods)

John 13 - Jesus, the Loving Servant

Alexander Maclaren wrote of this remarkable section, John 13-17: "Nowhere else is His speech at once so simple and so deep. Nowhere else have we the heart of God so unveiled to us... The immortal words which Christ spoke in that upper chamber are His highest self-revelation in speech, even as the Cross to which they led up is His most perfect self-revelation in act."

A. Jesus washes the disciples' feet.

1. (1) Jesus and His disciples at a last meeting before His arrest.

Now before the feast of the Passover, when Jesus knew that His hour had come that He should depart from this world to the Father, having loved His own who were in the world, He loved them to the end.

a. **Now before the feast of the Passover**: This gives us a time reference. Jesus was about to share a meal with His disciples, and scholars disagree whether this meal was actually on the Passover, or if it was the Passover meal, but celebrated the day before.

i. The chronology is an issue because in some passages, it seems that Jesus was crucified *on* the day of Passover. In other passages, it seems that Jesus was crucified the day *after* Passover. There are scores of potential solutions to the problem, but it's hard to say which one is the final answer.

ii. "The verbs for 'reclining' [John 13:23] ... suggest that, although this meal fell 'before the (official) festival of the Passover' (verse 1) it was nevertheless treated by the participants as a Passover meal." (Bruce)

iii. This debate has contributed to one practical difference among Christians. "From time immemorial western Christendom uses for the Eucharist unleavened bread, eastern Christendom has from time immemorial insisted on the bread being leavened. The East asserts, and rightly, that the Last Supper was eaten on the night before the nation

246

ate the Passover, and infers that it was, therefore, eaten with ordinary leavened bread. The West asserts, and rightly, that the Passover eaten by our Lord and the Twelve was a genuine Passover, as He Himself calls it (Luke 22:15) and as all the Synoptists agree in calling it, and infers that it was, therefore, eaten with full Mosaic ritual and therefore with unleavened bread." (Trench)

b. **Jesus knew that His hour had come**: Jesus lived His life in anticipation of this **hour**. He knew when it had not yet come (John 2:4). Up to this point, Jesus enjoyed a unique protection because His hour had not yet come (John 7:30, 8:20). Now, **Jesus knew that His hour had come**. He spoke of this awareness in John 12:23-27 and even said that *for this purpose I came to this hour.*

i. Indeed, **His hour had come**. Jesus' public ministry was over. In close to 24 hours, Jesus would hang on the cross. This was the beginning of the end, and Jesus used these last precious hours to serve and prepare His disciples.

c. **That He should depart this world to the Father**: The cross is not *specifically* mentioned in John 13:1, but casts a shadow over almost every word. We see the shadow of the cross over **His hour had come**. We see the shadow of the cross over **loved them to the end**. But we also see the shadow of the cross over **depart this world**. It is phrased softly, but there is an iron-hard reality underneath the soft cover. Jesus would only **depart this world** through the cross.

i. "When one is leaving for a distant country, and has transacted all necessary business with the outside world, he is fain to spend the few remaining hours in the sweet intimacy of the family circle." (Morrison)

d. **Having loved**: Surely, Jesus had **loved** His disciples. He led them, taught them, cared for them, and protected them. What Jesus gave them was already more than any other teacher or leader would or could give his followers.

e. **Having loved His own**: There is a love Jesus has for all people, and then there is a love for **His own**. It isn't so much that Jesus' *love* is different, but the dynamic of the love relationship is different. The love of Jesus for **His own** is greater because it has a response, and love answers to love.

i. Jesus has done *some* things for *all* men. He has also done *all* things for *some* men - **His own who were in the world**.

ii. "God's wider love for 'the world' (John 3:16) is not displaced by this concentrated love of Jesus for his friends, but it is they who experience it in its fullness." (Bruce)

iii. These disciples and all disciples were and are really **His own**, belonging to Jesus.

- They were **His own** because He chose them.
- They were **His own** because He gave Himself to them.
- They were **His own** because His Father gave them to Him.
- They were **His own** because He would soon purchase them.
- They were **His own** because He conquered them.
- They were **His own** because they yielded themselves to Him.

f. **He loved them to the end**: Jesus had **loved His own**. But He hadn't finished loving them. He would love **them to the end**. The idea behind the phrase **to the end** is "to the fullest extent, to the uttermost."

i. "'To the fullest extent' is a better rendering of the original *eis telos* than KJV 'unto the end.' It does not mean that Jesus continued to love his disciples only up to the end of his career but that his loved has no limits." (Tenney)

ii. **To the end** means *to the end of Jesus' earthly life*. Though the disciples gave up on Him, He never gave up on them. Though they stopped thinking about Jesus, and were only thinking of themselves, He never stopped thinking of them. Whose problems were worse - Jesus' or the disciples'? Who was concerned more for the other? He loved them **to the end**.

iii. **To the end** means a *love that will never end*. Jesus will never stop loving **His own**. It isn't a love that comes and goes, that is here today and gone tomorrow.

iv. **To the end** means a *love that reaches to the fullest extent*. Some translations have "He loved them to the uttermost." Jesus poured out the cup of His love to the bottom for us.

2. (2-3) The heart of Judas and the heart of Jesus.

And supper being ended, the devil having already put it into the heart of Judas Iscariot, Simon's *son*, to betray Him, Jesus, knowing that the Father had given all things into His hands, and that He had come from God and was going to God,

a. **Supper being ended**: Some ancient manuscripts have *supper was now in progress* instead of **supper being ended**. This probably makes more sense, and the difference is one letter in the ancient Greek manuscripts.

i. "'Supper was now in progress' is a preferable reading to the variant 'Supper having ended,' chiefly because the sequel (verses 13:30) makes it plain that supper had not ended. The point is that supper had already begun when Jesus rose from the table and began to wash the disciples' feet." (Bruce)

ii. "Some MSS read *being ended* (*genomenou*) and others 'while still in progress' (*ginomenou*). Both readings are well-attested." (Tasker)

b. **The devil having already put it into the heart of Judas**: It may be that a better translation is *the devil had already made up his mind that Judas Iscariot, Simon's son, should betray him.* Satan looked for a man to betray Jesus, and had probably cultivated Judas for a long time. Now the choice was made. Judas was his man.

i. Bruce favors the reading that it was the *devil's* **heart** that held the evil impulse against Jesus, and that the **devil** impressed it from his heart to Judas.

c. **Jesus, knowing that the Father had given all things into His hands**: This wasn't something that Jesus came to know just at this hour. Several years before in His ministry, Jesus said *The Father loves the Son, and has given all things into His hand.* (John 3:35) But this means that at this particular time, and in this particular circumstance, it was *important* that Jesus knew **the Father had given all things into His hands**.

i. It was important because of the *hour*. Jesus was about to face the agony of crucifixion and the terror of standing in the place of guilty sinners before the righteous wrath of God the Father. At the same time, Jesus went into this situation as a *victor*, not as a *victim*. He could have backed out any time He wanted to, because **the Father had given all things into His hands**.

ii. It was important because of the *circumstance*. Jesus was about to lower Himself, literally stooping in humble service to His disciples. As He served in this humble way, He did not do it from *weakness*. He did it from a position of *all authority*, because **the Father had given all things into His hands**.

iii. The Gospel accounts often don't tell us the *motive* or the *thinking* behind what Jesus did. This is different. John told us exactly why Jesus washed their feet and spoke to them with so much love in the following chapters. Perhaps he asked Jesus, and Jesus told him.

iv. "John says much more about the inner consciousness of Jesus than the Synoptics do, either because he was more observant or because Jesus confided in him." (Tenney)

d. **And that He had come from God and was going to God**: Jesus didn't only know His *authority*, He also knew His *relationship* with God. He knew His identity, as one who **had come from God**, and as one who **was going to God**. Knowing His past with God the Father, and His future with God the Father, He determined to glorify Him in the present.

i. Sometimes in demanding better treatment people think or say, "Do you know who I am?" Jesus knew His greatness more than anyone, and it made Him give better treatment to others instead of expecting it Himself.

ii. "It was not *in spite of* but *because of* His consciousness of His divine origin and destination, that He rose from supper, and assumed the dress and posture of a slave; for s servant in truth He was, being none other than the ideal Servant delineated in Isaiah's prophecy." (Tasker)

3. (4-5) Jesus washes the feet of His disciples.

Rose from supper and laid aside His garments, took a towel and girded Himself. After that, He poured water into a basin and began to wash the disciples' feet, and to wipe *them* with the towel with which He was girded.

a. **Rose from supper and laid aside His garments**: With short, vivid statements John described the remarkable thing Jesus did on that unforgettable night. We have the sense that when John wrote this many years after the fact he could still remember every detail.

i. "John's account reads like that of an eye-witness who had watched with wonder and suspense -- short staccato sentences." (Trench)

ii. "Each step in the whole astounding scene is imprinted on the mind of John. 'Next He pours water into the basin,' *the* basin which the landlord had furnished as part of the necessary arrangements." (Dods)

b. **Began to wash the disciples' feet**: At this moment of deep meaning, Jesus did something that must have almost seemed crazy. He began to do the job of the lowest servant in the household. He **began to wash the disciples' feet**.

i. At this critical moment, at this evening before the torture of the cross, Jesus did not think of Himself. He thought about His disciples. Truly, this was *loving them to the end*. After all, Jesus' disciples treated Him badly and were about to treat Him even worse, forsaking Him completely; yet He loved them.

ii. Jesus *completely* gave Himself to washing their feet. He was thorough in the work. First, He **rose from supper**. Then Jesus **laid aside His garments**, which had to remind Him of what waited in just a few hours, when He would be stripped of **His garments** and be crucified.

Jesus then **took a towel and girded Himself**. Finally Jesus **poured water into a basin**. If Jesus wanted to just display the *image* of a servant, He would have had a servant or one of the disciples do all this preparation work. He then would have quickly wiped a damp cloth on a few dirty feet and consider the job done. That would give the *image* of servanthood and loving leadership, but Jesus gave Himself *completely* to this work.

iii. This was an *extreme* act of servanthood. According to the Jewish laws and traditions regarding the relationship between a teacher and his disciples, a teacher had no right to demand or expect that his disciples would wash his feet. It was absolutely unthinkable that the Master would wash His disciple's feet.

c. **And to wipe them with the towel with which He was girded**: As Jesus went around the table, washing and drying the feet of His disciples, it was a dramatic scene. Luke 22:23 says that the disciples entered the room debating who was greatest. By what He did, Jesus illustrated true greatness.

i. It was customary that the lowest servant of the house would wash the feet of the guests as they came into the house, especially for a formal meal like this. For some reason, this didn't happen when Jesus and the disciples came into the room. They ate their meal with dirty feet.

ii. This was more awkward than we might think. First, because of the sandals they wore and the roads they walked on, the feet were dirty. Second, the disciples ate a formal meal like this at a table known as a *triclinium*. This was a low (coffee-table height), U-shaped table. The guests sat and their status at the meal was reflected by how close they were to the host or leader of the meal. Because the table was low, they didn't sit on chairs. They leaned on pillows, with their feet behind them. The unwashed feet were easily seen and perhaps smelled.

iii. None of the disciples were interested in washing each other's feet. Any of them would have gladly washed Jesus' feet. But they could not wash *His* without having to be available to wash the others' feet, and that would have been an intolerable admission of inferiority among their fellow competitors for the top positions in the disciples' hierarchy. So no one's feet got washed.

d. **Began to wash the disciples' feet**: In all of this, Jesus acted out a parable for the disciples. Jesus knew actions speak louder than words. So when He wanted to teach the proud, arguing disciples about true humility, He didn't just *say* it - He *showed* it. He showed it in a way that illustrated His whole work on behalf of *His own*.

- Jesus **rose from supper**, a place of rest and comfort.

- Jesus rose from His throne in heaven, a place of rest and comfort.

- Jesus **laid aside His garments**, taking off His covering.

- Jesus laid aside His glory, taking off His heavenly covering.

- Jesus **took a towel and girded Himself**, being ready to work.

- Jesus took the form of a servant, and came ready to work.

- Jesus **poured water into a basin**, ready to clean.

- Jesus poured out His blood to cleanse us from the guilt and penalty of sin.

- Jesus *sat down again* (John 13:12) after washing their feet.

- Jesus sat down at the right hand of God the Father after cleansing us,

    i. "It is a parable in action, setting out that great principle of lowly service which finds its supreme embodiment in the cross." (Morris)

    ii. "'Knowing that He came from God, and went to God,' and that even when He was kneeling there before these men, 'the Father had given all things into His hands,' what did He do? Triumph? Show His majesty? Flash His power? Demand service? 'Girded Himself with a towel and washed His disciples' feet'!" (Maclaren)

    iii. "The form of God was not *exchanged for* the form of a servant; it was *revealed in* the form of a servant. In the washing of their feet the disciples, though they did not understand it at the time, saw a rare unfolding of the authority and glory of the incarnate Word, and a rare declaration of the character of the Father himself." (Bruce)

    iv. Decades later, when Peter wrote to Christians about humility, he put it like this: *Yes, all of you be submissive to one another, and be clothed with humility* (1 Peter 5:5). More literally, Peter wrote: "wrap the apron of humility around yourself." What Jesus did here remained in his mind and heart.

4. (6-8) Jesus overcomes Peter's objections and washes his feet.

Then He came to Simon Peter. And *Peter* said to Him, "Lord, are You washing my feet?" Jesus answered and said to him, "What I am doing you do not understand now, but you will know after this." Peter said to Him, "You shall never wash my feet!" Jesus answered him, "If I do not wash you, you have no part with Me."

a. **You shall never wash my feet**: Perhaps Peter thought, "All these other disciples missed the point by letting Jesus wash their feet. He wants us to protest, and proclaim that He is too great, and we are too unworthy, to have Him wash our feet." So, Peter made this dramatic statement.

i. "This was an immoderate modesty, a proud humility." (Trapp)

ii. At the same time, Peter clearly felt uncomfortable with having Jesus perform such a humble act of service for him. This example of the servant's heart of Jesus made Peter and the others look proud by comparison.

iii. "The word **my** is not emphatic. The having his feet washed is a matter of course; it is the Person who is about to do it that offends him." (Alford)

b. **If I do not wash you, you have no part with Me**: Peter *had to* accept this from Jesus. He became a pattern for us. If we do not accept the humble service of Jesus to cleanse us, we have **no part** with Him.

- Peter preached the good news of the kingdom and cast out devils in Jesus' name - *and still needed his feet washed.*

- Peter saw Jesus transfigured in His glory together with Moses and Elijah, an amazing spiritual experience - *and still needed his feet washed.*

- Peter's own feet walked on the water in an amazing act of faith - *and still needed his feet washed.*

i. This foot washing was a powerful lesson in humility but it was more than that. It also shows that Jesus has no fellowship, no deep connection with those who have not been cleansed by Him.

ii. "The same well-meaning but false humility would prevent him (and does prevent many) from stooping to receive at the hands of the Lord that spiritual washing which is absolutely necessary in order to have any part in Him." (Alford)

iii. We are grateful Jesus did not say, *If you do not have great holiness, you have no part with Me.* We are happy He did not say, *If you are not a Bible expert, you have no part with Me.* Having a part with Jesus begins simply with *receiving* something from Him, not achieving something our self.

iv. This statement of Jesus also shows us that the literal foot washing was not so important. Judas had his feet literally washed, but he had **no part** with Jesus because Judas did not let Jesus **wash** him in the sense Jesus meant here.

v. "It is not the area of skin that is washed that matters but the acceptance of Jesus' lowly service." (Morris)

5. (9-11) Peter tells Jesus to wash him completely.

Simon Peter said to Him, "Lord, not my feet only, but also *my* hands and *my* head!" Jesus said to him, "He who is bathed needs only to wash *his* feet, but is completely clean; and you are clean, but not all of you." For He knew who would betray Him; therefore He said, "You are not all clean."

a. **Lord, not my feet only, but also my hands and my head!** Peter, in his request to be fully washed, was still reluctant to let Jesus do as He wanted. Peter wanted to tell Jesus what to do. Jesus - though the servant of all - still was and is God's appointed leader. He would not allow Peter to dominate this situation and set things on a wrong course.

i. "Peter's humility is true enough to allow him to see the incongruity of Jesus washing his feet: not deep enough to make him conscious of the incongruity of his thus opposing and dictating to his Master." (Dods)

ii. "A moment ago he told his Master He was doing too much: now he tells Him He is doing too little." (Dods)

iii. Sometimes we show a servant's heart by accepting the service of others for us. If we only serve, and refuse to be served, it can be a sign of deeply rooted and well-hidden pride. "Man's humility does not begin with the giving of service; it begins with the readiness to receive it. For there can be much pride and condescension in our giving of service." (Temple)

b. **He who is bathed needs only to wash his feet**: Speaking in the long Biblical tradition of using physical washing as an illustration of spiritual cleansing, Jesus taught there is an initial bathing that is distinct from an ongoing washing. We need to be **bathed** by our trust in Jesus and what He did for us on the cross; there is a sense in which that is done once for all. Yet afterward we must continually have our feet washed in ongoing relationship with and trust upon Jesus.

i. "The priest of God, when consecrated first, was washed from head to foot, and so baptised into the service of the sanctuary; but each time he went to offer sacrifice be washed his feet and his hands in the brazen laver." (Spurgeon)

6. (12-14) Jesus explains what He did, and calls His disciples to follow His example.

So when He had washed their feet, taken His garments, and sat down again, He said to them, "Do you know what I have done to you? You call Me Teacher and Lord, and you say well, for *so* I am. If I then, *your*

Lord and Teacher, have washed your feet, you also ought to wash one another's feet."

a. **Do you know what I have done to you**: Jesus entire life was a lesson and example to the disciples. Here He felt it was important to specifically draw attention to the lesson of what He had just done. The washing of their feet *meant something* and Jesus would not leave the understanding of that up to chance.

b. **You call Me Teacher and Lord, and you say well, for so I am**: Jesus recognized and encouraged the commitment of the disciples to Him. He was their **Teacher** and He was their **Lord** and in this sense they had no other **Teacher** or **Lord**.

c. **You also ought to wash one another's feet**: As their **Teacher and Lord** Jesus commanded them to show the same humble, sacrificial love to one another. The example of Jesus should mark their *attitude* and their *action*. This was and is true for every follower of Jesus Christ (all who call Him **Teacher and Lord**), but should be even more so for those who are or desire to be leaders among God's people.

i. "If there be any deed of kindness or love that we can do for the very meanest and most obscure of God's people, we ought to be willing to do it -- to be servants to God's servants." (Spurgeon)

ii. **You also ought to wash one another's feet**: Some try to fulfill this with foot washing ceremonies. Surely, if this is done with the right heart it can be a blessing, but Jesus didn't refer to a ceremony here. "Every year they hold a theatrical feet-washing, and when they have discharged this empty and bare ceremony they think they have done their duty finely and are then free to despise their brethren. But more, when they have washed twelve men's feet they cruelly torture all Christ's members and thus spit in the face of Christ Himself. This ceremonial comedy is nothing but a shameful mockery of Christ. At any rate, Christ does not enjoin an annual ceremony here, but tells us to be ready all through our life to wash the feet of our brethren." (Calvin, cited in Morris)

iii. "The studied formality of the *pedilavium* on Maundy Thursday, when bishops, abbots and sovereigns have traditionally washed the feet of paupers, may commemorate our Lord's action but in the nature of the case it can scarcely fulfill its spirit." (Bruce)

d. **Wash one another's feet**: We, like the disciples, would gladly wash the feet of Jesus. But He tells us to wash **one another's** feet. Anything we do for each another that washes away the grime of the world and the dust of defeat and discouragement is foot washing.

i. It is easy for us to criticize those with dirty feet instead of *washing them*. "In the world they criticize: this is the business of the public press, and it is very much the business of private circles. Hear how gossips say, 'Do you see that spot? What a terrible walk that man must have had this morning: look at his feet! He has been very much in the mire you can see, for there are the traces upon him.' That is the world's way. Christ's way is very different. He says nothing, but takes the basin and begins to wash away the stain. Do not judge and condemn, but seek the restoration and the improvement of the erring." (Spurgeon)

ii. If we are going to wash one another's feet, we should be careful of the temperature of the water. Sometimes we try to wash someone with our water too *hot* - we are too fervent and zealous. Sometimes our water is too *cold* - we are cold and distant in heart to them. The temperature needs to be in the middle. We should also remember that we cannot *dry-clean* someone else's feet. Jesus washed us *with the washing of water by the word* (Ephesians 5:26), we should use the same "water" in ministering to others.

7. (15-17) The importance of following Jesus' example of humble service.

"For I have given you an example, that you should do as I have done to you. Most assuredly, I say to you, a servant is not greater than his master; nor is he who is sent greater than he who sent him. If you know these things, blessed are you if you do them."

a. **For I have given you an example, that you should do as I have done to you**: Jesus was far more than an example to the disciples and they needed more than an example. Yet Jesus *certainly was an example* to those disciples and all who would follow Him. They must take Him as **an example** for both attitude and action.

i. "There are too many of us who profess to be quite willing to trust to Jesus Christ as the Cleanser of our souls who are not nearly so willing to accept His Example as the pattern for our lives." (Maclaren)

b. **A servant is not greater than his master; nor is he who is sent greater than he who sent him**: If Jesus - who is our **master** and who sends us - if this Jesus humbly served in this way, it is even more appropriate for His servants and sent ones to do so.

i. **He who is sent**: "This occurrence of the noun translated 'one who is sent' (Greek *apostolos*) is the only one in this Gospel, and it is used in no official sense." (Bruce)

ii. "He gives the assurance that those whom He sends as His apostles will be identified with Himself and with God." (Dods)

c. **If you know these things, blessed are you if you do them**: The *theory* of being humble and being a servant isn't worth very much. But the *practice* of being a servant pleases God, fulfills our calling, bringing blessing and happiness.

i. "If there is a position in the church where the worker will have to toil hard and get no thanks for it, take it, and be pleased with it. If you can perform a service, which few will ever seek to do themselves, or appreciate when performed by others, yet occupy it with holy delight. Covet humble work, and when you get it be content to continue in it. There is no great rush after the lowest places, you will rob no one by seeking them." (Spurgeon)

B. Jesus sends Judas away after favoring him.

1. (18-20) Jesus reveals that one at the table will betray Him.

"I do not speak concerning all of you. I know whom I have chosen; but that the Scripture may be fulfilled, 'He who eats bread with Me has lifted up his heel against Me.' Now I tell you before it comes, that when it does come to pass, you may believe that I am *He*. Most assuredly, I say to you, he who receives whomever I send receives Me; and he who receives Me receives Him who sent Me."

a. **I know whom I have chosen**: When Jesus chooses a person He knows them. He does not choose apart from His knowledge of who they are and what they will do. It was important for Jesus to tell the disciples that He was not surprised by the betrayal that would soon happen.

b. **Lifted his heel against me**: Jesus had Psalm 41:9 in mind as He said this. It had the sense of a treacherous, unexpected attack or taking cruel advantage of someone. In Biblical culture the code of hospitality and a shared table meant that if one who **eats bread with Me** did afterward lift **up his heel against Me**, it was great betrayal and treachery.

c. **I tell you before it comes, that when it does come to pass, you may believe that I am**: Jesus didn't tell His disciples that one of them would betray Him because He just learned about it. He knew it all along. Jesus told them this so the *faithful* disciples would remain confident in Him.

d. **He who receives whomever I send receives Me; and he who receives Me receives Him who sent Me**: Jesus reminded all His disciples - the faithful ones and Judas - that His work was *not* finished. Judas would not win; the work of Jesus would continue and they would be sent as His representatives. He also wanted Judas to know that rejecting Him meant rejecting the God who **sent** Jesus.

2. (21-26) Jesus identifies Judas as His betrayer, and shows Judas love one last time.

When Jesus had said these things, He was troubled in spirit, and testified and said, "Most assuredly, I say to you, one of you will betray Me." Then the disciples looked at one another, perplexed about whom He spoke. Now there was leaning on Jesus' bosom one of His disciples, whom Jesus loved. Simon Peter therefore motioned to him to ask who it was of whom He spoke. Then, leaning back on Jesus' breast, he said to Him, "Lord, who is it?" Jesus answered, "It is he to whom I shall give a piece of bread when I have dipped *it.*" And having dipped the bread, He gave *it* to Judas Iscariot, *the son* of Simon.

a. **He was troubled in spirit**: Judas' betrayal of Jesus **troubled** Him. Jesus was not unfeeling or emotionally detached from the events surrounding His passion. He loved Judas, and was troubled for Judas' sake, much more than His own.

i. "Though John pictures Jesus as in control of the situation he does not want us to think of Him as unmoved by the events through which He is passing." (Morris)

b. **Most assuredly, I say to you, one of you will betray Me**: By revealing that one of them was a traitor, Jesus showed that He was in control of these events; He was not taken by surprise.

c. **Perplexed about whom He spoke**: It was not obvious to the other disciples that Judas was the one. There was nothing suspicious about him in this sense. They wondered if Jesus meant some kind of accidental, unintended betrayal, one that any of them might commit (Matthew 26:22).

d. **Simon Peter therefore motioned to him to ask who it was of whom He spoke**: Peter's question to John (here mentioned as the disciple **whom Jesus loved**) may have been prompted by a desire to take preventative action. Peter couldn't discreetly ask Jesus, so he asked John.

i. "The fact that Peter *beckoned* to the disciple whom Jesus loved in an attempt to obtain information about the identity of the traitor suggests that he was not next to Jesus; otherwise he could have spoken to Him directly." (Tasker)

ii. **Whom Jesus loved**: John referred to himself with this phrase four times in his Gospel, each connected with the cross in some way.

- Here in the upper room (John 13:23).
- At the cross of Jesus (John 19:26).
- At the empty tomb (John 20:2).
- With the risen Jesus at the Sea of Galilee (John 21:20).

iii. "We know that it must have been John, for many reasons; but still he does not say so. He hides John behind the love of Jesus, which proves that John gloried in the love of Christ, but did not boast of it egotistically." (Spurgeon)

e. **Leaning back on Jesus' breast, he said to Him**: At a special or ceremonial meal like this they would lay on their stomachs around a U-shaped table, leaning on their left elbow and eating with their right hand. It seems that from John's position next to Jesus, he could lean back and be close enough to speak quietly to Jesus and still be heard.

i. A disciple sat at each side of Jesus. "One of them was John the divine, and the other was Judas the devil. One of them was the seer of the Apocalypse, the other was the son of perdition." (Spurgeon)

ii. "The place of honor was to the left of, and thus slightly behind the principal person. The second place was to his right, and the guest there would have his head on the breast of the host. Plainly this was the position occupied by the beloved disciple." (Morris)

iii. "The normal posture at a table was sitting, as rabbinical sources indicate, clearly enough; reclining was the posture reserved for special meals, such as parties, wedding feasts, and the like." (Bruce)

iv. "The verbs for 'reclining' suggest that, although this meal fell 'before the (official) festival of the passover' (John 13:1), it was nevertheless treated by the participants as a passover meal." (Bruce)

f. **It is he to whom I shall give a piece of bread when I have dipped it**: The giving of the dipped bread designated special honor, something like a toast at a banquet. It was a mark of courtesy and esteem.

i. "It seems not unlikely that Judas was in the chief place. From Matthew's account it seems clear that Jesus could speak to him without being overhead by the others (Matthew 26:25)." (Morris)

ii. "When Jesus offers Judas a special morsel from the common dish, such as it was customary for a host to offer to an *honoured* guest, it is a mark of divine love which ever seeks to overcome evil with good." (Tasker)

iii. Sometimes we imagine people are against us when they are not and it makes us suspicious, unpleasant, and afraid. Jesus *knew* Judas was against Him yet His love and goodness seemed to become *greater* instead of lesser. Jesus even gave Judas the chance to repent without revealing him as the traitor to all the other disciples.

iv. Earlier at this dinner, the washing of feet displayed a degree of sacrificial love and service not seen before the cross. Now, the giving of the dipped bread to Judas showed the height of love for enemies, previous to the cross.

v. Jesus identified the betrayer to John, and seemingly to none of the other disciples. John did not stop or oppose Judas and he did not explain why. Perhaps he did not immediately grasp what Jesus said or found it so shocking that it momentarily confused him.

3. (27-30) The departure of Judas.

Now after the piece of bread, Satan entered him. Then Jesus said to him, "What you do, do quickly." But no one at the table knew for what reason He said this to him. For some thought, because Judas had the money box, that Jesus had said to him, "Buy *those things* we need for the feast," or that he should give something to the poor. Having received the piece of bread, he then went out immediately. And it was night.

a. **After the piece of bread, Satan entered him**: It was already in the heart of Judas to betray Jesus (John 13:2). Yet when Judas rejected the love and favor of Jesus it broke some barrier within him and **Satan entered him**.

i. "In accepting *the sop* Judas shows himself completely impervious to the appeal of love; and from that moment he is wholly the tool of Satan." (Tasker)

ii. "Satan could not have entered into him had he not granted him admission. Had he been willing to say 'No' to the adversary, all of his Master's intercessory power was available to him there and then to strengthen him." (Bruce)

b. **What you do, do quickly**: Jesus knew Judas was now past any appeal to conscience or heart. Set on his course, it was best to get it done with. Judas believed that *he* was the master now; that Jesus would have to deal with what *Judas* did. The sooner this delusion reached its end, the better.

i. Matthew 26:25 tells us something else Jesus said to Judas. When Jesus said one of them would betray Him (John 13:21), they all asked, *Is it I?* (Matthew 26:22). When Judas - sitting right next to Jesus - asked this, Jesus said to him privately, *You have said it* (Matthew 26:25). The point is, *Judas knew that Jesus knew* that this disciples would betray his Master.

ii. "Two things, then, appealed to him at the moment: one, the conviction that he was discovered; the other, the wonderful assurance that he was still loved, for the gift of the morsel was a token of friendliness. He shut his heart against them both; and as he shut his heart against Christ he opened it to the devil." (Maclaren)

c. **No one at the table knew**: If they (especially Peter) *had* known they would have stopped Judas. They believed Judas had business to do on behalf of the group, either to pay the expenses for the dinner or to **give something to the poor**.

i. **That he should give something to the poor**: "It is well known that our Lord and his disciples lived on *public charity*; and yet they gave *alms* out of what they had thus received. From this we learn that even those who live on charity themselves are expected to divide a little with those who are in deeper distress and want." (Clarke)

d. **He went out immediately**: With the taste of **the piece of bread** that showed the love and favor of Jesus still in his mouth, Judas left his fellow disciples, left his Master and went out into the **night**. Perhaps the events earlier at the dinner made Judas decide that he didn't want anything to do with a foot-washing Messiah, with a Messiah who would perform such a humble act.

i. "His act, however, was more than an incidental act of treachery; he sold himself to the power of evil." (Tenney)

ii. Judas shows us that fallen man needs more than an example and even more than good teaching. Judas had the best example and the greatest Teacher, and was still lost.

C. A new commandment.

1. (31-32) Jesus declares the cross as supreme glorification, not supreme humiliation.

So, when he had gone out, Jesus said, "Now the Son of Man is glorified, and God is glorified in Him. If God is glorified in Him, God will also glorify Him in Himself, and glorify Him immediately."

a. **Now the Son of Man is glorified**: When Judas left Jesus knew that everything was set in motion for His arrest, trials, humiliation, condemnation, beatings, crucifixion, and burial. He spoke of coming death as glorification (John 12:23). Now it was to happen.

i. "It was not that the *presence of* Judas, as some have thought, hindered the great consummation imported by this *glorification*, but that the work on which he was gone out, was the ACTUAL COMMENCEMENT *of that consummation.*" (Alford)

b. **Glorified... glorified... glorified... glorify... glorify**: Jesus made five references to glory in the space of two verses. With good reason, the world looked at the cross and could only say, *humiliated, disgraced, cursed.* Jesus looked at the cross and knowing what would be accomplished at it could truthfully say, **glorified**.

i. The cross most perfectly made known the heart of Jesus; and for Jesus, to be known was to be glorified. The love of Jesus was about to be revealed in a new way. "If His death is His glorifying, it must be because in that death something is done which was not completely by the life, however fair; by the words, however wise and tender; by the works of power, however restorative and healing." (Maclaren)

ii. "Jesus is looking to the cross as He speaks of glory. Origen employs the striking phrase 'humble glory' to express this idea of glory." (Morris)

iii. "He calls his death his glory, esteems his crown of thorns more precious than Solomon's diadem; looks upon his welts as spangles, his blows on the face as ingots, his wounds as gems, his spittings on as sweet ointment, his cross as his throne." (Trapp)

2. (33) Jesus plainly reveals His soon departure.

"Little children, I shall be with you a little while longer. You will seek Me; and as I said to the Jews, 'Where I am going, you cannot come,' so now I say to you."

a. **Little children**: This is the only place in the Gospels where Jesus addressed His disciples as **little children**. He didn't mean it as an insult. He meant it with a sense of tenderness, care, and recognition of their present dependence and immaturity.

b. **I shall be with you a little while longer... Where I am going, you cannot come**: This would have been like an earthquake to the disciples. They had literally left everything to follow Jesus, and expected to be high-ranking officials in His government when He took political control of Israel as Messiah. After three years they now heard Him say He would leave.

3. (34-35) Jesus tells of a **new commandment**.

"A new commandment I give to you, that you love one another; as I have loved you, that you also love one another. By this all will know that you are My disciples, if you have love for one another."

a. **A new commandment**: The specific ancient Greek work used here for **new** here implies freshness, or the opposite of outworn, rather than recent or different. It isn't that this **commandment** was just invented, but it will be presented in a new, fresh way.

> i. "'New' (*kainen*) implies freshness, or the opposite of 'outworn' rather than simply 'recent' or 'different.'" (Tenney)

> ii. "The 'new commandment' (*mandatum novum* in the Vulgate) has given its name to the anniversary of the Last Supper: Maundy Thursday." (Bruce)

b. **That you love one another**: We might have thought the new commandment was for us to *love Jesus* in an outstanding way. Instead, Jesus directed them and us to **love one another**, emphasizing that there should be a special presence of love among followers of Jesus Christ.

c. **As I have loved you**: The *command* to love wasn't new; but the *extent* of love just displayed by Jesus was new, as would be the display of the cross. Love was newly defined from His example.

> i. "We are to love our neighbor as ourselves, but we are to love our fellow-Christians as, Christ loved us, and that is far more than we love ourselves." (Spurgeon)

d. **By this all will know that you are My disciples**: Jesus said that love would be the identifying mark of His disciples. It wasn't that love for the outside world was not important or relevant, but it wasn't *first*. There are other measures of discipleship, but they come after this mark.

- Jesus would mark us as His disciples by our **love** for **one another**.
- We can mark ourselves as His disciples by our **love** for **one another**.
- The world can mark us as His disciples by our **love** for **one another**.

> i. "So Tertullian reports the pagans of his day (a century after this Gospel was published) as saying of Christians, 'See how they love one another!'" (Bruce)

4. (36-38) Peter's denial of Jesus is predicted.

Simon Peter said to Him, "Lord, where are You going?" Jesus answered him, "Where I am going you cannot follow Me now, but you shall follow Me afterward." Peter said to Him, "Lord, why can I not follow You now? I will lay down my life for Your sake." Jesus answered him, "Will you lay down your life for My sake? Most assuredly, I say to you, the rooster shall not crow till you have denied Me three times."

a. **Lord, where are You going**: Peter (and the other disciples) did not yet understand Jesus. Peter perhaps thought that Jesus was going on a long journey without them. Peter wanted more of an explanation.

b. **Where I am going you cannot follow Me now, but you shall follow Me afterward**: Peter didn't understand, but Jesus did. Jesus understood that Peter *could not* **follow** Him unto death now, but **afterward** he would.

c. **Lord, why can I not follow You now**: Peter knew he was the disciple of Jesus, and the disciple's duty was the **follow** the rabbi. Peter felt so committed to his discipleship to Jesus that not only would he **follow** Him, but also **lay down my life for Your sake.**

> i. *We believe Peter.* He *would* have died for Jesus right then but he later failed because his devotion was based on emotion, and in the soon-to-come crisis emotion would fail him.

> ii. We might say that Judas' denial of Jesus was *deliberate* and planned; Peter's denial of Jesus was accidental and spontaneous. Peter's denial was terrible, but it wasn't the same as what Judas did.

> iii. We see a different Peter when his walk is no longer built on emotion, but on the work of Jesus on the cross and the power of the Holy Spirit. "Christ must first die for Peter, before Peter can die for him." (Clarke)

d. **Till you have denied Me three times**: Peter confidently said that he would follow Jesus and even die for him. Yet when the test came he could not stand being laughed at for Jesus' sake. To him, a servant-girl's tongue was sharper than an executioner's sword. Before the next morning dawned he would deny he even *knew* Jesus **three times**.

> i. "When Peter protested, our Lord showed him that He knew all the weakness lurking within him better than he himself could know it." (Morgan)

> ii. "Cockcrow was the third of the four Roman night-watches, halfway between midnight and dawn." (Bruce)

> iii. The denial was burnt in his memory. When Peter preached in Acts 3, he charged them with denying Jesus (Acts 3:14). Towards the end of his life he described some dangerous men as those who denied the Lord (2 Peter 2:1).

John 14 - The Departing Jesus

A. Calming troubled hearts with trust and hope in Jesus.

1. (1) A command to calm the troubled heart.

"Let not your heart be troubled; you believe in God, believe also in Me."

a. **Let not your heart be troubled**: The disciples had reason to be troubled. Jesus had just told them that one of them was a traitor, that all of them would deny Him, and that He would leave them that night. All of this would legitimately trouble the disciples, yet Jesus told them, **let not your heart be troubled**.

    i. Jesus never wanted us to have life without trouble, but He promised that we could have an untroubled heart even in a troubled life.

    ii. This was in some sense a command. "The form of the imperative *me tarassestho* implies that they should 'stop being troubled.' 'Set your heart at ease' would be a good translation." (Tenney)

    iii. Jesus didn't say, "I'm happy you men are troubled and filled with doubts. You're doubts are wonderful." "He takes no delight in the doubt and disquietude of his people. When he saw that because of what he had said to them sorrow had filled the hearts of his apostles, he pleaded with them in great love, and besought them to be comforted." (Spurgeon)

    iv. "His disciples felt His departure like a torture. And it was then that He consoled them with such simple and glorious speech that all Christendom is the debtor to their agony." (Morrison)

b. **You believe in God, believe also in Me**: Instead of giving into a troubled heart, Jesus told them to firmly put their trust in God and in Jesus Himself. This was a radical call to trust in Jesus *just as* one would trust in God the

265

Father, and a radical promise that doing so would bring comfort and peace to a **troubled** heart.

i. "What signalizes Him, and separates Him from all other religious teachers, is not the clearness or the tenderness with which He reiterated the truths about the Father's love, or about morality, and justice, and truth, and goodness; but the peculiarity of His call to the world is, 'Believe in Me.'" (Maclaren)

ii. "One who seems a man asks all men to give Him precisely the same faith and confidence that they give to God." (Meyer)

iii. There is some debate as how the verb tenses of this verse should be regarded. It is possible that Jesus meant, *You must believe in God, you must also believe in Me* (imperative) or it is possible that He meant, *You do believe in God, you also do believe in Me* (indicative). On balance, the best evidence seems to be that Jesus meant this as a command or an instruction to the disciples.

- "The verb **believe** *both times is imperative*." (Alford)
- "In view of the preceding imperative it is in my judgment best to take both forms as imperative. Jesus is urging His followers to continue to believe in the Father and to continue to believe also in Him." (Morris)

iv. "Jesus' solution to perplexity is not a recipe; it is a relationship with him." (Tenney)

2. (2-4) Reasons for calming the troubled heart: a future reunion in the Father's house.

"In My Father's house are many mansions; if *it were* not *so,* I would have told you. I go to prepare a place for you. And if I go and prepare a place for you, I will come again and receive you to Myself; that where I am, *there* you may be also. And where I go you know, and the way you know."

a. **In My Father's house are many mansions**: Jesus spoke with complete confidence about heaven, here spoken of as His **Father's house**. Jesus didn't wonder about the life beyond this earth; He knew it and told His disciples that there was room for all in heaven (**many mansions**).

i. "Plato tells of the last hours of Socrates in prison before he drank the poison....Like Christ, Socrates is going to die. Like Christ, his thoughts run on immortality. He discusses it with his friends, who come to visit him; he speculates, he argues, and he wonders. What a perfect and stupendous contrast between that and the attitude of Christ." (Morrison)

b. **Many mansions**: In light of the ancient Greek, **mansions** is better translated "dwelling places." The noun *mone* (connected to the verb *meno*, "stay" or "remain") means "a place to stay." In light of God's nature, it is better to translate it **mansions**. Whatever dwelling place God has for us in heaven, it will be as glorious as a mansion.

i. There will be **many** such dwelling places. Jesus could see what the disciples never could - millions upon millions, even billions from every tribe, language, nation in His Father's house. He may have even smiled when He said, **many mansions - many** indeed!

ii. "*Mansions, monai*, came into the AV and RV through the influence of the Vulgate *mansions*, which can mean 'stations' or 'temporary lodgings' where travellers may rest at different stages in their journey. In the light of this, many scholars, especially Westcott and Temple, following Origen, assume that the conception of heaven in this passage is that of a state of progress from one stage to another till the final goal is reached. This was not however the interpretation generally given to the word by the ancient Fathers, and by derivation it would seem to denote much more the idea of permanence. It is found once more in the New Testament, in John 14:23, where the permanent dwelling of the Father and the Son in the hearts of loving disciples is stressed." (Tasker)

c. **I go to prepare a place for you:** Love prepares a welcome. With love, expectant parents prepare a room for the baby. With love, the hostess prepares for her guests. Jesus prepares **a place** for His people because He loves them and is confident of their arrival.

i. James Barrie was the man who wrote *Peter Pan*, among other works. One of his books was about his mother, Margaret Ogilvy, and his growing up in Scotland. His mother endured a lot of misery in life, including the tragic death of one of her sons. According to Morrison, Barrie wrote that his mother's favorite Bible chapter was John 14. She read it so much that when her Bible was opened and set down, the pages naturally fell open to this place. Barrie said that when she was old and could no longer read these words, she would stoop down to her Bible and kiss the page where the words were printed.

ii. **I go** speaks of Jesus' own planning and initiative. He wasn't taken to the cross; He went there. "*They* thought that His death was an unforeseen calamity. Christ taught them that it was the path of His own planning." (Morrison)

d. **I will come again to receive you to Myself**: Jesus promised to come again for the disciples. This was not only in the sense of His soon resurrection or in the coming of the Holy Spirit. Jesus also had in mind the great gathering together of His people at the end of the age.

i. "They were not to think of Him as having ceased to be when they could not see Him. He had only gone to another abiding-place to prepare for their coming; and moreover, He would come back to receive them." (Morgan)

ii. "The reference to the second advent should not be missed. It is true that John does not refer to this as often as do most other New Testament writers, but it is not true that it is missing from his pages." (Morris)

iii. "This was a very precious promise to the early Church, and Paul may well be echoing it when he informs the Thessalonians 'by the word of the Lord' that Jesus will descend from heaven and gather believers unto Himself to be with Him for ever (see 1 Thessalonians 4:15-17)." (Tasker)

e. **That where I am, there you may be also**: The entire focus of heaven is being united with Jesus. Heaven is heaven not because of streets of gold, or pearly gates, or even the presence of angels. Heaven is heaven because Jesus is there.

i. We take comfort in knowing that even as He prepares a place for us, Jesus also prepares us for that place.

3. (5-6) Jesus is the exclusive way to the Father.

Thomas said to Him, "Lord, we do not know where You are going, and how can we know the way?" Jesus said to him, "I am the way, the truth, and the life. No one comes to the Father except through Me."

a. **Lord, we do not know where You are going**: Thomas should be praised for honestly and clearly explaining his confusion. He thought Jesus was simply going to another place, as if it were another city.

i. "Though a necessity of human language compels Jesus to speak of 'going away' and of 'a way to the Father', these terms have no spatial or material significance." (Tasker)

ii. "Thus we notice how they speak to him with a natural, easy familiarity; and he talks to them in full sympathy with their weakness, teaching them little by little as they are able to learn. They ask just such questions as a boy might ask of his father. Often they show their ignorance, but never do they seem timid in his presence, or ashamed

to let him see how shallow and hard of understanding they are."
(Spurgeon)

b. **I am the way, the truth, and the life**: Jesus didn't say that He would show us a way; He said that He *is* the way. He didn't promise to *teach us a* truth; He said that He *is* the truth. Jesus didn't offer us the secrets to life; He said that He *is* the life.

- *I'm wandering about; I don't know where I'm going.* Jesus is the way.
- *I'm confused; I don't know what to think.* Jesus is the truth.
- *I'm dead inside and don't know if I can go on.* Jesus is the life.

i. In light of soon events, this declaration was a paradox. Jesus' *way* would be the cross; He would be convicted by blatant *liars*; His body would soon lie *lifeless* in a tomb. Because He took that way, He is **the way** to God; because He did not contest the lies we can believe He is **the truth**; because He was willing to die He becomes the channel of resurrection - **the life** to us.

ii. "Without the way there is no going; without the truth there is no knowing; without the life there is no living. I am the way which thou must follow; the truth in which thou must believe; the life for which thou must hope." (a' Kempis, cited by Bruce)

c. **No one comes to the Father except through Me**: Jesus made this remarkable statement, claiming that He was the only way to God. In this He set aside the temple and its rituals, as well as other religions. It was a claim to have an exclusive **way**, **truth**, and **life** - the only pathway to God the **Father**, the true God in heaven.

i. Understood plainly, this was one of the more controversial things Jesus said and the Gospel writers recorded. Many people don't mind saying that Jesus is one legitimate way to God, but other religions and even individuals have their own legitimate ways to God. Many think it isn't *fair* for God to make only one way.

ii. Nevertheless, this is a consistent theme in the Bible. The Ten Commandments begin, *I am the LORD your God, who brought you out of the land of Egypt, out of the house of bondage. You shall have no other gods before Me* (Exodus 20:2-3). Throughout the Old Testament God denounced and mocked the supposed gods others worshipped (Isaiah 41:21-29; 1 Kings 18:19-40). The Bible consistently presents *One True God*, and Jesus is consistently presented as *the only true way to the One True God*.

d. **No one comes to the Father except through Me**: Simply put, if Jesus is not *the only* way to God, then He is not *any way* to God. If there are many roads to God, then Jesus is not one of them, because He absolutely claimed there was only one road to God, and He Himself was that road. If Jesus is not the only way to God, then He was not a honest man; He was most certainly not a true prophet. He then would either be a madman or a lying devil. There is no middle ground available.

i. Sometimes people object and say, "I believe Jesus was an honest man, and I believe He was a true prophet. But I don't actually believe He said those things about Himself in the Gospels. I believe Christians added those things in later on all by themselves." But there is no *objective* reason for a person to make a distinction between "Jesus really said this" or "Jesus really didn't say that." We have no ancient texts showing us just the *supposedly true* sayings of Jesus. Any such distinction is based *purely* on subjective reasons - "I personally don't think Jesus would have said that, therefore He did not say that - later Christians only put those words in His mouth."

ii. If it is all up to personal opinion - if we can determine what Jesus said or didn't say on our own whims - then we should reject the Gospels completely. It really is an all-or-nothing deal. Either we take the words of Jesus as recorded by these historically reliable and accurate documents, or we reject them completely.

iii. But is Christianity bigoted? Certainly, there are some who claim to be Christians who are in fact bigots. But Biblical Christianity is the most pluralistic, tolerant, embracing of other cultures religion on earth. Christianity is the one religion to embrace other cultures, and has the most urgency to translate the Scriptures into other languages. A Christian can keep their native language and culture, and follow Jesus in the midst of it. An early criticism of Christianity was the observation that they would take *anybody*! Slave or free; rich or poor; man or woman; Greek or Barbarian. All were accepted, but on the common ground of the truth as revealed in Jesus Christ. To leave this common ground in Jesus is spiritual suicide, for both now and eternity.

iv. "If this seems offensively exclusive, let it be borne in mind that the one who makes this claim is the incarnate Word, the revealer of the Father." (Bruce)

v. The Christian faith will receive *anyone* who comes through Jesus. Jesus said, **through Me**: "It is not 'through believing certain propositions regarding me' nor 'through some special kind of faith,' but 'through me'." (Dods)

4. (7-8) Knowing the Father and knowing the Son.

"If you had known Me, you would have known My Father also; and from now on you know Him and have seen Him." Philip said to Him, "Lord, show us the Father, and it is sufficient for us."

a. **If you had known Me, you would have known My Father also**: Jesus explained *why* He was the only way to God; because He was and is the *perfect representation* of God. To know Jesus is to know God.

b. **And from now on you know Him and have seen Him**: The disciples certainly had learned and known much about God in their three years of apprenticeship under Jesus. Yet Jesus understood that since they had not yet seen the full revelation of God's *love* at the cross and His *power* at the resurrection, there was a sense in which they would only **now** know and see God.

c. **Lord, show us the Father and it is sufficient**: Philip had seen and experienced much in following Jesus, but had not yet *seen* God the Father with his physical eyes. Perhaps he thought that such an experience would bring life-changing assurance and courage.

5. (9-11) Jesus again explains His unity with and dependence on the Father.

Jesus said to him, "Have I been with you so long, and yet you have not known Me, Philip? He who has seen Me has seen the Father; so how can you say, 'Show us the Father'? Do you not believe that I am in the Father, and the Father in Me? The words that I speak to you I do not speak on My own *authority*; but the Father who dwells in Me does the works. Believe Me that I *am* in the Father and the Father in Me, or else believe Me for the sake of the works themselves."

a. **Have I been with you so long, and yet you have not known Me**: This means that Philip had been close to Jesus yet still did not understand Him. The same is possible and true for many today.

b. **He who has seen Me has seen the Father**: This gentle rebuke reminded Philip of what Jesus often said; that to know Him was to know God the Father. To see the love of Jesus was to see the love of God the Father; seeing Jesus in action was seeing the Father in action.

i. "It is difficult interpret it without seeing the Father and the Son as in some sense one. These are words which no mere man has a right to use." (Morris)

ii. **He who has seen Me has seen the Father**: "No material image or likeness can adequately depict God. Only a person can give knowledge of him since personality cannot be represented by an impersonal object."

(Tenney) This forever finishes the idea that the Hebrew Scriptures present a cruel God and Jesus showed us a nicer God. Rather, Jesus shows us the same love, compassion, mercy, and goodness that was and is in God the Father. Exodus 34:5-9, among other passages, shows this nature of God the Father in the Old Testament.

iii. **He who has seen Me has seen the Father**: "Could any *creature* say these words? Do they not evidently imply that Christ declared himself to his disciples to be the everlasting God?" (Clarke)

c. **The words that I speak to you I do not speak on My own authority**: Jesus repeated something emphasized in the Gospel of John; that Jesus lived and spoke in constant dependence upon God the Father and did nothing outside His authority and guidance (John 5:19, 8:28).

d. **Believe Me... or else believe Me for the sake of the works themselves**: Jesus presented two solid foundations for our trust in Him. We can believe Jesus simply because of His person and words, or we can also believe Him **for the sake of the works** that He miraculously did.

i. **The Father who dwells in Me does the works**: "We are not only *one* in *nature*, but *one* also in *operation*. The works which I have done bear witness of the infinite perfection of my nature. Such miracles as I have wrought could only be performed by unlimited power." (Clarke)

ii. **Believe Me**: "Here Jesus calls on Philip and the others (note the change to the plural) to believe Him, not only to believe in Him. Faith includes a recognition that what Jesus says is true." (Morris)

iii. "Our Saviour allegeth for himself the Divinity both of his word and works. He was mighty, saith Peter, both in word and deed. Ministers also must, in their measure, be able to argue and approve themselves to be men of God, by sound doctrine and good life." (Trapp)

B. Three assurances for troubled disciples.

1. (12-14) When Jesus departs to the Father, His work will continue on earth.

"Most assuredly, I say to you, he who believes in Me, the works that I do he will do also; and greater *works* than these he will do, because I go to My Father. And whatever you ask in My name, that I will do, that the Father may be glorified in the Son. If you ask anything in My name, I will do *it*."

a. **Most assuredly**: Jesus began the first of three assurances given to His disciples on the night of His departure. The first assurance answered their fear, "This is the end. The work is over and we all got fired." They didn't get fired; they got promoted, and promoted to greater things.

b. **He who believes in Me**: Jesus just encouraged the disciples to trust in, rely on, and cling to Him in faith, because of who He is, the words He spoke, and the miracles He has done. Now Jesus described the benefit or blessing that comes to this one who believes.

c. **The works I do he will do**: Jesus expected those who believe in Him to carry on His work in the world. He did not expect the disciples to disband after His departure, but to carry on His work in even greater magnitude (**greater works than these he will do**).

> i. "The 'greater works' of which he now spoke to them would still be his own works; accomplished no longer by his visible presence among them but by his Spirit within them." (Bruce)

d. **Greater works than these he will do**: Jesus did not mean **greater** in the sense of *more sensational*, but *greater in magnitude*. Jesus would leave behind a victorious, working family of followers who would spread His kingdom to more people and places than Jesus ever did in His life and ministry.

> i. This promise seems impossible; yet after Peter's first sermon there were more converted than are recorded during Jesus' entire ministry.

> ii. "The literal rendering of the word translated by av *greater works* is 'greater things'; and probably this should be retained. The works of the apostles after the resurrection were not greater in kind than those of Jesus, but greater in the sphere of their influence." (Tasker)

> iii. "The word 'works' does not actually occur. There is no word at that point, so our best translation would be 'and greater *things*.' The point is that Christians will do something greater even than the works of Jesus." (Boice)

> iv. "What Jesus means we may see in the narratives of the Acts. There there are a few miracles of healing, but the emphasis is on the mighty works of conversion. On the day of Pentecost alone more believers were added to the little band of believers than throughout Christ's entire earthly life. There we see a literal fulfillment of 'greater works than these shall he do.'" (Morris)

> v. William Barclay considered the difficult of taking this to mean that Jesus intended His followers to do more miracles and more impressive miracles than He Himself did: "Though it could be said that the early Church did the things which Jesus did, it certainly could not be said that it did greater things than he did." (Barclay)

> vi. There are some who believe that Jesus meant that individual believers can and should do more spectacular works than Jesus did in the years

of His earthly ministry. We earnestly await proof of those who have repeatedly done **greater works** than walking on water, calming storms with a word, multiplying food for thousands, raising people from the dead (more than the three recorded in Jesus' work). Even if it were proved that *one person* after Jesus had done such things, it still does not explain why there are not now or have been thousands of people who have fulfilled this wrong and sometimes dangerous understanding of what Jesus meant when He said, **greater works than these he will do**.

e. **Because I go to My Father**: Jesus would soon explain that when He ascended to heaven, He would send the Holy Spirit (John 14:16, 14:26, 15:26, 15:7-9, 15:13). It was because Jesus went to the Father that the Holy Spirit came upon His people, enabling them to do these **greater works**.

> i. "*The reason why you shall do these greater works is, on account of the all-powerful Spirit of grace and supplication which My going to the Father shall bring down upon the Church.*" (Alford)

f. **Whatever you ask in My name, that I will do**: Jesus further explained how **greater works** would be possible for His followers. It would be possible because Jesus would do His work through His prayerful people, who asked and acted in His **name**. He promised to do **anything** that His trusting followers asked for in His **name**; that is, according to His character and authority.

> i. **In My name** is not a magic incantation of prayer; it speaks of both an endorsement (like a bank check) and a limitation (requests must be in accordance with the character of the name). We come to God in Jesus' **name**, not in our own.

> ii. "The test of any prayer is: Can I make it in the name of Jesus? No man, for instance, could pray for personal revenge, for personal ambition, for some unworthy and unchristian object *in the name of Jesus*." (Barclay)

> iii. "To ask 'in His name' or do anything 'in His name' argues a unity of mind with His, a unity of aim and of motive." (Trench)

g. **That the Father may be glorified in the Son**: These **greater works** Jesus promised would bring glory to both the Father and the Son. Prayers prayed with a passion for the glory of Jesus and God the Father will truly be in the name of Jesus and be the kind of prayer God will answer.

2. (15-17) When Jesus departs, He will send the Holy Spirit.

"If you love Me, keep My commandments. And I will pray the Father, and He will give you another Helper, that He may abide with you

**forever—the Spirit of truth, whom the world cannot receive, because
it neither sees Him nor knows Him; but you know Him, for He dwells
with you and will be in you."**

a. **If you love Me, keep My commandments**: Jesus had just demonstrated
His remarkable love to the disciples by washing their feet (John 13:1-
5). He told them what their loving response should be; to **keep** His
commandments.

- He commanded them to wash one another's feet, after the example
  He just displayed (John 13:14-15).

- He commanded them to love one another after the pattern of His
  love to them (John 13:34).

- He commanded them to put their faith in God the Father and in
  Jesus Himself (John 14:1).

  i. Keeping the commandments of Jesus does speak to our personal
  morality, yet His emphasis was on love for others and faith in Him as
  demonstrations of obedience to His **commandments**.

  ii. This is a fair measure of our love for Jesus. It is easy to think of
  loving Jesus in merely sentimental or emotional terms. It is wonderful
  when our love for Jesus has sentiment and passion, but it must always
  be connected to keeping His commandments, or it isn't **love** at all.

  iii. For the believer, disobedience is not only a failure of performance
  or a failure of strength. In some sense, it is also a failure of love. Those
  who love God most obey Him most joyfully and naturally. To say, "I
  really love Jesus. I just don't want Him to tell me how to live my life" is
  a terrible misunderstanding of both Jesus and love to Him.

  iv. Jesus also spoke to the proper source of our obedience. It isn't fear,
  pride, or desire to earn blessing. The proper source of obedience is
  love. "Obedience must have love for its mother, nurse, and food. The
  essence of obedience lies in the hearty love which prompts the deed
  rather than in the deed itself." (Spurgeon)

  v. "Some persons think that if they love Jesus, they must enter a
  convent, retire to a cell, dress themselves queerly, or shave their
  heads. It has been the thought of some men, 'If we love Christ we
  must strip ourselves of everything we possess, put on sackcloth, tie
  ropes round our waists, and pine in the desert.' Others have thought it
  wise to make light of themselves by oddity of dress and behavior. The
  Savior does not say anything of the kind; but, 'If ye love me, keep my
  commandments.'" (Spurgeon)

b. **I will pray the Father, and He will give you another Helper**: This was the second in this series of three assurances. The disciples feared, "Jesus is abandoning us. When He leaves we won't know what to do." They wouldn't have less help; they would have *more help* because the Father would send **another Helper**.

i. Jesus understood that His disciples (both those with Him on that evening and those across the centuries) would need God's presence and power to keep His commandments. God the Son promised to pray to God the Father and ask for the giving of God the Holy Spirit to the believer to accomplish this.

ii. This statement is one wonderful example of the Trinitarian idea of God woven into the fabric of the New Testament. Jesus didn't intend to give a complicated lecture on the Trinity; He simply spoke of how the Persons of the Trinity interact and work for the good of God's people and the furtherance of His plan.

iii. The sense is that this prayer would be made when Jesus ascended to heaven. "**I will pray** betokens, probably, a manner of asking implying *actual presence and nearness*, -- and is here used of the mediatorial office in Christ's *ascended state*." (Alford)

c. **He will give you another Helper**: The word **Helper** translates the ancient Greek word *parakletos*. This word has the idea of someone called to help someone else, and it could refer to an advisor, a legal defender, a mediator, or to an intercessor.

i. The King James Version translates *parakletos* with the word *Comforter*. That translation made more sense understanding the meaning of the word in older English. "Wicliff, from whom we have our word **Comforter**, often used 'comfort' for the Latin *confortari*, which means to strengthen…Thus the idea of *help and strength* is conveyed by it, as well as of consolation." (Alford)

ii. One way to understand the work of the **Helper** is to understand the *opposite* of that work. "The devil is called the accuser, in full opposition to this name and title given here to the Holy Spirit." (Trapp)

iii. **Another Helper**: The word **another** is the ancient Greek word *allen*, meaning "another of the same kind" (Tenney) in contrast to another of a *different* kind. Just as Jesus shows the nature of God the Father, so the Holy Spirit - being *another of the same kind* - would show the nature of Jesus.

iv. "That our Lord here calls the Holy Spirit 'another Comforter (αλλον παρακλητο)' implies that He Himself claimed to be also a παρακλητο, as John in his first epistle (1 John 2:1) calls Him." (Trench)

v. It would be wonderful to live the Christian life with Jesus beside us each step of the way. Jesus promised that the Holy Spirit would fulfill just that role for us, being sent to empower and help the believer. The greater work described in John 14:12-14 is impossible without the empowering described in John 14:15-18.

d. **That He may abide with you forever**: Jesus would give the Holy Spirit so that **He** (indicating a person, not a thing) **may abide** in us permanently and not temporarily, as in giving of the Holy Spirit in the Old Testament.

i. "The Advocate will be with the disciples 'for ever'. The new state of affairs will be permanent. The Spirit once given will not be withdrawn." (Morris)

e. **Whom the world cannot receive**: The world cannot understand or receive the Spirit, because He is Holy and true. **The Spirit of truth** is not popular in an age of lies, and the world cannot perceive the Spirit and does not **know Him.**

i. "If the world cannot receive the Holy Spirit, shall we wonder that we in our collective worldliness see and show collectively so little of His power?" (Trench)

f. **But you know Him, for He dwells with you and will be in you**: Jesus spoke of three aspects of a disciple's relationship to the Holy Spirit.

- In contrast to the world, the disciple of Jesus *should* **know** the Holy Spirit.

- In contrast to the world, the disciple of Jesus *should* have the Holy Spirit **with** them.

- In contrast to the world, the disciple of Jesus *should* have the Holy Spirit **in** them.

i. For those 11 disciples, the Holy Spirit was already **with** them, and would later be **in** them. This was fulfilled when Jesus breathed on them and they received the Holy Spirit, when they were regenerated and born again (John 20:22).

ii. In addition to **with** and **in**, Jesus used a third preposition to describe the relationship of the disciple to the Holy Spirit: *you shall receive power when the Holy Spirit has come upon you* (Acts 1:8). This *upon* experience is the baptism of the Holy Spirit, the outpouring of the Spirit.

iii. "Between Christ on earth and his disciples what a distance there was! In his condescension he came very near to them; but yet you always perceive a gulf between the wise Master and the foolish disciples. Now the Holy Ghost annihilates that distance by dwelling in us." (Spurgeon)

3. (18-21) When Jesus departs, He will make Himself known to His disciples.

"I will not leave you orphans; I will come to you. A little while longer and the world will see Me no more, but you will see Me. Because I live, you will live also. At that day you will know that I *am* in My Father, and you in Me, and I in you. He who has My commandments and keeps them, it is he who loves Me. And he who loves Me will be loved by My Father, and I will love him and manifest Myself to him."

a. **I will not leave you orphans; I will come to you**: Jesus began His third assurance. The disciples feared, "When Jesus leaves, then our discipleship program is over and it has barely started." Their discipleship program wasn't finished; it was only just beginning.

i. "The disciples of a particular teacher among the Hebrews called him *father*; his *scholars* were called his *children*, and, on his *death*, were considered as *orphans*." (Clarke)

ii. Spurgeon considered several ways that the followers of Jesus are not like orphans.

- An orphan has parents who are dead; the Spirit shows us Jesus is alive.
- An orphan left alone; the Spirit draws us close to God's presence.
- An orphan has lost their provider; the Spirit provides all things.
- An orphan is left without instruction; the Spirit teaches us all things.
- An orphan has no defender; the Spirit is protector.

b. **I will come to you**: Jesus again promised to **come to** the disciples (previously in John 14: 3). This was a broad promise fulfilled by His resurrection, by the sending of the Spirit, and by the promise of His bodily return to this earth.

i. "Every phase of his promised coming is embraced in this assurance: 'I am coming to you.'" (Bruce)

c. **The world will see Me no more, but you will see Me**: This was true in one sense when Jesus rose from the dead. Yet it true even when He ascended to heaven. Jesus would reveal Himself to the disciples in a real and powerful way after His departure. They would **see** Him a way even greater than seeing Him with physical sight.

> i. The Apostle Paul later wrote, *Even though we have known Christ according to the flesh, yet now we know Him thus no longer* (2 Corinthians 5:16). There was something *more* compelling about knowing Jesus by the Spirit than even knowing Him in the flesh.

d. **Because I live, you will live also**: The disciples would not only **see** Jesus by the Spirit, they would also continue to **live** in Jesus through the work of the Holy Spirit. Their dependence on the life of Jesus would not end when He departed; it would continue in greater measure through the Holy Spirit.

> i. "A man is saved because Christ died for him, he continues saved because Christ lives for him. The sole reason why the spiritual life abides is because Jesus lives." (Spurgeon)

e. **You will know that I am in My Father, and you in Me, and I in you**: Through the Holy Spirit they would know a life of relationship, shared life, and union with God the Father, God the Son, and in the disciple.

- This union is marked by knowledge of God's will (**has My commandments**).

- This union is marked by obedience to God's will (**and keeps them**).

- This union is marked by love (**is he who loves me**).

- This union is marked by relationship and reception of love with God the Father (**will be loved by My Father**).

- This union is marked by a revelation of Jesus Himself (**and manifest Myself to him**).

- All this flows from the union with God in the disciple through the Holy Spirit.

> i. This relationship is for the disciple's experience *now*, not only in the age to come. "For he reserves not all for the life to come, but gives a grape of Canaan in this wilderness, such as the world never tasted of." (Trapp)

> ii. **He who has My commandments and keeps them, it is he who loves Me**: "The love to which Christ promises a manifestation of Himself is not an idle sentiment or shallow fancy, but a principle prompting obedience." (Dods)

> iii. **He who has My commandments**: "The man who loves Christ is the one who 'has' His commandments and keeps them. To 'have'

commandments is an unusual expression and does not seem to be exactly paralleled (though *cf.* 1 John 4:21). The meaning appears to be to make the commandments one's own, to take them into one's inner being." (Morris)

4. (22-24) Answering the question of Judas (not Iscariot).

Judas (not Iscariot) said to Him, "Lord, how is it that You will manifest Yourself to us, and not to the world?" Jesus answered and said to him, "If anyone loves Me, he will keep My word; and My Father will love him, and We will come to him and make Our home with him. He who does not love Me does not keep My words; and the word which you hear is not Mine but the Father's who sent Me."

a. **How is it that You will manifest Yourself to us**: Judas asked an excellent question. The idea of **manifest** is to reveal, to make plain. It wasn't immediately apparent how in His departure Jesus could reveal Himself to His disciples and not to the world at large.

i. Judas had heard Jesus teach that all the earth would see the Messiah in His glory (Matthew 24:30). It was hard for him to understand Jesus when He now spoke of a revealing of Himself that the world would *not* see.

ii. "*Judas* is called 'Judas of James' in Luke 6:16 and Acts 1:13; and on each occasion AV translates 'the brother of James', and RV and RSV, more naturally, 'the son of James'. He seems to be identical with the Thaddaeus of Matthew 10:3 and Mark 3:18. Some of the apostles clearly had more than one name." (Tasker)

iii. "The words **not Iscariot** are in reality superfluous, after John 13:30, but are added by St. John from his deep horror of the Traitor who bore the same name." (Alford)

b. **If anyone loves Me, he will keep My word**: In answering Judas, Jesus repeated the themes from the previous verses. Jesus would be revealed to and among the disciples through love, obedience, and union with the Father and the Son. These were not and are not primarily mystical or ecstatic experiences, but real life lived out in the presence and work of the Holy Spirit.

• The love is personal; Jesus said, **if anyone loves Me**.

• The love has a reverent regard for the teaching of Jesus; Jesus said, **he will keep My word**.

i. **He will keep My word**: "That is more than a 'commandment,' is it not? Christ's 'word' is more than *precept*. It includes all His sayings, and it includes them all as in one vital unity and organic whole. We are not to go picking and choosing among them; they are one." (Maclaren)

ii. **We will come to him and make Our home with him**: "Where love and obedience are shown, the presence of God and of Christ is realized; the Father and the Son together make their home with each of the children." (Bruce)

c. **The word which you hear is not Mine but the Father's who sent Me**: Jesus again emphasized His total reliance upon and submission to God the Father. Jesus openly stated both His equality with the Father (John 14:1, 14:3, 14:7, 14:9).

C. As Jesus departs, He gives the gift of the Holy Spirit and His peace.

1. (25-27) The departing Jesus leaves the gifts of the Holy Spirit and His peace.

"These things I have spoken to you while being present with you. But the Helper, the Holy Spirit, whom the Father will send in My name, He will teach you all things, and bring to your remembrance all things that I said to you. Peace I leave with you, My peace I give to you; not as the world gives do I give to you. Let not your heart be troubled, neither let it be afraid."

a. **The Helper, the Holy Spirit, whom the Father will send in My name**: Jesus first mentioned the **Helper** in John 14:16. He returned to the wonderful promise that as He left them with His physical presence, Jesus would ask the Father to send the Holy Spirit to *help* His disciples.

i. **Will send in My name**: The Holy Spirit is sent to the disciples on the *merits* of Jesus and in the *nature,* the *character* of Jesus. "The Spirit would be Jesus' officially designated representative to act in his behalf." (Tenney)

- The disciple does not have to ask for the Spirit on his or her own merit; they can receive Him in the merit of Jesus.

- The disciple should expect that the work of the Spirit would look like the nature and character of Jesus as revealed in God's Word.

ii. This is another wonderful example of the truth of the Trinity woven into the fabric of the New Testament. God the Father sends God the Holy Spirit at the request of God the Son.

iii. **The Holy Spirit**: "This characteristic designation, found throughout the New Testament, does not draw attention to the power of the Spirit, His greatness, or the like. For the first Christians the important thing was that He is holy." (Morris)

b. **He will teach you all things, and bring to your remembrance all things that I said to you**: In His departure, Jesus finished His direct work of teaching the disciples as a rabbi taught disciples. Their training was not finished, but would be continued by the **Helper, the Holy Spirit.**

i. The Holy Spirit would teach the disciples what more they needed to know and would also supernaturally bring to **remembrance** the words of Jesus, both for their own benefit and for the writing of the Gospels.

ii. This means that the work of the Spirit would be a work of *continuation*. His teaching would continue what Jesus already taught. The Spirit does not wipe clear the previous teaching of Jesus and begin again. "The Spirit will not dispense with the teachings of Jesus. The teaching to be recalled is His." (Morris)

iii. There is something *general* in this promise for every believer. The Holy Spirit teaches us and brings God's word to our remembrance (if we are careful to receive it). Yet the *fullness* of this promise was reserved for those first-generation disciples and apostles, upon whom Jesus established the church (Ephesians 2:20).

iv. "*It is on the fulfillment of this promise to the Apostles, that their sufficiency as Witnesses of all that the Lord did and taught, and consequently* THE AUTHENTICITY OF THE GOSPEL NARRATIVE, *is grounded.*" (Alford)

c. **Peace I leave with you, My peace I give to you**: In one sense this was a common thing to say at a departure in that culture, to wish **peace** (*shalom*) to others as you left them. Jesus took this normal good-bye and filled it with deep strength and meaning.

i. "It was customary to take leave with wishes of peace: -- so 1 Samuel 1:17; Luke 7:50; Acts 16:36; 1 Peter 5:14; 3 John 15." (Alford) "'Peace (*shalom*) be with you' was (and is) the usual Jewish greeting when friends met and parted." (Bruce)

ii. **Not as the world gives do I give to you**: When someone in that ancient culture said *peace* as they departed, they said it without any special meaning. It was like when we say *goodbye*. Literally that means, *God be with you* - but we don't really mean it that way. Jesus wanted them to know that when He said **peace I leave with you**, it wasn't in the casual, empty way that most people said it.

iii. The peace of this world is often based on distraction or deliberate blindness and lies. Jesus offers a better peace, a real **peace**.

iv. Jesus had no inheritance or fortune to leave to His followers in a last will and testament. Yet Jesus gave them two things greater than any fortune: the presence and power of the Holy Spirit, and the **peace** of Jesus Himself. This is the peace of God the Son, with His complete trusting love in God the Father.

v. "He carefully described the peace as 'My peace.' His peace was a heart untroubled and unfearful in spite of all the suffering and conflict ahead of Him." (Morgan)

vi. "In the Bible the word for *peace, shalom,* never means simply the absence of trouble. It means everything which makes for our highest good. The peace which the world offers us is the peace of escape, the peace which comes from the avoidance of trouble and from refusing to face things." (Barclay)

d. **Let not your heart be troubled**: Jesus returned to the theme recorded in the first verse of John 14. With faith in God and His Son, with the receiving of His Spirit and His peace, we can have an untroubled **heart** in a quite troubled life.

2. (28-29) The goodness of Jesus' departure to the Father.

"You have heard Me say to you, 'I am going away and coming *back* to you.' If you loved Me, you would rejoice because I said, 'I am going to the Father,' for My Father is greater than I. And now I have told you before it comes, that when it does come to pass, you may believe."

a. **If you loved Me, you would rejoice**: The disciples were troubled at the news of Jesus' departure. In faith, they should instead **rejoice**, for the sake of Jesus, for their own sake, and for the sake of the world. The work of Jesus through the sent Holy Spirit would be greater than His work during the years of His earthly ministry.

- Jesus, when I think of all You gave up, all You took upon Yourself when You came from heaven to earth - it makes me happy that You are **going to the Father** to have it all restored to You.

- Jesus, when I think of all You will give to me and all Your people when You ascend to glory and from there send forth the Holy Spirit, pray for Your church, and prepare a place for us - it makes me happy that You are **going to the Father**, also for my sake.

b. **Because I said, "I am going to the Father"**: We sense a joyful anticipation in Jesus, happy in His soon return to heaven's fellowship between Father and Son.

c. **My Father is greater than I**: The Father **is greater** than the Son in *position*, especially in regard to the incarnation. Yet the Father is *not* greater than the Son in *essence* or *being*; They are both equally God.

i. It is remarkable that Jesus should even say this. "That it should require to be explicitly affirmed, as here, is strongest evidence that He was Divine." (Dods)

3. (30-31) Jesus goes forth willingly, not as one who is being overwhelmed by Satan.

"I will no longer talk much with you, for the ruler of this world is coming, and he has nothing in Me. But that the world may know that I love the Father, and as the Father gave Me commandment, so I do. Arise, let us go from here."

a. **The ruler of this world is coming**: Jesus knew that *Satan was coming for Him*. At that moment Judas Iscariot was arranging the arrest of Jesus in the Garden of Gethsemane. The loving, others-centered calm of Jesus in such circumstances is remarkable.

b. **He has nothing in Me**: Jesus could confidently and truthfully say that Satan had absolutely no hook, no foothold, no toehold of deception in Him. Satan could not push Jesus to the cross; Jesus went in loving obedience to God the Father and out of love for the world (**that the world may know that I love the Father, and as the Father gave Me commandment, so do I**).

i. "**Has nothing in Me** -- no point of appliance whereon to fasten his attack." (Alford)

ii. "Jesus goes to death not crushed by the machinations of Satan, 'but that the world may know that I love the Father and as the Father has commanded me.'" (Dods)

c. **Arise, let us go from here**: At this point, Jesus and His disciples left the table and slowly made their way toward the Garden of Gethsemane. It is clear they did not immediately leave (John 18:1), but here began to.

i. "Anyone who has tried to get a group of a dozen or so to leave a particular place at a particular time will appreciate that it usually takes more than one brief exhortation to accomplish this." (Morris)

ii. "Probably the rest of the discourse, and the prayer, chapter 17, were delivered when now all were standing ready to depart." (Alford)

iii. "Whether chapters 15-17 were spoken en route to Gethsemane or whether he and the disciples lingered while he finished the discussion is not plain." (Tenney)

iv. Notably, *they got ready to go together*. "One would have thought that on such a night as that, the deepest craving of Jesus would have been to be alone... He could not leave them to go out alone. He loved them far to deeply for that. They might forsake Him, as they were soon to do. It was impossible for Him to forsake them." (Morrison)

John 15 - The Departing Jesus Teaches His Disciples about Life in Him

"It must occur to all who read these discourses preserved by John how simple the text looks, and yet how transcendent is the thought when it is even dimly understood. John is sailing sky-high: are we? It is the strongest food in the Bible." (Trench)

A. Relating to Jesus when Jesus departs.

1. (1-3) Jesus as the **true vine**.

"I am the true vine, and My Father is the vinedresser. Every branch in Me that does not bear fruit He takes away; and every *branch* that bears fruit He prunes, that it may bear more fruit. You are already clean because of the word which I have spoken to you."

a. **I am the true vine**: This was a familiar symbol. God repeatedly used a **vine** as a symbol of His people in the Hebrew Scriptures (one example is Psalm 80:8-9). Yet it was often used in a negative sense (as in Isaiah 5:1-2, 7 and Jeremiah 2:21). Just in the previous week Jesus publicly taught about Israel being like a vineyard in the Parable of the Vineyard (Matthew 21:33-44).

i. Jesus spoke this to His disciples, probably as they stood in the upper room and prepared to leave. He used the picture of the **vine** because there were grapevines everywhere in ancient Israel. Also, there was a large golden vine set as a prominent decoration on the front of the temple communicating the idea that Israel was God's vine. As well, "The vine was a recognized symbol also of the Messiah." (Dods)

ii. In contrast, Jesus is **the true vine**. We must be rooted in Him (not in Israel) if we will bear fruit for God. In the New Covenant community, our first identification is in *Jesus Christ Himself*, not in Israel or even in the church as such.

ii. In contrast, Jesus is **the true vine**. We must be rooted in Him (not in Israel) if we will bear fruit for God. In the New Covenant community, our first identification is in *Jesus Christ Himself*, not in Israel or even in the church as such.

iii. Of the many pictures of the relationship between God and His people, the **vine** and **branch** picture emphasizes complete dependence and the need for constant connection. The branch depends on the vine even more than the sheep depends on the shepherd or the child depends on the father. As Jesus was about to depart from His disciples, this was important encouragement. He would remain united to them and they to Him as truly as branches are connected to the main vine.

b. **And My Father is the vinedresser**: In the Old Testament use of the vine as a picture of Israel, God the Father was also presented as the One who cultivated and managed the vine. God fulfills this role also for the believer under the New Covenant.

i. The New Covenant participant has relationship with both the **Father** and the Son; with both the **vine** itself and the **vinedresser**.

c. **Every branch in Me that does not bear fruit He takes away**: The branches that are taken away were never properly abiding in the vine, demonstrated by the fact that they did **not bear fruit**.

i. There is an alternative understanding of this passage that bears some consideration. James Montgomery Boice (among others) believes that the ancient Greek verb *airo*, translated, **takes away** is more accurately translated *lifts up*. The idea is that the Father lifts up unproductive vines off of the ground (as was common in the ancient practices of vineyard care). Those caring for ancient grape vines made sure to lift them up off the ground that they might get more sun and bear fruit better.

ii. "The verb translated 'cut off' (*aireo*) means literally 'to lift up' or 'to take away'; the second, 'trims clean' (*kathaireo*), a compound of the first, means 'to cleanse' or 'to purify.'" (Tenney)

d. **Every branch that bears fruit He prunes**: This word for **prunes** is the same word translated *cleanse* in other places. The same word could apply to either "pruning" or "cleansing" in ancient Greek. The vinedresser cleans up the fruit-bearing vine so it will bear more fruit.

i. "Left to itself a vine will produce a good deal of unproductive growth. For maximum fruitfulness extensive pruning is essential." (Morris)

ii. "Dead wood is worse than fruitlessness, for dead wood can harbor disease and decay...God removes the dead wood from his church and disciplines the life of the believer so that it is directed into fruitful activity." (Tenney)

iii. "And if it be painful to bleed, it is worse to wither. Better be pruned to grow than cut up to burn." (Trapp)

e. **You are already clean because of the word which I have spoken to you**: The work of pruning, of cleansing, had already begun in the eleven disciples Jesus spoke to. They had heard and received much of His teaching and were in some sense **already clean because of the word**.

i. In saying **you are already clean**, Jesus repeated an idea from earlier in the evening: that there is an initial cleansing, and then a continuing cleansing (John 13:10).

ii. The word of God is a cleansing agent. It condemns sin, it inspires holiness, it promotes growth, and it reveals power for victory. Jesus continues to wash His people through the word (Ephesians 5:26).

iii. "The means by which pruning or cleaning is done is by the Word of God. It condemns sin; it inspires holiness; it promotes growth. As Jesus applied the words God gave him to the lives of the disciples, they underwent a pruning process that removed evil from them and conditioned them for further service." (Tenney)

2. (4-5) The vital relationship between the branch and the vine.

"Abide in Me, and I in you. As the branch cannot bear fruit of itself, unless it abides in the vine, neither can you, unless you abide in Me. I am the vine, you *are* the branches. He who abides in Me, and I in him, bears much fruit; for without Me you can do nothing."

a. **Abide in Me, and I in You**: Jesus emphasized a *mutual* relationship. It isn't only that the disciple abides in the Master; the Master also abides in the disciple. Something of this close relationship is described in Song of Solomon 6:3: *I am my beloved's, and my beloved is mine.*

i. Jesus used this picture to assure His disciples of continued connection and relationship even though He was about to depart from them. Yet He spoke this in a way that also indicated an aspect of *choice* on their part. Abiding was something they must *choose*.

ii. "When our Lord says: *Abide in me* he is talking about the will, about the choices, the decisions we make. We must decide to do things which expose ourselves to him and keep ourselves in contact with him. This is what it means to abide in him." (Boice)

b. **As the branch cannot bear fruit of itself, unless it abides in the vine**: It is impossible for the branch to bear grapes if it isn't connected to the

vine. The disciple can't do true good for God and His kingdom if they do not consciously connect with and abide in Jesus.

i. "All our sap and safety is from Christ. The bud of a good desire, the blossom of a good resolution, and the fruit of a good action, all come from him." (Trapp)

c. **I am the vine, you are the branches**: Jesus perhaps spoke so perhaps because they were so accustomed to thinking of *Israel* as the vine and thought mainly in terms of their connection to Israel. They now had to think of *Jesus* as the vine, and emphasize their connection to Him.

d. **He who abides in Me, and I in him, bears much fruit**: Fruit bearing is inevitable with abiding. The quality and quantity of the fruit may differ, but the presence of fruit will be inevitable.

i. The purpose of the branch is to bear fruit. Though there are uses for grape leaves, people don't raise grape vines to look at the pretty leaves. They take the trouble to cultivate, plant, water and tend the vines so that fruit can be enjoyed. In this sense, we can say that fruit represents Christian character (such as the fruit of the Spirit in Galatians 5). God's work in us and our connection to Him should be evident by **fruit**, and perhaps by **much fruit**.

ii. Fruit also implies inherent reproduction. Virtually every piece of fruit has seeds within it, seeds that are meant to reproduce more fruit.

iii. The concept of abiding is not restricted to our abiding in Jesus; it also includes His abiding in us (**and I in him**). It is a mutual dynamic that expects our life to be spiritually and practically in vital connection with Jesus, *and* that expects Him to indwell us in an active, real way. In no way is the responsibility for abiding only upon the believer.

e. **Without Me you can do nothing**: It isn't that they disciples could do no *activity* without Jesus. They could be active without Him, as were the enemies of Jesus and many others. Yet they and we could **do nothing** of real, eternal value without Jesus.

i. "The 'I am' comes out in the personal word 'me,' and the claim of all power unveils the Omnipotent. These words mean Godhead or nothing." (Spurgeon)

ii. "It is only by union with Him that any branch can bear fruit: once that union is broken, the sap no longer flows; and *fruit* in that branch is no longer possible, though the remains of the sap that lay in it may be enough to bear leaves and so for a time give semblance of life." (Trench)

iii. "Paul does not use the Johannine idiom but he expresses the same truth when he says, 'It is no longer I who live, but Christ who lives in me' (Galatians 2:20), and 'I can do all things in him who strengthens me' (Philippians 4:13)." (Bruce)

iv. "'Without me ye can do nothing;' if this be true of apostles, much more of opposers! If his friends can do nothing without him, I am sure his foes can do nothing against him." (Spurgeon)

3. (6-8) The price of not abiding and the promise to those who do abide.

"If anyone does not abide in Me, he is cast out as a branch and is withered; and they gather them and throw *them* into the fire, and they are burned. If you abide in Me, and My words abide in you, you will ask what you desire, and it shall be done for you. By this My Father is glorified, that you bear much fruit; so you will be My disciples."

a. **If anyone does not abide in Me, he is cast out as a branch and is withered**: Jesus warned His disciples that failing to abide means that life fails. A **branch** only has life as it is connected to the stock of the vine; a disciple only spiritually lives as they are connected to the Master.

i. These verbs describe a progression for the one who doesn't abide: cast out, withered, gathered, thrown, and burned. Like other parables, the picture Jesus used here was not meant to describe a whole theological system. Yet the progression described is a sober and significant warning of the danger of not abiding.

ii. The phrasing Jesus used here was important. He didn't say, *If anyone does not bear fruit he is cast out.* He said, **if anyone does not abide in Me, he is cast out.** *He* knows who abides and who does not, and this can't be perfectly discerned by our outward estimation of fruit.

b. **They gather them and throw them into the fire**: The lifeless branch bears no fruit and even its wood is good for nothing but burning. This reference to burning and **fire** raises the association of punishment in the life to come and warns of the great consequences of failing to abide.

i. We think of how these words would impact the eleven disciples who first heard them. Jesus told them He would depart; yet they would not be disconnected from Him. The work of the Holy Spirit, sent by the Father, would be to keep them connected to Jesus. If they were disconnected from Him, they would be ruined - perhaps as Judas was.

ii. This passage is interpreted at least three ways regarding the security of the professed disciple's position in Jesus.

- The first view believes **cast out** branches are ones who, though once true believers, end up in hell for lack of abiding and fruit. They were once disciples, but are now **cast out**.

- The second view is that the **cast out** branches are ones who only appeared to be disciples, and who never really abided in Jesus, and therefore go to hell (like Judas).

- The third view sees the **cast out** branches as fruitless disciples who live wasted lives that are in effect burnt up, and this passage doesn't refer to their eternal destiny (like Lot, Abraham's nephew).

iii. The emphasis seems plain: there are no true disciples who do not abide. The branch must remain connected to the vine or it has no life and is of no lasting good.

iv. **Are burned**: "Not, 'is burned,' in any sense of being *consumed*; '*and must burn*,' as Luther renders it." (Alford)

c. **If you abide in Me, and My words abide in you, you will ask what you desire and it shall be done for you**: Jesus connected the principle of abiding to two ideas previously mentioned in this upper room talk.

- **My words abide in you**: Jesus connected abiding to the idea of *faithfulness to His words*, as previously mentioned in John 14:23-24.

- **You will ask what you desire**: Jesus connected abiding to the idea of *answered prayer*, as previously mentioned in John 14:13-14. "Prayer comes spontaneously from those who abide in Jesus... Prayer is the natural outgushing of a soul in communion with Jesus." (Spurgeon)

i. Abiding in Jesus means abiding in His **words**, and having His words live in the disciple. "We should not overlook the importance of the reference to 'my words'. The teaching of Christ is important and is not lightly to be passed over in the interests of promoting religious feeling." (Morris)

ii. "The connection is maintained by obedience and prayer. To remain in Christ and to allow his words to remain in oneself means a conscious acceptance of the authority of his word and a constant contact with him by prayer." (Tenney)

iii. This faithful, abiding disciple should expect answered prayer as part of their relationship with Jesus. A failure to see prayer answered means something is not right in the disciple's relationship. Perhaps something is not right in the *abiding*, and prayers are amiss and unanswered.

Perhaps something is not right in the *asking* and there is no perception of what Jesus wants to do in and through His disciple.

iv. **It shall be done for you**: "It becomes safe for God to say to the sanctified soul, 'Ask what thou wilt, and it shall be done unto thee.' The heavenly instincts of that man lead him right; the grace that is within his soul thrusts down all covetous lustings and foul desires, and his will is the actual shadow of God's will. The spiritual life is master in him, and so his aspirations are holy, heavenly, Godlike." (Spurgeon)

d. **By this my Father is glorified, that you bear much fruit**: The purpose of fruit bearing is to bring glory to God, not to the disciple. A branch that bears **much fruit** brings honor to one who cares for the vine, and a disciple who bears **much fruit** in a spiritual sense brings honor to God.

i. "Branches and clusters have no self-seeking, no aim outside the Vine and the Husbandman's glory: all other aims are cast out as unworthy." (Trench)

ii. **By this My Father is glorified**: "Or, *honoured*. It is the honour of the husbandman to have good, strong, vigorous vines, plentifully laden with fruit: so it is the honour of God to have strong, vigorous, holy children, entirely freed from sin, and perfectly filled with his love." (Clarke)

iii. Real fruitfulness is only determined over an extended period of time. "Genuine conversion is not measured by the hasty decision but by long-range fruitfulness." (Erdman) This principle is displayed in the Parable of the Soils (Matthew 13).

4. (9-11) The link between love and obedience.

"As the Father loved Me, I also have loved you; abide in My love. If you keep My commandments, you will abide in My love, just as I have kept My Father's commandments and abide in His love. These things I have spoken to you, that My joy may remain in you, and *that* your joy may be full."

a. **As the Father loved Me, I also have loved you**: Jesus deliberately loved His disciples according to the way God the Father **loved** Him. We know that Jesus **loved** His disciples by teaching them, protecting them, guiding them, sacrificially serving them, and using His power and authority to do these things. In some way, the Father also did all those things for Jesus and Jesus did them for the disciples after that pattern.

i. The love of Jesus for His people is so remarkable, that *this* is the analogy or illustration that He must make. He didn't say, "I love you as a mother loves her baby" or "I love you the way a husband loves his wife" or "I love you the way the soldier loves his buddy" or even "I love you the way an addict loves his dope." The only way He could paint the picture was to use the love of the Father for the Son.

ii. **As the Father loved Me, I also have loved you**: "This surely is Christ's superlative word concerning His love for His own. It leaves nothing more to be said. What the love of the Father is for the Son, who can tell? The very suggestion fills the soul with the sense of profound depths which cannot be fathomed." (Morgan)

iii. "Beloved, you do not, dare not, could not, doubt the love of the Father to his Son. It is one of those unquestionable truths about which you never dreamed of holding an argument. Our Lord would have us place his love to us in the same category with the Father's love to himself. We are to be as confident of the one as of the other." (Spurgeon)

iv. The Father loved the Son with a love:

- That has no beginning.
- That has no end.
- That is close and personal.
- That is without measure.
- That is unchanging.

b. **Abide in My love**: There is no single way to describe the nature and character of Jesus. He is filled with power, wisdom, truth, holiness, devotion, submission, sacrifice, and dozens of other qualities. Of all these to emphasize, Jesus said **abide in My love**. When the disciple stays connected to the love of Jesus the relationship stays strong.

i. **You will abide in My love**: "Notice that this is done as an explanation of the means of abiding in His love. This is not some mystical experience. It is simple obedience. It is when a man keeps Christ's commandments that he abides in Christ's love." (Morris)

c. **If you keep My commandments, you will abide in My love**: *Again,* Jesus connected true discipleship with obedience to His command and honoring His word. Jesus fulfilled this in regard to His Father; the disciple must fulfill it in regard to Jesus.

i. As noted previously (John 14:15) what Jesus did and taught that evening in the upper room emphasized the **commandments** of Jesus mainly in love for fellow disciples, sacrificial service for fellow disciples, and trusting love for God the Father and Jesus the Son.

d. **These things I have spoken to you, that My joy may remain in you, and that your joy may be full**: When the disciple fails to abide in the love of Jesus and thereby fails to keep His commandments, that disciple will not experience the fullness of joy Jesus promised to those who do abide in His love and obedience.

i. "No one is more miserable than the Christian who for a time hedges in his obedience. He does not love sin enough to enjoy its pleasures, and does not love Christ enough to relish holiness. He perceives that his rebellion is iniquitous, but obedience seems distasteful. He does not feel at home any longer in the world, but his memory of his past associations and the tantalizing lyrics of his old music prevent him from singing with the saints. He is a man most to be pitied; and he cannot forever remain ambivalent." (Carson)

e. **That My joy may remain in you**: The joy of Jesus isn't the same as what is commonly understood as *happiness* or *excitement*. The joy of Jesus is not the pleasure of a life of ease; it is the exhilaration of being right with God, and consciously walking in His love and care. We can have that **joy** - we can have *His* **joy** - and have it as an abiding presence.

i. **My joy**: "Not '*joy concerning Me*,' nor '*joy derived from Me*,' nor '*My joy over you*,' but **My joy**, properly speaking...His own holy exultation, the joy of the Son in the consciousness of the love of God." (Alford)

ii. When Jesus spoke of His joy, "Nobody ever asked Him what He meant. They did not look at each other in perplexity. To them it seemed entirely natural that the Master should make reference to His gladness. From this we gather that the joy of Christ was something they were perfectly familiar with." (Morrison)

f. **That your joy may be full**: This is the result of abiding in Jesus' love, and obedience flowing from that abiding relationship.

i. **That your joy may be full**: "Or, *complete*-πληρωθη, *filled up*: a metaphor taken from a vessel, into which water or any other thing is poured, till it is full to the brim. The religion of Christ expels *all misery* from the hearts of those who receive it in its fulness. It was to drive wretchedness out of the world that Jesus came into it." (Clarke)

ii. "God made human beings, as he made his other creatures, to be happy. They are capable of happiness, they are in their right element when they are happy; and now that Jesus Christ has come to restore the ruins of the Fall, he has to bring back to us the old joy, — only it shall be even sweeter and deeper than it could have been if we had never lost it." (Spurgeon)

B. Relating to each other when Jesus departs.

1. (12-15) Jesus speaks of the extent of His love that they are to imitate.

"This is My commandment, that you love one another as I have loved you. Greater love has no one than this, than to lay down one's life for his friends. You are My friends if you do whatever I command you. No longer do I call you servants, for a servant does not know what his master is doing; but I have called you friends, for all things that I heard from My Father I have made known to you."

a. **That you love one another as I have loved you**: As Jesus spoke these words to the disciples as they stood in the upper room, having risen from the table, we sense the emphasis created by repetition. Jesus *really cared* that His disciples **love one another**, and that they do so according to the measure and quality of His love for them.

i. "Perhaps they expected minute, detailed instructions such as they had received when first sent out (Matthew 10). Instead of this, love was to be their sufficient guide." (Dods)

ii. "We are sent out into the world to love one another. Sometimes we live as if we were sent into the world to compete with one another, or to dispute with one another, or even to quarrel with one another." (Barclay)

iii. **As I have loved you**: "His love was at once the source and the measure of theirs." (Dods)

iv. "Unity instead of rivalry, trust instead of suspicion, obedience instead of self-assertion must rule the disciples' common labors." (Tenney)

v. **This is My commandment, that you love one another**: "So deeply was thus commandment engraved on the heart of this evangelist that St. Jerome says, lib. iii. c. 6, Com. ad *Galat.*, that in his extreme old age, when he used to be carried to the public assemblies of the believers, his constant saying was, *Little children, love one another*. His disciples, wearied at last with the constant repetition of the same words, asked him, Why he constantly said the same thing? 'Because (said he) it is the commandment of the Lord, and the observation of it *alone* is sufficient.'" (Clarke)

b. **Greater love has no one than this, than to lay down one's life for his friends**: Jesus described the measure and quality of His love for them, to use as a pattern for the way they should love each other. His love is complete and of surpassing greatness, laying down its **life**.

i. "No man can carry his love for his friend farther than this: for, when he gives up his life, he gives up all that he has. This proof of my love for you I shall give in a few hours; and the doctrine which I recommend to you I am just going to exemplify myself." (Clarke)

c. **I have called you friends**: Jesus descried the measure and quality of His love for them as a love that treats **servants** as **friends**. In the relationship between a disciple and his rabbi of that time, it wasn't expected to be a friendship. Yet Jesus the rabbi called His disciples, His servants **friends**.

i. In the thinking of the ancient world a slave could be a useful and trusted tool but could never be thought of as a *partner*. It was possible that a slave and a friend might be of similar help, but a friend could be a *partner* in the work in a way a slave never could.

ii. "John Wesley, looking back on his conversion in later years, described it as a time when he exchanged the faith of a servant for the faith of a son." (Bruce)

d. **You are My friends if you do whatever I command you**: They were **friends** because they were obedient (though not perfectly so). Friendship with Jesus can't be disconnected from obedience to His commands.

i. "It must be active obedience, notice that. 'Ye are my friends, if ye do whatsoever I command you.' Some think it is quite sufficient if they avoid what he forbids. Abstinence from evil is a great part of righteousness, but it is not enough for friendship." (Spurgeon)

e. **I have called you friends, for all things that I heard from My Father I have made known to you**: They were **friends** because Jesus didn't keep secrets from them, but openly revealed what He had received from God the Father.

i. "The friend is a confidant who shares the knowledge of his superior's purpose and voluntarily adopts it as his own." (Tenney)

2. (16-17) Chosen to bear fruit and to love one another.

"You did not choose Me, but I chose you and appointed you that you should go and bear fruit, and *that* your fruit should remain, that whatever you ask the Father in My name He may give you. These things I command you, that you love one another."

a. **You did not choose Me, but I chose you**: Jesus just spoke of great privilege for the disciples - friendship with the Master, answered prayer, bearing much fruit, knowing things from the Father. The disciples should rightly treasure these without becoming proud as if they had earned them.

They were all rooted in the fact that Jesus **chose** them, not that they chose Him.

> i. "We are in Christ, not because we hold Him, but because He holds us." (Meyer)

> ii. "It was not they who chose Him, as was normally the case when disciples attached themselves to a particular Rabbi. Students the world over delight to seek out the teacher of their choice and attach themselves to him. But Jesus' disciples did not hold the initiative. On the contrary it was He who chose them." (Morris)

> iii. **That you should go and bear fruit**: "The word **go** probably merely expresses the activity of living and developing principle; not the missionary journeys of the Apostles, as some have explained it." (Alford)

b. **Appointed you that you should go and bear fruit, and that your fruit should remain**: Jesus chooses disciples not simply so they would have the thrill of knowing they are chosen, but so that they would **bear fruit** that remains, to the glory of God the Father.

> i. "Much of their fruit will be necessarily the winning of others to Christ: but that is not *the prominent* idea here." (Alford)

c. **That whatever you ask**: Again, Jesus connected fruit bearing with answered prayer. When He departed from them their experience of asking and receiving would not end but would change, and Jesus prepared His disciples for this.

d. **That you love one another**: Again, Jesus commanded love among the disciples. When He departed from them they must not disband or turn against each other, and Jesus prepared them to stay together and **love one another**.

C. Relating to the world when Jesus departs.

1. (18-20) The world may reject the disciples because of who they are.

"If the world hates you, you know that it hated Me before *it hated* you. If you were of the world, the world would love its own. Yet because you are not of the world, but I chose you out of the world, therefore the world hates you. Remember the word that I said to you, 'A servant is not greater than his master.' If they persecuted Me, they will also persecute you. If they kept My word, they will keep yours also."

a. **If the world hates you**: Jesus told the disciples that the world would often hate them. As wonderful as Jesus was and His message was, they should expect to be rejected when Jesus departed, just was much as they were often opposed while Jesus was with them.

i. The disciples Jesus spoke to that night would know the hatred of the world. They were persecuted and all of them died as martyrs in Jesus' name, except for John -- whom they tried to kill, but he miraculously would not die at their hands.

ii. The earliest Christians would know the hatred of the world. "Tacitus spoke of the people 'hated for their crimes, whom the mob call Christians.' Suetonius had spoken of 'a race of men who belong to a new and evil superstition.'" (Barclay)

iii. "It is an odd fact that the world soon justified its hostility to them by imputing to them the initiative in hatred. The earliest extant reference to Christians in pagan literature charges them with 'hatred of the human race'." (Tacitus, *Annals*, 15.44.5) (Bruce)

iv. Christians through the centuries have known the hatred of the world, and millions have died for Jesus. It is said that more died as martyrs for Jesus in the 20th century than in all previous centuries combined.

v. "It is not without significance that the disciples are to be known by their love, the world by its hatred." (Morris)

b. **You know that it hated Me before it hated you**: Jesus hoped to comfort the disciples with the knowledge that the world's hatred was first directed toward Him. Jesus attracted attention from great multitudes and devotion from individuals of all kinds; yet as a whole, the world **hated** Jesus.

i. **You know**: "*Ye know* can also be read as an imperative *know ye*. The sense is therefore either 'Ye are aware', or 'Be very sure', so that (on either interpretation) the hatred of the world for them will not take them by surprise." (Tasker)

ii. **It hated Me**: "The perfect tense of the verb 'hate' (*memiseken*) implies that the world's hatred is a fixed attitude toward him -- an attitude that carries over to his disciples as well." (Tenney)

iii. When Jesus spoke to Saul of Tarsus on the Road to Damascus, He asked Saul: *Why do you persecute Me?* (Acts 9:4) "The Lord who was personally persecuted on earth continued to be persecuted, even in his exultation, in the person of his persecuted followers." (Bruce)

iv. **It hated Me**: "He and the world are antagonistic. The world is glad to forget God: He came to bring men back to God." (Trench)

c. **Because you are not of the world**: Jesus said this both as a fact and an explanation. This further explained why the world would hate the disciples of Jesus. It was also to be a factual description of the disciples - that in many ways they were different than **the world**.

> i. **But I chose you out of the world**: "The hatred of the world, instead of being depressing, should be exhilarating, as being an evidence and guarantee that they have been chosen by Christ." (Dods)

d. **If they persecuted Me, they will also persecute you**: Jesus was mostly persecuted by the religious establishment, which mainly reflected the values and goals of the world in opposition to God. One may be religious and very much part of the world.

> i. **If they kept My word, they will keep yours also**: "The force of the last clause in this verse is well brought out by Knox 'they will pay the same attention to your words as to mine; that is, none'." (Tasker)

2. (21-25) The world may reject disciples because of who Jesus is.

"But all these things they will do to you for My name's sake, because they do not know Him who sent Me. If I had not come and spoken to them, they would have no sin, but now they have no excuse for their sin. He who hates Me hates My Father also. If I had not done among them the works which no one else did, they would have no sin; but now they have seen and also hated both Me and My Father. But *this happened* that the word might be fulfilled which is written in their law, 'They hated Me without a cause.'"

a. **Because they do not know Him who sent Me**: If people do not know God as He really is, they often attack and persecute those who represent God in some way. This should cause sympathy in the persecuted for their persecutors.

> i. "Men may prefer to evolve an idea of their universal Father, but that idea of theirs will take their own colour and the colour of their Age. The only true idea of Him is to be got from The Son." (Trench)

b. **Now they have no excuse for their sin**: Because Jesus did come to and speak to the world, *they knew something of God that they did not know before*. This made them without **excuse** for hating and rejecting Jesus and His Father in heaven. Jesus did **among them the works which no one else did**, and they still hated and rejected Him.

> i. **Spoken to them... done among them the works**: "By both his life and his words he rebukes human sin and condemns it. He uncovers the inner corruption and hypocrisy of men, and they react violently to the disclosure." (Tenney)

ii. **Spoken to them... done among them the works**: "So then He puts before us two forms of His manifestation of the divine nature, by His words and His works. Of these two He puts His words foremost, as being a deeper and more precious and brilliant revelation of what God is than are His miracles." (Maclaren)

c. **They hated Me without a cause**: Jesus quoted this line from Psalm 69:4 (and possibly Psalm 35:19) to show the Scriptural precedent and prophetic fulfillment that there was no just **cause** for the world to hate Jesus and His Father as they did.

i. "Their unreasonable hatred both of Himself and His Father is inexplicable except as a corroboration of the truth of the Psalmist's words *They hated me without a cause* (Psalm 35:19; 69:4)." (Tasker)

ii. "The irony of his quotation is clear: the men who posted as the champions of the Law were fulfilling the prophecy concerning the enemies of God's servant." (Tenney)

iii. As the disciples of Jesus expect some measure of hatred and rejection from the world, they should live in such a way that it is also **without a cause**. Peter communicated some of this heart in his letter: *If you are reproached for the name of Christ, blessed are you, for the Spirit of glory and of God rests upon you. On their part He is blasphemed, but on your part He is glorified. But let none of you suffer as a murderer, a thief, an evildoer, or as a busybody in other people's matters. Yet if anyone suffers as a Christian, let him not be ashamed, but let him glorify God in this matter.* (1 Peter 4:14-16)

3. (26-27) The witness of the Holy Spirit and the disciples.

"But when the Helper comes, whom I shall send to you from the Father, the Spirit of truth who proceeds from the Father, He will testify of Me. And you also will bear witness, because you have been with Me from the beginning."

a. **When the Helper comes**: Jesus previously spoke of the sending of the **Helper** (John 14:16, 14:26). The departing Jesus knew the disciples would need the presence and the power of the Holy Spirit to face the opposition the world would bring.

i. **Who proceeds from the Father**: This line is one source of a historic controversy between the eastern and western branches of Christianity, debating if the Spirit **proceeds from the Father** alone or from the Father and the Son.

ii. "Although the coming of the Advocate is clearly stated to be dependent upon the initiative of the Son, He is only said to 'proceed' from the Father. Hence the long controversy between East and West over the *filoque* clause in the Nicene Creed." (Tasker)

iii. "The western expansion of the clause, 'who proceeds from the Father and the Son' (*filioque*), could be justified by the fact that the Son as well as the Father is said to send the Spirit; the basic objection to it was that it was unwarranted for one part of the church to make such an alteration in the wording of the ecumenical creed without reference to the rest of the church." (Bruce)

b. **He will testify of Me:** Jesus had told them that the **Helper**, the Holy Spirit, would continue the teaching work of Jesus (John 14:26). Here He explained that the **Helper** would speak of and about Jesus.

i. Everything the Holy Spirit does is consistent with the testimony of the nature of Jesus. His job is to tell us, and to show us, who Jesus is. If spiritual things happen that are not consistent with the nature of Jesus, it isn't the Holy Spirit doing it. He is the One who will **testify of** Jesus in all that He does.

c. **And you also will bear witness:** The disciples were not left in the world merely to endure the world's hatred. Empowered by the **Helper** and His testimony about Jesus, they will **bear witness** of who Jesus is and what He did to rescue the world.

i. "The witness of the Advocate and the witness of the apostles are in effect a single witness." (Tasker)

ii. "Their witness is linked with that of the Holy Spirit. It is the same Christ to whom they bear witness, and it is the same salvation of which they bear witness. At the same time it is *their* witness. They cannot simply relax and leave it all to the Spirit." (Morris)

iii. This bearing of witness may have had special application to the apostles. "This verse alludes to the historical witness which the Holy Ghost in the ministers and eye-witnesses of the word, Luke 1:2, should enable them to give, -- which forms the *human side* of this great testimony of the Spirit of truth, and OF WHICH OUR INSPIRED GOSPELS ARE THE SUMMARY: the *Divine side* being, His own indwelling testimony in the live and heart of every believer in all time." (Alford)

d. **Because you have been with Me:** The disciples were qualified to **bear witness** of Jesus because they trusted Him, had the Holy Spirit, and had simply been with Jesus - they were part of His life and He was part of their life.

John 16 - The Departing Jesus' Final Teaching

A. More on the work of the Holy Spirit.

1. (1-4) The reason for Jesus' warning: certain persecution.

"These things I have spoken to you, that you should not be made to stumble. They will put you out of the synagogues; yes, the time is coming that whoever kills you will think that he offers God service. And these things they will do to you because they have not known the Father nor Me. But these things I have told you, that when the time comes, you may remember that I told you of them. And these things I did not say to you at the beginning, because I was with you."

a. **They will put you out of the synagogues**: Jesus warned His disciples of coming opposition because He did not want them to be surprised and stumbled by it. He also did not expect that His disciples would immediately leave **the synagogues**, or leave them by their own choice. They would be forced out of the synagogues for Jesus' sake.

i. **Stumble**: "A *skandalethron* was not a stumbling-block which might trip you up… It is used of the spring of a trap which might 'go off' when you were least expecting it." (Tasker)

ii. "At the time when the Gospel was written these words had acquired a special relevance from the inclusion in the synagogue prayers of a curse on the Nazarenes, which was intended to ensure that the followers of Jesus could take no part in the service." (Bruce)

b. **The time is coming that whoever kills you will think that he offers God service**: That time quickly came, as the life of Saul of Tarsus before his conversion showed (Acts 8:1-3, 22:3-5, 26:9-11). Since then there have been many who persecute and kill the true followers of Jesus because they think God is pleased.

i. **Offers God service**: "The word Jesus uses for service is *lateria*, which is the normal word for the service that a priest rendered at the altar in the Temple of God and is the standard word for religious service." (Barclay)

ii. In the 20th Century most Christian martyrs were victims of the atheistic, communist state. Historically, this was unusual. Through most of history, most Christian martyrs were targets of those from other religions or even sects within Christendom.

c. **When the time comes, you may remember that I told you of them**: Jesus did well to forewarn, because it comes as a great shock that a gospel so glorious is hated so passionately. He did not tell His disciples these things **at the beginning**, but He certainly told them.

i. "During the earlier part of His ministry Jesus had spoken comparatively little to His disciples about the persecution which awaited them, because He had been in their company, and as long as He was with them the world's hatred must inevitably be drawn to Himself." (Tasker)

ii. "While He was with them they leant upon Him and could not apprehend a time of weakness and persecution." (Dods)

2. (5-7) Jesus explains the benefits of His departure.

"But now I go away to Him who sent Me, and none of you asks Me, 'Where are You going?' But because I have said these things to you, sorrow has filled your heart. Nevertheless I tell you the truth. It is to your advantage that I go away; for if I do not go away, the Helper will not come to you; but if I depart, I will send Him to you."

a. **None of you asks Me, "Where are You going"**: Peter *had* asked this question earlier (John 13:36) and Thomas asked a similar question (John 14:5). Therefore Jesus must mean not only the *words* of the question, but the heart of it. Their previous asking was in the sense, *what will happen to us when You leave*, not in the sense Jesus meant here - *what will happen to You when You leave*.

i. "A difficulty is posed by His statement that nobody asks, 'Whither goest thou?' in the light of Simon Peter's earlier question, 'Lord, wither goest thou?' (John 13:36). But that question had not really indicated a serious inquiry as to Jesus' destination. Peter was diverted immediately and he made no real attempt to find out where Jesus was going. He had been concerned with the thought of parting with Jesus, not with that of the Master's destination. He had in mind only the consequences for himself and his fellows." (Morris)

b. **But because I have said these things to you, sorrow has filled your heart**: Jesus excused their lack of interest in *His* fate, knowing their great **sorrow**. They had sorrow at the moment, but their future was brighter. The disciples could only see the sorrow of Jesus leaving; but Jesus' departure was an essential step in their growth as disciples.

c. **It is to your advantage that I go away**: This had to be difficult for the disciples to believe. When a loved one is near death we often think it is the best to let death take its course. We say, "It will be better for them to go, and to stop the suffering. It is to their advantage to go away." But when someone we love is near death, we usually don't think that it is to *our* advantage that they go. Yet Jesus here said that it wasn't for *His* advantage, but **to your advantage that I go away**.

i. If the disciples really understood what was about to happen, it would be even more difficult for them to believe.

- *To your advantage* that Jesus is arrested?

- *To your advantage* that Jesus' ministry of teaching and miracles is stopped?

- *To your advantage* that Jesus is beaten?

- *To your advantage* that Jesus is mocked?

- *To your advantage* that Jesus is sentenced for execution?

- *To your advantage* that Jesus is nailed to a cross?

- *To your advantage* that Jesus dies in the company of notorious criminals?

- *To your advantage* that His lifeless body is laid in a cold grave?

d. **Nevertheless**: This word meant a challenge to their sorrow and even their unbelief. **Nevertheless** is one of the great words of the Bible, meaning *despite all of that*. Jesus knew they were filled with sorrow because of what He told them. But, *despite all of that* He wanted them to know that it was **to** their **advantage**.

i. "**It is expedient for you**, implies that the dispensation of the Spirit is a more blessed manifestation of God than was even the bodily presence of the risen Saviour." (Alford)

e. **I tell you the truth**: Jesus didn't say this because He lied most of the time. He said this because He wanted them to make a concerted effort to trust Him at this point. Jesus knew this was difficult to believe.

f. **For if I do not go away, the Helper will not come to you**: Jesus had a plan, but they couldn't understand it. With 2,000 years of hindsight we see that when Jesus went away He then sent the Spirit of God, which had and has a broader and more effective ministry in the entire world.

i. "The withdrawal of the bodily presence of Christ was the essential condition of His universal spiritual presence." (Dods)

g. **I will send Him to you**: Jesus promised to send the Holy Spirit to His disciples when He departed. This is what would make it to their **advantage** that He departed from them. Jesus meant that the presence and work of the Holy Spirit would actually be better for believers than the physical, bodily presence of Jesus.

i. It was better because Jesus could be with every believer all the time. Jesus promised, *For where two or three are gathered together in My name, I am there in the midst of them* (Matthew 18:20). That was not a promise He could keep after flesh, but only after the Spirit. He had to go away for that promise to be made true. If Jesus were present bodily on this earth, there would be some Christians who would be overjoyed – those in His immediate presence. But for most Christians, they would have the overwhelming sense that Jesus was *not* with them. Truly, it was all **to your advantage**.

ii. It was better because now we can understand Jesus better. If Jesus were present bodily on this earth, there would be no end to His words for us. We wouldn't have a Bible; we would have the library of congress. Secretaries would follow Him constantly to record His every word. It would all be written down and preserved. We would have all of it, and the mass of it would be just plain unmanageable. Truly, it was all **to your advantage**.

iii. It was better because now we can have a more trusting relationship with God. If Jesus were present bodily on this earth, there would be a great challenge to our walk of faith. Paul said, *Even though we have known Christ according to the flesh, yet now we know Him thus no longer.* (2 Corinthians 5:16) God wants us to walk by faith, and not by sight, and if Jesus were here bodily, there would be great temptation to walk by sight, and not by faith. Truly, it was all **to your advantage**.

iv. It was better because Jesus' work is better understood as He is enthroned in the heavens. If Jesus were present bodily on this earth, it would be confusing to us. Jesus does not continue to suffer; He finished His work on the cross. Yet it might be difficult for us to see a Savior who never suffered when we are in distress; it might make us think that Jesus was unsympathetic. God didn't want us to struggle with this dilemma, so Jesus is no longer bodily on this earth. He is enthroned in the heavens. Truly, it was all **to your advantage**.

v. Before Jesus left the disciples were confused, thick headed, afraid, selfish and self-centered. After Jesus left and after the Helper had come they were wise, surrendered, bold, and giving. Truly, it was **to your advantage** that Jesus left.

3. (8-11) The work of the Holy Spirit in the world.

"And when He has come, He will convict the world of sin, and of righteousness, and of judgment: of sin, because they do not believe in Me; of righteousness, because I go to My Father and you see Me no more; of judgment, because the ruler of this world is judged."

a. **He will convict the world of sin, and of righteousness, and of judgment**: **Sin** is the truth about man, **righteousness** is the truth about God, **judgment** is the inevitable combination of these two truths.

i. "Each man's conscience has some glimmering of light on each of these; *some* consciousness of guilt, *some* sense of right, *some* power of judgment of what is transitory and worthless; but all these are unreal and unpractical, till the convicting work of the Spirit has wrought in him." (Alford)

b. **He will convict**: The ancient Greek work translated **convict** has a broader range of meaning than simply our word **convict**, especially as it is understood in a legal sense. It also carries the ideas to *expose*, to *refute*, and to *convince* (Bruce). This is the work of the Holy Spirit in the world and in individual hearts; to convince and convict of these truths.

i. **He will convict**: "Or undeceive the world, by refuting those odd conceits and erroneous opinions, that men had before drunk in, and were possessed of." (Trapp)

ii. It is a serious thing to resist and reject this work of the Holy Spirit, which is especially prominent and powerful in seasons of great spiritual advance (sometimes called revival or spiritual awakening).

iii. Before the convicting work of the Holy Spirit one may say, *I make a lot of mistakes. Nobody's perfect.* After the convicting work of the Holy Spirit one may say, *I'm a lost rebel, fighting against God and His law - I must rely on Jesus to get right with God.*

iv. "The Spirit does not merely accuse men of sin, he brings to them an inescapable sense of guilt so that they realize their shame and helplessness before God." (Tenney)

v. "The Spirit is the 'advocate' or helper of those who believe in Jesus, their counsel for the defence. But in relation to unbelievers, to the godless world, he acts as counsel for the prosecution." (Bruce) It's important to have the Spirit of God to defend rather than to convict.

vi. In the great awakening of 1860-61 in Great Britain, a high-ranking army officer described the conviction of sin in his Scottish town: "Those of you who are ease have little conception of how terrifying a sight it is when the Holy Spirit is pleased to open a man's eyes to see the real state of heart. Men who were thought to be, and who thought themselves to be good, religious people... have been led to search into the foundation upon which they were resting, and have found all rotten, that they were self-satisfied, resting on their own goodness, and not upon Christ. Many turned from open sin to lives of holiness, some weeping for joy for sins forgiven." (J. Edwin Orr, *The Second Evangelical Awakening in Britain*)

c. **Of sin, because they do not believe in Me**: It is unbelief, the rejection of Jesus, which ultimately proves one to be guilty. The Holy Spirit will tell the world of the importance of trusting in, relying on, and clinging to Jesus to avoid this sin.

i. "The essence of sin is unbelief, which is not simply a casual incredulity nor a difference of opinion; rather, it is a total rejection of God's messenger and message." (Tenney)

ii. "The basic sin is the sin which puts self at the centre of things and consequently refused to believe in Him." (Morris)

iii. "A sinner is a sacred thing: the Holy Ghost hath made him so. Your sham sinner is a horrid creature; but a man truly convinced of sin by the Spirit of God is a being to be sought after as a jewel that will adorn the crown of the Redeemer." (Spurgeon)

d. **Of righteousness, because I go to My Father**: The ascension of Jesus to heaven demonstrated that He had perfectly fulfilled the Father's will and had proven Himself righteous - and exposed the lack of **righteousness** in the world that rejected Him. The Holy Spirit shows the world the **righteousness** of Jesus and its own unrighteousness.

i. Many people today - even secular people - take the **righteousness** of Jesus as a given. Yet during His life Jesus was reviled as an imposter, as demon-possessed, as a wicked destroyer of the law, as a glutton, a drunk, and as illegitimate. The Holy Spirit persuades the work of the **righteousness** of Jesus.

ii. "Whereas righteousness had previously been defined by precepts, it now has been revealed in the incarnate Son, who exemplified it perfectly in all his relationships." (Tenney)

e. **Of judgment, because the ruler of this world is judged**: The judgment of Satan himself means that there will be a final reckoning between God and His rebellious creature. The Holy Spirit warns the world of this coming judgment.

i. Normally conviction is followed by judgment. When the Holy Spirit works, there is an in-between step: the revelation of the righteousness of Jesus Christ, which can satisfy the judgment for the convicted person.

ii. "The world, the prince of it, is 'judged'. To adhere to it rather than to Christ is to cling to a doomed cause, a sinking ship." (Dods)

4. (12-15) The work of the Holy Spirit among the disciples.

"I still have many things to say to you, but you cannot bear *them* now. However, when He, the Spirit of truth, has come, He will guide you into all truth; for He will not speak on His own *authority,* but whatever He hears He will speak; and He will tell you things to come. He will glorify Me, for He will take of what is Mine and declare *it* to you. All things that the Father has are Mine. Therefore I said that He will take of Mine and declare *it* to you."

a. **I still have many things to say to you**: Jesus frankly admitted that His own teaching was incomplete, and anticipated the further instruction of the church by the Holy Spirit. This statement of Jesus leads us to anticipate the formation of the New Testament.

i. Here Jesus answered those who say, "I'll take what Jesus taught, but not what Paul or the others taught." Paul and the other New Testament writers taught us the **many things** that Jesus spoke of.

- For example, they didn't know that some of the customs and commands among the Jews would be fulfilled by the person and work of Jesus, and no longer be binding under the New Covenant.

- For example, they didn't know that God would bring Gentiles into the New Covenant community as equal partners, without have to first become Jews.

b. **He will guide you into all truth**: In one sense, this was fulfilled when the New Testament writings, divinely inspired by God, were completed. In another sense the Holy Spirit continues today to personally lead us into truth, but *never* in opposition to the Scripture, because God's supremely authoritative revelation is closed with the New Testament.

i. **Into all truth**: "The Greek means 'all *the* truth', i.e. the specific truth about the Person of Jesus and the significance of what He said and did. The New Testament is permanent evidence that the apostles were guided into truth about this." (Tasker)

ii. **He will tell you things to come**: "The promise must therefore refer to the main features of the new Christian dispensation. The Spirit would guide them in that new economy in which they would no longer have the visible example and help and counsel of their Master." (Dods)

c. **He will not speak on His own authority... He will glorify Me... He will take of what is Mine and declare it to you**: The Holy Spirit's ministry is revealing Jesus to us, to bear testimony of Jesus (John 15:26). He uses many different ways and many different gifts to accomplish this, but the purpose is always the same: to reveal Jesus.

i. One may speak of dream, visions, experiences, revelations and say they came from the Holy Spirit, but many of those supposed revelations of the Spirit say nothing or almost nothing about Jesus Himself.

ii. "This verse is decisive against all additions and pretended revelations subsequent to and besides Christ; it is being the work of the Spirit to testify and to declare the THINGS OF CHRIST; not any thing new and beyond Him." (Alford)

iii. **All things that the Father has are Mine**: "If Christ had not been equal to God, could he have said this without blasphemy?" (Clarke)

B. Jesus prepares the disciples for His coming challenge on the cross.

1. (16-18) Jesus tells them of His immediate, brief departure.

"A little while, and you will not see Me; and again a little while, and you will see Me, because I go to the Father." Then *some* of His disciples said among themselves, "What is this that He says to us, 'A little while, and you will not see Me; and again a little while, and you will see Me'; and, 'because I go to the Father'?" They said therefore, "What is this that He says, 'A little while'? We do not know what He is saying."

a. **A little while, and you will not see Me**: The disciples didn't understand that the arrest of Jesus was only an hour or two away, and then His crucifixion would follow. Yet because He must **go to the Father**, they would **see** Him again as He rose from the dead.

i. **You will not see Me**: "During the interval between His death and resurrection the disciples lost their faith and spiritual vision, and no more *beheld* Him than did the world." (Trench)

ii. **You will see Me**: "'And again a little while shall elapse, and then *ye-shall-see Me, i.e.* with bodily eyes.' When the short interval between His death and resurrection had elapsed, then they should see Him with their bodily eyes." (Trench)

b. **We do not know what He is saying**: The disciples were both troubled and confused. They probably thought Jesus spoke with unnecessary mystery about where He was going and what He would do. They didn't understand what He meant about not seeing Him and then seeing Him.

i. **We do not know what He is saying**: "A different word is used here in the Greek for *saith* from that used in the first part of the verse. Hence, RSV, rightly, 'we do not know what he means'." (Tasker)

ii. "The use of the imperfect tense in 'kept asking' [**they said**] (*elegon*) shows that they must have held a consultation among themselves about it and that the discourse did not proceed as an uninterrupted lecture." (Tenney)

iii. "Where for us, all is clear, for them all was mysterious. If Jesus wishes to found the Messianic kingdom, why go away? If He does not wish it, why return?" (Godet, cited in Morris)

2. (19-22) Jesus explains of coming sorrow being turned into joy.

Now Jesus knew that they desired to ask Him, and He said to them, "Are you inquiring among yourselves about what I said, 'A little while, and you will not see Me; and again a little while, and you will see Me'? Most assuredly, I say to you that you will weep and lament, but the world will rejoice; and you will be sorrowful, but your sorrow will be turned into joy. A woman, when she is in labor, has sorrow because her hour has come; but as soon as she has given birth to the child, she no longer remembers the anguish, for joy that a human being has been born into the world. Therefore you now have sorrow; but I will see you again and your heart will rejoice, and your joy no one will take from you."

a. **Jesus knew that they desired to ask Him**: Jesus understood that the disciples wanted more clarity; but He also knew that they needed more than information. They needed their hearts and minds prepared to endure the coming crisis.

i. "Jesus, perceiving their embarrassment, and that they wished to interrogate Him, said to them: 'Are you inquiring among yourselves?'" (Dods)

b. **You will be sorrowful, but your sorrow will be turned into joy**: Jesus knew they would be plunged into deep and dark **sorrow** in the next few hours. He also knew that God would, by His power and grace, turn their **sorrow** into **joy**.

   i. The words, **you will be sorrowful** were certainly true.

- Sorrowful at the loss of relationship.
- Sorrowful at the humiliation of their Master and Messiah.
- Sorrowful at the seeming victory of His enemies.
- Sorrowful because all they hoped for was taken away.

   ii. The crucifixion and all that went with it was not a bump in the road on the way to fulfilling God's plan, as if it were an obstacle to overcome. It was the way the plan would be fulfilled. That sorrow would turn into joy.

   iii. God's work was not to *replace* their sorrow with joy, but to *turn* sorrow **into joy**, as He often does in our lives. The sorrow would be directly connected to their coming joy, even as the sorrow of a woman in childbirth is directly connected to her joy that her child **has been born into the world**.

   iv. "It is most remarkable and instructive that the apostles do not appear in their sermons or epistles to have spoken of the death of our Lord with any kind of regret. The gospels mention their distress during the actual occurrence of the crucifixion, but after the resurrection, and especially after Pentecost, we hear of no such grief." (Spurgeon)

c. **I will see you again and your heart will rejoice**: They didn't fully understand the separation, so they could not fully understand the joy of the coming reunion. Yet when it happened, no one could deny their joy-filled testimony of the resurrection. It was testimony so sure that they endured death because of it. It was **joy no one will take from you**.

   i. **Your joy no one will take from you**: "Our Lord's meaning appears to have been this: that his resurrection should be so *completely demonstrated* to them, that they should never have a doubt concerning it; and consequently that their joy should be great and permanent." (Clarke)

   ii. "That he should suffer was cause for grief, but that he has now suffered all is equal cause for joy. When a champion returns from the wars bearing the scars of conflict by which he gained his honors, does anyone lament over his campaigns?" (Spurgeon)

3. (23-27) Jesus promises greater joy regarding their coming access to God after Jesus' departure.

"And in that day you will ask Me nothing. Most assuredly, I say to you, whatever you ask the Father in My name He will give you. Until now you have asked nothing in My name. Ask, and you will receive, that your joy may be full. These things I have spoken to you in figurative language; but the time is coming when I will no longer speak to you in figurative language, but I will tell you plainly about the Father. In that day you will ask in My name, and I do not say to you that I shall pray the Father for you; for the Father Himself loves you, because you have loved Me, and have believed that I came forth from God."

a. **In that day you will ask Me nothing**: Jesus probably meant that they would be so overcome with joy and relief at the resurrection that they would be speechless when it came to making requests of Jesus. Yet the pathway to audience with God and answered prayer was more open, not more closed.

i. **Until now you have asked nothing in My name**: "Ye have not as yet considered me the great *Mediator* between God and man; but this is one of the truths which shall be *more fully revealed* to you by the Holy Spirit." (Clarke)

b. **Whatever you ask the Father in My name He will give you**: Because of Jesus' great work, disciples have unlimited, undeniable access to God through Him. The disciples had yet to really pray in the **name** of Jesus, but He would teach them.

i. "The meaning is that the atoning death of Jesus will revolutionize the whole situation. On the basis of the Son's atoning work men will approach God and know the answers to their prayers." (Morris)

c. **But I will tell you plainly about the Father**: The disciples should trust that in this time of restored joy and open access to Jesus, they would know the Father Himself, and know about Him more than ever.

i. **Figurative language**: "Used here to cover the cryptic expression 'a little while' and the metaphor of childbirth used in verse 21." (Tasker)

d. **For the Father Himself loves you**: Jesus makes it clear that the Son did not need to persuade an angry Father to be gracious; but His work would provide a righteous basis for God's graciousness.

i. "Here Jesus is saying: 'You can go to God, because he loves you,' and he is saying that *before the Cross*. He did not die to change God into love; he died to tell us that God is love. He came, not because God so hated the world, but because he so *loved* the world. Jesus brought to men the love of God." (Barclay)

ii. "The reason that Christ will not intercede for them is now given. There will be no need. The Father *Himself* loves them. He does not need to be persuaded to be gracious. In this case the ground of acceptance is the relationship in which they stand to Jesus." (Morris)

e. **Because you have loved Me**: The Father did not love the disciples on the basis of their love for Jesus, but their love for Jesus was evidence of the Father's love for them.

i. A pulse doesn't make the heart pump, but it is evidence of it. Our love for God doesn't make Him love us, but it is evidence that He loves us.

4. (28-32) The disciples proclaim their faith; Jesus places it in perspective.

"I came forth from the Father and have come into the world. Again, I leave the world and go to the Father." His disciples said to Him, "See, now You are speaking plainly, and using no figure of speech! Now we are sure that You know all things, and have no need that anyone should question You. By this we believe that You came forth from God." Jesus answered them, "Do you now believe? Indeed the hour is coming, yes, has now come, that you will be scattered, each to his own, and will leave Me alone. And yet I am not alone, because the Father is with Me."

a. **I came forth from the Father**: Jesus repeated themes from previously in this great talk with His disciples, telling them again about His departure from this **world** and unto His **Father**. John 16:28 is a remarkable summary of the work of Jesus.

- **I have come forth from the Father**: Jesus is God, having existed in heaven's glory and goodness before He ever came to the earth.

- **And have come into the world**: Jesus was born as a man, having added humanity to deity.

- **Again I leave the world**: Jesus would die.

- **And go to My Father**: Jesus would rise from the dead and ascend to heaven.

    i. "In those sentences we have a declaration of the whole redemptive progress of the Son of God. From the Father into the world; from the world unto the Father." (Morgan)

    ii. "Here is the sum of the Christian Faith in four fundamental propositions, which, with their several *why* and *how* and *result*, form the whole body of Christian verity." (Trench)

b. **Now we are sure that You know all things**: The summary statement in the previous sentence made the disciples feel that *now* they understood.

They seem to have been sincere, but more confident in their faith than they should have been.

> i. "They declared that their belief in the Divinity of His mission was confirmed. They were perfectly sincere. They felt that they had at last passed beyond the region where it would be possible to doubt. How much better He knew them than they knew themselves!" (Morgan)

c. **Do you now believe… You will be scattered**: Jesus did not doubt the belief of the disciples, but warned them that their faith would be shaken before it was finally settled upon Him. They would find it much easier to believe on Him in the upper room than in the Garden of Gethsemane, where they would all flee **each to his own, and** would **leave** Jesus **alone**.

> i. This wasn't to make an *I told you so* moment. "The very fact that He had known and had foretold the course of events, would be something to hold on to, and the memory of it would help them back again to faith." (Morgan)

> ii. "The words *Do you now believe?* can also be taken as a statement. This is preferable, as it brings out better the emphasis laid upon *now* in the original. 'You do *now* believe, but your belief will soon be shaken.'" (Tasker)

> iii. "Jesus read their hearts better than they knew. Not only could he answer their unspoken questions: he could assess the strength of their belief in him. It was sincere and genuine, bound up with their love for him, but it was about to be exposed to a test such as they had not imagined." (Bruce)

d. **You will be scattered, each to his own, and will leave Me alone**: The crisis would come soon, and when it did the disciples would think, *every man for himself* and abandon Jesus **alone**.

> i. "When he did not need their friendship, they were his very good friends. When they could do nothing for him if they tried, they were his faithful followers. But the pinch has come; now might they watch with him one hour, now might they go with him amid the rabble throng, and interpose at least the vote of the minority against the masses; but they are gone." (Spurgeon)

> ii. "There he stands. They have left him alone; but there he is, still standing to his purpose. He has come to save, and he will save. He has come to redeem, and he will redeem. He has come to overcome the world, and he will overcome it." (Spurgeon)

e. **Yet I am not alone, because the Father is with Me**: Jesus relied upon His close relationship with God all the way to the cross, and even upon it.

In the loneliest moments imaginable, He understood that the Father was with Him.

> i. "I remember that passage about Abraham going with Isaac to mount Moriah, where Isaac was to be offered up. It is written, 'So they went both of them together.' So did the Eternal Father and his Well- beloved Son when God was about to give up his own Son to death. There was no divided purpose; they went both of them together." (Spurgeon)

5. (33) The triumphant conclusion to Jesus' farewell discourse to His disciples and to all of Jesus' teaching before the cross.

"These things I have spoken to you, that in Me you may have peace. In the world you will have tribulation; but be of good cheer, I have overcome the world."

a. **These things I have spoken to you**: In a moment Jesus would pray for His disciples. Before He did, He summarized the purpose of the long talk He had with those disciples: to bring them peace and the settled assurance of overcomers.

b. **That in Me you may have peace**: Jesus offered His disciples **peace**. He made the offer in the most unlikely circumstances. At that very minute, Judas met with Jesus' enemies to plot His arrest. Jesus knew that He would be arrested, forsaken, rejected, mocked, humiliated, tortured and executed before the next day was over. We think that the disciples should have comforted Him - yet Jesus had **peace**, and enough to give to others.

> i. Jesus did not *promise* peace; He *offered* it. He said, "**you *may* have peace**." People may follow Jesus yet deny themselves this peace. We gain the peace Jesus offered by finding it *in Him*. Jesus said, "**that in Me you may have peace**." We won't find real peace anywhere else other than in Jesus.

> ii. Jesus made the way to **peace** with God: *Having been justified by faith, we have peace with God through our Lord Jesus Christ.* (Romans 5:1)

> iii. Jesus made the way to **peace** with others: *For Jesus is our peace, who has made the both one and broken down the middle wall of division between us.* (Ephesians 2:14)

> iv. This word of peace is especially meaningful set in the context of conflict - **tribulation** and **overcome** both speak of battles to fight. "He promises a peach which co-exists with tribulation and disturbances, a peach which is realized in and through conflict and struggle." (Maclaren)

v. This promise was especially powerful for those eleven disciples. "He predicted their desertion in the very saying in which He assured them of the peace He would give them. He loved them for who they were and despite their shortcomings." (Morris)

c. **In the world you will have tribulation**: Jesus also made the promise of **tribulation**. Peace is offered to us, but tribulation is *promised*. When we become Christians we may bring fewer problems upon ourselves, but we definitely still have them.

i. Understanding this removes a false hope. Struggling Christians often hope for the day when they will laugh at temptation and there will be one effortless victory after another. We are promised struggle as long as we are in this world; yet there is peace in Jesus.

ii. "There is no avoiding it; it is not a paradise, but a purgatory to the saints. It may be compared to the Straits of Magellan, which is said to be a place of that nature, that which way soever a man set his course, he shall be sure to have the wind against him." (Trapp)

d. **Be of good cheer, I have overcome the world**: Jesus proclaimed the truth of His victory. This was an amazing statement from a man about to be arrested, forsaken, rejected, mocked, tortured and executed. Judas, the religious authorities, Pilate, the crowd, the soldiers or even death and the grave could not overcome Him. Instead, Jesus could truly say, "**I have overcome the world**." If it was true then, it's even truer now.

i. When Jesus wanted to comfort and strengthen His disciples, He spoke of *His* victory, not directly *their* victory. This wasn't "cheer up" or "try harder." Jesus knew that His victory would be theirs.

ii. "He overcame the world in three areas: in His life, in His death, and in His resurrection." (Boice)

iii. "This statement, spoken as it is in the shadow of the cross, is audacious… He goes to the cross not in fear or in gloom, but as a conqueror." (Morris)

iv. "He overcame the world when nobody else had overcome it." (Spurgeon)

v. The thought that Jesus has **overcome** became precious to John. "*Nikeo* occurs only here in the Gospel, but twenty-two times in the Johannine Epistles and Apocalypse." (Dods)

vi. "The world conquers me when it comes between me and God, when it fills my desires, when it absorbs my energies, when it blinds my eyes to the things unseen and eternal." (Maclaren)

vii. Knowing that Jesus has **overcome the world** brings us **good cheer**. It is the foundation for our **peace** in Him. We see that Jesus is in control, we see that although He leaves He does not abandon, we see that He loves, and we see that the victory is His. We can **be of good cheer** indeed.

John 17 - Jesus' Great Prayer

"John Knox, on his death-bed in 1572, asked his wife to read to him John 17, 'where', he said, 'I cast my first anchor.'" (Bruce)

A. Jesus prays concerning Himself.

1. (1a) Introduction.

Jesus spoke these words, lifted up His eyes to heaven, and said:

a. **Jesus spoke these words**: The Bible is filled with great prayers. We are impressed with Solomon's prayer (1 Kings 8), Abraham's prayer (Genesis 18), and Moses' prayer (Exodus 32), but this prayer is by far the greatest recorded in the Bible.

i. Most of us know what it is to hear a true man or woman of God deep in prayer; there is something holy and awesome about it. Far beyond all that was this prayer Jesus prayed unto His God and Father, which is *the only long, continuous prayer of Jesus recorded in the Gospels*. The sentences are simple, but the ideas are deep, moving, and meaningful.

ii. "There is no voice which has ever been heard, either in heaven or in earth, more exalted, more holy, more fruitful, more sublime, than the prayer offered up by the Son to God Himself." (Melanchthon, cited in Boice)

iii. Genuine prayer often reveals a person's innermost being. John 17 is an unique opportunity to see the nature and heart of Jesus. In this prayer, Jesus will touch on many of themes developed in this Gospel: *glory, glorify, sent, believe, world, love.*

iv. Many of the same concerns of what is commonly called the Lord's Prayer (Matthew 6:9-13) are here in this prayer.

- Prayer is repeatedly directed to God the Father.
- There is recognition of and concern for God's name.

- There is concern for the work of the kingdom of God.
- There is concern for keeping from evil.

v. Yet there is something different in this prayer; Jesus did not pray just as He told His disciples to pray. "The request of our Lord thus given in John's seventeenth chapter is clearly no prayer of an inferior to a superior: constantly there is seen in it the co-equality of the Speaker with The Father. The Two have but one mind… Where the Son speaks He is not seeking to bend The Father to Him: rather is He voicing the purpose of the Godhead." (Trench)

vi. The New Testament tells us that Jesus has an ongoing, present work of intercession for His people (Romans 8:34, Hebrews 7:25). "The object being not so much to let us know what He said on a special occasion, as to show the constant attitude of His mind, the informing idea of His unceasing 'intercession' for us during the time of His absence." (Trench)

b. **Lifted up His eyes to heaven**: This indicates the physical posture of Jesus as He prayed. This is a posture that we don't usually associate with deep prayer. In the prayer customs of the western world, we often bow our head and close our eyes. Jesus prayed with the customs of prayer common in His own day (John 11:41, Mark 7:34, Psalm 123:1).

i. "In the sacred record, however, much more space is taken up by our Lord's intercessions as he nears the end of his labors. After the closing supper, his public preaching work being ended, and nothing remaining to be done but to die, he gave himself wholly unto prayer. He was not again to instruct the multitude, nor to heal the sick, and in the interval which remained, before he should lay down his life, he girded himself for special intercession. He poured out his soul in life before he poured it out unto death." (Spurgeon)

ii. The words **lifted up His eyes to heaven** also indicate that Jesus looked **up** in a hopeful sense and was not gloomy or downcast in this prayer. This is actually a prayer of faith and confidence, even victory - all the while acknowledging the reality of the conflict. "We so often understand this payer as though it were rather gloomy. It is not. It is uttered by One who has just affirmed that He has overcome the world (John 16:33), and it starts from this conviction." (Morris)

iii. This remarkable prayer is made with a heart and mind looking **up** towards **heaven**. Jesus made no mention of His problems or the decisions He must make. His heart and mind were fixed on the highest things, pledging Himself to the absolutely fulfillment of God the

Father's will no matter what the cost, so that eternal life could come to others.

2. (1b) Jesus asks to be glorified.

"Father, the hour has come. Glorify Your Son, that Your Son also may glorify You,"

a. **Father, the hour has come**: Before, Jesus' hour of glorification (beginning with His death) had not yet come (John 2:4; 7:8; 7:30; 8:20). Now, **the hour has come** (as Jesus said before at John 12:23).

i. Note the words: **Father... Your Son... Your Son... You**. This is a prayer deep and rich with *relationship*. Jesus prayed with a full and deep sense of the familial relationship and the natural hierarchy or order that exists between God the **Father** and God the **Son**.

ii. **Father**: "And herein he sets us an example: in all times of tribulation let us fall back upon our sonship, our adoption, and the fatherhood of our great God. To our Father let us go, for to whom else should a child so naturally fly?" (Spurgeon)

iii. **The hour**: "His faith thinks it but an hour: the midnight of Gethsemane, the morning of the scourging, the day of the crucifixion, all are but an hour, a short space. Now is he in trouble, for his time of travail is come; but he counts it as an hour, for joy of that which shall be born into the world by his grievous pangs. Thus his love and patience make him despise the time of shame and reckon it but a brief interval." (Spurgeon)

b. **Glorify Your Son**: Jesus prayed first for Himself, but His petition was not selfish. His concern for Himself was actually a concern for the glory of the Father. The Son can only **glorify** the Father if the Father first answers the prayer of the Son, "**Glorify Your Son**."

i. "It will bring no glory to the Father if Jesus' sacrifice on the cross is not acceptable, or if the Son is not restored to his rightful place in the presence of the Father's unshielded glory. That would mean the divine mission had failed, the purposes of grace forever defeated." (Carson)

ii. "Father, the hour has come: glorify Thy Son: *i.e.* make plain to these there that the Man Jesus is also the God-Man; make it plain by His resurrection and ascension." (Trench)

iii. "This glorification embraced His death, resurrection, and session at God's right hand, as accredited Mediator." (Dods)

iv. Jesus gave several *reasons* or *grounds* for this prayer, "**Glorify Your Son**." If the God the Son made use or reasons or grounds in praying to

God the Father, we should much more give attention to giving reasons and grounds for our requests before the throne of God.

- Because the hour has come (John 17:1).

- Because the Father will be glorified (John 17:1).

- Because authority had already been given to grant eternal life (John 17:2).

- Because Jesus is the only way to life (John 17:3).

- Because it finishes the work the Father sent the Son to perform (John 17:3).

c. **The hour has come... Glorify Your Son**: It is the *cross* (see John 12:27-33, 13:30-33, 21:18-19) that will glorify the Son. The cross was utter humiliation to the world, but it was an instrument of glorification in God's eyes. This is an aspect of the foolishness and weakness of the cross (1 Corinthians 1:18, 1:23-25).

i. "To men the cross appeared an instrument of shame. To Christ it was the means of true glory." (Morris)

ii. *This prayer was wonderfully answered.* "Yes, the Father glorified his Son, even when it pleased him to bruise him and to put him to grief. With one hand he smote, and with the other hand he glorified. There was a power to crush, but there was also a power to sustain working at the self-same time. The Father glorified his Son." (Spurgeon)

iii. *How different are most our prayers.* "In one form or another we are constantly asking the Father to glorify us. Glorify me, O Father, we cry, by giving me the largest congregation in the town; by commencing a great revival in my mission, by increasing my spiritual power, so that I shall be greatly sought after. Of course, we do not state our reason quite so concisely; but this is really what we mean. And then we wonder why the answer tarries." (Meyer)

d. **That Your Son also may glorify You**: In its counter-intuitive work, the cross glorified Jesus the Son and displayed the wisdom and the power of God (1 Corinthians 1:23-25). Yet it *also* glorified God the Father, by displaying His wise plan and great sacrifice in giving the Son to do such a work.

i. "The Son glorified the Father by revealing in this act [the cross] the sovereignty of God over evil, the compassion of God for men, and the finality of redemption for believers." (Tenney)

ii. *"Christ's motive should be ours.* When you ask a blessing from God, ask it that you may glorify God by it. Do you pine to have your health back again? Be sure that you want to spend it for him. Do you desire temporal advancement? Desire it that you may promote his glory. Do you even long for growth in grace? Ask it only that you may glorify him." (Spurgeon)

3. (2-3) Jesus speaks of the source and nature of eternal life.

"As You have given Him authority over all flesh, that He should give eternal life to as many as You have given Him. And this is eternal life, that they may know You, the only true God, and Jesus Christ whom You have sent."

a. **You have given Him authority over all flesh**: Jesus claimed to have **authority over all flesh** with the ability to **give eternal life** to mankind. *This is a clear and startling claim to deity*; no One but God could truthfully and knowingly make this claim.

i. Jesus here claimed "authority to determine the ultimate destiny of men." (Takser)

ii. This gives us new hope for evangelism and missionary work, knowing that Jesus has **authority over all flesh**. Even for those who reject Jesus or are ignorant of Him, even if *they* do not know it or acknowledge it, Jesus has **authority over** them. We can pray in faith and ask Jesus to exercise that authority over those who have yet to repent and believe.

iii. **You have given Him authority over all flesh**: Philippians 2:5-11 is a demonstration of this, that *all* will recognize the authority of Jesus; every knee will bow and every tongue confess that Jesus Christ is Lord.

iv. The believer understands and glories in the **authority** of Jesus, especially considering the alternative. "Men and women cannot operate without authority. So if you put out one authority, another will come in. If you reject the authority of God, human authority will emerge." (Boice)

b. **That He should give eternal life to as many as You have given Him**: Jesus understood that He was and is the One who grants **eternal life** to those **given** to Him by the Father.

i. "Christians often think of Jesus as God's gift to us; we rarely think of ourselves as God's gift to Jesus." (Carson)

ii. This indicates something that we can dimly understand as a division of labor in the work of salvation between the Persons of the Godhead. Here we see that the Father gives some unto the Son, and the Son gives them **eternal life** through His work on the cross. Of course, the Holy

Spirit also has His work in salvation, unmentioned in this particular passage.

iii. "Here the doctrines of a general and a particular redemption sweetly blend 'As thou hast given him power over all flesh,' they are all under Christ's mediatorial government by virtue of his matchless sacrifice; but the object in view is specially the gift of everlasting life to the chosen people: 'that he should give eternal life to as many as thou hast given him.'" (Spurgeon)

c. **And this is eternal life, that they may know You:** Eternal life is found in an experiential knowledge (*ginosko*) of both God the Father and Jesus Christ, God the Son.

i. "In this world we are familiar with the truth that it is a blessing and an inspiration to know certain people. Much more is it the case when we know God." (Morris)

ii. "Life is active involvement with environment; death is the cessation of involvement with the environment, whether it be physical or personal." (Tenney) Eternal life means that we are alive and active to God's environment. If God and His spiritual environment does not affect (and even dominate) our life, then it can be said that we do not have or experience **eternal life**. If this is true, then we live life in the same dimension that animals live, and we exist as if we are dead to God and His environment.

iii. **That they may know You:** "In the Greek the verb is in the present subjunctive indicating the 'knowledge' is a growing experience." (Tasker)

4. (4-5) The request is again stated, full of faith: **Glorify Me.**

"I have glorified You on the earth. I have finished the work which You have given Me to do. And now, O Father, glorify Me together with Yourself, with the glory which I had with You before the world was."

a. **I have glorified You on the earth:** Jesus did not wait until His work on the cross to glorify God the Father. His entire life **glorified** God **on the earth**.

i. Jesus **glorified** the Father through His whole life, from His circumcision and dedication at the temple (Luke 2:21-23) through His quiet years of obedience in Nazareth (Matthew 2:23, 13:55).

ii. Jesus **glorified** the Father through His faith, obedience, and work through the years of His earthly ministry. Every sermon preached, every blind or sick person healed, every bit of instruction and training for the disciples, every confrontation with the corrupt religious leaders, every question answered, every loving touch - they all **glorified** God the Father.

b. **I have finished the work**: Jesus, with divine confidence and assurance, saw the work on the cross as already finished. There was (of course) a sense in which the work was not **finished**; but since Jesus is *the Lamb slain from the foundation of the world* (Revelation 13:8), there is a greater sense in which the work was already **finished**, completed in the heart and mind of God. Now it just had to be *done*.

i. There is a similar sense in which God sees our own work of transformation and perfection as already complete, before the fact. Now it has to be *done*.

ii. "There is a quiet recognition that Jesus has completed His task adequately, and brought glory to the Father in the process." (Morris)

c. **Glorify Me together with Yourself**: Jesus asked the Father to **glorify** Him, but with the *same glory* that the Father Himself has. Jesus' prayer was in no way an expression of *independence*, but of utter and continued dependence upon God the Father.

i. There are many men who cry out "glorify me," and sometimes they even direct the cry to God under a more spiritual terminology. Yet their cry "glorify me" is almost always completely different than Jesus prayer, "**Glorify Me together with Yourself**" and the difference is normally between dependence and independence.

d. **With the glory which I had with You before the world was**: Jesus was aware of His pre-existence, and of the nature of that pre-existence. Jesus understood there was a time in eternity past when God the Son and God the Father enjoyed a shared glory.

i. Jesus could not truthfully or sanely pray this if He were not Yahweh Himself, equal with God the Father. In Isaiah 42:8 and 48:11, Yahweh proclaimed that He shares His glory with *no one*. If God the Father and God the Son share their glory, they must *both* be Yahweh.

ii. "He had one main petition: that the Father would receive him back to the glory he had relinquished to accomplish his task. This petition for a return to his pristine glory implies unmistakably his preexistence and equality with the Father. It confirms his claim that he and the Father are one (John 10:30)." (Tenney)

iii. The Gospel of John has emphasized the glory of Jesus throughout its record. John was careful to record the many ways Jesus referred to His own glory in this prayer.

- The life of Jesus was a manifestation of God's glory, and the disciples beheld this glory (John 1:14).
- The miracles of Jesus manifested His glory (John 2:11).
- Jesus only ever sought the glory of His Father (John 7:18, 8:50).
- The revelation of glory is the reward of faith (John 11:40).
- Many times Jesus spoke of His coming passion and crucifixion as His coming glorification (John 7:39, 12:16, 12:23, 13:31).
- God the Son seeks to glorify God the Father (John 12:28).
- God the Father glorifies God the Son (John 13:31-32).

B. Jesus prays concerning the disciples.

Having taught and encouraged the disciples as much as He could on the eve of their despair, Jesus now did the great thing: He committed them to the Father in prayer.

1. (6-8) Jesus speaks of His mission among the disciples and their reception of it.

"I have manifested Your name to the men whom You have given Me out of the world. They were Yours, You gave them to Me, and they have kept Your word. Now they have known that all things which You have given Me are from You. For I have given to them the words which You have given Me; and they have received *them*, and have known surely that I came forth from You; and they have believed that You sent Me."

a. **I have manifested Your name to the men whom You have given Me**: Jesus thought about the three or so years of ministry and teaching with His chosen disciples, and summarized it with this phrase. It indicates that Jesus did not simply *teach* about the **name** (character) of God, He **manifested** (displayed) that character.

i. Jesus *lived out* the love and goodness and righteousness and grace and holiness of God the Father; He **manifested** God's **name** to them. "'I manifested Thy Name,' *i.e.* I revealed Thy nature. For any adequate *name* of a person or thing is the complete connotation of that person or thing." (Trench)

ii. Believers today have a similar call and duty. Paul wrote that believers are like living letters, read by the world (1 Corinthians 3:2-3), with the responsibility to manifest the name and nature of God to a watching world.

b. **The men You have given Me out of the world**: Jesus chose His disciples after a night of prayer, expressing His total dependence upon God the Father in the choosing of the men (Luke 6:12-16). Truly, it could be said that God the Father *gave* these men to Jesus, and gave them **out of the world**.

> i. Judas had departed from this group of disciples sometime earlier that evening (John 13:26-30). With Judas gone, Jesus could truly say, "**The men You have given Me out of the world**."

c. **They were Yours, You gave them to Me**: Here is another hint at the workings of the Persons of the Trinity in what could be called a division of labor. There was some sense in which the disciples first belonged to God the Father, then were given to God the Son.

d. **They have kept Your word**: One might say that Jesus generously judged His disciples; but He saw a genuine work of God in them. For all their failures and faults, they had **kept** God's **word**.

> i. "He looked at them with the insight of faith, hope, and love, and realized their present devotion and their potential for the future." (Bruce)

e. **Now they have known that all things which You have given Me are from You**: Jesus plainly told His disciples this shortly before (John 14:10-11) and in the more distant past (John 8:28-29). Jesus did or said nothing on His own initiative, but did and said all in complete dependence upon His God and Father.

f. **They have known surely that I came forth from You**: The disciples obviously did not understand everything about Jesus and His work, but at this point they were convinced of Divine origin of Jesus and His teaching.

> i. "It is a rare and holy privilege to observe the divine Son of God not only formulating his prayers but formulating the *grounds* for his petitions. These grounds reflect the essential unity of Father and Son, and reveal that Jesus' prayers for his followers trace their argument back to the inscrutable purposes of Deity." (Carson)

g. **They have believed that You sent Me**: One might say that in these few verses, Jesus looked at salvation from two points of view. Each perspective is true from its point of view.

- John 17:6 explains their salvation in the election of God (**the men You have given Me out of the world**), seeing it from God's point of view.

- John 17:8 explains their salvation in their faith (**they have believed that You sent Me**), seeing it from humanity's point of view.

2. (9-10) Jesus directs His prayer.

"I pray for them. I do not pray for the world but for those whom You have given Me, for they are Yours. And all Mine are Yours, and Yours are Mine, and I am glorified in them."

a. **I pray for them. I do not pray for the world**: Jesus specifically had His disciples in mind in this prayer. He did not pray in a general sense for the world; instead, Jesus prayed for the disciples who would carry His message of love and redemption to the world.

> i. **I pray for them**: Trench says that the "I" is emphatic in this sentence.

> ii. When Jesus said, **I do not pray for the world** it was not because He did not care for a lost and fallen world; it was to focus on His own disciples. "He was praying for the instrument He was creating, through which He would reach the world." (Morgan)

> iii. "If he does not pray for the world, it is not because he had no concern for the world; he is, indeed, the Saviour of the world (John 4:42; cf. 3:17; 12:47). But the salvation of the world depends on the witness of those whom the Father has given him 'out of the world' (see verses 21, 23), and it is they who need his intercession at this junction." (Bruce)

> iv. "I am now wholly employed for my disciples, that they may be properly qualified to preach my salvation to the ends of the earth. Jesus here imitates the high priest, the second part of whose prayer, on the day of expiation, was for the *priests*, the *sons of Aaron*." (Clarke)

b. **But for those whom You have given Me**: One might say that this has in mind more than simply the eleven disciples, but also those who would believe on their testimony (as is specifically mentioned in John 17:20). Jesus had special focus upon them in prayer because He knew those disciples belonged to the Father (**for they are Yours**).

> i. "There is an old proverb, and I cannot help quoting it just now; it is, 'Love me, love my dog.' It is as if the Lord Jesus so loved the Father that even such poor dogs as we are get loved by him for his Father's sake. To the eyes of Jesus we are radiant with beauty because God hath loved us." (Spurgeon)

c. **All Mine are Yours, and Yours are Mine**: Jesus already spoke of the shared *glory* between God the Father and God the Son (John 17:5). Here He spoke of their shared role in the life of the redeemed, that believers *belong* to both God the Father and God the Son.

> i. Everything *we* have belongs to God, but not everything *He* has belongs to us. Anyone can say to God the Father "**all mine are Yours**"; but only Jesus could say "**and Yours are Mine**."

ii. "Each has full title to the possessions of the other; they share the same interests and responsibilities." (Tenney)

d. **I am glorified in them**: In a sense, this is what it means to be a believer, to be born again, to be a true follower of Jesus Christ - to have Him **glorified** in us. Jesus does not merely want to *dwell* in or *live in* the believer, but to be **glorified** in them.

i. "Just as the world's values were all wrong concerning the cross, so were the world's values all wrong concerning the apostolic band. In them the Son of God, none less, was actually glorified." (Morris)

ii. The Apostle Paul later understood this, using phrases such as *Christ in you, the hope of glory* (Colossians 1:27) and noting that God's work in us moves *from glory to glory, just as by the Spirit of the Lord* (2 Corinthians 3:18).

iii. No one other than Jesus should be glorified in the believer. Leaders have a tendency to glorify *themselves* in their followers, but it should only be Jesus.

3. (11-12) Jesus' first request for the disciples: *Father, keep them.*

"Now I am no longer in the world, but these are in the world, and I come to You. Holy Father, keep through Your name those whom You have given Me, that they may be one as We *are*. While I was with them in the world, I kept them in Your name. Those whom You gave Me I have kept; and none of them is lost except the son of perdition, that the Scripture might be fulfilled."

a. **Now I am no longer in the world, but these are in the world**: Jesus prayed this entire prayer with His soon departure in mind. He realized that He would no longer remain **in the world**, but His disciples would. They therefore needed special prayer.

- They needed prayer because the unique three years of discipleship during His earthly ministry would be over.

- They needed prayer because of the circumstances surrounding the departure of Jesus; His betrayal, arrest, trial, beatings, crucifixion, resurrection, and ascension.

- They needed prayer because Jesus would not be there in His bodily presence to help them.

- They needed prayer because of the necessary role of the Holy Spirit; both for the sending of the Spirit and their constant reliance upon Him.

i. "Jesus is no longer in the world, already He has bid farewell to it, but the disciples remain in it, exposed without His accustomed counsel and defence." (Dods)

b. **And I come to You**: This was not a phrase used to focus Jesus' thoughts as He prayed, so that He might be conscious of praying in the presence of His Father. This was His recognition that His work on earth was almost done, and He was on His way to heaven.

c. **Holy Father, keep through Your name those whom You have given Me**: The disciples needed the prayer of Jesus and the power of God the Father to **keep** them.

i. They must be kept, continuing as disciples of Jesus. This was not obvious; in the Jewish world of that day no one continued as a disciple to a dead rabbi. Yet these disciples were to continue, to be kept as disciples to Jesus.

ii. "You have been redeemed; but you must still be kept. You have been regenerated; but you must be kept. You are pure in heart and hands; but you must be kept." (Spurgeon)

iii. *We* need Jesus our intercessor (Romans 8:34, Hebrews 7:25) to pray for us, asking God the Father to **keep** us. Our continuing on in Jesus is not left to our own efforts alone. The world, the flesh, and the devil are so mighty, so pervasive, and so seductive that we could never keep ourselves in our own efforts. If we stay with Jesus, it is because Jesus has prayed for us *"Father, keep them."*

- We need keeping from division: *Keep them that they may be one.*
- We need keeping from error.
- We need keeping from sin.
- We need keeping from hypocrisy.

iv. **Keep through Your name**: Jesus didn't pray, "keep through an angel" or "keep through a church leader" or "keep through their own effort." The work of keeping a believer is so significant that it takes the **name** of God - the whole character and authority of God.

v. There is some debate (mainly from Westcott and Hort) if the idea in John 17:11 is **keep through Your name those whom You have given Me** or *keep through Your name which You have given Me*. Westcott and Hort believed strongly that in this verse it was the *name* that was given, not the *disciples* - with the idea, "keep them in Me who am Thy name, They connotation, revelation, manifestation: keep them in unity with Me." (Trench)

d. **That they may be one as We are**: The keeping work of God the Father in the disciples would not only keep them in Him, but it would also keep them together. Jesus prayed that they would be **one**, and **one** after the pattern of the unity of God the Father and God the Son (**that they may be one as We are**).

i. "The unity mentioned here is not simply a unity achieved by legislation. It is a unity of nature because it is comparable to that of the Son and the Father." (Tenney)

ii. Their continued unity could not be assumed; it would make more sense for the disciples to scatter after the death of Jesus than it would for them to stay together.

iii. The unity Jesus prayed for among His people has a pattern. Even as the Father and the Son are one yet are not the same, we do not expect that genuine Christian unity will mean uniformity or unity of structure. It will mean unity of spirit, unity of heart, unity of purpose, and unity of destiny.

e. **While I was with them in the world, I kept them in Your name**: Jesus thought back over His three years of service with and unto the apostolic band. During that time He protected and guided them; He **kept them**. That keeping work Jesus did in the **name** of His Father, with His authority and power and according to His will.

i. "The Lord here, as Cyril remarks, compares *His* keeping of His own, to that by *the Father* - in a way only accountable by both Persons being of equal Power and Dignity." (Alford)

ii. "By the Father's power, imparted to Jesus, Jesus himself has guarded them as a treasure entrusted to him by the Father, and now he gives an account of his stewardship." (Bruce)

iii. Jesus did not keep His own disciples in and through His own name, but in total reliance upon God the Father. It is far more foolish for us to think we can keep ourselves or others in our own name, but our own effort or authority or will.

iv. The basis of Jesus' request was rooted in the **name** (character) of God *and* in His ownership of the disciple (**those whom You gave Me**).

f. **None of them is lost except the son of perdition**: There was one exception to Jesus' work in keeping the disciples, Judas. This was because in fulfillment of the Scriptures; Judas was **the son of perdition**, the one destined to evil and destruction.

i. "Remark, it is not "*I lost* none, but the son of perdition.' - *Christ* did not *lose* him (compare chapter 18:9, where there is no exception), but *he lost himself.*" (Alford)

ii. "It may be well to notice, for the English reader, that in the original, the noun **perdition** is the derivative of the verb **perished**. None perished but the one who *should perish*; whose very state and attribute it was to perish." (Alford)

iii. "'The son of perdition' points to character rather than destiny. The expression means that he was characterized by 'lostness', not that he was predestined to be 'lost'." (Morris)

g. **That the Scripture might be fulfilled**: The Scriptures fulfilled by the betrayal of Judas were especially Psalm 41:9 and Psalm 109:8, especially noted in Acts 1:20. The treachery and treason of Ahithophel against King David was a prophesy of the treachery and treason of Judas against the Son of David.

4. (13-16) Jesus elaborates on the first request: **keep them in My joy** and **away from the evil one.**

"But now I come to You, and these things I speak in the world, that they may have My joy fulfilled in themselves. I have given them Your word; and the world has hated them because they are not of the world, just as I am not of the world. I do not pray that You should take them out of the world, but that You should keep them from the evil one. They are not of the world, just as I am not of the world."

a. **But now I come to You**: Jesus again used this phrase, first noted in John 17:11. He prayed this prayer in full recognition of the soon accomplishment of His earthly work.

b. **That they may have My joy fulfilled in themselves**: Jesus prayed not only for the keeping of and the unity of His disciples, as if He only longed to leave behind good employees. He deeply cared for and prayed for **joy fulfilled** in their life. Specifically, Jesus prayed for *His own* **joy** to be fulfilled in His life.

i. "Their joy will be greater for remembering that Jesus, on the night he was betrayed, prayed for his followers." (Carson)

ii. Jesus had a life filled with joy; He could speak of **My joy**. If He did not, this part of the prayer would make no sense. Truly Jesus was *a man of sorrows and acquainted with grief* (Isaiah 53:3). Nevertheless there was a joy and a satisfaction in the life experience of Jesus that surpassed the joy of any other who ever lived.

- His joy was rooted in unbroken fellowship with God His Father.

- His joy was the fruit of true faith and confidence in His Father.

- His joy came from seeing the great things God had done.

- His joy was never diminished by His own sin.

- His joy was never diminished by deception.

- His joy was never diminished by allowing even the smallest foothold to the devil.

iii. If Jesus was so concerned for joy among His disciples that He prayed for it, we can know that He is also concerned that we have joy. God's purpose is to multiply joy in our lives, not to subtract it. The world, the flesh, and the devil would tell us something different, but God wants **joy fulfilled** in our lives.

c. **I have given them Your word**: Jesus faithfully delivered the **word** from God the Father unto His own disciples. *Even Jesus saw Himself as a messenger.*

i. **I have given them Your word**: "Not merely the oral teaching, but the whole revelation of The Father as manifested in the words and acts and personality of Jesus Christ." (Trench)

ii. "See how the Lord Jesus himself takes all his teaching from the Father. You never hear from him any boast about being the originator of profound thoughts. No, he just repeated to his disciples the words he had received from the Father: 'I have given unto them the words which thou gavest me.' If Jesus acted thus, how much more must the messengers of God receive the word from the Lord's mouth, and speak it as they receive it!" (Spurgeon)

d. **I do not pray that You should take them out of the world**: This prayer of Jesus cautions us against seeking refuge in Christian isolation; in modern day monasteries. Our goal is to be in the world but not of it or of the evil one; even as a ship is to be in the ocean, but not allowing the ocean to be in the ship.

- If we were taken from the world, the world would be in utter darkness and would perish; Jesus said, "You are the light of the world." *So, shine.*

- If we were taken from the world, the world would not have us as a witness, to be a means of salvation unto them. *So, win others to Jesus.*

- If we were taken from the world, we would be denied the opportunity to serve Jesus in the same place we have sinned against Him. *So, serve Jesus.*

- If we were taken from the world, we would not see that there are aspects of God's wisdom, truth, power and grace that are better appreciated on earth rather than in heaven. *So, see the glory of the Lord.*

- If we were taken from the world, we would be denied the place to prepare for heaven. There is no purgatory; our preparation is *now*. *So, get ready for heaven.*

- If we were taken from the world, we could not show the power of God's grace to preserve us in the midst of difficulty. *So, continue on.*

i. Job and Moses and Elijah and Jonah all prayed that they would be taken out of the world, but God did not answer. He also wants us to stay in the world, to complete the work He gives us to do.

e. **I do not pray that You should take them out of the world, but that You should keep them from the evil one**: Jesus definitely wanted us to be in the world, but He did not want us to be evil, or marked by **the evil one**. Jesus didn't pray that we would be taken out of the battle, but that we would be strengthened and protected in it.

i. "The genitive *ponerou* might indeed be construed as neuter ('keep them from evil') rather than masculine ('from the evil one'); but the reference is more probably to the being who has been thrice mentioned already as 'the ruler of this world' (John 12:31; 14:30; 16:11)." (Bruce)

ii. Jesus prayed for His own to be kept **from the evil one**, the world he rules, and of all of his evil schemes and strategies.

- Kept from the evil of apostasy.
- Kept from the evil of worldliness.
- Kept from the evil of unholiness.
- It is *not* to be kept from the evil of trouble or hardship.

iii. "The evil one, apparently, often operates through the hatred of the world (cf. 15:18-16:4); and the disciples are going to need protection against such malice." (Carson)

iv. *All* need to be kept. If we think of the young man, we appreciate how he must be kept from sin. The young have their own evil to battle against. Passions are strong, lusts seem to burn hot, and the pressure to conform to the world seems so much greater. Yet there is great danger for the older man. There is no description in the Scriptures of a young man falling into sin; think of Joseph and Daniel, and how they resisted sin. The examples of sin are from the lives of middle-aged men, like David and Solomon and Lot and many others.

v. In a sermon speaking on this text, Spurgeon spoke to those who are in sin, yet do not feel it to be evil: "There are some of you who do not feel sin to be an evil; and shall I tell you why? Did you ever try to pull a bucket up a well? You know that, when it is full of water, you can pull it easily so long as the bucket remains in the water; but when it gets above the water, you know how heavy it is. It is just so with you. While you are in sin, you do not feel it to be a burden, it does not seem to be evil; but if the Lord once draws you out of sin, you will find it to be an intolerable, a heinous evil. May the Lord, this night, wind some of you up! Though you are very deep down, may he draw you up out of sin, and give you acceptance in the Beloved!" (Spurgeon)

f. **They are not of the world, just as I am not of the world**: Because Jesus could see His disciples as *in Him*, He could see them as **not of the world**, even as Jesus was **not of the world**. His call to His disciples was for them to *be* what they really *were* in Him.

i. Jesus didn't simply say that His people were not of the world; He said they were **not of the world** *even as He was not of the world* - in other words, after the same pattern of Jesus' not being of the world.

ii. It's possible for someone to not be of the world, but in a very different way that Jesus was not of the world. They can be crazy, they can be violent, they can be weird, or it can be many things. But there was a particular way that Jesus was not of the world.

- Jesus was not of the world in His *nature*.
- Jesus was not of the world in His *office*.
- Jesus was not of the world in His *character*.

5. (17-19) Jesus' second request for the disciples: **sanctify them**.

"Sanctify them by Your truth. Your word is truth. As You sent Me into the world, I also have sent them into the world. And for their sakes I sanctify Myself, that they also may be sanctified by the truth."

a. **Sanctify them by Your truth**: **Sanctify** means to be set apart for God's special pleasure and use. It implies holiness, being set apart *from* the corruption of the world and *for* God's use.

i. "The word *hagios* (rendered 'sanctify,' 'hallow,' 'consecrate') means to set-apart-and-devote-to-God: whether it be things, or sacrificial animals, or men for His service." (Trench)

ii. Jesus didn't just leave the disciples to sanctify themselves. He prayed for their sanctification. This process, as the keeping process, is not left to us alone; it is a work of God in us and through us.

b. **Sanctify them by Your truth. Your word is truth**: The dynamic behind sanctification is **truth**. The word of God read, heard, understood and applied.

i. "Sanctification is not effected apart from divine revelation." (Morris)

ii. "The more truth you believe, the more sanctified you will be. The operation of truth upon the mind is to separate a man from the world unto the service of God." (Spurgeon)

c. **As You sent Me into the world, I also have sent them into the world**: The thought of service is sandwiched by sanctification. The sanctification Jesus had in mind here was not primarily personal holiness (though that is included), but more so being set apart for God's service and mission.

i. "He does not merely *leave* them into the world, but *sends* them into it, to witness to this same truth of God." (Alford) "The word 'mission' comes from the Latin verb *mitto, mittere, misi, missum*, which means 'to send' or 'dispatch.' A mission is a sending forth." (Boice) "They not merely remain in it because they can do nothing else; they are positively sent into it as their Master's agents and messengers." (Bruce)

ii. "Christ was the great Missionary, the Messiah, the Sent One; we are the minor missionaries, Sent out into the world to accomplish the Father's will and purpose." (Spurgeon)

iii. "Christ's commission is on a higher scale than ours; for he was sent to be a propitiation and covenant-head, and so came into positions which it would be presumption for us to dream of occupying. Still, there is a likeness though it be only that of a drop to the sea." (Spurgeon)

iv. Think of how Jesus came, and connect it to the way that He sends us **into the world**:

- Jesus did not come as a philosopher like Plato or Aristotle, though He knew higher philosophy than them all.

- Jesus did not come as an inventor or a discoverer, though He could have invented new things and discovered new lands.

- Jesus did not come as a conqueror, though He was mightier than Alexander or Caesar.

- Jesus came to teach.

- Jesus came to live among us.

- Jesus came to suffer for truth and righteousness.

- Jesus came to rescue men.

v. "If Jesus does not explicitly pray for the world at this time (verse 9), yet his prayer for the disciples involves hope for the world." (Bruce)

d. **And for their sakes I sanctify Myself:** One should not think that Jesus was *unsanctified* up to this point. Yet now He was about to enter a new aspect of being set aside for God the Father and His purpose: to complete the work of the cross. It was through that finished work that the word of God and work of God would become fully effective in the lives of the disciples (**that they also may be sanctified by the truth**).

i. **And for their sakes I sanctify Myself:** "As both priest, altar, and sacrifice; and this Christ did from the womb to the tomb; at his death especially." (Trapp)

ii. "Chrysostom paraphrases 'I sanctify myself' as 'I offer myself in sacrifice'. Here is a Johannine counterpart to the Gethsemane prayer." (Bruce)

C. Jesus prays concerning all believers.

1. (20) Jesus broadens the scope of His prayer.

"I do not pray for these alone, but also for those who will believe in Me through their word;"

a. **I do not pray for these alone:** Jesus prayed for His eleven disciples, but He also had the heart and the vision to pray beyond them. He prayed for those who would come to faith by the testimony of these disciples. He prayed for us.

i. "He prayed for them. He prays for us. He knew His intercession for them would prevail. He knows His intercession for us will prevail. Then let us rest in Him, with the rest of loving obedience and of surest confidence." (Morgan)

b. **Those who will believe in Me through their word:** This shows that Jesus expected that the disciples' soon failure would be only temporary. Others *would* hear from them, and many would come to belief in Jesus through the testimony of the disciples.

i. i. Jesus went to the cross *knowing* His work would endure. He didn't have a vague hope in what God would do through the disciples. Jesus left His earthly work full of confidence in the work of God through the disciples.

ii. "The last section of Jesus' prayer shows that he expected the failure of the disciples to be only temporary. The entire tone of the farewell discourse is built on the assumption that after the resurrection they would renew their faith and carry on a new ministry is the power of the Holy Spirit." (Tenney)

iii. "By worldly standards of success Jesus had little to show for his mission." (Bruce) Yet Jesus left His earthly work full of confidence in the work of God through the disciples.

2. (21) Jesus prays for unity among all believers, even as among the original disciples.

"That they all may be one, as You, Father, *are* in Me, and I in You; that they also may be one in Us, that the world may believe that You sent Me."

a. **That they all may be one**: Jesus envisioned the great multitude before the throne of God of every nation, race, language, class, and social level (Revelation 7:9-10). Jesus prayed that they might rise above their different backgrounds and understand their unity; that **they may all be as one**.

i. It's as if Jesus prayed with this in mind: "Father, I have prayed for the unity of the disciples You gave Me. Yet they are all Galileans, from this time and place. There will be countless others who also become disciples, and they will come from every nation, every language, every culture, every class, every status, from every age through the rest of history. Father, make *them* one."

ii. "We are to be faithful to truth; but we are not to be of a contentious spirit, separating ourselves from those who are living members of the one and indivisible body of Christ. To promote the unity of the church, by creating new divisions, is not wise. Cultivate at once the love of the truth and the love of the brethren." (Spurgeon)

iii. "Why are we not one? Sin is the great dividing element. The perfectly holy would be perfectly united. The more saintly men are, the more they love their Lord and one another; and thus they come into closer union with each other." (Spurgeon)

iv. "Christ will have all his members to be *one* in *spirit, one* in *rights* and *privileges*, and *one* in the *blessedness* of the future *world*." (Clarke)

b. **That they all may be one, as You, Father are in Me, and I in You**: Earlier in this prayer Jesus prayed specifically that the eleven disciples present at His prayer remain unified (*that they may be one as We are*, John 17:11). Here Jesus broadened the sense of that prayer to **all** believers, **that they all may be one**.

i. As in the previous prayer for the eleven, Jesus prayed that their unity would follow the pattern of the unity of the Godhead, specifically in the relationship between God the Father and God the Son. "If the Father is in him and he is in them, then the Father is in them: they are drawn into the very life of God, and the life of God is perfect love." (Bruce)

ii. The repetition and extension of this prayer to all future believers is important. It shows that unity among the broader body of Jesus Christ was and is *very* important to Jesus.

iii. **As You, Father, are in Me, and I in You** also speaks to the truth that the foundation of our unity is the same as the foundation of unity between the Father and the Son: equality of person. We are all on the same ground at the cross.

iv. "Beloved, those in whom Christ lives are *not uniform, but one*. Uniformity may be found in death, but this unity is life. Those who are quite uniform may yet have no love to each other, while those who differ widely may still be truly and intensely one. Our children are not uniform, but they make one family." (Spurgeon)

c. **That they also may be one in Us**: The oneness Jesus had in mind was the unity that comes from the shared life in both God the Father and God the Son.

i. As before, Jesus did not pray for uniformity or institutional unity among believers, but for unity rooted in love and a shared nature, bringing together the many different parts of Jesus' one body. This isn't a legislated uniformity seeking to unite wheat and tares, nor is it the unity of institutions. Jesus had in mind the true unity of the Spirit (Ephesians 4:3).

ii. We must believe that this prayer was answered, and that they church *is* one. Our failure is in failing to recognize and walk in that divine fact.

d. **That the world may believe that You sent Me**: This was a remarkable statement. Jesus essentially gave the world permission to judge the validity of *His* ministry based on the unity of His people. Unity among God's people helps the **world** to **believe that** the Father **sent** the Son.

i. "Even when he prays for their unity, he looks beyond their unity to the still unconverted world which stands in need of the witness generated by that unity." (Carson)

3. (22) Jesus prays that the church would be marked by glory.

"And the glory which You gave Me I have given them, that they may be one just as We are one:"

a. **The glory which You gave Me I have given them**: As God the Father shared His glory with God the Son (John 17:5), so Jesus gave glory unto His people.

i. There are many ways that Jesus gives His glory to His people.

- The glory of His presence.
- The glory of His Word.
- The glory of His Spirit.
- The glory of His power.
- The glory of His leadership.
- The glory of His preservation.

ii. In all these aspects, there is the essential aspect of the *presence* of Jesus, God the Son. Scripturally speaking, when God gives or displays His glory to His people, it is some type of manifestation of God's *presence*. God's glory is, in some way, the radiance or shining of His presence, His essential nature.

iii. The Apostle Paul also understood that Jesus gives His glory to His people: *For it is the God who commanded light to shine out of darkness, who has shone in our hearts to give the light of the knowledge of the glory of God in the face of Jesus Christ.* (2 Corinthians 4:6)

b. **The glory which You gave Me**: It is important to remember that the **glory** that God the Father gave to God the Son was **glory** that often appeared humble, weak, and suffering. It was glory that was ultimately displayed in radical sacrifice. The glory of Jesus is almost the opposite of the self-glory and vainglory of man.

i. The glory of Jesus was ultimately displayed in His work on the cross. Jesus often referred to it as His glorification (John 7:39, 12:16, 12:23).

ii. "Just as His true glory was to follow the path of lowly service culminating in the cross, so for them the true glory lay in the path of lowly service wherever it might lead them." (Morris)

c. **That they may be one**: The presence of glory - among the Persons of the Godhead and the member of Jesus' Church - this **glory** contributes to the oneness and unity of God's people.

i. Where there is a sense of God's glory, unity is so much easier. Lesser things that often divide us are set far in the background when there is a sense of God's glory at work.

4. (23) Jesus prays for a unity founded in love.

"I in them, and You in Me; that they may be made perfect in one, and that the world may know that You have sent Me, and have loved them as You have loved Me."

a. **I in them, and You in Me; that they may be made perfect in one**: Jesus again referred to the living, organic unity He prayed would exist among His people. This isn't the totalitarian unity of coercion or fear, and it isn't the unity of compromise. Jesus prayed for a unity of love and common identity *in Him*.

i. "Like sanctification, this oneness is simultaneously something already achieved and something that needs perfecting." (Carson)

b. **That the world may know that You have sent Me, and have loved them as You have loved Me**: Jesus here took the idea introduced in John 17:21 (*that the world may believe that You sent Me*) and expanded it. The *repetition* is notable, and so is the *expansion*.

i. The idea that the unity of God's people would display to the world that Jesus was truly sent from God the Father was so important to Jesus that He repeated it in the same short prayer.

ii. Then Jesus expanded the idea, now praying that the unity among generations of believers to come would also demonstrate to the world that Jesus loves His people, and loves them after the pattern of God the Father's love for God the Son (**and have loved them as You have loved Me**).

iii. This reminds us of the importance of unity and love among Christians. It is as if Jesus gave the world permission to doubt both His mission and His love if the world does not see unity and love among believers.

- This is difficult, because sometimes the most unloving and critical among the followers of Jesus *directly justify* their divisiveness and sharp criticism as love, as in "I only demand that you be exactly as I am because I love you."

- This is difficult, because *sometimes it is true* that there must be criticism, correction, and rebuke in the name of love.

- This is difficult, because even as we understand the words of Jesus here, we also understand that there are many, many other reasons why people do not believe (2 Corinthians 3:13-16, Ephesians 4:17-19, Romans 1:20-21). Christians have a great responsibility to display Jesus to the world through their love and unity, but often Christians are too quick to blame one another for an unbelieving world.

iv. "But what a sad thing was it, that a heathen should soon after have cause to say, No beasts are so mischievous to men, as Christians are to one another." (Trapp)

5. (24) Jesus prays to be with His people, and for them to see His glory.

"Father, I desire that they also whom You gave Me may be with Me where I am, that they may behold My glory which You have given Me; for You loved Me before the foundation of the world."

a. **I desire that they also whom You gave Me may be with Me where I am**: Jesus asked that the unity between Himself and His people be completed, even as He promised His disciples that it would be (John 14:2-3).

i. The words "**I desire**" mean something. They mean that Jesus *longs for* the consummation of all things, greatly desiring for His people to be gathered to Him in heaven. *Jesus longed for heaven's completion of all things.*

ii. **Where I am**: Jesus was not yet in heaven, yet He spoke as if He already were there. In a sense, we are called to do the same, understanding that we are seated with Jesus in heavenly places even as we remain on earth (Ephesians 1:3 and 2:6).

iii. "Was he not carried away by the fervor of his devotion? Where was he when he uttered the words of our text? If I follow the language I might conclude that our Lord was already in heaven. He says, 'rather, I will that they also, whom thou hast given me, be with me where I am; that they may behold my glory.' Does he not mean that they should be in heaven with him? Of course he does; yet he was not in heaven; he was still in the midst of his apostles, in the body upon earth; and he had yet Gethsemane and Golgotha before him ere he could enter his glory. He had prayed himself into such an exaltation of feeling that his prayer was in heaven, and he himself was there in spirit." (Spurgeon)

iv. Jesus promised something to His disciples (John 14:2-3) and then prayed that God the Father would perform it. Jesus did *everything* in dependence upon God the Father.

b. **That they may behold My glory which You have given Me**: This is what Jesus said would occupy the attention of His people in heaven - to **behold** the **glory** of Jesus. There must be something so deep, so enthralling, so vast to the **glory** of Jesus that it can occupy the attention of God's people in eternity.

c. **For You loved Me before the foundation of the world**: Jesus said this in connection with the **glory** that God the Father gave to God the Son. This **glory** was given in the context of a love relationship, and a love relationship extending into eternity past.

i. This tells us that before anything was created, there was a love relationship between the Persons of the Godhead, the Trinity. Even if Jesus had not specifically told us this, we might have understood it by other Biblical truths, understanding that God is eternal (Micah 5:2) and that God is love (1 John 4:8 and 4:16). There was never a time when God did not love and was not love.

ii. Genuine love must have an object outside of itself to love; therefore love existed between the Persons of the Godhead before anything was created. The Triune nature of God is a not only Scripturally correct, it is a logical necessity given what we know of God through His revealed Word.

6. (25-26) The triumphant conclusion to Jesus' prayer.

"O righteous Father! The world has not known You, but I have known You; and these have known that You sent Me. And I have declared to them Your name, and will declare *it,* that the love with which You loved Me may be in them, and I in them."

a. **O righteous Father!** Jesus was about to go to the cross and undergo the entire ordeal of His passion - all of it planned and sent by God the Father. Yet Jesus, full of love and honor towards God the Father cried out in concluding this prayer, "**O righteous Father!**"

i. Jesus understood that His present and soon-to-be-endured pain did not diminish the righteousness of God the Father in even the smallest way.

b. **The world has not known You, but I have known You**: Jesus understood both that the world did not know and understand God the Father, and that He did know and understand Him.

c. **And these have known that You sent Me**: Jesus repeated the idea first mentioned in this prayer at John 17:8. Whatever their weaknesses and failings, the disciples understood that God the Father sent God the Son.

d. **I have declared to them Your name, and will declare it**: Jesus ended this great prayer on a note of faith and even triumph. He knew that He had done His work, and would finish His course.

i. In one sense, the entire work of Jesus could be summed up in saying that He **declared** to the disciples and to the world the **name** of God the Father. That is, He revealed and lived out the character and nature of God the Father as the *brightness of His glory and the express image of His person* (Hebrews 1:3).

ii. The world called Jesus a blasphemer (John 10:33), a drunk, a glutton, and an associate of sinners (Matthew 11:19), a demon-possessed pagan (John 7:20 and 8:48), and an illegitimate child (John 8:41). *Jesus believed none of it, because none of it was true.* At the end He could confidently say, "**I have declared to them Your name, and will declare it.**"

e. **That the love with which You loved Me may be in them:** Jesus received love from God the Father, and this love relationship was the strength and sustenance of His life. Here, concluding His great prayer, Jesus prayed that the same love that was His strength and sustenance would fill His disciples (both near and far).

i. This speaks to the essential place of **love** in the Christian life and community. Jesus thought it so important that He specifically prayed for **love** when He might have prayed for many other things.

- Take love from joy and you have only hedonism.
- Take love from holiness and you have self-righteousness.
- Take love from truth and you have bitter orthodoxy.
- Take love from mission and you have conquest.
- Take love from unity and you have tyranny.

f. **And I in them:** Jesus prayed that His disciples would not only be filled with the love of God the Father, but that they would also know the indwelling presence of Jesus Himself. This continues the emphasis on abiding and the indwelling Jesus from the words of Jesus earlier that evening (John 15:1-8).

John 18 - Jesus' Arrest and Trial

A. Betrayal and arrest in the garden.

1. (1-3) Jesus enters the garden, followed by Judas and his troops.

When Jesus had spoken these words, He went out with His disciples over the Brook Kidron, where there was a garden, which He and His disciples entered. And Judas, who betrayed Him, also knew the place; for Jesus often met there with His disciples. Then Judas, having received a detachment *of troops,* and officers from the chief priests and Pharisees, came there with lanterns, torches, and weapons.

a. **Over the Brook Kidron**: When Jesus went from the city of Jerusalem, and crossed the **Brook Kidron**. This small stream was the drainage from the temple, and would be reddish from the blood of thousands of Passover lambs. This would have been a vivid reminder to Jesus of His soon sacrifice.

i. "From the altar there was a channel down to the brook Kedron, and through that channel the blood of the Passover lambs drained away. When Jesus crossed the brook Kedron it would still be red with the blood of the lambs which had been sacrificed." (Barclay)

ii. "The very brook would remind him of his approaching sacrifice, for through it flowed the blood and refuse from the temple." (Spurgeon)

b. **There was a garden**: John did not name this as the Garden of Gethsemane, but the other Gospel writers did (Matthew 26:36 and Mark 14:32). Jesus **often met there with His disciples**, perhaps to sleep for the night under the shelter of the olive trees or in a nearby cave.

i. Luke 21:37 says that during this Passover week, Jesus spent the nights with His disciples on the Mount of Olives. Yet, probably not only during that week but they **often met there**. This "would be a curious way of referring to Jesus' custom on the present visit only. It probably indicates that He had been in the habit of using the garden through the years." (Morris)

ii. *It was a familiar place.* "It is plain that, having consecrated himself for the impending sacrifice, he now made no attempt to hide from his enemies, but went to the place where Judas would normally expect to find him." (Bruce)

iii. "St. John mentions nothing of the agony in the garden; probably because he found it so amply related by all the other evangelists." (Clarke)

c. **Then Judas, having received a detachment of troops**: Judas came to the garden with team of soldiers to seize and arrest Jesus. He led both **a detachment of troops** (a large number of Roman soldiers), and **officers** from the temple security force. *Why* they came with such force is not directly answered; the religious leaders or the Romans must have expected or feared some kind of battle or conflict.

i. **Lanterns, torches**: "With these they had intended to search the corners and caverns, provided Christ had hidden himself; for they could not have needed them for any other purpose, it being now the fourteenth day of the moon's age, in the month Nisan, and consequently she appeared *full* and *bright*." (Clarke)

ii. This **detachment of troops** was well armed with swords and clubs, and Jesus noted how unnecessary it was: *Have you come out, as against a robber, with swords and clubs to take Me? I sat daily with you, teaching in the temple, and you did not seize Me* (Matthew 26:55).

iii. **Detachment**: "That word, if it is correctly used, can have three meanings. It is the Greek word for a Roman cohort and a cohort had six hundred men. If it was a cohort of auxiliary soldiers, a *speira* had one thousand men, two hundred and forty cavalry and seven hundred and sixty infantry. Sometimes, much more rarely, the word is used for the detachment of men called a maniple which was made up of two hundred men." (Barclay)

iv. "The article in *ten speiran* [**detachment**] points to the battalion which garrisoned the Antonia fortress in Jerusalem. The 'officers' (*hyperetas*) are members of the Temple police, a body of men drawn from the tribe of Levi." (Trench)

v. This shows that Judas misunderstood the nature of Jesus and at the same time underestimated His power. Had Jesus been of the nature to physically battle against Judas and the devil driving the betrayer, the **detachment of troops** was not enough.

vi. A sinless Man in an appointed garden was about to do battle with Satan's representative (Luke 22:3). The first time this happened, the sinless man failed. The Second Adam would not fail.

2. (4-6) Jesus speaks to Judas and the detachment of troops.

Jesus therefore, knowing all things that would come upon Him, went forward and said to them, "Whom are you seeking?" They answered Him, "Jesus of Nazareth." Jesus said to them, "I am *He.*" And Judas, who betrayed Him, also stood with them. Now when He said to them, "I am *He,*" they drew back and fell to the ground.

a. **Jesus, therefore, knowing all things that would come upon Him**: Judas hoped to catch Jesus by surprise, but this was impossible. Jesus' entire life was prepared for this hour, and He was ready for it.

b. **Whom are you seeking**: Taking the lead, Jesus said this for at least two reasons. He wanted any potential violence to be directed to Him and not to His disciples, so He wanted to identify Himself. Jesus also wanted Judas and the detachment of troops to *announce* their evil intention.

c. **Jesus of Nazareth**: This was the common name that Jesus was known by. Jesus wasn't normally identified by His role as a rabbi or a carpenter, and not by His apparent parentage (Jesus ben Joseph). Jesus chose and received the title that identified Him with **Nazareth**.

i. "They called him Jesus of Nazareth by way of reproach. He takes it upon him, and wears it for a crown. And should not we do likewise?" (Trapp)

d. **I am**: Jesus answered them with this curious phrase, two words in both English and in the original language (*ego eimi*). It is curious because Jesus didn't say *I am He*, but simply **I am** - the *He* was added by the translators and is not in the original text. With this Jesus consciously proclaimed that He was God, connecting His words to the many previous **I am** statements recorded in the Gospel of John, especially in John 8:58 (but also John 6:48, 8:12, 9:5, 10:9, 10:11-14, 10:36, 11:25, 14:6).

i. "The soldiers had come out secretly to arrest a fleeing peasant. In the gloom they find themselves confronted by a commanding figure, who so far from running away comes out to meet them and speaks to them in the very language of deity." (Morris)

ii. "The Greek *ego eimi* rendered *I am he* might well suggest divinity to those familiar with the Greek Bible, for it is the rendering in the LXX for the sacred name of God (see Exodus 3:14)." (Tasker)

e. **Now when He said to them, "I am He," they drew back and fell to the ground**: When Jesus declared His divine identity (in the words **I am**), Judas and soldiers all fell back. There was such a display of divine presence, majesty, and power in those two words that the enemies of Jesus were powerless to stand against Him.

i. "Here our Saviour let out a little beam of the majesty of his Deity, and 500 men fell before him." (Trapp)

ii. This shows that Jesus was completely in control of the situation. As a practical matter, Jesus did *not* have to go with this arresting army led by Judas. With God's power expressed through His words alone, Jesus could have overpowered them and easily escaped.

iii. "Our Lord chose to give them this proof of *his* infinite power, that they might know that *their* power could not prevail against him if he chose to exert his might, seeing that the very breath of his mouth confounded, drove back, and struck them down to the earth." (Clarke)

iv. "The question on the miraculous nature of this incident is not whether it was a miracle *at all* (for it is evident that it *must* be regarded as one), but whether it were an act *specially intended* by our Lord, or as a result of the superhuman dignity of His person, and the majestic calmness of His reply." (Alford)

v. "Wherever in our Lord's life any incident indicates more emphatically than usual the lowliness of His humiliation, there, by the side of it, you get something that indicates the majesty of His glory." (Maclaren)

- Jesus was born as a humble baby, yet announced by angels.
- Jesus was laid in a manger, yet signaled by a star.
- Jesus submitted to baptism as if He were a sinner, then heard the Divine voice of approval.
- Jesus slept when He was exhausted, but awoke to calm the storm.
- Jesus wept at a grave, then called the dead to life.
- Jesus surrendered to arrest, then declared "I am" and knocked all the troops over.
- Jesus died on a cross, but in it He defeated sin, death, and Satan.

3. (7-9) Jesus willingly goes with the arresting army.

Then He asked them again, "Whom are you seeking?" And they said, "Jesus of Nazareth." Jesus answered, "I have told you that I am *He*. Therefore, if you seek Me, let these go their way," that the saying might

be fulfilled which He spoke, "Of those whom You gave Me I have lost none."

a. **He asked them again**: Jesus didn't want the soldiers to panic and injure the disciples. Jesus called their attention back to Him, and **asked them again** a question they were probably hesitant to answer.

b. **I have told you that I am**: Jesus said the same words as before (**I am**, *ego eimi*) yet Judas and the troops did not fall to the ground as before. This shows that these were not magic words, but previously they all fell at the conscious display of God's power.

c. **If you seek Me, let these go their way**: After the display of power described in John 18:6, Jesus did not continue to oppose His arrest. Jesus willingly gave Himself up to protect His disciples. This was the same sacrificial love that would find its ultimate peak at the cross. It also shows *why* Jesus knocked the soldiers to the ground; the show of power was to protect the *disciples*, not Jesus Himself.

i. **Let these go their way**: "These words are rather words of *authority*, than words of *entreaty*. I *voluntarily* give myself up to you, but you must not molest one of these my disciples. At your peril injure them. Let them go about their business. I have already given you a sufficient proof of my power: I will not exert it in my own behalf, for I will lay down my life for the sheep; but I will not permit you to injure the least of *these*." (Clarke)

ii. "In a sense, he sacrificed himself for their safety. He had promised the Father that he would protect them (John 17:12) and he fulfilled the guarantee of the voluntary surrender of his life." (Tenney)

iii. The disciples took the words **let these go their way** as their signal to leave. They probably left as fast and as quietly as they could.

d. **Of those whom You gave Me I have lost none**: In doing this, Jesus fulfilled what He had already said at John 6:39 and John 17:12.

4. (10-12) Peter attacks one among the party arresting Jesus.

Then Simon Peter, having a sword, drew it and struck the high priest's servant, and cut off his right ear. The servant's name was Malchus. So Jesus said to Peter, "Put your sword into the sheath. Shall I not drink the cup which My Father has given Me?" Then the detachment *of troops* and the captain and the officers of the Jews arrested Jesus and bound Him.

a. **Simon Peter, having a sword**: The disciples apparently sometimes carried swords, and Luke 22:38 indicates that they had at least two on this occasion. **Having a sword** made sense when there were robbers and violent men to consider.

b. **Drew it and struck the high priest's servant**: Each of the other Gospel accounts mention that one of the disciples did this, but John is the only Gospel writer to say that it was **Simon Peter** who made this attack. Peter wanted to fulfill his previous promise to defend Jesus at all cost: *Even if I have to die with You, I will not deny You!* (Matthew 26:35).

> i. "It is exceedingly thoughtless in Peter to try to prove his faith by the sword, while he could not do so by his tongue." (Calvin, cited in Morris)

> ii. "But it was a sad omen (saith a noble and renowned writer, Lord Brook) that Peter's sword should cut off the ear of Malchus, which signifies a king or kingly authority. How the pope hath lifted up himself...above all that is called Augustus, or emperor, is better known than that it need be here related." (Trapp)

c. **And cut off his right ear**: It has been noted (but not proved) that this meant Peter, holding the sword in his right hand, must have attacked **the high priest's servant** from behind, because it would be near impossible to **cut off his right ear** if he was facing the servant **Malchus**. It is entirely possible that Peter deliberately chose a non-solider, and attacked him from behind. This was not a shining display of courage.

> i. It may be significant that John alone mentioned the **high priest's servant** by name, **Malchus**. This is another piece of evidence that John had connections to those in the household of the high priest (John 18:16). It may also indicate that **Malchus** later became a Christian, because often people in the Gospels and Acts are named because they were known among the early Christian community.

d. **Put your sword into the sheath**: Jesus did not praise Peter for what he did; He told him to *stop*. This was to protect Peter as much as to protect those who came to arrest Jesus. Most of all, it was that Jesus could **drink the cup** the Father gave to Jesus, the measure of suffering and judgment He would endure.

> i. "Peter's impulsive action was more likely to get himself and his companions into serious trouble than to do his Master any good, but even if it had a better chance of success, Jesus would allow nothing to stand in the way of his bringing to completion the work which his Father had given him to do." (Bruce)

ii. John the Gospel writer named Peter as the offender, but did not tell that Jesus miraculously healed the cut-off ear of the **high priest's servant** (Luke 22:51).

e. **The captain and officers of the Jews arrested Jesus and bound Him**: This describes two different groups. The **captain** was the Roman commander and the **officers of the Jews** were the temple security force.

i. **The captain**: "The 'commander' (*chiliarchos*) was the officer in charge, possible the executive of the Roman garrison in Jerusalem (cf. the use of the same term in Acts 22:24, 26, 27, 28; 23:17, 19, 22). The technical expression strengthens the impression that the Romans supported the action of the Jewish hierarchy." (Tenney)

f. **And bound Him**: They regarded Jesus dangerous enough to send many soldiers after Him, so in custody they **bound** Jesus, treating Him as if He were a threat. Yet Jesus remained **bound** only because He surrendered to His Father's will; hands that healed the sick and raised the dead could certainly break bonds.

i. We could say that in spiritual application, there were two ways that Jesus was bound.

- Jesus was bound with the cords of love.
- Jesus was bound with our bonds.

ii. "This was done as Irenaeus hath it, while the Deity rested; for he could as easily have delivered himself as he did his disciples, but this sacrifice was to be bound with cords to the altar; he was pinioned and manacled, as a malefactor." (Trapp)

iii. "I do not find any indication that His bonds were unloosed by Annas, or that he had even a moment's relief or relaxation granted to him; but, with the cruel ropes still binding him fast, he was sent across the great hall into the other wing of the palace in which Caiaphas resided." (Spurgeon)

B. Jesus' trial before Annas; Peter's denial.

1. (13-14) Jesus is lead away to Annas.

And they led Him away to Annas first, for he was the father-in-law of Caiaphas who was high priest that year. Now it was Caiaphas who advised the Jews that it was expedient that one man should die for the people.

a. **They led Him away to Annas first**: Annas was not the official High Priest but as father-in-law to Caiaphas, he was the one who put Caiaphas in office.

i. "Annas was the power behind the throne in Jerusalem. He himself had been High Priest from A.D. 6 to 15. Four of his sons had also held the high priesthood and Caiaphas was his son-in-law." (Barclay)

ii. "There is a passage in the *Talmud* which says: 'Woe to the house of Annas! Woe to their serpent's hiss! They are High Priests; their sons are keepers of the treasury; their sons-in-law are guardians of the Temple; and their servants beat the people with staves.' Annas and his household were notorious." (Barclay)

iii. "At any rate, the Lord is led to Annas *first*, and we feel sure that there was a motive for that act. Annas, in some sense, had a priority in the peerage of enmity to Jesus; he was malignant, cruel, and unscrupulous enough to be premier in the ministry of persecutors." (Spurgeon)

b. **It was Caiaphas who advised the Jews that it was expedient that one man should die for the people**: This unknowing prophecy of Caiaphas is recorded in John 11:49-53. Without knowing, Caiaphas spoke the truth that it was good for Jesus to **die for the people**.

i. In that unknowing prophecy Caiaphas spoke logically (the good of the many outweigh the good of the one) but not morally (it was wrong to put an innocent Man, God's Messiah, to death).

ii. One reason John reminds us of what Caiaphas said in John 11:49-52 is to show that the judgment against Jesus was already decided. It would not be a fair trial. "Jesus might expect little from such a judge. Here was no idealist ready to see that justice was one, but a cynical politician who had already spoken in favor of Jesus' death." (Morris)

2. (15-16) Peter and John follow Jesus to the house of the high priest.

And Simon Peter followed Jesus, and so *did* another disciple. Now that disciple was known to the high priest, and went with Jesus into the courtyard of the high priest. But Peter stood at the door outside. Then the other disciple, who was known to the high priest, went out and spoke to her who kept the door, and brought Peter in.

a. **Simon Peter followed Jesus, and so did another disciple**: Peter embarrassed himself at the Garden of Gethsemane with his sword and the ear of the high priest's servant. Hoping for a second chance to show his loyalty, he followed Jesus to where He was held. Most believe that the **other disciple** was John himself, who had previous connections with the high priest and his household (**was known to the high priest**).

i. "It may be that the family had connections with the priesthood, either by business relationships or possibly by marital ties." (Tenney)

ii. "Perhaps for that he and his father Zebedee were wont to serve the fat priests with the best and daintiest fish (for this other disciple was John, who had first fled with the rest, and now came sculking in to see what would become of his master)." (Trapp)

b. **Spoke to her who kept the door, and brought Peter in**: John's connection to the high priest and his servants explains how Peter and John had any access to the property of the high priest on such a night.

3. (17-18) Peter denies his relationship to Jesus the first time.

Then the servant girl who kept the door said to Peter, "You are not also *one* of this Man's disciples, are you?" He said, "I am not." Now the servants and officers who had made a fire of coals stood there, for it was cold, and they warmed themselves. And Peter stood with them and warmed himself.

a. **You are not also one of this Man's disciples, are you**: A simple **servant girl** who minded the door to the courtyard of the high priest's house questioned Peter. This first test of Peter's loyalty seemed easy; he could have answered nothing, mumbled something, or said, "I know Him."

i. **You are not also one of this Man's disciples**: The **also** means that John was already known to her as a disciple of Jesus. "The servant-girl presumably knew the 'other disciple' to be a follower of Jesus, and when she saw him bringing in Peter, she said, in effect: 'Oh no, not another!'" (Bruce)

ii. **This Man's disciples**: "*This man's* in the Greek is contemptuous, more akin to 'this fellow's' or 'this person's'." (Tasker)

iii. "A silly wench is too hard for this stout stickler." (Trapp)

b. **I am not**: Peter responded to her negative statement with a negative of his own. Instead of being loyal to Jesus, he denied being His disciple. This seems to have happened at the door and may have been a quick exchange that Peter did not give much thought to, yet even that was a clear denial of association with Jesus.

i. "The first denial was to all appearance rashly and almost inadvertently made, from a mere feeling of shame." (Alford)

c. **Peter stood with them and warmed himself**: The sense is that Peter was there not only because **it was cold** and he wanted warmth. Peter also wanted to blend into the small crowd so that he would not stand out and want to be noticed. It was *dangerous* to be noticed, because he was a disciple of the man arrested and in serious trouble.

i. **Peter stood**: "Luke is quite definite that they and Peter were *sitting*: so too Matthew as to Peter. John seems to speak of them and Peter as *standing*: but these words used by John are so frequently idiomatic to mean merely 'to be stationary,' 'to continue,' 'to be there,' 'to be,' exactly like the Italian *stare*, that the *standing* cannot be pressed -- no more here than *e.g.* in the other nineteen places where they occur in John's gospel." (Trench)

4. (19-21) Annas interrogates Jesus.

The high priest then asked Jesus about His disciples and His doctrine. Jesus answered him, "I spoke openly to the world. I always taught in synagogues and in the temple, where the Jews always meet, and in secret I have said nothing. Why do you ask Me? Ask those who have heard Me what I said to them. Indeed they know what I said."

a. **The high priest then asked Jesus about His disciples and His doctrine**: Annas wanted to know about Jesus' **disciples**, perhaps because of fear or jealousy. Then he wanted to know about **His doctrine**, what Jesus taught that might be of concern to the religious establishment.

i. Annas basically brought the prisoner before him and asked, "Tell us all what You're guilty of and everyone who is with You." In His reply, Jesus did not mention His disciples at all. He protected them in every way possible.

ii. "Annas bore a very promising name, for it signifies *clement* or *merciful*, yet he was the man to begin the work of ensnaring the Lord Jesus in his speech, if he could be ensnared." (Spurgeon)

b. **I spoke openly to the world**: Jesus told Annas that He did not have secret doctrine or teaching that could be revealed under interrogation. His teaching was open, **in synagogues and in the temple**. Jesus could even say, **in secret I have said nothing**.

i. "Truth is bold and barefaced; when heresy hides itself, and loathes the light." (Trapp)

c. **Why do you ask Me? Ask those who have heard Me what I said to them**: In saying this, Jesus wasn't being uncooperative, only asserting His legal right. There was to be no formal charge against the accused until witnesses had been heard and been found to be truthful.

i. It was the high priest's duty to call forth the witnesses first, beginning with those for the defense. These basic legal protections for the accused under Jewish law were not observed in the trial of Jesus. "Jesus therefore claimed that, if his teaching was in question, evidence should be heard in the normal way." (Bruce)

ii. "For the *Talmud* states, Sanhedrin. C. iv. S. 1, that-'Criminal processes can neither commence not terminate, but during the course of the *day*. If the person be acquitted, the sentence may be pronounced during that day; but, if he be condemned, the sentence cannot be pronounced till the next day. But no kind of judgment is to be executed, either on the eve of the Sabbath, or the eve of any festival.'" (Clarke)

5. (22-24) The end of Jesus' appearance before Annas.

And when He had said these things, one of the officers who stood by struck Jesus with the palm of his hand, saying, "Do You answer the high priest like that?" Jesus answered him, "If I have spoken evil, bear witness of the evil; but if well, why do you strike Me?" Then Annas sent Him bound to Caiaphas the high priest.

a. **One of the officers who stood by**: This anonymous official began the physical abuse of Jesus that would end in His crucifixion. In His deity, Jesus knew his name; but as one of those who did not know what they did against God's Messiah (Luke 23:34), his name was graciously not recorded.

b. **Struck Jesus with the palm of his hand**: His name was not recorded, but his crime was. Without warning he strongly slapped Jesus **with the palm of his hand** and accused Him of disrespect to the high priest.

i. "This blow was a signal for the indignities which followed." (Alford)

c. **If I have spoken evil, bear witness of the evil, but if well, why do you strike Me**: Jesus asked both the unnamed official and Annas to justify this physical abuse. Jesus exposed the shameful truth, that they did not follow their own standards and practice of justice with Jesus of Nazareth.

d. **Annas sent Him bound to Caiaphas the high priest**: Annas had nothing to answer to Jesus. He sent Jesus on to a more official trial to the man who held the actual office of high priest, and sent Jesus **bound** as if He were a dangerous criminal.

6. (25-27) Peter denies Jesus twice more.

Now Simon Peter stood and warmed himself. Therefore they said to him, "You are not also *one* of His disciples, are you?" He denied *it* and said, "I am not!" One of the servants of the high priest, a relative *of him* whose ear Peter cut off, said, "Did I not see you in the garden with Him?" Peter then denied again; and immediately a rooster crowed.

a. **Peter stood and warmed himself**: Watching Jesus from a distance at the house of Annas, Peter hoped to mix into the small crowd and remain unnoticed. Yet because Peter was with them, **therefore** they noticed him.

i. Luke 22:61 indicates that Peter could see Jesus, probably at a distance. Peter likely saw the hard slap unexpectedly put upon Jesus, and understood that this whole incident was going to be more violent and messy than he had thought. The shock of this sight increased the level of stress and panic for Peter as he **stood and warmed himself**.

b. **You are not also one of His disciples, are you**: This unnamed one at the fire asked the same question as the servant girl at the door (John 18:17), even placing it in the negative as she did. For a second time, Peter said **I am not** and denied any association with Jesus.

i. **You are not also one of His disciples**: For a second time we see that there was another disciple present - John, no doubt. Peter knew John was present and known as a disciple of Jesus, but *he* didn't want to be known.

c. **One of the servants of the high priest, a relative of him whose ear Peter cut off**: This is the kind of thing that John would know, having connection with the high priest and his household (John 18:15-16).

d. **Did I not see you in the garden with Him**: The relative of Malchus would pay special notice of the man who attacked his kin. Even in the light of the night fire in the courtyard he though he recognized Peter as the man who attacked Malchus with a sword from behind.

i. **Did I not see you**: "The 'I' is emphatic in the original: as we say, *Did I not see thee with my own eyes?*" (Alford)

e. **Peter then denied again**: Matthew 26:74 tells us that Peter denied this third time with cursing and swearing, hoping that this would make them think even more that he was not associated with Jesus. We could say that at this point it was not the *faith* of Peter that failed, but his *courage*.

f. **Immediately a rooster crowed**: This fulfilled what Jesus said in John 13:38, and must have immediately reminded Peter of the prediction Jesus made in the upper room.

C. Jesus is brought before Pilate.

1. (28) Jesus is brought to the Roman leader.

Then they led Jesus from Caiaphas to the Praetorium, and it was early morning. But they themselves did not go into the Praetorium, lest they should be defiled, but that they might eat the Passover.

a. **They led Jesus from Caiaphas**: After interrogation, Annas sent Jesus to Caiaphas (John 18:24) for a trial in two parts. The first was a hastily gathered assembly of the council recorded in Matthew 26:57-68. The second was the official, daylight meeting of the Sanhedrin (Luke 22:66).

i. The Gospel of John mentions only that Jesus was sent to Caiaphas, and then Caiaphas sent Jesus on to Pilate. John focused on the appearance of Jesus before the Roman leader, Pontius Pilate.

b. **To the Praetorium**: This word described the headquarters of Pilate in Jerusalem, likely at the Roman Fortress Antonia, where Pilate held court and conducted public business.

i. "The term 'praetorium' denotes the headquarters of a Roman military governor (as the governor of Judea was). In a Roman camp, the praetorium was the commander's headquarters in the centre of the camp." (Bruce)

ii. "Philo tells us that on one occasion Pilate hung up shields in Herod's palace (*Leg. Ad Gai.*, 299). Some years later Florus when governor lodged in the same palace (Josephus, *Bell*. Ii, 301, 328). The evidence is not enough to prove that Pilate must have lodged there and the whole matter must be regarded as uncertain." (Morris)

c. **They themselves did not go into the Praetorium, lest they should be defiled**: John used an ironic touch to expose the hypocrisy of the Jewish rulers. They refused to break relatively small commands regarding ceremonial defilement, but broke much greater commands in rejecting God's Messiah and condemning an innocent Man to death.

i. "The examination began therefore in the open air in front of the building." (Dods)

ii. "Putrid hypocrisy! they stand upon legal defilements, and care not to defile their consciences with innocent blood. What is this, but to strain at a gnat and swallow a camel?" (Trapp)

iii. "Westcott conjectures that John may well have entered the Praetorium and this have been in a position to observe what was going on." (Morris)

d. **That they might eat the Passover**: This statement introduces a controversy, namely this - was the Last Supper a Passover meal, and was Jesus crucified on the Passover or the day following? This statement in John 18:28 seems to indicate that Passover was the coming day, the day Jesus would be crucified and that the Last Supper was the day *before* Passover. Yet several passages seem to indicate that the Last Supper *was* a Passover meal (Matthew 26:18, Mark 14:12, 14:16, Luke 22:15). The best solution to this difficult chronological problem seems to be that Jesus was crucified on the Passover, and the meal they had the night before *was* as Passover meal, held after sunset (the *start* of the day in Jewish reckoning). We can speculate that Passover lambs were sacrificed on both days, a necessity due to the massive number of lambs sacrificed in Jerusalem at the temple on Passover (later described by Josephus as being more than 200,000).

i. "Bishop *Pearce* supposes that it was lawful for the Jews to eat the paschal lamb any time between the evening of Thursday and that of Friday. He conjectures too that this permission was necessary on account of the immense number of lambs which were to be killed for that purpose." (Clarke)

ii. Tasker suggested another possibility: "It may be, however, that by *the passover* in this verse the whole Passover festival, which lasted seven days, is meant; and that the expression *eat the passover* refers not to the main Passover meal which may have already taken place, but to the remaining meals that would be taken in the Passover season."

2. (29-32) The religious leaders explain the matter to Pilate.

Pilate then went out to them and said, "What accusation do you bring against this Man?" They answered and said to him, "If He were not an evildoer, we would not have delivered Him up to you." Then Pilate said to them, "You take Him and judge Him according to your law." Therefore the Jews said to him, "It is not lawful for us to put anyone to death," that the saying of Jesus might be fulfilled which He spoke, signifying by what death He would die.

a. **Pilate then went out to them**: The religious leaders had reason to expect a favorable result as they brought Jesus to the Roman governor Pontius **Pilate**. Secular history presents Pilate as a cruel, ruthless man, completely insensitive to the moral feelings of others.

i. Pilate had married a granddaughter of Caesar Augustus. "If it were not for his influential connections through marriage, he would never have come even to the relatively insignificant post he held as procurator of Judea." (Boice)

ii. Philo, the ancient Jewish scholar from Alexandria, described Pilate: "His corruption, his acts of insolence, his rapine, his habit of insulting people, his cruelty, his continual murders of people untried and uncondemned, and his never-ending gratuitous and most grievous inhumanity." (Barclay)

iii. "He was a weak man who tried to cover up his weakness by a show of obstinacy and violence...his period of office was marked by several savage outbreaks of bloodshed (cf. Luke 13:1)." (Bruce)

b. **What accusation do you bring against this Man**: Consistent with Roman character, Pilate spoke directly to the matter at hand. He demanded to know the accusation. John recorded their *evasion* of the question: **If He were not an evildoer, we would not have delivered Him up to you**.

> i. "They had had his cooperation in making the arrest. Now they apparently expected that he would take their word for it that the man the Romans had helped to arrest was dangerous and should be executed." (Morris)

> ii. "So they did not wish to make Pilate the judge, but the executor of the sentence which they had already illegally passed." (Clarke)

> iii. "'We have condemned Him; that is enough. We look to you to carry out the sentence at our bidding.' So the 'ecclesiastical authority' has often said to the 'secular arm' since then, and unfortunately the civil authority has not always been as wise as Pilate was." (Maclaren)

c. **You take Him and judge Him according to your law**: Pilate responded to their evasion by telling them to resolve the matter themselves. If they would not bring Pilate an accusation that mattered to *him*, then *they* would have **judge Him according** to their own law and not bother the Romans.

> i. John does not record it, but eventually the religious leaders did give a more specific answer to Pilate's demand for an accusation: *We found this fellow perverting the nation, and forbidding to pay taxes to Caesar, saying that He Himself is Christ, a King* (Luke 23:2).

d. **It is not lawful for us to put anyone to death**: Without yet answering Pilate's demand for a specific accusation, the religious leaders explained why they did not want to **judge Him according** to their own law. They wanted Jesus dead, and the Romans did not allow them to execute the guilty under their own law.

> i. "Josephus tells us, that it was lawful to hold a court of judgment in capital cases, without the consent of the Procurator." (Alford)

> ii. There were times when the religious leaders risked the disapproval of the Roman authorities and executed those they considered guilty without permission. Acts 7:54-60 records one such execution by stoning. When the Jewish leaders did put someone to death in this unauthorized way, it was generally by stoning.

> iii. The religious leaders may have, in part, pressed for crucifixion to bring the curse of Deuteronomy 21:22-23 upon Jesus. He did bear that curse, to redeem us from the curse of the law (Galatians 3:13).

> iv. "The power of life and death was in all probability taken from the Jews when *Archelaus*, king of Judea, was banished to Vienna, and Judea

was made a Roman province; and this happened more than *fifty* years before the destruction of Jerusalem." (Clarke)

e. **That the saying of Jesus might be fulfilled**: Their demand that Jesus die a *Roman* death of crucifixion would fulfill Jesus' own words (*if I be lifted up*, John 3:14). If the Jews had put Jesus to death, He would have been stoned to death and this prophecy about the manner of His death would not have been fulfilled.

i. John pointed to the answer of a question: If the enemies of Jesus were among the Jewish religious leaders, then why did He die a Roman death of crucifixion? John described much opposition to Jesus, but none of it from the Romans. The series of events leading to His death by crucifixion was somewhat strange and interesting.

3. (33-35) Pilate questions, Jesus clarifies.

Then Pilate entered the Praetorium again, called Jesus, and said to Him, "Are You the King of the Jews?" Jesus answered him, "Are you speaking for yourself about this, or did others tell you this concerning Me?" Pilate answered, "Am I a Jew? Your own nation and the chief priests have delivered You to me. What have You done?"

a. **Then Pilate entered the Praetorium again**: John combined two appearances of Jesus before Pilate, separated by an appearance of Jesus before Herod Antipas (Luke 23:8-12). Pilate hoped to give this problem to Herod because he ruled over Galilee, where Jesus was from. Herod sent Jesus back to Pilate, and this is the likely start of the second appearance.

b. **Are You the King of the Jews**: Pilate was already involved in this case, having sent a detachment of many Roman troops to arrest Jesus (John 18:3). This was his first look at the Man the religious leaders claimed was dangerous. Yet, Pilate's question revealed doubt.

i. Pilate had seen wild revolutionaries who claimed to be kings. "Speaking of the anarchy in Judea which followed Herod's death in 4 BC, Josephus says: 'Any one might make himself king by putting himself at the head of a band of rebels whom he fell in with.'" (Bruce)

ii. He asked this question because Jesus didn't *look* like a revolutionary or a criminal. These were the only types who would be foolish enough to claim to be the King of the Jews in the face of Roman domination. Pilate had seen these kinds of men before, and knew Jesus was not like them.

iii. "Pilate had expected to meet a sullen or belligerent rebel and met instead the calm majesty of confident superiority. He could not reconcile the character of the prisoner with the charge brought against him." (Tenney)

c. **Are you speaking for yourself**: Jesus wanted to know if Pilate really wanted to know or if he asked the question on behalf of those who already condemned Jesus. The answer could be different depending on where his question came from.

i. "If Pilate asked it of himself, the question would have meant, 'Art thou a political King, conspiring against Caesar'! If he had asked it of Caiaphas' prompting, it would have meant, 'Art Thou the Messianic King of Israel?' The answer to the first question would have been 'No'. The answer to the second question, 'Yes.'" (Pilcher, cited in Morris)

d. **What have You done**: Pilate said that he, as a Roman, had no interest in Jewish spiritual or social ideas. Pilate simply understood that if the religious leaders wanted Jesus dead, He must have **done** something wrong and he wanted to find out what that was.

i. Jesus could have given a wonderful answer to the question, **what have You done?**

- He was without sin, never doing wrong against God or man.

- He healed the sick, gave sight to the blind, calmed the storm, walked on the water, fed the multitude, defeated demons, and raised the dead.

- He taught the truth so clearly and powerfully that it astonished His listeners.

- He fearlessly confronted corruption.

- He poured His life into a few men who were destined, in God's plan, to turn the world upside down (or right side up).

- He did not come to be served, but to serve - and to give His life a ransom for many.

ii. "Strange to ask the Prisoner what He had done! It had been well for Pilate if he had held fast by that question, and based his judgment resolutely on its answer!" (Maclaren)

4. (36) Jesus explains His kingdom to Pilate.

Jesus answered, "My kingdom is not of this world. If My kingdom were of this world, My servants would fight, so that I should not be delivered to the Jews; but now My kingdom is not from here."

a. **My kingdom is not of this world**: Jesus plainly told Pilate that He *was* a king and could say, **My kingdom**. He also plainly told Pilate that His kingdom *was not* a rival political kingdom; it was and **is not of this world**.

- In contrast to the kingdoms of this world, the kingdom of Jesus *originates* in heaven (**My kingdom is not of this world**).

- In contrast to the kingdoms of this world, the kingdom of Jesus has *peace* for its foundation (**If My kingdom were of this world, My servants would fight**).

    i. "There is no denial that His Kingdom is *over* this world; but that it is to be established by this world's power." (Alford)

b. **My kingdom is not from here**: We may imagine that Pilate was relieved and satisfied to hear that the kingdom of Jesus was **not from here**. Pilate may have concluded that Rome therefore had nothing to fear from Jesus and His kingdom.

    i. Romans *thought* they knew about kingdoms and their might; that armies, navies, swords, and battles measured the strength of kingdoms. What Jesus knew was that His kingdom - though **not of this world** - was mightier than Rome and would continue to expand and influence when Rome passed away.

    ii. **My kingdom is not from here**: Augustine observed from this verse that earthly kingdoms are based upon force, pride, the love of human praise, the desire for domination, and self interest - all displayed by Pilate and the Roman Empire.

    iii. The heavenly kingdom, exemplified by Jesus and the cross, is based on love, sacrifice, humility, and righteousness - and is *to the Jews a stumbling block, and to the Gentiles foolishness* (1 Corinthians 1:23).

    iv. "The obvious inference from his words would be that he came in to the world from another realm, that whoever did not listen to him would not be characterized by truth, and that if Pilate really wanted to know what truth was, he would give Jesus his earnest attention." (Tenney)

5. (37-38) Jesus and Pilate discuss truth.

Pilate therefore said to Him, "Are You a king then?" Jesus answered, "You say *rightly* that I am a king. For this cause I was born, and for this cause I have come into the world, that I should bear witness to the truth. Everyone who is of the truth hears My voice." Pilate said to Him, "What is truth?" And when he had said this, he went out again to the Jews, and said to them, "I find no fault in Him at all."

a. **Are You a king then**: This was the statement that interested Pilate. He didn't mind religious leaders among the Jews, even crazy ones, as long as they kept the peace and did not challenge the rule of Rome. A rival **king** might challenge, and Pilate wanted to investigate this.

i. "The word **thou**, in Pilate's question, is emphatic and sarcastic. 'Art THOU, thus captured, bound, standing here as a criminal in peril of thy life, A KING?'" (Alford)

ii. "The question could scarcely have been more sarcastic. Pilate, in his heart, despised the Jews as such, but here was poor Jew, persecuted by his own people, helpless and friendless; it sounded like mockery to talk of a kingdom in connection with him." (Spurgeon)

b. **You say rightly that I am a king**: Jesus did not deny that He was a **king**. He insisted that He was **born** a king, and to be a different kind of King. He came to be a King of Truth, that He **should bear witness to the truth**.

i. "He made an appeal to Pilate, not for acquittal or mercy, but for recognition of truth." (Tenney)

ii. "It is by *truth* alone that I influence the minds and govern the manners of my subjects." (Clarke)

c. **For this cause I was born, and for this cause I have come into the world**: Decades after this, Paul urged young Timothy with these words: *Christ Jesus who witnessed the good confession before Pontius Pilate* (1 Timothy 6:13). The *good confession* of Jesus was that He was a king, His kingdom came from heaven, and that it was a kingdom of eternal truth in contrast to earthly power.

i. **For this cause I was born, and for this cause I have come into the world**: "'I,' is both times emphatic, and majestically set against the preceding scornful **thou** of Pilate." (Alford)

ii. "Our Lord implies that He was *born* a King, and that He was born with a definite purpose. The words are a pregnant proof of an Incarnation of the Son of God." (Alford)

iii. "Both statements can be paralleled elsewhere, but the combination us unusual, and in such a situation, unexpected." (Morris)

d. **What is truth**: Pilate's cynical question showed he thought Jesus claim to be a King of Truth was foolish. Probably, Pilate did not mean that there was no truth, but that there was no **truth** in the kind of spiritual kingdom Jesus represented. For Pilate, soldiers and armies were truth, Rome was truth, Caesar was truth, and political power was truth.

i. "Pilate knew his business, and to discuss the nature of truth formed no part of it. So he broke off the interrogation with the curt dismissal." (Bruce)

ii. "It was a way of dismissing the subject. Pilate has learned what he wants to know. Jesus is no revolutionary. He represents no danger to the state. He may be safely released, and indeed He ought in common justice to be released." (Morris)

iii. **What is truth**: Many in our day ask Pilate's question, but from a different perspective. Noting that many things are true only on the basis of personal preference or perspective, they think *all* truth is personal, individual. They think there is no *true truth* about God; there is only *my truth* and *your truth* and one is as good as the other. Though this thinking is strong in our day, it denies the One who said: **For this cause I was born, and for this cause I have come into the world, that I should bear witness to the truth**.

e. **I find no fault in Him at all**: Pilate spoke to the religious leaders who wanted Jesus dead and clearly told them that Jesus was *not guilty*. Pilate went far beyond saying that Jesus was not guilty of a crime worthy of death; he found **no fault in Him at all**. Pilate *knew* Jesus was innocent.

6. (39-40) Pilate tries to release Jesus, but the crowd cries for Barabbas.

"But you have a custom that I should release someone to you at the Passover. Do you therefore want me to release to you the King of the Jews?" Then they all cried again, saying, "Not this Man, but Barabbas!" Now Barabbas was a robber.

a. **You have a custom that I should release someone to you at the Passover**: Judging there was something different – and innocent – about Jesus, Pilate hoped this custom of releasing a prisoner might help deliver this Man whom Pilate knew was innocent.

i. "Of which we have no information elsewhere; although Josephus (*Antiquities* 20.9,3) relates that at a passover Albinus released some robbers." (Dods)

ii. "Nothing relative to the origin or reason of this custom is known. Commentators have swam in an ocean of conjecture on this point. They have lost their labour, and made nothing out." (Clarke)

b. **Do you therefore want me to release to you the King of the Jews**: Pilate phrased the question this way to appeal to the Jewish crowd. He thought they would *want* a Man named as their own **King** to be spared death by crucifixion.

i. "Like all weak men, he was not easy in his conscience, and made a futile attempt to get the right thing done, yet not suffer for doing it." (Maclaren)

c. **Not this Man, but Barabbas**: The crowd rejected Jesus and chose **Barabbas** instead. Pilate hoped they would spare Jesus, but the crowd instead condemned Him.

i. Matthew 27:20 says that this was not a spontaneous response from the crowd, but one deliberately promoted by the religious leaders: *But the chief priests and elders persuaded the multitudes that they should ask for Barabbas and destroy Jesus* (also Mark 15:11).

ii. When the crowd chose Barabbas instead of Jesus, it reflected the fallen nature of all humanity. The name **Barabbas** sounds very much like *son of the father*. They chose a false, violent *son of the father* instead of the true Son of the Father. This prefigures the future embrace of the ultimate Barabbas - the one popularly called the Antichrist.

iii. People today still reject Jesus and choose another. Their Barabbas might be lust, it might be intoxication, it might be self and the comforts of life. "This mad choice is every day made, while men prefer the lusts of their flesh before the lives of their souls." (Trapp)

d. **Barabbas was a robber**: Mark 15:7 tells us he was one of several *insurrectionists*, who had *committed murder in the insurrection*. The Romans would have thought of Barabbas as a terrorist and many Jews would think of him as a freedom fighter.

i. "It would seem that Barabbas was a member of the local resistance movement. Because of his opposition to the Romans he would be a hero to many of the Jews." (Morris)

ii. "He uses the term almost certainly to denote (as Josephus habitually does) a Zealot insurgent. In Mark 15:27 (cf. Matthew 27:38) the same word is used of the two men who were crucified along with Jesus." (Bruce)

iii. "Quite likely Barabbas was a guerrilla 'resistance fighter' who had been captured by the Romans and was being held for execution." (Tenney)

iv. Barabbas was accused of at least three crimes: Theft (John 18:40), insurrection (Mark 15:7), and murder (Mark 15:7). "You and I may fairly take our stand by the side of Barabbas. We have robbed God of his glory; we have been seditious traitors against the government of heaven: if he who hateth his brother be a murderer, we also have been guilty of that sin." (Spurgeon)

v. If anyone knew what it meant that Jesus died in his place, it was **Barabbas**. He was a terrorist and a murderer, yet he was set free while Jesus was crucified. The cross Jesus hung upon was probably originally intended for Barabbas.

John 19 - Jesus Is Crucified

A. Jesus is condemned to crucifixion.

1. (1-4) Pilate hopes to satisfy the mob by having Jesus whipped and mocked.

So then Pilate took Jesus and scourged *Him*. And the soldiers twisted a crown of thorns and put *it* on His head, and they put on Him a purple robe. Then they said, "Hail, King of the Jews!" And they struck Him with their hands. Pilate then went out again, and said to them, "Behold, I am bringing Him out to you, that you may know that I find no fault in Him."

a. **So then Pilate took Jesus and scourged Him**: Previously Pilate said of Jesus, *I find no fault in Him at all* (John 18:38), yet he commanded this severe, brutal punishment for a Man he knew was innocent. It has been suggested that Pilate wanted to *help* Jesus, hoping the mob would be satisfied with the scourging.

b. **Scourged Him**: Pilate gave the order, so Jesus was **scourged** according to Roman practice. The blows came from a whip with many leather strands, each having sharp pieces of bone or metal at the ends. It reduced the back to raw flesh, and it was not unusual for a criminal to die from a scourging, even before crucifixion.

i. Scourging had three purposes. It was used to punish prisoners, and to gain confessions of crimes from prisoners. Also, in cases of crucifixion scourging was used to weaken the victim so he would die more quickly on the cross. Pilate hoped that this punishment of his prisoner would satisfy the crowd. "Neither, then, as part of the capital punishment, nor in order to elicit the truth; but in the ill-judged hope that this minor punishment might satisfy the Jews, Pilate ordered the scourging." (Dods)

ii. "The victim of this severe punishment was bound in a stooping attitude to a low column and beaten with rods or scourged with whips, the thongs of which were weighted with lead, and studded with sharp-pointed pieces of bone, so that frightful laceration followed each stroke." (Dods)

iii. "It literally tore a man's back into strips. Few remained conscious throughout the ordeal; some died; and many went raving mad." (Barclay)

iv. "It is a further example of the reserve of the Gospels that they use but one word to describe this piece of frightfulness. There is no attempt to play on our emotions." (Morris)

c. **The soldiers twisted a crown of thorns and put it on His head, and they put on Him a purple robe. Then they said, "Hail, King of the Jews!"**: Everything about this was intended to humiliate Jesus. The Jewish rulers had already mocked Jesus as the Messiah (Matthew 26:67-68). Now the Roman powers mocked him as king.

- **The soldiers twisted a crown of thorns**: Kings wear crowns, but not crowns of torture. The specific thorn-bushes of this region have long, hard, sharp thorns. This was a crown that cut, pierced, and bloodied the head of the King who wore it.

- **Put on Him a purple robe**: Kings and rulers often wore **purple**, because the dyes to make fabrics that color were expensive. The **purple robe** was intended as cruel irony.

- **"Hail, King of the Jews!"** Kings are greeted with royal titles, so in their spite they mocked Jesus with this title. It was meant to humiliate Jesus, but also the **Jews** - saying, "This is the best King they can bring forth."

- The soldiers also **struck Him with their hands**, beating and mocking Jesus simply to gratify cruelty and wickedness.

- The Gospel of Matthew adds that Jesus was stripped, given a reed as mocking royal scepter, that the soldiers bowed their knee before Jesus, offering mocking homage and honor to Him, that they spat on Jesus.

i. We can also decide to do the opposite of what these did to Jesus. "Oh, that we were half as inventive in devising honor for our King as these soldiers were in planning his dishonor! Let us offer to Christ the real homage that these men pretended to offer him." (Spurgeon)

d. **That you may know that I find no fault in Him**: Pilate repeated the statement first recorded at John 18:38, declaring Jesus innocent of any wrongdoing. As a judge Pilate had both reason and responsibility to set Jesus free with no punishment instead of the humiliation and brutality that He endured.

i. "Pilate made *five* several attempts to release our Lord; as we may learn from Luke 23:4, 15, 20, 22; John 19:4, 12, 13." (Clarke)

2. (5-6) Pilate presents Jesus to the crowd.

Then Jesus came out, wearing the crown of thorns and the purple robe. And *Pilate* said to them, "Behold the Man!" Therefore, when the chief priests and officers saw Him, they cried out, saying, "Crucify *Him*, crucify *Him!*" Pilate said to them, "You take Him and crucify *Him*, for I find no fault in Him."

a. **Jesus came out, wearing the crown of thorns and the purple robe**: Pilate presented Jesus to the crowd as One beaten and mocked, with blood, sweat, and spit all over His body. Perhaps Pilate hoped the sad sight would make the crowd feel sorry for Jesus.

i. "This crown He continued to wear to the end: both Origen and Tertullian, two of the earliest Fathers of the Church of east and west, assert that He was crucified with it on His head." (Trench)

ii. "Many a crown has been secured by blood, and so is this, but it is his own blood; many a throne has been established by suffering, and so is this, but he himself bears the pain." (Spurgeon)

b. **Behold the Man**: Pilate invited the crowd to *look at this suffering One*, and to look with careful consideration (**behold**). There is a sense in which Pilate spoke for God here, who invites all humanity to **behold the Man**, to see the Man of men, the Perfect Man, the tested and approved Ideal of all humanity.

i. "*The man* is contemptuous. Pilate is saying in effect 'Here he is - the poor fellow. Can you really think that such a caricature of a king is really a danger either to Israel or Rome?'" (Tasker)

ii. "If ye be men, take pity upon a man so miserably misused; and if ye be good men, let him go who is innocent." (Trapp)

iii. Pilate though he might save Jesus through humiliating Him. Some modern people also do that; they think that by saying Jesus is not God or that He wasn't right about everything they can "save" Jesus, keeping Him relevant to a modern, progressive, scientific age. Such attempts are as wrong as what Pilate did.

iv. "Whatever Pilate's intention, the vision of Jesus failed to arouse in the hearts of the multitude any pity for Him, and the clamored for His death." (Morgan)

c. **When the chief priests and officers saw Him**: We aren't told the immediate reaction of the crowd; perhaps they did feel a moment of sympathy for this remarkable, strong man in such circumstances. Whatever the crowd felt, the religious leaders immediately screamed "**Crucify Him, crucify Him!**" This was pure hatred, man's hatred of God.

i. "Some pity may have stirred in the crowd, but the priests and their immediate dependents silenced it by their yell of fresh hate at the sight of the prisoner." (Maclaren)

ii. "So afterwards the primitive persecutors cried out, *Ad bestias, ad bestias, Christianos ad leones,* To the beasts, to the beasts, Christians, to the lions, imputing the cause of all public calamities to them, as Tertullian testifieth." (Trapp)

d. **You take Him and crucify Him, for I find no fault in Him**: For the third time, Pilate pronounced Jesus innocent of all charges.

i. "Pilate must have realized that the Sanhedrin could not execute the sentence. His apparent relegation of Jesus to them was an act of sarcasm." (Tenney)

3. (7-11) Pilate learns of the charge against Jesus.

The Jews answered him, "We have a law, and according to our law He ought to die, because He made Himself the Son of God." Therefore, when Pilate heard that saying, he was the more afraid, and went again into the Praetorium, and said to Jesus, "Where are You from?" But Jesus gave him no answer.

a. **Because He made Himself the Son of God**: In John's account, with this the religious leaders showed their true charge against Jesus. They wanted Him dead not because He claimed to be King of the Jews, but because He claimed to be God, the unique **Son of God**.

i. "It is certain that the Jews understood this in a very peculiar sense. When Christ called himself *the Son of God*, they understood it to imply positive *equality* to the Supreme Being." (Clarke)

b. **He was the more afraid**: Pilate was not *angry* or *amused* when he learned that Jesus **made Himself the Son of God**, he was **more afraid** of Jesus than ever. Pilate saw something in Jesus - even beaten, bloodied, and spat upon - that made him think that it could be true that the Man before him was more than a man.

i. "It may be that the comparative *the more afraid* should be given a superlative force, such as it often has in New Testament Greek, and rendered 'exceedingly afraid'." (Tasker)

ii. "He can scarcely be called a religious man, but the news that his prisoner had made divine claims scared the governor...every Roman or that day knew of stories of the gods or their offspring appearing in human guise." (Morris)

c. **Where are You from**: Pilate wanted Jesus to defend Himself and give Pilate *more* reasons to let an innocent Man free. He wanted Jesus to explain what made Him different than the dozens of other prisoners Pilate had judged. Yet Jesus already told Pilate that He was King of a kingdom *not of this world* (John 18:36); Jesus *already* said where He was from. Therefore, **Jesus gave him no answer**.

i. Though he already had the answer, one could say Pilate asked the right question. "His question is almost the most pertinent question that can be asked about Him, for to know where Jesus comes from is to know the most important thing about Him." (Tasker)

4. (10-11) Pilate and Jesus speak about power.

Then Pilate said to Him, "Are You not speaking to me? Do You not know that I have power to crucify You, and power to release You?" Jesus answered, "You could have no power at all against Me unless it had been given you from above. Therefore the one who delivered Me to you has the greater sin."

a. **Are You not speaking to me**: Pilate couldn't believe that Jesus would not speak to defend Himself. He couldn't believe that Jesus would not beg for His life as many others had done. Pilate also couldn't believe that Jesus was not awed and intimidated by the representative of Rome who judged Him.

i. "*Me* is very emphatic in the Greek; it is the refusal of Jesus to speak to one who possesses such supreme human authority that amazes Pilate." (Tasker)

ii. The general silence of Jesus before His accusers and judges fulfilled the prophecy of Isaiah 53:7: *And as a sheep before its shearers is silent, so He opened not His mouth.*

b. **Do You not know that I have power**: Pilate was amazed that Jesus was not intimidated by his **power** as judge to condemn and crucify. In his understanding of power, Pilate felt that he held the power position and was mystified that Jesus didn't see it.

i. Pilate thought he had power, but what he had was the power to do wrong, to do harm. He didn't have the power to do what was right. The right thing to do was to release an obviously innocent Man instead of sending Him to death, but Pilate was weak before the strength of the religious leaders and the crowd they commanded. To say, "I have power to do what the crowd wants me to do" is to say you have no power at all.

ii. The same man who claimed to have all power tried to wash his hands of the decision (Matthew 27:24) claiming, "I didn't really want to do this."

c. **You could have no power at all against Me unless it have been given you from above**: Jesus answered, explaining the true nature of power to Pilate. In the thinking of the Roman governor, *Rome* had the power. In reality, *God* held the power.

i. Jesus understood that Pilate had power; He simply insisted that this power was granted by God and not inherent in Pilate or Rome.

d. **The one who delivered Me to you has the greater sin**: Jesus didn't say Pilate was without **sin**; simply that the religious leaders were guilty of **greater sin**.

i. "*He that delivered me* could be a reference either to Judas or Caiaphas and the language of the evangelist seems to be deliberately vague." (Tasker)

ii. "The verb 'hand over' (Gk. *paradidomai*) has been used repeatedly in the earlier part of the narrative to denote Judas's act of betrayal." (Bruce)

5. (12-13) Pilate brings Jesus out for judgment.

From then on Pilate sought to release Him, but the Jews cried out, saying, "If you let this Man go, you are not Caesar's friend. Whoever makes himself a king speaks against Caesar." When Pilate therefore heard that saying, he brought Jesus out and sat down in the judgment seat in a place that is called *The* Pavement, but in Hebrew, Gabbatha.

a. **Pilate sought to release Him**: We sense panic in the Roman governor. The panic was greater when his wife told him to let the accused free because of a dream she had (Matthew 27:19-20). He knew this innocent Man, a Man not like any other prisoner he had seen before, *should* be set free - yet he felt the full force of the crowd and religious leaders demanding His crucifixion.

i. **From then on**: "Can be interpreted in either a temporal sense 'from that moment'; or inferentially, as in RSV, 'Upon this'. The latter is more probable. Pilate is flattered by what Jesus has said in verse 11 and in consequence tries still harder to release Him." (Tasker)

b. **If you let this Man go, you are not Caesar's friend**: By some accounts (such as Boice), Pilate was an unremarkable man who only had his position because he married the granddaughter of the emperor. Holding his position only by relationship, Pilate would be greatly concerned that the relationship was damaged. The religious leaders and the crowd knew Pilate's weak point and they pressed upon it.

i. "Humanly speaking, the mention of Caesar sealed Jesus' fate." (Morris)

ii. "The phrase 'a friend of Caesar' was more than a casual allusion to Roman patriotism. It usually denoted a supporter or associate of the emperor, a member of the important inner circle." (Tenney)

iii. "He wanted so much to be a friend of Caesar. But he was not Caesar's friend; he barely knew Caesar. And what is even more significant, Caesar was not *his* friend at all." (Boice)

c. **He brought Jesus out and sat down in the judgment seat**: Pilate was ready to deliver his final judgment, presenting Jesus both before the crowd and the **judgment seat**. In truth it was *Pontius Pilate* who was on judgment, not Jesus Himself.

i. **Gabbatha**: "That is, *an elevated place*; from *gabah, high, raised up*; and it is very likely that the judgment seat was considerably *elevated* in the court, and that the governor went up to it by steps; and perhaps these very steps were what was called *the Pavement*." (Clarke)

6. (14-16) The crowd rejects Jesus and Pilate sentences Him to death.

Now it was the Preparation Day of the Passover, and about the sixth hour. And he said to the Jews, "Behold your King!" But they cried out, "Away with *Him*, away with *Him*! Crucify Him!" Pilate said to them, "Shall I crucify your King?" The chief priests answered, "We have no king but Caesar!" Then he delivered Him to them to be crucified. So they took Jesus and led *Him* away.

a. **It was the Preparation Day of the Passover**: This again raises the difficult chronological questions previous mentioned at John 18:28. John's point is nevertheless clear: *the Lamb of God who takes away the sin of the world* (John 1:29) is ready for sacrifice at **Passover**.

i. **About the sixth hour**: This introduces a point of some controversy, because Mark states the crucifixion was at the *third hour* (Mark 15:25). Several attempts have been made to reconcile John 19:14 and Mark 15:25.

- Some think John and Mark used different reckonings of time. "Westcott gives good reasons for supposing that this evangelist, instead of reckoning hours from 6 a.m. to 6 p.m., and 6 p.m. to 6 a.m., as was the Jewish custom, reckoned them from midnight to noon, and noon to midnight - a practice which we know from the *Martyrdom of Polycarp* was in use in Asia Minor at the time that document was written, and which is still followed in the West today. On this reckoning, it was… about 6 a.m. when Pilate passed sentence on Jesus." (Tasker)

- Some think that John and Mark never intended exact markers of time. "The 'third hour' may denote nothing more firm than a time about the middle of the morning, while 'about the sixth hour' can well signify getting on towards noon. Late morning would suit both expressions unless there were some reason for thinking that either was being given with more than usual accuracy. No such reason exists here." (Morris)

- Some think the problem is with early errors by copyists of the text and John originally wrote *the third hour*. "We must certainly suppose, as did Eusebius, Theophylact, and Severus, that there has been some very early erratum in our copies; whether the interchange of 3 and 6, which when expressed in Greek numerical letters, are not unlike one another, or some other, cannot now be determined." (Alford)

b. **Behold your King**: Pilate offered this sacrificial Lamb before the people for their inspection. He may have meant to *mock* Jesus and the crowd, presenting a thorn-crowned, bloodied and beaten Man with a purple rag across His ripped-open back as their **King**. The crowd saw Jesus in all His misery and dignity and responded by screaming, **Away with Him, away with Him! Crucify Him!**

i. "The words **Behold your King** seem to have been spoken in irony to the Jews - in the same spirit in which afterwards the title was written over the cross." (Alford)

ii. **But they cried out**: "Probably the well-attested imperfect tense should be followed, giving the sense 'they kept shouting'. It was the persistence of the Jews in making a political issue of the case that was wearing Pilate out." (Tasker)

iii. There are times when people are angry enough with God and His goodness that they think or wish Him dead. It is far more common for people to simply want God to disappear; for people to wish **away with Him, away with Him!**

c. **We have no king but Caesar**: The crowd rejected Jesus and chose Barabbas, a revolutionary against Rome. In the crazy and contradictory manner common among crowds, they both chose the revolutionary and swore allegiance to **Caesar**.

i. "Driven by hate, they deliberately disown their Messianic hope, and repudiate their national glory. They who will not have Christ have to bow to a tyrant. Rebellion against Him brings slavery." (Maclaren)

d. **Then he delivered Him to be crucified**: It appeared that Jesus was on trial before Pilate, but in an even greater sense Pilate was on trial before Jesus. Pilate failed his test. In fear of the crowd he sent a Man he knew to be innocent to a tortured death. Thus the ancient creed notes, Jesus was *crucified under Pontius Pilate*.

i. "You may do today exactly what Pilate did. He is simply an example of a man who lacks decision of character, who does not possess the courage of his convictions, who tries to compromise with wrong, who disobeys conscience through fear of personal loss." (Erdman)

B. The crucifixion of Jesus of Nazareth.

1. (17-18) Jesus is crucified.

And He, bearing His cross, went out to a place called *the Place* of a Skull, which is called in Hebrew, Golgotha, where they crucified Him, and two others with Him, one on either side, and Jesus in the center.

a. **And He, bearing His cross**: According to Roman custom Jesus carried His cross from the place of sentencing to the place of crucifixion, **the Place of a Skull**. Before the Romans put a man on a cross, they put the cross on the man, forcing him to carry it in a public procession intended to draw attention to the condemned, his crime, and his fate.

i. "It was normally the cross-piece (*patibulum*), and not the complete gibbet, that the condemned man carried into the place of execution; the upright stakes were probably standing there already." (Bruce)

ii. "Since Tertullian (*adv. Jud.*, 10) a type of this has been found in Isaac's carrying the wood for the sacrifice." (Dods)

b. **They crucified Him**: The Persians invented crucifixion, but one could say that the Romans perfected it and made it an institution. It was the form of execution reserved for the worst criminals and the lowest classes.

Crucifixion was designed to make the victim die publically, slowly, with great pain and humiliation. This was the form of death God ordained for Jesus to die, and the death that He submitted to in the will of God.

i. Crucifixion was so awful and degrading that polite Romans wouldn't talk about it in public. The Roman statesman Cicero said of crucifixion: "It is a crime to bind a Roman citizen; to scourge him is an act of wickedness; to execute him is almost murder: What shall I say of crucifying him? An act so abominable it is impossible to find any word adequately to express." The Roman historian Tacitus called crucifixion "A torture fit only for slaves."

ii. The Gospel writers do not give a detailed explanation of crucifixion. There were several reasons for this.

- Their original readers were familiar with the practice, so they needed no explanation.

- The Gospel writers take care to not use language or descriptions that could manipulate the emotions; they simply tell the story.

- The greater suffering of Jesus was inward and spiritual; even greater than His outward and physical suffering.

iii. Archaeologists discovered in 1968 the remains of a man crucified in Jesus' era. The study of the remains revealed that the victim was nailed to the cross in a sitting position, both legs over sideways, with the nail penetrating the sides of both feet just below the heel. The arms were stretched out, each stabbed by a nail in the forearm. Dr. Nico Hass, Hebrew University anatomy professor described it as "a compulsive position, a difficult and unnatural posture," meant to increase the agony of the sufferer. (Tenney and others)

iv. "There was a horn-like projection (the *sedile*), which the crucified man straddled. This took some of the weight of the body and prevented the flesh from tearing from the nails." (Morris)

v. According to Dr. William Edwards in the *Journal of the American Medical Association*, death from crucifixion could come from many sources: acute shock from blood loss, being too exhausted to breathe any longer, dehydration, stress-induced heart attack, or congestive heart failure leading to a cardiac rupture. If the victim did not die quickly enough, the legs were broken, and the victim was soon unable to breathe and died of suffocation.

c. **And two others with Him, one on either side, and Jesus in the center:** There were three scheduled for crucifixion on that day, the **two others** and

Barabbas. Jesus took the place of Barabbas. This was another way that Jesus was identified with sinners in His death.

> i. "The whole of humanity was represented there: the sinless Saviour, the saved penitent, the condemned impenitent." (Plummer, cited in Dods)

d. **And Jesus in the center**: This was literally true; of the three crosses, Jesus was in the middle. Yet as a concept, there are many ways that it could be said that it was **Jesus in the center**.

- *Jesus was centered among humanity.* Jesus never distanced Himself from common men, and freely interacted with those thought to be great men. From His incarnation, through His whole life, He lived as one of us. Jesus died among men and women, Jews and Gentiles, rich and poor, high class and no class, the educated and the uneducated, the religious and the secular, the guilty and the innocent, the weepers and the mockers, those deeply moved and those indifferent, those who hated Him and those who loved Him.

- *Jesus was centered among sinful men.* His enemies thought this would make His sufferings worse. They thought it would bother Him more to see the low company He died with. In His death the righteously religious mocked Him and His disciples forsook Him; yet Jesus was centered among sinners to the end.

- *Jesus was centered among confusion.* Matthew 27:46-49 says tells us that when Jesus cried out in agony to His Father, the people around Him didn't understand and some even thought it kind of amusing.

- *Jesus was centered between believing and rejecting.* Matthew 27:44 told us that both robbers mocked Him, but Luke 23:39-41 tells us of a change in one of the criminals. The last human voice testifying to Jesus was a criminal converted right before his death. The disciples were gone and all Jesus healed and taught were nowhere to be found. The religious leaders mocked Him and spit upon Him, and even the faithful women were silenced by their grief. Yet there was one lone human voice that told the truth about Jesus when all others were silent.

- *Jesus was centered between saved and perishing.* The thief on the cross was the last companion of Jesus on this earth before His death - and Jesus brought Him to salvation. Not with a sermon, but with every sermon He had already preached, every righteous deed He had done before. This was perhaps the only comfort to Jesus on the cross. Still, one thief was saved, but one was lost, and Jesus was in the center between them. To pass between one side and the other, *you must go through Jesus.*

- *Jesus was centered between God and man.* Jesus on the cross took all the punishment our sin deserved. At the cross Jesus was both the priest and the offering.

- *Jesus was centered in all God's history and work.* We do not look at Jesus in the center with pity, as if we should all feel sorry for poor Jesus. He was the winner at the cross. This was the greatest victory of all time.

2. (19-22) Pilate's public description of Jesus and His supposed crime.

Now Pilate wrote a title and put *it* on the cross. And the writing was: Jesus of Nazareth, the King of the Jews. Then many of the Jews read this title, for the place where Jesus was crucified was near the city; and it was written in Hebrew, Greek, *and* Latin. Therefore the chief priests of the Jews said to Pilate, "Do not write, 'The King of the Jews,' but, 'He said, "I am the King of the Jews."'" Pilate answered, "What I have written, I have written."

a. **Now Pilate wrote a title and put it on the cross**: This was according to Roman custom. The one to be crucified had his crime written out and the title hung around his neck as he carried his cross to the place of death. Then the **title** was placed at the top of the cross, so all would know the reason for the crucifixion.

   i. "It was customary for the condemned person to wear a placard giving his name and the nature of his crime." (Tenney)

   ii. "A board whitened with gypsum such as were commonly used for public notices." (Dods)

b. **The writing was: Jesus of Nazareth, the King of the Jews**: Pilate wrote the *name* of Jesus, the same name by which He was identified and arrested in the Garden of Gethsemane (John 18:5). He also wrote what was said to be the *crime* of Jesus, (at least in the original charge brought to him) that He claimed to be **King of the Jews** (John 18:33-34).

   i. Even in His death, Jesus was identified with humble and obscure **Nazareth**. Even in His death, Jesus was recognized as a **King**. Kings of this world take their throne through others dying. Jesus was proclaimed as King to the whole world through His own death.

   ii. The title was also a proper justification of the sinless nature of Jesus. On either side were criminals with descriptions of their crimes; on the cross of Jesus it simply described who He was, which was no crime at all *because it was true.*

c. **Many of the Jews read this title, for the place where Jesus was crucified was near the city**: The Romans wanted crucifixion to be a public event. They wanted **many** to see the wretched victim, read of their crime, and be warned. This also confirms that Jesus was crucified outside the walls of the city (Hebrews 13:12), but close to the city and likely close to an often-used road.

d. **It was written in Hebrew, Greek, and Latin**: Pilate wanted this statement regarding Jesus to be as public as possible. This is also an unknowing prophecy of how the message of Jesus Christ and Him crucified and reigning as King would be published to every nation and language, that it was from the beginning intended as a global message.

i. "Aramaic, for the local inhabitants; Latin, for the officials; Greek, the lingua franca of the eastern Mediterranean world." (Tenney)

ii. "In Hebrew, for the Jews who gloried in the law; in Greek, for the Grecians who gloried in wisdom; in Latin, for the Romans who most gloried in dominion and power." (Trapp)

iii. Ancients such as the Romans often used abbreviations, so it may be difficult to recreate the exact letters. Nevertheless, Adam Clarke renders it so:

- In Hebrew, ישוע נצריא מלכא דיהודריא
- In Greek, ιησους ο ναζωρεος ο βασιλευς των ιουδαιων
- In Latin, *iehsus nazarenus rex iudaeorum*

e. **Do not write, "The King of the Jews," but, "He said, 'I am the King of the Jews'"**: The religious leaders objected to Pilate's title. They felt it was *false*, because they did not believe that Jesus was **the King of the Jews**. They also believed it was *demeaning*, because it showed Rome's power to humiliate and torture even the "**King of the Jews**."

f. **What I have written, I have written**: Pilate finally found the courage to stand up to the Jewish rulers, but on a relatively unimportant matter. One may say that despite himself, Pilate honored the King of Truth (John 18:37) with this true description of who He was, in both His humility and His glory.

i. "That is, I will not alter what I have written. The Roman laws forbad the sentence to be altered when once pronounced; and as this inscription was considered as the *sentence* pronounced against our Lord, therefore, it could not be changed." (Clarke)

3. (23-24) Soldiers divide Jesus' clothing in fulfillment of prophecy.

Then the soldiers, when they had crucified Jesus, took His garments and made four parts, to each soldier a part, and also the tunic. Now the tunic was without seam, woven from the top in one piece. They said therefore among themselves, "Let us not tear it, but cast lots for it, whose it shall be," that the Scripture might be fulfilled which says:

"They divided My garments among them,
And for My clothing they cast lots."

Therefore the soldiers did these things.

a. **Then the soldiers**: A Roman crucifixion was supervised by soldiers, both to keep order and to make sure the condemned actually died.

b. **Took His garments**: On the cross, Jesus retained no material possessions. Even the clothes on his back were taken and His tunic was awarded by a bit of petty gambling.

> i. "Men were ordinarily crucified naked (Artemidorus II. 61). Jewish sensitivities, however, dictated that men ought not to be publicly executed completely naked, and men condemned to stoning were permitted a loin-cloth (M. *Sanhedrin* VI. 3). Whether the Romans were considerate of Jewish feelings in this matter is unknown." (Lane, commentary on Luke)

> ii. "Apuleius has the comparison 'naked as a new-born babe or as the crucified.'" (Dods)

> iii. This shows that Jesus came all the way down the ladder to accomplish our salvation. He let go of everything - even His last bit of clothing - becoming completely poor for us that we could become completely rich in Him. 2 Corinthians 8:9 says it like this: *For you know the grace of our Lord Jesus Christ, that though He was rich, yet for your sakes He became poor, that you through His poverty might become rich.*

c. **The tunic was without seam, woven from the top in one piece**: The main garment Jesus wore (**the tunic**) was made well enough that it was better to not tear it into **four parts**, as each of the four soldiers had already received one of His other garments.

> i. Jesus' seamless tunic reminds us of His role as our great High Priest, because Exodus 28:31-32 tells us that the High Priest wore a seamless garment.

d. **Let us not tear it, but cast lots for it, whose it shall be**: The soldiers did this in an unknowing fulfillment of the prophecy of Psalm 22:18. As the Son of God died for the sins of the world men carelessly laughed and played games at His feet.

4. (25-27) Jesus entrusts His mother into John's care.

Now there stood by the cross of Jesus His mother, and His mother's sister, Mary the *wife* of Clopas, and Mary Magdalene. When Jesus therefore saw His mother, and the disciple whom He loved standing by, He said to His mother, "Woman, behold your son!" Then He said to the disciple, "Behold your mother!" And from that hour that disciple took her to his own *home*.

a. **There stood by the cross of Jesus His mother**: It is difficult to comprehend the agony of Mary as she saw her Son crucified. She was witness to the pain, humiliation, shame, suffering, and death of her Son.

> i. As Mary and Joseph brought their newborn son Jesus to the temple for dedication, a godly man named Simeon saw Jesus, took Him in his arms, and blessed the baby Jesus. Yet he also said this to Mary: *Yes, a sword will pierce through your own soul also* (Luke 2:35). Mary experienced this throughout the ministry of her Son as He was rejected, opposed, slandered, and plotted against. Yet this was the ultimate fulfillment of that solemn promise. Of all those who looked upon Jesus at the cross, none suffered as Mary did.

b. **His mother's sister, Mary the *wife* of Clopas, and Mary Magdalene**: These faithful women were there with Jesus through His agony on the cross, to honor Him and to support His mother Mary. **Mary the wife of Clopas** and **Mary Magdalene** were also among those who first discovered the empty tomb, evidence of the resurrection of Jesus.

> i. "It is probable that 'his mother's sister' here is to be equated with Salome (Mark 15:40), and that she was 'the mother of the sons of Zebedee' (Matthew 27:56), who was standing at a distance with the other women when Jesus died." (Morris)

c. **The disciple whom He loved standing by**: This was the author John's humble way to refer to himself in the story, as he does four times in his Gospel (John 13:23, 19:26, 21:7, 21:20). John told us that he was at Jesus' crucifixion and saw these things with his own eyes (John 19:35).

d. **He said to His mother, "Woman, behold your son"**: Jesus consciously cared for His mother to the end, showing that even on the cross His attention was directed to others and not upon Himself. If there was ever a moment when Jesus deserved to be *self*-focused, this was it; yet He remained *others-centered* to the end.

i. Clarke on **Woman, behold your son**: "It conveys no idea of *disrespect*, nor of unconcern, as has been commonly supposed. In the way of compellation, *man*! and *woman*! were titles of as much respect among the Hebrews as *sir*! and *madam*! are among us." (Clarke)

ii. Clarke also suggested that Jesus did not call her *mother* from the cross because the sound of that name in those circumstances would only add to her agony.

iii. "There was no specific direction given to John to entertain Mary. It was quite enough for the Lord to call his attention to her by saying 'Behold thy mother.' How I wish we were always in such a state of heart that we did not need specific precepts, a hint would suffice." (Spurgeon)

e. **From that hour that disciple took her to his own home**: John and Mary each obeyed this solemn command of Jesus from the cross, though it was a remarkable thing that Jesus commanded. Mary had other children born after Jesus, and there are references to both the half brothers and sisters of Jesus (Matthew 12:46-47, 13:55-56, John 2:12 and 7:3-10). Despite this, Jesus left the care of His mother Mary to John the disciple and apostle.

• Perhaps Jesus did this to emphasize that our relationships in Him and in the Kingdom are even more important than those by blood.

• Perhaps Jesus did this to honor the one disciple (we know of) who was courageous enough to stand with Jesus and be present at the crucifixion.

• Perhaps Jesus did this because His siblings did not follow Him as disciples during His earthly ministry and did not yet believe on Him, and Jesus wanted to leave His mother with a believer.

• Perhaps Jesus did this knowing that John was the only disciple who would die a natural death and would outlive even the siblings of Jesus.

• Perhaps Jesus did this out of simple wisdom and foresight.

i. **Behold your mother!** Significantly, Jesus did not need to tell John, "Take care of My mother." All Jesus needed to do was describe *the* new *relationship* and He knew the rest would properly follow. In the same way, there are many commands for a holy life that Jesus need not specifically give to us; if the relationship is ordered right, the conduct will flow from it.

ii. "There was no specific direction given to John to entertain Mary. It was quite enough for the Lord to call his attention to her by saying 'Behold thy mother.' How I wish we were always in such a state of heart that we did not need specific precepts, a hint would suffice." (Spurgeon)

5. (28-30) Jesus' great proclamation and death.

After this, Jesus, knowing that all things were now accomplished, that the Scripture might be fulfilled, said, "I thirst!" Now a vessel full of sour wine was sitting there; and they filled a sponge with sour wine, put *it* on hyssop, and put *it* to His mouth. So when Jesus had received the sour wine, He said, "It is finished!" And bowing His head, He gave up His spirit.

a. **Knowing that all things were now accomplished**: Jesus knew that His great work, His life and death work on the cross was fulfilled. He then made preparation to yield His life and die, having finished the work.

- There was a time *before* all things were accomplished (Luke 12:50).

- There was a time *when* all things were accomplished, when Jesus actually became the target of God's wrath and judgment of sin, when He *who knew no sin* became *sin for us, that we might become the righteousness of God in Him* (2 Corinthians 5:21).

- There was a time *after* all things **were now accomplished** and Jesus successfully offered Himself as a substitute sin offering for humanity.

b. **I thirst**: Jesus didn't accept a pain-numbing drink at the beginning of His ordeal (Mark 15:23), but now He accepted a taste of greatly diluted wine, to wet parched lips and a dry throat so He could make one final announcement to the world with a clear, loud voice.

i. "Thirst is a common-place misery, such as may happen to peasants or beggars; it is a real pain, and not a thing of a fancy or a nightmare of dreamland. Thirst is no royal grief, but an evil of universal manhood; Jesus is brother to the poorest and most humble of our race." (Spurgeon)

ii. "Appetite was the door of sin, and therefore in that point our Lord was put to pain. With 'I thirst' the evil is destroyed and receives its expiation." (Spurgeon)

iii. **A vessel full of sour wine was sitting there**: "The mention of the vessel betrays the eye-witness." (Dods)

iv. **Sour wine**: "It is, of course, not to be confused with the drugged wine, the 'wine mingled with myrrh' of Mark 15:23, which Jesus refused, but was the wine take to the cross by the soldiers for their own refreshment during what normally was a long time of waiting." (Tasker)

v. **Put it on hyssop**: "The very mention of *hyssop* would take the thoughts of any Jew back to the saving blood of the Passover lamb." (Barclay)

vi. We can connect **all things were now accomplished** with the words **I thirst**. When Jesus said **I thirst**, the worst was over - the price had been paid and He was ready to announce it. When the sinner says "I thirst" the worst is over, because if they bring their thirsty soul to Jesus He will satisfy.

c. **It is finished!** Jesus' final word (*tetelestai* in the ancient Greek) was the cry of a winner. Jesus had finished the eternal purpose of the cross. It stands today as a finished work, the foundation of all Christian peace and faith, paying in full the debt we righteously owed to God and making peace between God and man.

i. A single word can change everything. "Not guilty" in a court of law changes everything. "Fair" on the playing field changes everything. When a woman says "Yes" to a marriage proposal it changes everything. "Goodbye" can change everything. Yet, there has never been a single-word said that has impacted history than what Jesus said in John 19:30.

ii. At some point before He died, before the veil was torn in two, before He cried out **it is finished**, an awesome spiritual transaction took place. God the Father laid upon God the Son all the guilt and wrath our sin deserved, and He bore it in Himself perfectly, totally satisfying the wrath of God for us.

iii. "It was a Conqueror's cry; it was uttered with a loud voice. There is nothing of anguish about it, there is no wailing in it. It is the cry of One who has completed a tremendous labor." (Spurgeon)

iv. "Jesus died with the cry of the Victor on His lips. This is not the moan of the defeated, nor the sigh of patient resignation. It is the triumphant recognition that He has now fully accomplished the work that He came to do." (Morris)

v. "The verb τελεω (*teleo*, 'to finish') was used in first and second centuries in the sense of 'fulfilling' or 'paying' a debt and often appeared in receipts. Jesus' statement 'It is finished' (τετελεσται, *tetelestai*) could be interpreted as 'Paid in full.'" (Tenney)

vi. It was all **finished**, paid in full, accomplished.

- The types, promises, and prophecies were finished.

- The sacrifices and ceremonies of the priesthood were finished.
- His perfect obedience was finished.
- The satisfaction of God's justice was finished.
- The power of Satan, sin, and death was finished.

vii. "From the gates of Eden the blood of sacrifice had begun to flow, augmented by the confluent streams of the years. From that moment, however, not another drop need be shed. The types were finished now that the Antitype had been realized." (Meyer)

viii. "Has he finished his work for me? Then I must get to work for him, and *I must persevere until I finish my work, too;* not to save myself, for that is all done, but because I am saved." (Spurgeon)

d. **Bowing His head**: This speaks of a peaceful act, like lying down on a pillow to sleep. Jesus did not hang His head in defeat; He bowed it in peace.

i. "Elsewhere in the Gospels the same phrase as is here used of Jesus' reclining his head in death us used of reclining one's head in sleep (Matthew 8:20; Luke 9:28, 'the Son of Man has nowhere to lay his head'); the implication here may be that he voluntarily reclines his head, ready now to sleep the sleep of death." (Bruce)

ii. **Bowing His head**: "We have the minuteness of an eye-witness, on whom every particular of this solemn moment made and indelible impression." (Alford)

e. **Gave up His spirit**: No one took Jesus' life from Him; He, in a manner unlike any man, **gave up His spirit**. Death had no righteous hold over the sinless Son of God. He stood *in the place* of sinners, but was never a sinner Himself. So He could not die unless He **gave up His spirit**.

i. As Jesus said, *I lay down My life that I may take it again. No one takes it from Me, but I lay it down of Myself. I have power to lay it down, and I have power to take it again.* (John 10:17-18)

ii. "He gave up his life because He willed it, when He willed it, and as He willed it." (Augustine)

iii. "No one took His life from Him: His death was a voluntary surrender: a surrender which He had authority to make, because the authority to surrender His life was accompanied with an authority to resume it (John 10:18)." (Trench)

iv. Jesus work as a substitute on the cross, connected to His yielding to death on the cross, made for the the most important act of this most important life. This is reflected even in ancient secular histories. The existing mentions of Jesus in ancient extra-biblical literature each highlight His death on the cross.

- A letter written by Mara bar Serapion to his son (ca. AD 73).
- Josephus, the Jewish historian (ca. AD 90).
- Tacitus, the Roman historian (ca. AD 110-120).
- The Babylonian Talmud (ca. AD 200).

C. Immediately after the death of Jesus by crucifixion.

1. (31-32) The need to remove the bodies from their crosses.

Therefore, because it was the Preparation *Day*, that the bodies should not remain on the cross on the Sabbath (for that Sabbath was a high day), the Jews asked Pilate that their legs might be broken, and *that* they might be taken away. Then the soldiers came and broke the legs of the first and of the other who was crucified with Him.

a. **Because it was the Preparation Day**: This refers back to John's statement at John 19:14 and raises the same difficult chronological questions previous mentioned at John 18:28.

b. **That the bodies should not remain on the cross on the Sabbath**: Normally those executed by crucifixion remained affixed to their cross for days as a grim warning of the consequences of disobeying the Roman government. Yet because of the approaching **Sabbath** (and because it was **a high day**, associated with Passover and its week), the religious leaders demanded that the Romans take away the disgusting sight of three crucified men.

> i. "Their consciences were not wounded by the murder of Jesus, but they were greatly moved by the fear of ceremonial pollution. Religious scruples may live in a dead conscience." (Spurgeon)

c. **The Jews asked Pilate that their legs might be broken**: The breaking of the legs of a crucified man hastened his death because he could not support himself from his legs or feet helping him to take a better breath.

> i. "The only way a crucified man would obtain a full breath of air was to raise himself by means of his legs to ease the tension on his arms and chest muscles. If the legs were broken, he could not possibly do so; and death would follow shortly because of lack of oxygen." (Tenney)

d. **The soldiers came and broke the legs of the first and of the other**: Answering the request of the religious leaders, the **soldiers** hastened the death of the men on either side of Jesus.

i. This was brutal work for rough men. They likely used an iron bar or a heavy club. "To secure speedy death the *crucifragium*, breaking of the legs with a heavy mallet or bar, was sometimes resorted to: as without such means the crucified might in some cases linger for thirty-six hours." (Dods) This breaking of the legs

must have been terrifying for a man still alive on a cross.

ii. "*Lactantius* says. l. iv. c. 26, that it was a common custom to break the legs or other bones of criminals upon the cross; and this appears to have been a kind of *coup de grace*, the sooner to put them out of pain." (Clarke)

iii. The archeological finding referenced at John 19:18 "Was apparently subjected to this treatment: one of his legs had sustained a clean fracture from a single blow with also cracked the other." (Bruce)

iv. "The penitent thief entered into Paradise that very day, but it was not without suffering; say, rather, that the terrible stroke was the actual means of the prompt fulfillment of his Lord's promise to him. By that blow he died that day; else might he have lingered long." (Spurgeon)

2. (33-34) The confirmation of the death of Jesus of Nazareth.

But when they came to Jesus and saw that He was already dead, they did not break His legs. But one of the soldiers pierced His side with a spear, and immediately blood and water came out.

a. **They came to Jesus and saw that He was already dead**: These soldiers had (presumably) supervised many executions on the cross. They knew when a man had died and when he was still alive. It was their experienced judgment that said Jesus **was already dead**.

i. Mark 15:44-45 add that Pontius Pilate asked the supervising centurion for confirmation of the death of Jesus, and the centurion confirmed that He was dead.

b. **One of the soldiers pierced His side with a spear**: The customary way to make sure of the death of a crucified man was to club and break the legs. After doing so to the first two victims, it was entirely normal for this soldier to do the same to Jesus - he was even presumably *ordered* to do it. Yet he did not; instead he **pierced His side with a spear** and unwittingly fulfilled several prophecies, mentioned below.

i. "As the wound inflected by this spear thrust seems to have been a hand-breadth wide (John 20:25) it may be presumed the soldier meant to make sure that Jesus was dead by giving Him a thrust which itself would have been fatal." (Dods)

c. **Immediately blood and water came out**: This was taken as absolute confirmation that Jesus was dead. The gash in His side from the point of the spear flowed forth with a substance that looked like **blood**, and a substance that looked like **water**.

i. There are some who regard this as something of an on-the-spot autopsy of Jesus, revealing that His actual cause of death was of a ruptured (burst) heart. The thinking is that in such cases, the sack surrounding the heart (normally filled with a watery substance) fills with blood. If that sack is opened and its contents allowed to flow outside the body, it would look like an issue of blood and water (because the two substances do not mix, something like oil and water). Normally this would be a trickle; perhaps there was something supernatural at work to demonstrate this sign.

ii. Augustus Toplady used this image in his great hymn, *Rock of Ages*:

Rock of Ages, cleft for me,
Let me hide myself in Thee
Let the water and the blood,
From Thy riven side which flowed
Be of sin the double cure,
Cleanse me from its guilt and power

iii. Toplady's idea is prominent under the Old Covenant, where both blood and water were often used in the priestly service of atoning for and cleansing of sin. "Take all the types of the Old Testament together, and you will gather this, that *the purification of sin was typically set forth by blood and water*. Blood was conspicuous always, you have no remission of sin without it: but water was exceedingly prominent also." (Spurgeon)

iv. Spurgeon gave an additional thought of what this shows us: "One of these old divines says that Jesus Christ was typified by our first father, Adam. As Adam fell asleep, and out of his side Eve was taken, so Jesus slept upon the cross the sleep of death, and from his side, where the spear was thrust, his Church was taken."

3. (35-37) John's solemn assurance; the fulfillment of Scripture.

And he who has seen has testified, and his testimony is true; and he knows that he is telling the truth, so that you may believe. For these things were done that the Scripture should be fulfilled, "Not *one* of His bones shall be broken." And again another Scripture says, "They shall look on Him whom they pierced."

a. **He who has seen has testified, and his testimony is true; and he knows that he is telling the truth, so that you may believe**: John gave solemn assurance that he was present at the crucifixion of Jesus and saw these things with his own eyes. He also explained the reason for his testimony: **so that** the reader **may believe**.

> i. In particular, the sight of the *blood and water* mentioned in the previous verses had an impact on John. Later in one of his letters (1 John 5:6) he described Jesus as *He who came by water and blood*. This description has puzzled many commentators, unsure if John meant the waters of baptism or the water mentioned in John 19:34.

> ii. Nevertheless, *the manner and certainty of the death of Jesus is an essential part of our Christian belief*. This is truly **so that you may believe**. What John has told us about the death of Jesus to this point already leads us to belief.

> • The innocence of Jesus leads us to believe.
> • His great dignity under suffering leads us to believe.
> • The manner of His death - crucifixion - leads us to believe.
> • The title on His cross leads us to believe.
> • The gambling for His clothes leads us to believe.
> • The love for His mother leads us to believe.
> • The cry, "It is finished!" leads us to believe.
> • His peaceful giving up of His spirit leads us to believe.
> • The certainty of His death leads us to believe He was really resurrected from the dead.

b. **These things were done that the Scripture should be fulfilled**: Remarkably, what seemed to be a random choice by an anonymous Roman soldier - to pierce the side of Jesus instead of breaking His legs - was **done that the Scripture should be fulfilled**.

c. **Not one of His bones shall be broken**: This prophecy of Psalm 34:20 (as well as Exodus 12:46 and Numbers 9:12) was unknowingly and accidently (on man's part) fulfilled. Nevertheless, its *exact* fulfillment shows the providence and guidance of God, and leads us to **believe**.

> i. The Roman soldier was *commanded* to break the legs of the crucified men, yet for some reason he did not break Jesus' legs. This was a remarkable fulfillment of prophecy.

d. **They shall look on Him whom they pierced**: This prophecy of Zechariah 12:10 and 13:6 was unknowingly and accidently (on man's part) fulfilled. Nevertheless, its *exact* fulfillment shows the providence and guidance of God, and leads us to **believe**.

> i. "The *piercing* has been done, but the 'looking upon' with 'mourning' and 'supplication,' such as Zechariah foretells, lies in the yet future." (Trench)

4. (38-42) Jesus is lovingly buried by two hesitant disciples.

After this, Joseph of Arimathea, being a disciple of Jesus, but secretly, for fear of the Jews, asked Pilate that he might take away the body of Jesus; and Pilate gave *him* permission. So he came and took the body of Jesus. And Nicodemus, who at first came to Jesus by night, also came, bringing a mixture of myrrh and aloes, about a hundred pounds. Then they took the body of Jesus, and bound it in strips of linen with the spices, as the custom of the Jews is to bury. Now in the place where He was crucified there was a garden, and in the garden a new tomb in which no one had yet been laid. So there they laid Jesus, because of the Jews' Preparation *Day,* for the tomb was nearby.

> a. **Joseph of Arimathea, being a disciple of Jesus, but secretly**: In this final step of the earthly work of Jesus before His resurrection, the Son of God remained passive. God raised up two previously secret disciples (**Joseph of Arimathea** and **Nicodemus**) to receive the body of Jesus and give it the best burial they could in the short time they had before sundown and the start of Sabbath (Luke 23:54).

> b. **Asked Pilate that he might take away the body of Jesus**: Customarily, the bodies of crucified criminals were left on their crosses to rot or be eaten by wild animals. But the Jews wanted no such horror displayed during the Passover season, and Romans were known to grant the corpses of executed men to friends or relatives for proper burial.

> > i. "The Roman custom was to leave the body to birds and beasts of prey." (Dods)

> > ii. "The Jews of that day regarded proper burial of the dead as most important. Many went out of their way to see that fellow-countrymen received proper burial, and this may have had something to do with Joseph's action." (Morris)

> > iii. God used these men to protect the body of Jesus. "As Achilles dragged Hector by the heels round the walls of Troy, so would Satan have liked that men should have mauled the dead body of Christ. He would have cast him to the dogs or to the kites if he could have had his way; but so it must not be." (Spurgeon)

c. **Then they took the body of Jesus**: It is not precisely said, but the implication is that Joseph and Nicodemus did this *themselves*. They were wealthy and influential men (Matthew 27:57, Mark 15:43, John 3:1) who could find servants to do the work for them; yet *they* did this themselves.

i. "The narrative implies, though it does not mention (as St. Mark and St. Luke do), that Joseph himself took the Body from the cross." (Alford)

ii. The removal of the bloody, dirty body of Jesus from the cross and the iron spikes that held it must have been difficult both practically and emotionally.

d. **Bound it in strips of linen with the spices, as the custom of the Jews is to bury**: Joseph and Nicodemus did what they could to wrap the body of Jesus with the **myrrh and aloes, about a hundred pounds** Nicodemus brought. Before the body was wrapped it had to be prepared. One of the customs of the Jews in preparing a body for burial is the requirement to remove all foreign matter from the body and to carefully wash it.

i. They examined His entire body and found broken pieces of thorn all over the head. They saw His bloody, matted hair; the terrible bruising of the face, the areas of beard pulled out, the dry and cracked lips. They turned the body over to see His shoulders and arms are riddled with splinters; each one was removed with care. The back, from the shoulders down, was a bloody open wound from the terrible scourging suffered before the crucifixion. His hands and feet were smashed and bloodied. On the front – just beneath the rib cage – there was a gaping wound made from the spear thrust that confirmed His death. Worst of it all were the eyes that did not open; the voice that did not speak.

ii. We can only imagine what deep, life-long impressions this left upon both men and how for the rest of their life the smell of those particular spices would bring back every mental detail.

iii. As these two men did this – men who were experts in the law – they must have known that they were fulfilling prophecy; the prophecy in Isaiah 53:9 that said the Messiah would be *with the rich at His death*. Here the body of Jesus was, at the hands of two rich men – who customarily would have had a servant do such humble, bloody work. Yet they knew they *had* to do it themselves.

iv. This was a strange work for these two men to do; yet it was also strange that Jesus, in the plan of Godhead, passively submitted to it. Conceivably, after Jesus accomplished all things and yielded His life, Jesus could have sprung from the cross in a super-hero like flash of power and glory five minutes – or five seconds – after His death. Yet in the plan of God the Father, He hung lifeless on the cross for some period of time – long enough for Joseph to gain an audience with Pilate and receive permission to take the body. He hung on that cross until His body was laboriously removed, and hurriedly buried according to Jewish custom.

v. In God's plan this burial of Jesus was so important that it is said to be one of the essential components of the gospel itself (1 Corinthians 15:3-4. We can consider many reasons for this.

- This burial fulfilled the Scripture. Isaiah 53:9 says, *And they made His grave with the wicked*; so that meant the Messiah would be buried in a grave – and He was.

- This burial fulfilled the promise, the prediction of Jesus. Jesus said that He, like Jonah, would be buried away for three days (Matthew 12:40), and so it had to be fulfilled.

- This burial demonstrated that Jesus was truly dead; it was proof of the glory of the coming resurrection. No one could tell Joseph of Arimathea or Nicodemus that Jesus did not really die.

- This burial was important because burial spices and preparations protected His holy body from decay; as it was said in Psalm 16:10: *You will not allow Your Holy One to see decay.*

- This burial gave both Joseph of Arimathea and Nicodemus a way to proclaim their relationship with Jesus; it called them out of their state of secret discipleship.

- This burial and the days of Jesus in the tomb tested the faith and devotion of the disciples; it made them die a certain kind of death for those days they knew Jesus lay in the tomb.

- This burial and the days of Jesus in the tomb were ways to prove that at the cross Jesus defeated not only sin, but also death. The burial and the empty tomb show that Jesus conquered sin *and* death.

- The days in the tomb were important because there was important work for Jesus to do during that time in the tomb. 1 Peter 3:18-20 tells us that Jesus *went and preached to the spirits in prison*; though there isn't as much explanation on all this as we would like to have, it seems that as the body of Jesus lay lifeless in the tomb, His Spirit went to Hades, the abode of the dead. There He led the faithful dead to heaven, in light of His then-completed work on the cross. He also preached a message of judgment and coming condemnation to the evil spirits that were imprisoned in the depths.

- This burial was another great and final connection of the Son of God with the humility of man. There was a *transaction* aspect to the great work of Jesus on the cross; but there was so much more. There is also a radical *identification* aspect; where Jesus connects with *you* in every way possible, and He invites *you* to connect with Him. He was buried with us, in the humiliation of utter humanness. We are buried with Him – spiritually by faith, ceremonially by baptism. He identified with us; we by faith identify with Him.

vi. **Myrrh and aloes, about a hundred pounds**: "The enormous quantity has been accounted for as a rich man's expression of devotion, or as required if the entire body and all the wrappings were to be smeared with it." (Dods)

vii. "The quantity of one hundred Roman pounds (75 lbs. avdp.) revealed both Nicodemus's wealth and appreciation of Jesus." (Tenney)

e. **The garden tomb in which no one had yet been laid**: Matthew 27:60 tells us that this tomb belonged to Joseph of Arimathea himself. A rich man like Joseph would probably have a tomb that was carved into solid rock; this tomb was in a **garden** near the place of crucifixion.

i. A typical tomb of this type had a small entrance and perhaps one or more compartments where bodies were laid out after being somewhat mummified with spices, ointments, and linen strips. Customarily, the Jews left these bodies alone for a few years until they decayed down to the bones, then the bones were placed in a small stone box known as an ossuary. The ossuary remained in the tomb with the remains of other family members.

ii. The door to the tomb was typically made of a heavy, circular shaped stone, running in a groove and settled down into a channel, so it could not be moved except by several strong men. This was done to ensure that no one would disturb the remains.

iii. **In the place where He was crucified there was a garden**: "To a deep-seeing eye like that of John, this proximity was more than a coincidence. John felt that there was an inward harmony between the garden and the cross." (Morrison)

iv. "The fall of the first Adam took place in a garden; and it was in a garden that the second Adam redeemed mankind from the consequences of Adam's transgression." (Tasker)

v. **In which no one had yet been laid**: "If they buried him in an old tomb, the Jews would say that he had touched the bones of some prophet or other holy man, and so came to life." (Spurgeon)

John 20 - An Empty Tomb and A Risen Jesus

A. Discovery of the empty tomb

1. (1-2) Mary Magdalene comes upon Jesus' tomb, finds it empty and tells the disciples about it.

Now on the first *day* of the week Mary Magdalene went to the tomb early, while it was still dark, and saw *that* the stone had been taken away from the tomb. Then she ran and came to Simon Peter, and to the other disciple, whom Jesus loved, and said to them, "They have taken away the Lord out of the tomb, and we do not know where they have laid Him."

a. **Now on the first day of the week Mary Magdalene went to the tomb early**: Jesus was crucified on Friday (or on Thursday by some accounts). After His entombment, the tomb was sealed and guarded by Roman soldiers (Matthew 27:62-66). The tomb stayed sealed and guarded until discovered **on the first day of the week... early, while it was still dark**.

b. **Mary Magdalene... she ran and came to Simon Peter**: Other gospels explain she was not the only woman to come to the tomb that morning (at least three other women accompanied her). Mary was the one who ran back and told the disciples about the empty tomb, so John mentions her.

    i. Jesus had cast *seven* demons out of this Mary (Luke 8:2, Mark 16:9). Her troubled past didn't disqualify her from being the first witness of the resurrected Jesus and His first commissioned messenger of His resurrection.

    ii. The women came to complete the work begun by Joseph and Nicodemus. "Probably, in view of the lateness of the hour and the nearness of the sabbath, Nicodemus was not able to use all the spices he had brought in the way intended." (Morris)

c. **They have taken away the Lord out of the tomb**: When she saw the empty tomb, Mary's first reaction was to think the body of Jesus was stolen. She wasn't wishing for or anticipating the resurrection of Jesus, and she certainly did not imagine it out of hope.

i. **We do not know where**: "The plural may naturally be accepted as confirming Mark's account that she was not alone." (Dods)

2. (3-4) Peter and John run to the tomb.

Peter therefore went out, and the other disciple, and were going to the tomb. So they both ran together, and the other disciple outran Peter and came to the tomb first.

a. **Peter therefore went out, and the other disciple**: Peter and John heard the news from Mary and immediately started for the tomb. In keeping with the author's humility, John did not refer to himself directly, but only as **the other disciple**.

b. **They both ran together, and the other disciple outran Peter and came to the tomb first**: John was humble enough to avoid the mention of his own name, but competitive enough to tell us that he **outran Peter** to the tomb.

i. By tradition, Peter was older than John. We might picture a man in his late forties or early fifties like Peter running to the tomb with great labor, and a man and his mid-twenties easily outrunning him.

ii. This shows that they both ran hard. Peter and John had just heard life-changing news: that the tomb was empty. They couldn't be indifferent or detached to this news; they *had to* see for themselves.

3. (5-10) Peter and John examine the empty tomb.

And he, stooping down and looking in, saw the linen cloths lying *there*; yet he did not go in. Then Simon Peter came, following him, and went into the tomb; and he saw the linen cloths lying *there*, and the handkerchief that had been around His head, not lying with the linen cloths, but folded together in a place by itself. Then the other disciple, who came to the tomb first, went in also; and he saw and believed. For as yet they did not know the Scripture, that He must rise again from the dead. Then the disciples went away again to their own homes.

a. **Stooping down and looking in**: Arriving first at the tomb, John was **looking in** (the ancient Greek word *blepei* meaning "to clearly see a material object"), and he saw the grave wrappings of Jesus still in the tomb (**saw the linen cloths lying there**). John *clearly* saw this, and there was no mistake about what he saw.

i. **Yet he did not go in**: Something kept John from actually going into the tomb. "Having seen that the graveclothes were still within, the other disciple probably concluded that the body was also there and so refrained from entering. Either he felt that he should not enter the tomb out of respect for the dead, or else he feared the ceremonial defilement of touching a corpse." (Tenney)

ii. A typical rich man's tomb of that time would be large enough to walk into, with a place to lay out the body on one side and a bench for mourners on the other side. The entrance might be an opening only 3 feet (1 meter) high and 2.5 feet (.75 meters) wide. It was large enough to get into, yet there was a bit of bowing and turning necessary. There was some *commitment* needed to go inside the tomb, and for some reason John **did not go in**.

b. **Then Simon Peter came, following him, and went into the tomb**: Whatever ever kept John from going in didn't stop Peter. When he finally arrived he immediately **went into the tomb**. This action-oriented impulsiveness was characteristic of Peter. John wanted to stop and think about it but Peter went right in.

c. **He saw the linen cloths lying there**: Going in, Peter then **saw** (the ancient Greek word *theorei* meaning "to contemplate, observe, scrutinize") that the cloths were still orderly and neat. It looked as if the body evaporated out of the burial wrappings without disturbing their place.

i. The phrasing of **linen cloths lying there** and **folded together in a place by itself** indicates the orderly arrangement of the burial wrappings. Prepared for burial, those strips of **linen cloths** were smeared with ointments and aloes and spices, and the **linen cloths** were applied in several layers. The burial of Jesus on the day of His death was hurried, and the women came early Sunday morning to apply more layers.

ii. The mixture of ointments and aloes and spices would dry and harden the **linen cloths**, making something of a mummy or a cocoon. The normal removal of these burial wrappings would require some tearing or cutting; Peter saw that it was no normal removal of the burial wrappings. "The whole point of the description is that the grave-clothes did not look as if they had been put off or taken off; they were lying there in their regular folds as if the body of Jesus had simply evaporated out of them." (Barclay)

iii. The neat, orderly arrangement of the **linen cloths** showed that a human hand, at least not in any way that was immediately apparent, did not remove the burial wrappings of Jesus. All this demonstrated that something absolutely unique had happened in that now-empty tomb.

- The linen cloths were there - the body had not been removed with them.

- The linen cloths were orderly - not removed in any normal way by the person wrapped in them.

- The linen cloths were orderly - not removed by grave robbers or vandals.

iv. It has been suggested that the burial wrappings of Jesus have been preserved in the Shroud of Turin. The Shroud of Turin can probably never be positively proved to be part of the burial wrappings of Jesus. But, "The evidence thus far indicates the probable conclusions that the shroud is ancient (perhaps from the first century), that it does not contradict the NT accounts, and that the image is not a fake. It may well be the actual burial garment of Jesus." (*Evangelical Dictionary of Theology*)

v. The image on the shroud is of a crucified male, bearded, 5'11" in height, weighing about 175 pounds. His physique was muscular and well built, and he is an estimated age of 30-35 years. His long hair is tied into a pigtail and there is no evidence on decomposition on the cloth. Results of the Shroud of Turin Research Project in October 1978 determined that the Shroud is *not* a painting or a forgery. They determined that its blood is real blood and the image seems to be some type of scorch, though they cannot account for how it was made.

vi. The Shroud of Turin is an interesting object, yet there are also reasons for skepticism.

- John described two aspects of the grave wrappings: the **linen cloths** and **the handkerchief that had been around His head**. This would imply that the head and the body of Jesus were wrapped separately, while the Shroud of Turin presents an image of an entire body on one cloth. It is possible that the Shroud was *underneath* those two sets of wrappings and unmentioned by John, but we can't say that John describes a fabric such as the Shroud of Turin.

- However, Trench suggests: "The winding sheet which had been folded over all (Matthew, Mark, Luke) must have been unfolded and laid back along either side so as to leave the bandage-casing exposed."

- We may suppose a good reason why God would not want or allow the preservation of Jesus' burial wrappings, not wanting to leave behind a relic that would be inevitably worshipped.

vii. **The handkerchief that had been around His head**: "This means the headcloth still retained the shape the contour of Jesus' head had given it and that It was still separated from the other wrappings by a space that suggested the distance between the neck of the deceased and the upper chest, where the wrappings of the body would have begun." (Tenney)

d. **The other disciple… he saw and believed**: After Peter went into the tomb John also went in. He then **saw** (the ancient Greek word *eiden* meaning, "to understand, to perceive the significance of") and then John **believed**. The distinctive arrangement of the burial wrappings convinced him.

i. Generally, the very first Christians did not believe in the resurrection only because the tomb was empty, but because *they saw and met* the resurrected Jesus. John was something of an exception; he believed simply by seeing the empty tomb, before meeting the resurrected Jesus.

ii. "He believed *that Jesus was risen from the dead*. He received into his mind, embraced with his assent, THE FACT OF THE RESURRECTION, for the first time. He did this, on the *ocular testimony before him*; for as yet neither of them *knew the Scripture*." (Alford)

iii. "John believed, but Peter was still in the dark. Again the former had outrun his friend." (Maclaren)

iv. "Some of the best books on the Resurrection have been written by lawyers, some of whom originally set out to disprove it. I am thinking of men like Frank Morrison, Gilbert West, J.N.D. Anderson, and others. Sir Edward Clark, another English jurist, once wrote: 'As a lawyer I have made a prolonged study of the evidences for the first Easter day. To me the evidence is conclusive, and over and over again in the High Court I have secured the verdict on evidence not nearly so compelling. … As a lawyer I accept it unreservedly as the testimony of men to facts that they were able to substantiate.'" (Boice)

e. **For as yet they did not know the Scripture, that He must rise again from the dead**: At this point Peter and John were persuaded of the *fact* of the resurrection; they **believed**. Yet because **they did not know the Scripture, that He must rise again from the dead**, they did not understand the *meaning* of the resurrection.

i. Knowing the *fact* of the resurrection is an important start, but not enough. We need to let the Bible tell us the *meaning* and the *importance* of Jesus' resurrection.

- The resurrection means that Jesus was *declared to be the Son of God with power, according to the Spirit of holiness, by the resurrection from the dead* (Romans 1:4).

- The resurrection means that we have assurance of our own resurrection: *For if we believe that Jesus died and rose again, even so God will bring with Him those who sleep in Jesus* (1 Thessalonians 4:14).

- The resurrection means that God has an eternal plan for these bodies of ours. "There was nothing in the teaching of Jesus approaching the Gnostic heresy that declared that the flesh is inherently evil. Plato could only get rid of sin by getting rid of the body. Jesus retains the body; and declares that God feeds the body as well as the soul, that the body is as sacred thing as the soul, since the soul makes it its sanctuary." (Morgan)

- The resurrection means that Jesus has a continuing ministry: *He is also able to save to the uttermost those who come to God through Him, since He ever lives to make intercession for them* (Hebrews 7:25).

- The resurrection means that Christianity and its God are unique and completely different and unique among world religions.

- The resurrection proves that though it looked like Jesus died on the cross as a common criminal He actually died as a sinless man, out of love and self-sacrifice to bear the guilt of our sin. The death of Jesus on the cross was the payment, but the resurrection was the receipt, showing that the payment was perfect in the sight of God the Father.

B. Mary Magdalene meets the risen Jesus.

1. (11-13) Mary, stricken with grief, sees two angels in the empty tomb.

But Mary stood outside by the tomb weeping, and as she wept she stooped down *and looked* into the tomb. And she saw two angels in white sitting, one at the head and the other at the feet, where the body of Jesus had lain. Then they said to her, "Woman, why are you weeping?" She said to them, "Because they have taken away my Lord, and I do not know where they have laid Him."

a. **Mary stood outside the tomb weeping**: Peter and John examined the evidence of the empty tomb and John was persuaded that Jesus rose from the dead, though he did not yet understand the *meaning* of it all. Mary did not yet have the confidence that Jesus was resurrected, so she wept.

b. **As she wept she stooped down and looked into the tomb**: Mary wanted to see what Peter and John saw, so she made her own examination. Yet in the moment between their examination and Mary's, something was different in the tomb.

c. **She saw two angels in white sitting**: Mary didn't notice the burial wrappings and their curious arrangement; now there were **two angels** in the tomb. Mary didn't seem to react with shock or fear; she probably did not immediately perceive that they were angels (Hebrews 13:2).

> i. "The presence of angels was a trifle to Mary, who had only one thought - the absence of her Lord." (Maclaren)

> ii. "Sent for her sake, and the rest, to certify them of the resurrection. It is their office (and they are glad of it) to comfort and counsel the saints still, as it were by speaking and doing after a spiritual manner." (Trapp)

> iii. **One at the head and the other at the feet**: "So were the cherubim placed at each end of the mercy-seat: Exodus 25:18, 19." (Clarke)

d. **They have taken away my Lord, and I do not know where they have laid Him**: Mary wasn't thinking or dreaming that Jesus was alive. She believed He was still dead, and only wanted to know where He was so she could do the final work of preparing His body for burial. This is more evidence that she didn't notice the burial cloths because of the angels.

2. (14-16) Mary meets Jesus.

Now when she had said this, she turned around and saw Jesus standing *there*, and did not know that it was Jesus. Jesus said to her, "Woman, why are you weeping? Whom are you seeking?" She, supposing Him to be the gardener, said to Him, "Sir, if You have carried Him away, tell me where You have laid Him, and I will take Him away." Jesus said to her, "Mary!" She turned and said to Him, "Rabboni!" (which is to say, Teacher).

a. **She turned around and saw Jesus standing there**: Mary wondered and worried about where Jesus was, but He wasn't far away.

> i. "Perhaps Mary withdrew abruptly. She may have heard a movement behind her. Or, as many commentators from Chrysostom down have held, the angels might have made some motion at the sight of the Lord behind Mary. We do not know." (Morris)

b. **Did not know that it was Jesus**: Mary certainly knew who Jesus was, and it was strange that she did not immediately recognize Him. Some think it was because she was emotionally distressed and had tears in her eyes. Others speculate it was because Jesus looked somewhat different, retaining at least some of the marks of His suffering.

i. "She did not *expect Him to be there*, and was wholly preoccupied with other thoughts." (Alford)

ii. "Not merely because her eyes were dim with tears, but because He was altered in appearance; as Mark (16:12)." (Dods)

iii. "There seems to have been something different about the risen Jesus so that He was not always recognized." (Morris)

c. **Why are You weeping? Whom are you seeking?** Jesus did not immediately reveal Himself to Mary. It wasn't to play some trick on her; it was to break through her unbelief and forgetfulness of Jesus' promise of resurrection.

d. **Tell me where You have laid Him, and I will take Him away**: It's possible that Mary was a large, strong woman and was physically capable of carrying away the body of a dead man. It is more likely that she was simply so filled with sorrow and devotion that she isn't thinking through her plans carefully.

i. "Her words reveal her devotion. She never paused to consider how she would carry the corpse of a full-grown man or how she would explain her possession of it." (Tenney)

ii. "How true is the proverb, *Love feels no load*! Jesus was in the prime of life when he was crucified, and had a hundred pounds weight of spices added to his body; and yet Mary thinks of nothing less than carrying him away with her, if she can but find where he is laid!" (Clarke)

e. **Jesus said to her, "Mary!"** Jesus had only to say one word, and all was explained. She heard in the name and the tone the voice of her beloved Messiah, and instantly called Him **Rabboni** (as did another Mary in John 11:28).

i. "Jesus says to her, 'Mariam,' the Hebrew name, of which the Greek form is Maria." (Trench) Jesus didn't reveal Himself to Mary by telling her who *He* was, but by telling her who *she* was to Him.

ii. Her eyes failed her, but her ears could not mistake that voice saying her name. "Many had called her by that name. She had been wont to hear it many times a day from many lips; but only One had spoken it with that intonation." (Meyer)

iii. "Never was a one-word utterance more charged with emotion than this." (Tasker) "Jesus can preach a perfect sermon in one word." (Spurgeon)

iv. "In the garden of Eden, immediately after the Fall, the sentence of sorrow, and of sorrow multiplied, fell upon the woman. In the garden where Christ had been buried, after his resurrection, the news of comfort — comfort rich and divine, — came to a woman through the woman's promised Seed, the Lord Jesus Christ. If the sentence must fall heavily upon the woman, so must the comfort come most sweetly to her." (Spurgeon)

3. (17-18) Jesus sends Mary to tell the disciples.

Jesus said to her, "Do not cling to Me, for I have not yet ascended to My Father; but go to My brethren and say to them, 'I am ascending to My Father and your Father, and *to* My God and your God.'" Mary Magdalene came and told the disciples that she had seen the Lord, and *that* He had spoken these things to her.

a. **Do not cling to Me**: Some confusion has come regarding what Jesus meant, mostly owing to the phrasing of this in the older King James Version: *Touch me not*. Some think Jesus told Mary not to touch Him in any way, as if her contact would somehow defile Him. Yet the sense is that Mary immediately held on to Jesus and did not want to let Him go.

i. "Probably we should understand the Greek tense here in the strict sense. The present imperative with a negative means 'Stop doing something' rather than 'Do not do something'." (Morris)

ii. "Jesus was not protesting that Mary should not touch Him lest He be defiled, but was admonishing her not to detain Him because He would see her and the disciples again." (Tenney)

iii. "We need not be detained by that curiosity of exegesis which supposes that he still had to enter the heavenly holy of holies to complete the antitype of the Day of Atonement initiated by his sacrifice on the cross." (Bruce)

iv. This also shows that the resurrection body of Jesus was different, yet similar to His pre-resurrection body. It was definitely real and tangible, and Jesus was not a phantom.

b. **Go to My brethren and say to them**: Jesus made a woman the first witness of His resurrection. The law courts of that day would not recognize the testimony of a woman, but Jesus did.

i. This also argues for the historic truth of this account. If someone fabricated this story, they would not make the first witnesses to the resurrection *women*, who were commonly (if unfairly) regarded as unreliable witnesses.

ii. "Celsus, the anti-Christian polemicist of the later second century, dismisses the resurrection narrative as based on the hallucinations of a 'hysterical woman'." (Bruce)

iii. **My brethren**: It is touching that Jesus referred to His *disciples* - those who had all forsaken Him, except for John - as His **brethren**. It's also touching that Mary understood exactly who He meant.

iv. "I do not remember that the Lord Jesus ever called his disciples his brethren till that time. He called them 'servants'; he called them 'friends'; but now that he has risen from the dead, he says, 'my brethren.'" (Spurgeon)

c. **I am ascending to My Father and your Father, and to My God and your God**: Jesus did not say, *Our Father and God*, and therefore pointed out a difference between His relationship with God and the disciples' relationship with God. The One enthroned in the heavens is certainly their **Father** and **God**, but not in the identical way that He is **Father** and **God** to Jesus.

i. "He says not 'Our Father': in one sense therefore, He is mine, in another sense He is yours; by nature mine, by grace yours... my God, under whom I also am as a man; your God, between whom and you I am a mediator." (Augustine)

ii. He also made specific mention of His coming ascension. The word of His ascension let them know He was raised *never to die again*.

C. The disciples meet the risen Jesus.

1. (19) Jesus appears in their midst.

Then, the same day at evening, being the first *day* of the week, when the doors were shut where the disciples were assembled, for fear of the Jews, Jesus came and stood in the midst, and said to them, "Peace *be* with you."

a. **The same day at evening**: This took place on the same day that the tomb was found empty and Mary met the resurrected Jesus. We are told of five appearances of Jesus on the resurrection day.

- To Mary Magdalene (John 20:11-18).
- To the other women (Matthew 28:9-10).

- To the two on the road to Emmaus (Mark 16:12-13, Luke 24:13-32).
- To Peter (Luke 24:33-35, 1 Corinthians 15:5).
- To ten of the disciples, Thomas being absent (John 20:19-23).

b. **Where the disciples were assembled**: It was good that the disciples stayed together. Jesus told them that when He departed they must love one another, which assumes that they would stay together (John 15:17). He also prayed for their unity after their departure (John 17:11). This command was fulfilled and prayer was answered, at least in the days immediately after His crucifixion.

c. **When the doors were shut**: The sense is not only that the doors were **shut**, but secured and locked against any unwelcome entry. The idea is that the room was secure when suddenly **Jesus came and stood in the midst**. We aren't told *how* Jesus entered the room, but the sense is that it was not in any normal way and that He seemed to simply appear.

i. "When he tells us that the doors were 'shut' we should understand this to mean 'locked' as the following explanation, that this was due to fear of the Jews, shows." (Morris)

ii. The doors were shut and locked so they wouldn't get hurt. Those shut and locked doors also shut out Jesus. Thankfully, Jesus was greater than the shut and locked doors, and made His way in despite them. Still, it's better to unlock and open the door for Jesus.

iii. "Afterwards, when the Spirit came down upon them, they not only set open the doors, but preached Christ boldly in the temple without dread of danger." (Trapp)

iv. **Jesus came and stood**: "The word describes that *unseen arrival among them* which preceded His becoming visible to them." (Alford)

v. This strange and miraculous appearance of Jesus apparently was to demonstrate that resurrection bodies are not subject to the same limitations as our present bodies. Since we will be raised in the same manner as Jesus (Romans 6:4, 1 Corinthians 15:42-45), this gives us some hint of the nature of our future body in the resurrection.

vi. "We can scarcely say more than that John wants us to see that the risen Jesus was not limited by closed doors. Miraculously He stood in their midst." (Morris)

vii. Jesus might have gone anywhere and done anything after His resurrection, but He wanted to be with His people. He sought out His people.

d. **Peace be with you**: After their desertion of Jesus on the day of His crucifixion, the disciples probably expected words of rebuke or blame. Instead, Jesus brought a word of **peace**, reconciling **peace**.

i. "'Peace to you,' is an assurance that there is no cause to fear, and that all is well: for they (Luke 24:36) were alarmed by His manifestation." (Trench)

ii. "Our Master came to his cowardly, faithless disciples, and stood in the midst of them, uttering the cheering salutation, 'Peace be unto you!' My soul, why should he not come to thee, though thou be the most unworthy of all whom he has bought with his blood?" (Spurgeon)

2. (20-23) The risen Jesus serves His disciples.

When He had said this, He showed them *His* hands and His side. Then the disciples were glad when they saw the Lord. So Jesus said to them again, "Peace to you! As the Father has sent Me, I also send you." And when He had said this, He breathed on *them*, and said to them, "Receive the Holy Spirit. If you forgive the sins of any, they are forgiven them; if you retain the *sins* of any, they are retained."

a. **He showed them His hands and His side**: Jesus *assured* them He was actually Jesus of Nazareth and that He was really raised from the dead. Jesus did this for more than the 10 disciples present; Luke mentioned this gathering as including not only the disciples but also *those who were with them gathered together* (Luke 24:33) and that Jesus invited them to actually touch His body to see that it was real (Luke 24:39-40).

i. "Jesus did not come into their midst to show them a new thought, a philosophic discovery, or even a deep doctrine, or a profound mystery, or indeed anything but *himself*. He was a sacred egoist that day, for what he spake of was himself; and what he revealed was himself." (Spurgeon)

b. **Peace to you!** Jesus just gave them the blessing of His peace (John 20:19). Perhaps the emphasis there was to calm their fear and shock at the moment (Luke 24:36). The repetition of this promise makes this gift of **peace** much larger and more significant. *The resurrected Jesus brings* **peace**.

i. "He had faced and defeated all the forces which destroy the peace of man. As He said, 'Peace be unto you,' He was doing infinitely more than expressing a wish. He was making a declaration. He was bestowing a benediction. He was imparting a blessing." (Morgan)

- My sins are forgiven – peace.
- The slavery to sin is broken – peace.

- My Savior takes my fears and cares – peace.

- My life is settled for eternity – peace.

ii. "We must ourselves have peace both inwardly and outwardly, before we can effectively preach the gospel of peace to others." (Boice)

c. **As the Father has sent Me, I also send you**: Jesus gave His disciples a *mission*, to continue His work on this earth. This was the commission to do what Jesus had already prayed for in John 17:18: *As You sent Me into the world, I also have sent them into the world.*

i. This means that both then and now, disciples are sent after the pattern of the Father's sending of the Son. As previously observed on John 17:18, this means that disciples are *sent ones* - missionaries, after the Latin verb "to send."

ii. Luke 24:33 described this meeting on the evening of Resurrection Sunday and is important: *the eleven and those who were with them gathered together.* It means that it was not only the 10 disciples (lacking Judas and Thomas) who received from Jesus the Holy Spirit and this commission. It means that Jesus sends *every* believer into the world on mission.

iii. As with John 17:18, we think of how Jesus was sent and connect it with the truth, **I also send you**. We are sent the same way Jesus was.

- Jesus was not sent as a philosopher like Plato or Aristotle, though He knew higher philosophy than them all.

- Jesus was not sent as an inventor or a discoverer, though He could have invented new things and discovered new lands.

- Jesus was not sent as a conqueror, though He was mightier than Alexander or Caesar.

- Jesus was sent to teach.

- Jesus was sent to live among us.

- Jesus was sent to suffer for truth and righteousness.

- Jesus was sent to rescue men.

d. **Receive the Holy Spirit**: Jesus gave His disciples the *Holy Spirit*, bringing new life and the ability to carry out their mission. It seems John noted a deliberate connection between this breathing on the disciples and when at creation God breathed life into man. This was a work of re-creation, even as God breathed life into the first man. This is where the disciples were born again.

i. "Intimating, by this, that they were to be made *new* men, in order to be properly qualified for the work to which he had called them; for in this breathing he evidently alluded to the first *creation of man*, when God breathed into him the breath of lives." (Clarke)

ii. "The Greek word is the same as used by the LXX in those two pregnant phrases of the O.T., viz. Genesis 2:7, 'the Lord God *breathed into* man's nostrils the breath (or The Spirit) of Life'; and Ezekiel 37:9, '*breathe into* these slain and they shall live' (the vision of the Dry Bones)." (Trench)

iii. "At an earlier stage in Jesus' ministry the evangelist had said, 'the Spirit was not yet present, because Jesus had not yet been glorified' (John 7:3): now the time for imparting the Spirit has come." (Bruce)

iv. They received the *same* Holy Spirit that was in Jesus; the same Spirit that empowered and enabled all His words and works. "The breathing upon them was meant to convey the impression that His very own Spirit was imparted to them." (Dods)

e. **If you forgive the sins of any**: Jesus gave His disciples *authority* to announce forgiveness and to warn of guilt, as authorized by the Holy Spirit. We can say that Peter's preaching on Pentecost (Acts 2:38) was an exercise of this promised power to announce forgiveness of sins.

i. The connection with the reception of the Holy Spirit is important. "The words of Jesus emphasize that the Holy Spirit is not bestowed on the church as an ornament but to empower an effective application of the work of Christ to all men." (Tenney)

ii. This lays down the duty of the church to proclaim forgiveness to the repentant believer, and the duty of the church to warn the unbeliever that they are in danger of forfeiting the mercy of God. We don't create the forgiveness or deny it; we announce it according to God's word and the wisdom of the Spirit.

iii. "The Church collectively declares the conditions on which sins are remitted, and with the plenary powers of an ambassador pronounces their remission or their retention." (Trench)

iv. "He is saying that the Spirit-filled church has the authority to declare which are the sins that are forgiven and which are the sins that are retained. This accords with the Rabbinical reaching which spoke of certain sins as 'bound' and others as 'loosed'." (Morris)

v. The work of Jesus for His disciples on resurrection Sunday gives an ongoing pattern for His work among His people. Jesus wants to continue this fourfold ministry of *assurance, mission*, the *Holy Spirit* and *authority* to His people today.

3. (24-25) The skepticism of Thomas, the absent disciples.

Now Thomas, called the Twin, one of the twelve, was not with them when Jesus came. The other disciples therefore said to him, "We have seen the Lord." So he said to them, "Unless I see in His hands the print of the nails, and put my finger into the print of the nails, and put my hand into His side, I will not believe."

a. **Thomas... was not with them when Jesus came**: We are not told why Thomas was not with them and Thomas was not criticized for his absence.

b. **We have seen the Lord**: Thomas was not criticized for his absence, but he still missed out. There was a blessing for those present that Thomas did not receive.

> i. "Thomas did the very worst thing that a melancholy man can do, went away to brood in a corner by himself, and so to exaggerate all his idiosyncrasies, to distort the proportion of the truth, and hug his despair, by separating himself from his fellows. Therefore he lost what they got, the sight of the Lord." (Maclaren)

c. **Unless I see in His hands the print of the nails, and put my finger into the print of the nails, and put my hand into His side, I will not believe**: Thomas is often known as *Doubting Thomas*, a title that misstates his error and ignores what became of him. Here we could say that Thomas didn't doubt; he plainly and strongly *refused* to believe.

- Thomas refused the believe the testimony of *many* witnesses and *reliable* witnesses.

- Thomas made an extreme demand for evidence; evidence of not only *sight* but of *touch*, and to *repeatedly* touch the multiple wounds of Jesus.

- Thomas steadfastly refused to believe unless these conditions were met (**I will not believe**).

> i. "Normally this is taken to indicate that Thomas was of a more skeptical turn of mind than the others, and, of course, he may have been. But another possibility should not be overlooked, namely that he was so shocked by the tragedy of the crucifixion that he did not find it easy to think of its consequences as being annulled." (Morris)

> ii. "Perhaps he had abandoned hope; - the strong evidence of his senses having finally convinced him that the pierced side and wounded hands betokened such a death that revivification was impossible." (Alford)

iii. Adam Clarke called Thomas' unbelief *unreasonable, obstinate, prejudiced, presumptuous,* and *insolent.* Still, it was good and significant that Thomas still wanted to be around those who believed.

iv. The unbelief of Thomas was strong, but honestly spoken. It was good that he refused to *pretend* to believe when he did not believe.

v. Some find it interesting that Thomas made no mention of wounds in the *feet* of Jesus. "There is no mention in this Gospel, or in Matthew or Luke, of the piercing of the feet. That the feet of Jesus may have been nailed to the cross, rather than fastened with a rope, which was the common practice, is an inference from Luke 24:39." (Tasker)

4. (26-27) One week later, Jesus speaks to the skeptic Thomas.

And after eight days His disciples were again inside, and Thomas with them. Jesus came, the doors being shut, and stood in the midst, and said, "Peace to you!" Then He said to Thomas, "Reach your finger here, and look at My hands; and reach your hand *here,* and put *it* into My side. Do not be unbelieving, but believing."

a. **After eight days**: The idea is that Jesus had this meeting with the disciples now including Thomas on the following Sunday. Jesus entered the room in the same mysterious and remarkable way (**the doors being shut, and stood in the midst**). Jesus also gave the same greeting (**Peace to you!**).

i. The locked doors of their meeting room show that though they believed Jesus to be raised from the dead, that truth had yet to work its meaning and significance into every area of their thinking and actions.

ii. There is significance in that these two important meetings with Jesus and His assembled disciples took place on Sundays; this is the first indication we have of Sunday meetings of the disciples. "The memory of this coming of the Lord to his disciples may well have something to do with the church's early practice of meeting together on the evening of the first day of the week and bespeaking his presence with them in the words *Marana tha*, 'Our Lord, come!'" (Bruce)

b. **Reach your finger here, and look at My hands; and reach your hand here, and put it into My side**: Jesus granted Thomas the evidence he demanded. We suppose that Jesus was not *obligated* to do this; He could have rightly demanded faith from Thomas on the basis of the reliable evidence from others. Yet in mercy and kindness, Jesus gave Thomas what he asked for.

i. It must have been a surprise to Thomas that Jesus repeated back to him just was he said to the other disciples (John 20:25). *Jesus knew the demands and unbelief of Thomas.*

ii. "There is no surer way of making a good man ashamed of his wild words than just to say them over again to him when he is calm and cool." (Maclaren)

iii. Jesus' interaction with Thomas shows that the resurrected Jesus is full of love and graciousness and gentleness to His people. That didn't change. "The whole conversation was indeed a rebuke, but so veiled with love that Thomas could scarcely think it so." (Spurgeon)

iv. There is a clear lesson: When you want assurance, look to the wounds of Jesus. They are evidence of His love, of His sacrifice, of His victory, of His resurrection.

c. **Do not be unbelieving, but believing**: Jesus clearly commanded Thomas to stop his unbelief and to start believing. Jesus was generous and merciful to Thomas and his unbelief, but Jesus did not praise his unbelief. Jesus wanted to move him from doubt and unbelief to *faith*.

i. Jesus did not even credit to Thomas his *prior* belief, or his believe in the prior teaching and miracles of Jesus. Because Thomas did not believe in the resurrected Jesus, Jesus considered him **unbelieving**.

ii. Often God does not condemn our doubt and He also often reveals and does remarkable things to speak to our doubt and unbelief. But doubt and unbelief are not desired conditions for the disciple of Jesus. If they are checkpoints along a path leading to faith they should be dealt with a generous love; but doubt and unbelief should never be thought of as *destinations* for the disciple.

5. (28-29) Thomas responds in faith.

And Thomas answered and said to Him, "My Lord and my God!" Jesus said to him, "Thomas, because you have seen Me, you have believed. Blessed *are* those who have not seen and *yet* have believed."

a. **My Lord and my God**: Thomas made an immediate transition from declared unbelief (John 20:25) to radical belief. He addressed Jesus with titles of deity, calling Him **Lord** and **God**. It is also significant that *Jesus accepted these titles*, and did not tell Thomas, "Don't call Me *that*."

i. "Sight may have made Thomas believe that Jesus was risen, but it was something other and more inward than sight that opened his lips to cry, 'My Lord and my God!'" (Maclaren)

ii. "Thomas now avows the faith which a foretime he had disclaimed. 'I will not believe,' said he, 'except-except- except.' Now he believes a great deal more than some of the other Apostles did; so he openly avows it. He was the first divine who ever taught the Deity of Christ from his wounds." (Spurgeon)

iii. "The words are not a mere exclamation of surprise. That is forbidden by [greek text]; they mean, 'Thou are my Lord and my God'. The repeated pronoun lends emphasis." (Dods)

iv. "For a Jew to call another human associate 'my Lord and my God' would be almost incredible....Thomas, in the light of the Resurrection, applied to Jesus the titles of Lord (*kyrios*) and God (*theos*), both of which were titles of deity." (Tenney)

v. "In Pliny's letter to Trajan (112 A.D.) he describes the Christians as singing hymns to Christ as God." (Dods)

vi. Thomas was honest enough to say when he didn't believe (John 20:25), but also honest enough to follow the evidence to its full meaning. Thomas wasn't given to half-unbelief or half-faith.

vii. Spurgeon considered many aspects of Thomas' declaration.

- It was a devout expression of holy wonder.
- It was an expression of immeasurable delight.
- It indicates a complete change of mind.
- It was an enthusiastic profession of allegiance to Christ.
- It was a distinct and direct act of adoration, worship.

viii. "Whosoever will be saved, before all things it is necessary that he be able to unite with Thomas heartily in this creed, 'My Lord and my God.' I do not go in for all the minute distinctions of the Athanasian Creed, but I have no doubt that it was absolutely needful at the time it was written, and that it materially helped to check the evasions and tricks of the Arians. This short creed of Thomas I like much better, for it is brief, pithy, full, sententious, and it avoids those matters of detail which are the quicksands of faith." (Spurgeon)

b. **Thomas, because you have seen Me, you have believed**: Commentators divide over whether or not Thomas actually did as Jesus invited him, to actually touch the wounds of Jesus. That Jesus said, **because you have seen Me** and not *because you have seen and touched Me* gives some evidence to the idea that Thomas did *not* actually touch the wounds of Jesus.

c. **Blessed are those who have not seen and yet have believed**: There is a special promise blessing given to those who believe. Thomas demanded to see and touch before he would believe in the resurrected Jesus. Jesus understood that the testimony of reliable witnesses was evidence enough, and there was a blessing for those who accepted that sufficient evidence.

i. "I believe He is speaking, not of a subjective faith, but of a satisfied faith. He is speaking of faith that is satisfied with what God provides and is there fore not yearning for visions, miracles, esoteric experiences or various form of success as evidence of God's favor." (Boice)

ii. "From this we learn that to believe in Jesus, on the testimony of his apostles, will put a man into the possession of the very same blessedness which they themselves enjoyed. And so has God constituted the whole economy of grace that a believer, at eighteen hundred years' distance from the time of the resurrection, suffers *no loss* because he has not seen Christ in the flesh." (Clarke)

iii. These words of Jesus are another beatitude, and promise a great blessing. Spurgeon considered some ways that this blessing would be diminished.

- When we demand for a voice, a vision, a revelation to prove our faith.

- When we demand for some special circumstances to prove our faith.

- When we demand for some ecstatic experience.

- When we demand for an answer to every difficult question or objection.

- When we demand what men think of as success in our work of Jesus.

- When we demand that others support us in our faith.

iv. The faith of Thomas becomes the climax of the book. Throughout the Gospel of John Jesus has triumphed over sickness, sin, evil men, death and sorrow. Now with Thomas, Jesus conquered unbelief.

6. (30-31) The summary statement of the Gospel of John.

And truly Jesus did many other signs in the presence of His disciples, which are not written in this book; but these are written that you may believe that Jesus is the Christ, the Son of God, and that believing you may have life in His name.

a. **Jesus did many other signs**: John admits that he presented an incomplete collection. He couldn't possibly record in writing all that Jesus said and did (John 21:25).

i. One collects everything possible about a dead prophet; it is all one has of him. But one only tells enough of a living person to introduce one's hearers to him. John trusts that a personal relationship with Jesus will reveal more to the believer.

ii. **In this book**: "That this was the original or intended conclusion of the gospel is shown by the use of the words 'in this book,' which indicate that the writer was now looking back on it as a whole." (Dods)

b. **These are written that you may believe that Jesus is the Christ, the Son of God**: Though there were **many other signs**, John selected the signs presented in His Gospel to explain Jesus and bring readers to faith in Jesus as Messiah and God. This really isn't a book about *signs* - it is a book about Jesus. The signs are helpful as they reveal Jesus.

i. The Gospel - and all of the Bible - was written so that we may believe, not that we might doubt. "There is no text in the whole Book which was intended to create doubt. Doubt is a seed self-sown, or sown by the devil, and it usually springs up with more than sufficient abundance without our care." (Spurgeon)

ii. John 2:11 speaks of the *beginning of signs*, and throughout his Gospel John has listed at least seven signs.

- John 2:1-11 - Water into wine.
- John 4:46-54 - Healing of the nobleman's son.
- John 5:1-15 - Healing at the pool of Bethesda.
- John 6:1-14 - Feeding the 5,000.
- John 6:15-21 - Jesus walks on water.
- John 9:1-12 - Healing of the man born blind.
- John 11:1-44 - Lazarus raised from the dead.

iii. The greatest signs of all were the death and resurrection of Jesus. Collectively, these signs give strong foundation for faith in Jesus as Messiah and God. That faith isn't a blind leap; it is a reasonable step based on strong evidence.

iv. **The Son of God**: "The title does not, of course, imply biological descent like that of the Greco-Roman demigods; but the metaphor of sonship expresses the unity of nature, close fellowship, and unique intimacy between Jesus and the Father." (Tenney)

c. **And that believing you may have life in His name**: John understood that faith in Jesus as Messiah and God had value beyond the honorable recognition of truth. It also carried the promise of **life in His name**. This was life that transformed John himself, and he wanted that same life and transformation for all through his Gospel account.

i. This belief isn't complicated. Our response is as simple as ABC: *Accept*, *Believe*, and *Commit*. It isn't always easy, but it isn't complicated.

ii. **Life in His name**: "*Through his name* does not mean 'through the naming of His name', but through the power of the Person who bears the name. In the Bible the 'name' of God is not merely the name by which He is designated, but all that He is in Himself." (Tasker)

John 21 - The Restoration of Peter

A. A miraculous catch of fish.

1. (1-3) Peter and six other disciples return to fishing.

After these things Jesus showed Himself again to the disciples at the Sea of Tiberias, and in this way He showed *Himself*: Simon Peter, Thomas called the Twin, Nathanael of Cana in Galilee, the *sons* of Zebedee, and two others of His disciples were together. Simon Peter said to them, "I am going fishing." They said to him, "We are going with you also." They went out and immediately got into the boat, and that night they caught nothing.

a. **After these things Jesus showed Himself again to the disciples**: John recorded another of the several appearances of the resurrected Jesus to His disciples. This appearance took place in the Galilee region (**at the Sea of Tiberias**). Matthew 28:16 also records an appearance of the resurrected Jesus to His disciples in Galilee.

b. **Simon Peter**: Once again Peter was at the top of a list of the disciples. This time he was among seven who joined him in fishing at the Sea of Galilee.

i. **And two others of His disciples**: "There were 'two other,' and they are unnamed, and I believe purposely unnamed. They represent the anonymous and hidden multitudes of faithful souls, whose names are never published in human documents, whose deeds are never reported in human reports. To these He manifested Himself as surely as to the others. Those 'two other' represented the majority of the saints." (Morgan)

c. **I am going fishing**: Some believe that Peter was wrong to go fishing, and that this was a compromised return to a former occupation. Others believe Peter disobeyed no command of Jesus and was simply wise and practical.

In the end, only the attitude of Peter's heart could determine if he was disobedient to go back to fishing.

i. It is important to remember that they went to Galilee because Jesus told them to (Matthew 28:7, 28:10).

ii. Adam Clarke put their fishing enterprise in the best possible light: "Previously to the crucifixion of our Lord, the temporal necessities of himself and his disciples appear to have been supplied by the charity of individuals: Luke 8:3. As it is probable that the scandal of the cross had now shut up this source of support, the disciples, not fully knowing *how* they were to be employed, purposed to return to their former occupation of fishing, in order to gain a livelihood; and therefore the *seven*, mentioned John 21:2, embarked on the sea of Tiberias, otherwise called the sea of Galilee." (Clarke)

iii. At the best, it shows that Peter and the other disciples were uncertain as to what they should do next. "The fishing expedition plainly reveals the uncertainly of the disciples, an uncertainty which contrasts sharply with their assured sense of purpose from the day of Pentecost on." (Morris)

d. **That night they caught nothing**: They fished through the night and had no success. Whether their motives were good or bad, **that night they caught nothing**.

i. "All night they had toiled without one sign of fish; they had lost heart; they were weary, hungry, hopeless. 'Ah!' they would whisper, 'this lake is sadly changed; there used to be good fish in it. There doesn't seem to be one in it now.'" (Morrison)

ii. "To be a fisherman, a man must expect disappointments; he must often cast in the net and bring up nothing but weeds. The minister of Christ must reckon upon being disappointed; and he must not be weary in well-doing for all his disappointments, but must in faith continue in prayer and labor, expecting that at the end he shall receive his reward." (Spurgeon)

2. (4-6) Jesus directs their work.

But when the morning had now come, Jesus stood on the shore; yet the disciples did not know that it was Jesus. Then Jesus said to them, "Children, have you any food?" They answered Him, "No." And He said to them, "Cast the net on the right side of the boat, and you will find *some.* **So they cast, and now they were not able to draw it in because of the multitude of fish.**

a. **Jesus stood on the shore**: The previous three resurrection appearances in John's Gospel were each *unexpected*. This also seemed to be unexpected; the **disciples did not know that it was Jesus**.

   i. "It seems to indicate the suddenness of the appearance." (Dods)

   ii. It's wonderful to think that Jesus showed up at their work. He was interested in all their life, not just when they attended religious service. "The risen Redeemer and Ruler was showing men His interest and power in the commonplaces of their lives." (Morgan)

   iii. We don't know exactly why they **did not know that it was Jesus**. "Perhaps they were preoccupied with their failure, or because they could not see him clearly through the morning mist on the lake." (Tenney)

b. **Children, have you any food**: Jesus spoke to His disciples with a common greeting that working men used amongst themselves. Yet He also made them explain an unsuccessful night of fishing, causing them to answer Him **no**.

   i. "It should be 'lads'; παιδιον being the common term of address to men at work, see Aristophanes, *Clouds*, 137, *Frogs*, 33." (Dods)

   ii. "This he saith as seeming to be some housekeeper, who passing by fishermen, calls to them, as willing to buy their fish for the use of his family." (Trapp)

c. **Cast the net on the right side of the boat, and you will find some**: Jesus made a strange suggestion to His disciples. There was no logical reason why fishing in the morning light would be better than fishing at night. There was no reason why fishing on one side of the boat would be better than the other side. It wasn't even directly a test of trust in Jesus, because they did not know it was Him until the fish were caught. This was probably a test of their ability to find the guidance of God in small and unsuspected ways - such as a stranger calling out fishing instructions from the shore.

   i. "I have been unable to find any evidence which indicates which side of the boat was normally used by fishermen on the sea of Galilee so that it is difficult to know whether this was unusual or not." (Morris)

   ii. This account illustrates the principle that we should never be afraid to change our method, as long as it is at the direction of Jesus.

d. **They were not able to draw it in because of the multitude of the fish**: The disciples did as the Man on the shore asked and were successful beyond expectation. This shows a difference between doing work without Divine guidance and with Divine guidance.

i. "The experience must have reminded the disciples of a similar incident many months before, though on that occasion the net was broken and the boat began to sink (see Luke 5:1-11)." (Takser)

ii. "There is no need to seek symbolical meanings for the right and left side. The difference is not between right and left, but between working with and without Divine guidance." (Plummer)

iii. "The disciples' haul of fish is a parable of their missionary activity in the time that lies ahead. But this activity, with its pastoral sequel, will be attended by success only as they follow the directions of their risen Lord." (Bruce)

iv. We have even greater reason to expect blessing as He directs our service. Jesus never commanded these disciples to go fishing, but He commanded us to preach the Gospel and make disciples.

v. "Christ's presence, if he would but come among us in the fullness of his strength, would do so much more for us than anything that we have ever seen yet that we should be as much astounded by the increase as the apostles were by the two great draughts of fishes. Christ had but to will it, and the fish came swimming in shoals to the net, and he has but to will it, and souls will be converted by millions to himself and his gospel." (Spurgeon)

vi. "It is a miracle, certainly, but yet neither the fisherman, nor his boat, nor his fishing tackle are ignored; they are all used and all employed. Let us learn that in the saving of souls God worketh by means; that so long as the present economy of grace shall stand, God will be pleased by the foolishness of preaching to save them that believe." (Spurgeon)

vii. "Perhaps, if they had not fished at night, Christ would not, have given them fish in the day time. He does not often come to bless idlers; he acts sovereignly, as I have said, but he generally gives his blessing to those churches that do the most for him." (Spurgeon)

3. (7-8) The disciples recognize Jesus on the shore.

Therefore that disciple whom Jesus loved said to Peter, "It is the Lord!" Now when Simon Peter heard that it was the Lord, he put on *his* outer garment (for he had removed it), and plunged into the sea. But the other disciples came in the little boat (for they were not far from land, but about two hundred cubits), dragging the net with fish.

a. **It is the Lord**: John reached the tomb before Peter (John 20:4) and recognized the fact of Jesus' resurrection before Peter (John 20:8). Here John also recognized the identity of the stranger on the shore before Peter did. John knew that anything *this* wonderful had to come from Jesus.

b. **Plunged into the sea**: John was first in recognition, but Peter would be first in devotion. He threw on his **outer garment** and threw himself into the water to reach Jesus as soon as possible. The boat couldn't move quickly enough for Peter, and he didn't want John to be first *again*. Perhaps - *perhaps* - Peter thought he might walk on the water to the shore.

    i. "The probability here is that the word means that parts of the body normally covered were exposed so that Peter was not naked but rather 'stripped for work' (RSV, Barclay)." (Morris)

    ii. "He was rowing, then, with as little on as possible, probably only a *subligaculum* or loin-cloth, and now picks up his *ependyten*, a garment worn by fishers (Theophylact), and girds it on, and casts himself into the sea." (Dods)

    iii. "He looks up, recognizes Him, casts all other care aside, slips on his outer-garment, for no Oriental would appear in undress before his superior, girds it to him, and casts himself into the sea, so eager is his love for the Lord." (Trench)

c. **Dragging the net with fish**: The other disciples followed, doing the hard work of bringing the net full of fish with them.

4. (9-11) Jesus invites the disciples to breakfast.

Then, as soon as they had come to land, they saw a fire of coals there, and fish laid on it, and bread. Jesus said to them, "Bring some of the fish which you have just caught." Simon Peter went up and dragged the net to land, full of large fish, one hundred and fifty-three; and although there were so many, the net was not broken.

a. **They saw a fire of coals there, and fish laid on it, and bread**: When the disciples came to shore - including a wet Peter - they noticed that the resurrected Jesus was still a humble servant. He took the trouble to prepare a fire and cook the food for His disciples.

b. **Bring some of the fish which you have just caught**: The order of events shows that Jesus *had food for them* before the great catch of fish were brought it. What they caught *added* to the menu; it did not make it.

    i. **Simon Peter went up and dragged the net to land, full of large fish**: "One hundred and fifty-three fish plus a wet net would probably weigh as much as three hundred pounds, or more. The observation of the exact number of fish and the fact that the net did not break reflect both an eyewitness account and a fisherman's perspective." (Tenney)

    ii. "Peter's hauling it up single-handed is a tacit tribute to his physical strength." (Bruce)

c. **Full of large fish, one hundred and fifty-three**: Peter took the initiative and dragged the heavy net all by himself. The **net was not broken** and held a large catch of 153 fish. Through the centuries there have been many attempts to explain why the number was 153.

- Some interpreters (like Augustine) thought that because 153 is the sum of numbers 1 to 17, this catch of fish points towards the number 17 - which he thought to be the number of commandments (10) added to the sevenfold gifts of the Spirit.

- Some have noted that 153 is the added numerical value of the Greek words *Peter* and *fish.*

- Some note, "In Hebrew characters Simon Iona is equivalent to 118 + 35, *i.e.*, 153." (Dods)

- Some ancient writers (such as Jerome) believed there were 153 different types of fish in the world and this catch represented a full harvest of the entire world.

- Some (such as Cyril of Alexandria) thought that 100 stood for the Gentiles, 50 stood for Israel and 3 stood for the Trinity.

  i. The truth is that all we know for certain is that 153 represents *the number of fish in the net.* The many allegorical interpretations of the number warn us against creating hidden meanings in the Biblical text.

  ii. "Peter never landed a haul of fish without counting them, and John, fisherman as he was, could never forget the number of his largest takes." (Dods)

5. (12-14) The disciples eat breakfast with Jesus.

Jesus said to them, "Come *and* eat breakfast." Yet none of the disciples dared ask Him, "Who are You?"—knowing that it was the Lord. Jesus then came and took the bread and gave it to them, and likewise the fish. This *is* now the third time Jesus showed Himself to His disciples after He was raised from the dead.

a. **Jesus said to them, "Come and eat breakfast"**: We are again impressed at the servant nature of Jesus, even in His resurrection. He prepared breakfast for His disciples, no doubt a delicious one.

  i. Boice reflected on the many invitations of Jesus in the Gospels.

  - Come and see (John 1:39).
  - Come and learn (Matthew 11:28-29).
  - Come and rest (Mark 6:31).
  - Come and dine (John 21:12).

- Come and inherit (Matthew 25:34-36).

b. **Yet none of the disciples dared ask Him, "Who are You?"; knowing that it was the Lord**: This is another indication that there was something unusual about the appearance of Jesus after His resurrection. Possibly it was a result of the beatings He endured at the cross, the scars of which remained at least in part.

> i. "Formerly they would not have thought of asking him 'Who are you?' - but now they felt as if they ought to do so, because, after all, they *knew* who it was." (Bruce)

> ii. "The verb rendered **ask** signifies more: - **to question** or **prove** Him." (Alford)

> iii. "Not one of the disciples ventured to interrogate Him; *exetasai* is 'to examine by questioning'. Each man felt convinced it was the Lord, and a new reverence prevented them from questioning Him." (Dods)

c. **Jesus then came and took the bread**: Jesus is often seen eating with His disciples after His resurrection. This is a picture of intimate, friendly fellowship.

> i. **Gave it to them, and likewise the fish**: "Evidently there was something solemn and significant in His manner, indicating that they were to consider Him as the Person who supplied all their wants." (Dods)

> ii. "They ate the bread and fish that morning, I doubt not, in silent self- humiliation. Peter looked with tears in his eyes at that fire of coals, remembering how he stood and warmed himself when he denied his Master. Thomas stood there, wondering that he should have dared to ask such proofs of a fact most clear. All of them felt that they could shrink into nothing in his divine presence, since they had behaved so ill." (Spurgeon)

> iii. **The third time**: "This probably means the third of the appearances that he himself has recorded." (Takser)

B. The public restoration of Peter.

1. (15-16) Jesus inquires about Peter's love.

So when they had eaten breakfast, Jesus said to Simon Peter, "Simon, *son* of Jonah, do you love Me more than these?" He said to Him, "Yes, Lord; You know that I love You." He said to him, "Feed My lambs." He said to him again a second time, "Simon, *son* of Jonah, do you love Me?" He said to Him, "Yes, Lord; You know that I love You." He said to him, "Tend My sheep."

a. **Jesus said to Simon Peter**: After their breakfast Jesus spoke directly to Peter. Jesus had already met with Peter individually on the day of His resurrection (Luke 24:34, 1 Corinthians 15:5). We can only wonder at what Jesus and Peter talked about at that first meeting. Nevertheless, it was still important for Jesus to restore Peter in the presence of the other disciples.

b. **Simon, son of Jonah**: Jesus addressed the leader among the disciples as **Simon**, not as *Peter*. This perhaps was a subtle reminder that he had not stood as a *rock* in faithfulness to Jesus.

i. "There is an air of solemnity about John's use of the full name, Simon Peter, and then of his reporting Jesus as using the expanded form, Simon son of John." (Morris)

c. **Do you love Me more than these**: Jesus asked Peter to compare *his* love for Jesus to the love that the *other disciples* had for Jesus. Before he denied Jesus three times Peter claimed to love Jesus *more* than the other disciples did (Matthew 26:33). Jesus wanted to know if Peter still had a proud estimation of his love and devotion to Jesus.

i. It is possible that **these** referred to the fish and a fisherman's life. Some think that Jesus asked Peter if he was willing to give up fishing again to follow Him. Yet, Peter's previous claim to a greater love suggests that Jesus referred to the other disciples, not the fish.

ii. Jesus asked Peter not so that He would know - He already knew, and Peter was aware that Jesus knew. It was for Peter's self-examination the questions were asked.

d. **Do you love Me more than these... You know that I love You**: Jesus asked the question twice using the word *agapas*, which in its Biblical usage often speaks of an all giving, uncaused, unselfish **love**. Peter answered Jesus using the word *philio*, which in Biblical usage sometimes has in mind a more reciprocal **love**, a friendly affection. Some translations express Peter's answer as, "I am your friend."

i. Some commentators see no significant distinction between the two different ancient Greek words *agapeo* and *phileo* in this passage. Most believe that Peter was now more reserved in his proclamation of devotion. There is surely *some* significance that Jesus asked Peter this question twice, using the same ancient Greek word for **love**, and Peter answered twice using a different word for **love**.

ii. "He is simply saying that his heart is open to Christ and that Christ therefore knows that he loves Him with the best love of which he, a sinful human being, is capable." (Boice)

iii. "There are preachers of the gospel among us who have dragged a full net to shore, the great fishes have been many; they have been great and successful workers, but this does not prevent its being needful for the Lord to examine them as to their hearts. He bids them put by their nets for awhile and commune with him." (Spurgeon)

e. **Feed My lambs... Tend My sheep**: After Jesus asked and Peter answered, Jesus twice gave Peter an instruction regarding how he should act towards God's people. The idea was that Peter could demonstrate his claimed love for Jesus by feeding Jesus' **lambs** and by tending Jesus' **sheep**. Jesus emphasized that they were *His* sheep, not Peter's.

i. **Tend My sheep**: "The verb used here has a somewhat broader meaning. It is 'Exercise the office of shepherd' over against simply 'Feed'." (Morris)

ii. **Tend My sheep**: "By which he seems to intimate that it is not sufficient merely to *offer* the bread of life to the congregation of the Lord, but he must take care that the sheep be properly *collected, attended to, regulated, guided,* &c.; and it appears that Peter perfectly comprehended our Lord's meaning, and saw that it was a direction given not only to *him,* and to the rest of the *disciples,* but to all their *successors* in the Christian ministry." (Clarke)

2. (17) Jesus asks Peter a third time: **Do you love Me?**

He said to him the third time, "Simon, *son* of Jonah, do you love Me?" Peter was grieved because He said to him the third time, "Do you love Me?" And he said to Him, "Lord, You know all things; You know that I love You." Jesus said to him, "Feed My sheep."

a. **He said to him the third time**: The two previous questions Jesus asked Peter in the presence of the other disciples were not enough to accomplish what Jesus' wanted to do in the life of Peter. Jesus had to ask **him the third time**.

b. **Peter was grieved because He said to him the third time**: Peter understood the significance of the question being asked **the third time**. It was a plain reminder of his previous three-time denial.

i. "Peter had *thrice* denied his Lord, and now Christ gives him an opportunity in some measure to repair his fault by a *triple* confession." (Clarke)

c. **Do you love Me**: The third time Jesus slightly changed His question. He asked Peter if he did in fact have a brotherly love, a friendly devotion to Jesus (*phileis*).

i. "Peter in his first two answers uses a less exalted word, and one implying a consciousness of his own weakness, but a persuasion and deep feeling of personal love. Then in the third question, the Lord adopts the word of Peter's answer, the closer to press the meaning of it home to him." (Alford)

d. **Lord, You know all things; You know that I love You**: Peter did believe that he loved Jesus (using the word *philio*), yet he relied on Jesus' own knowledge of **all things**. Peter understood that Jesus knew him better than he knew himself.

i. Jesus didn't ask Peter, "Are you sorry?" nor "Will you promise never to do that again?" Jesus challenged Peter to *love*.

ii. "Jesus Christ asks each one of us, not for obedience primarily, not for repentance, not for vows, not for conduct, but for a *heart*; and that being given, all the rest will follow." (Maclaren)

e. **Feed My sheep**: Jesus restored Peter in the presence of the other disciples by causing him to face squarely his point of failure; *then* Jesus challenged Peter to set his eyes on the work ahead.

3. (18-19) Jesus' call on Peter's life.

"Most assuredly, I say to you, when you were younger, you girded yourself and walked where you wished; but when you are old, you will stretch out your hands, and another will gird you and carry *you* where you do not wish." This He spoke, signifying by what death he would glorify God. And when He had spoken this, He said to him, "Follow Me."

a. **Most assuredly**: Jesus prefaced these closing words to Peter with great assurance. What He was about to say needed to be remembered.

b. **When you were younger**: Jesus spoke of Peter's past, reminding him of his younger days when he had less responsibility and could do more as he pleased. Most of us know what these **younger** years were like.

c. **When you are old, you will stretch out your hands**: Jesus spoke of Peter's future, when another would bind him (**gird you**) and **carry** Peter to a place he would not want to go - a place with stretched out hands, crucified on a cross. It would be by this **death he would glorify God**.

i. "He will be restrained, no longer the master of his own movements." (Morris)

ii. Trusting that Peter understood what Jesus meant, this must have given him a great chill. *Peter, you will die on a cross.* John the Gospel-writer understood, but wrote this many years after Peter's death.

iii. Yet it also gave Peter *assurance*. In the crucial moment a few weeks before, Peter denied Jesus three times to save himself from the cross. Jesus assured Peter - **most assuredly** - he would face the challenge of the cross once again and he would embrace it. Jesus promised Peter that he would die in utter faithfulness to his Messiah and Lord.

iv. "Ancient writers state that, about thirty-four years after this, Peter was crucified; and that he deemed it so *glorious* a thing to die for Christ that he begged to be crucified with his *head downwards*, not considering himself worthy to die in the same posture in which his Lord did. So *Eusebius, Prudentius, Chrysostom*, and *Augustin*." (Clarke)

v. "Jerome says, that 'he was crowned with martyrdom under Nero, being crucified with his head downwards and his feet upwards, because he alleged himself to be unworthy of being crucified in the same manner as his Lord.'" (Alford)

vi. The Christian in death can **glorify God**. "Justin Martyr confesseth of himself, that seeing the piety of Christians in their lives and their patience in death, he gathered that that was the truth that they so constantly professed and sealed up with their blood." (Trapp)

d. **Follow Me**: In this dramatic moment, Jesus gave these last words to Peter. Years before He called Peter to follow Him (Matthew 4:18-19). Now Peter knew that continuing to follow Jesus would mean a certain cross. Peter was once again challenged to **follow** his Messiah, Teacher, and Lord.

i. "Jesus placed Peter in a category with himself - a life spent for God and ultimately sacrificed to glorify God. Similar language was used concerning Jesus earlier in the Gospel (John 12:27-32; 13:31). The command 'Follow me' is a present imperative, which literally means 'Keep on following me.'" (Tenney)

ii. "There is possibly significance in the use of the present tense here. 'Keep on following' will be the force of it. Peter had followed Christ, but not continuously in the past. For the future he was to follow steadfastly in the ways of the Lord." (Morris)

4. (20-23) What about John?

Then Peter, turning around, saw the disciple whom Jesus loved following, who also had leaned on His breast at the supper, and said, "Lord, who is the one who betrays You?" Peter, seeing him, said to Jesus, "But Lord, what *about* this man?" Jesus said to him, "If I will that he remain till I come, what *is that* to you? You follow Me." Then this saying went out among the brethren that this disciple would not die. Yet Jesus did not

say to him that he would not die, but, **"If I will that he remain till I come, what *is that* to you?"**

a. **But Lord, what about this man**: Jesus just renewed His challenge to Peter, *follow Me* (John 21:19). Peter's first response was not to tell Jesus yes, but **turning around** he looked at the other disciple, John. Peter first response to the personal challenge from Jesus was to deflect it by wondering what Jesus wanted to do regarding someone else.

> i. Peter represents most all of us. We find it easy to deflect any personal challenge from Jesus by wondering and even worrying about what *other* disciples are doing or what Jesus may require from them.

> ii. **What about** John? "His unique contribution will come later. After he has settled in the pagan, cosmopolitan city of Ephesus, he will recall men from drifting on the uncharted seas of vague religious experience and abstract speculation to the sure and certain anchorage of God's self-revelation in the historical figure of the Word-made-flesh." (Tasker)

> iii. "Paul might be the pioneer of Christ, Peter might be the shepherd of Christ, but John was the witness of Christ." (Barclay)

b. **If I will that he remain till I come, what is that to you**: Jesus answered Peter with another challenge. Though Peter was destined to die on a cross (John 21:18-19), Jesus wanted Peter to consider the possibility that He might have an entirely different destiny for John. Peter had to consider what Jesus required of him knowing that Jesus might require something different from John or other disciples.

> i. "There is a touch of human interest in His rebuke of Peter for attempting to discover the divine will concerning another man." (Morgan)

c. **You follow Me**: This was a powerful and pointed challenge to Peter. Without regard to how Jesus might deal with John or other disciples, Peter had to decide for himself whether or not he would **follow** Jesus. This is a challenge for every one of Jesus' disciples.

> i. "The use of the second person pronoun in Jesus' command makes the statement emphatic: '*You* must follow me'." (Tenney)

> ii. "I have come to the conclusion that, instead of trying to set all my Master's servants right at once, my first and most important work is to follow my Lord; and I think, my brother, that it will be wise for you to come to the same conclusion." (Spurgeon)

d. **Then this saying went out among the brethren that this disciple would not die**: The challenge Jesus gave to Peter gave rise to a rumor among early **brethren** in the Christian faith. The rumor was that Jesus said that John would not die until Jesus returned. The fact that John was the last surviving disciple, having survived attempts to kill him, gave strength to this rumor.

> i. This illustrates just how often and easily people misunderstand things, and how often **the brethren** misunderstand.

e. **Jesus did not say to him that he would not die**: One reason John added this appendix to his Gospel was to clarify what Jesus said about this and correct the rumor. Jesus **did not say to** John **that he would not die**, but simply used the possibility of that as an example to Peter.

> i. "Rumour had it that the Lord had prophesied that the beloved disciple would be alive when He came again, and the evangelist is anxious to make it perfectly clear that Jesus had only spoken hypothetically about such a possibility." (Tasker)

5. (24-25) The conclusion to the Gospel of John.

This is the disciple who testifies of these things, and wrote these things; and we know that his testimony is true. And there are also many other things that Jesus did, which if they were written one by one, I suppose that even the world itself could not contain the books that would be written. Amen.

a. **This is the disciple who testifies of these things, and wrote these things**: Here John explains that *he* was the unnamed disciple referred to in several previous places. John gave solemn testimony to the truth of what he wrote. **His testimony is true**.

b. **Even the world itself could not contain the books that would be written**: John wrote the truth about Jesus, but it was impossible for him or anyone else to write the *whole* truth about Jesus. There were **many other things that Jesus did**, and it would be impossible to write them all.

> i. "With this delightful hyperbole he lets us see that there is much more about Jesus than we know." (Morris)

> ii. The **many other things that Jesus did** includes His ongoing work among His disciples and in the world today. John thought of a book that continues to be written, with so many volumes that the world could not contain them all.

Bibliography - The Gospel of John

Alford, Henry *The New Testament for English Readers, Volume 1, Part 2* (Rivingtons: London, 1872)

Barclay, William *The Gospel of John, Volume 1* and *Volume 2* (Philadelphia: The Westminster Press, 1975)

Boice, James Montgomery *The Gospel of John, an Expositional Commentary, Five Volumes in One* (Grand Rapids: Zondervan, 1985)

Bruce, F.F. *The Gospel of John - Introduction, Exposition, and Notes* (Grand Rapids: Eerdmans, 1983)

Calvin, John *The Gospel According to St. John*—Parts One and Two, translated by T.H.L. Parker (Grand Rapids, Michigan: Eerdmans, 1961)

Carson, D.A. *The Farewell Discourse and Final Prayer of Jesus* (Grand Rapids, Michigan: Baker, 1980)

Clarke, Adam *The New Testament of Our Lord and Saviour Jesus Christ, Volume II* (New York: Eaton & Mains, 1832)

Dods, Marcus "The Gospel of St. John" *The Expositor's Greek Testament, Volume II* (Hodder and Stoughton: London, 1903)

Grieshaber, Erich and Jean *Expose of Jehovah's Witnesses* (Costa Mesa, California: Chapel Books, 1982)

Maclaren, Alexander *Expositions of Holy Scripture, Volume 10* and *Volume 11* (Grand Rapids, Michigan: Baker Book House, 1984)

Meyer, F.B. *Our Daily Homily* (Westwood, New Jersey: Revell, 1966)

Morgan, G. Campbell *An Exposition of the Whole Bible* (Old Tappan, New Jersey: Revell, 1959)

Morgan, G. Campbell *Searchlights from the Word* (New York: Revell, 1926)

Morris, Leon *The Gospel According to John* (Grand Rapids: Eerdmans, 1971)

Morrison, George H. *Morrison on John Volume 1* and *Morrison on John Volume 2* (AMG Publishers, 1977)

Reynolds, H.R. *The Gospel of St. John*, Volume 17 of *The Pulpit Commentary* (McLean, Virginia: MacDonald Publishing)

Spurgeon, Charles Haddon   *The New Park Street Pulpit, Volumes 1-6* and *The Metropolitan Tabernacle Pulpit, Volumes 7-63* (Pasadena, Texas: Pilgrim Publications, 1990)

Tasker, R.V.G. *The Gospel According to St. John, an Introduction and Commentary* (Leicester, England: Inter-Varsity Press, 1988)

Tenney, Merril C. "John" *The Expositor's Bible Commentary, Volume 9* (Grand Rapids. Michigan: Zondervan, 1984)

Trapp, John   *A Commentary on the Old and New Testaments, Volume Five* (Eureka, California: Tanski Publications, 1997)

Trench, G.H. *A Study of St John's Gospel* (London: John Murray, 1918)

Poole, Matthew   *A Commentary on the Holy Bible, Volume 1* (London, Banner of Truth Trust, 1968)

Ross, Hugh   *The Fingerprint of God* (Santa Ana, California, Promise Publishing, 1991)

Sailhamer, John H. "Genesis," *The Expositor's Bible Commentary, Volume 1* (Grand Rapids, Michigan: Zondervan, 1990)

Spurgeon, Charles Haddon   *The New Park Street Pulpit, Volumes 1-6 and The Metropolitan Tabernacle Pulpit, Volumes 7-63* (Pasadena, Texas: Pilgrim Publications, 1990)

Trapp, John   *A Commentary on the Old and New Testaments, Volume One* (Eureka, California: Tanski Publications, 1997)

As the years pass I love the work of studying, learning, and teaching the Bible more than ever. I'm so grateful that God is faithful to meet me in His Word.

Thanks to Nancy Aguilar for her editorial and proofreading work. Nancy showed remarkable endurance and grace in correcting the same mistakes over and over again. Nancy, thanks for making this much better.

Thanks to Brian Procedo for the cover design and all the graphics work. You can contact him at brianprocedo.com.

I am often amazed at the remarkable kindness of others, and thanks to all who give the gift of encouragement. With each year that passes, faithful friends and supporters become all the more precious. Through you all, God has been better to me than I have ever deserved.

David Guzik's Bible commentary is regularly used and trusted by many thousands who want to know the Bible better. Pastors, teachers, class leaders, and everyday Christians find his commentary helpful for their own understanding and explanation of the Bible. David and his wife Inga-Lill live in Santa Barbara, California.

You can e-mail David at
david@enduringword.com

For more resources by David Guzik, go to
www.enduringword.com